CHINA–US RELATIONS IN GLOBAL PERSPECTIVE

EDITED BY BO ZHIYUE

VICTORIA UNIVERSITY PRESS
for the New Zealand Contemporary China Research Centre

TE WHARE WĀNANGA O TE ŪPOKO O TE IKA A MĀUI

VICTORIA UNIVERSITY PRESS
Victoria University of Wellington
PO Box 600 Wellington
vup.victoria.ac.nz/

Copyright © Bo Zhiyue and contributors 2016
First published 2016

This book is copyright. Apart from
any fair dealing for the purpose of private study,
research, criticism or review, as permitted under the
Copyright Act, no part may be reproduced by any
process without the permission of
the publishers

National Library of New Zealand Cataloguing-in-Publication Data

China-US relations in a global perspective / ed. Bo Zhiyue.
Includes bibliographical references.
ISBN 978-1-77656-090-5
1. China—Relations—United States. 2. United States—Relations—China.
I. Bo, Zhiyue. II. Title.
327.51073—dc 23

Printed by printing.com, Wellington

Contents

Preface *The Right Honourable John Key, Prime Minister of New Zealand*	9
Foreword *Professor Grant Guilford, Vice-Chancellor of Victoria University of Wellington*	11
Notes on Contributors	13
List of Tables	26
List of Figures	26
Introduction: China and US: A tale of two civilisations *Wang Gungwu*	27

1. The China–US Bilateral Relationship

1. The China–US Relationship Matters *Wang Lutong*	43
2. US–China Relationship *Mark Gilbert*	46
3. China–US Relations after President Xi Jinping's State Visit to the US *Wu Jianmin*	51
4. Beyond Hegemony: The US–China Relationship in a Multi-Nodal World *Brantly Womack*	55
5. Two Roads, But One Destination? *Shao Yuqun*	75
6. Xi Jinping's US Policy: Building a 'New Type of Major-Country Relationship' *Bo Zhiyue*	80

2. China–US Economic Relations and the New World Economic Order

7. China's New Silk Roads: A New Global Financial Order in the Making? *Gerald Chan*	91

8. The Multilateral Development Banks: Innovation or Stagnation?   108
Susan Park

9. What the AIIB Means for the Development Finance System? A View of China–US Relations   126
Qiyuan Xu, Bei Gao and Dongmin Liu

3. Perspectives of Asian Countries (1)

10. The American Factor in Japan–China Relations   145
Akio Takahara

11. What do the United States and China present to South Korea?   154
Jaewoo Choo

12. Managing the Hermit Kingdom: China, North Korea and the Art of Strategic Patience   173
Jingdong Yuan

13. Rethinking Great Power Rivalry: US, China and the Challenge of Nuclear Proliferation in North Korea and Iran   196
Robert G. Patman and Laura Southgate

4. Perspectives of Asian Countries (2)

14. Not Too Hot, Not Too Cold: A Vietnamese Perspective on China–US Relations   215
Carlyle A. Thayer

15. The US–China–India Strategic Triangle   240
Manjeet S. Pardesi

5. Pacific Perspectives

16. China and the US: Trading Arrangements in a Post-TPP World   251
Crawford Falconer

17. Making Trans-Pacific Friends: New Zealand, China and the United States   260
Stephen Jacobi

18. How Robust is New Zealand's China–US Strategy?   268
    Robert Ayson

Conclusion: The Future of China–US Relations   276
    Bo Zhiyue, Wang Gungwu, Wu Jianmin, Charles Morrison,
    Bob Carr, Robert Ayson, Robert Sutter

About the New Zealand Contemporary China Research Centre   289

Editor's Acknowledgements   290

Index

Preface

The Right Honourable John Key

Prime Minister of New Zealand

To a country of 4.5 million people at the bottom of the South Pacific, the wider Asia-Pacific region is incredibly important.

We see immense opportunity in its diversity, its phenomenal economic growth and in the increasing flows of people, capital and ideas between our countries.

The 50-odd nations in the region are diverse but we share a common aspiration—better lives and greater opportunities for our people.

And we all share an interest in maintaining our region's continued stability and prosperity. It's why New Zealand works to maintain good relationships with our neighbours and be a constructive participant in regional forums like APEC, the East Asia Summit and the ASEAN Regional Forum.

For small trading countries like NZ, free trade agreements are not just nice to have—they are essential. This is why we work so hard to conclude free trade agreements like the Trans-Pacific Partnership (TPP) and are pushing for a high-quality Regional Comprehensive Economic Partnership.

The TPP represents an historic milestone with the US and other close Asia-Pacific partners. It provides a platform for wider regional economic integration, and supports the foundation of a free trade agreement in the Asia-Pacific.

Our free trade agreement with China continues to bring significant benefits to New Zealand. Since we signed it our exports to China have almost tripled, and our trade with China is now worth almost NZ$20 billion a year.

Perhaps no relationship is as important to our region as that between China and the US.

New Zealand welcomes greater US engagement in the Asia-Pacific. Having the world's largest economy more focused on our region will create greater opportunities from which we can all benefit.

And China's strong economic growth continues to contribute to the region's prosperity. We welcome its constructive diplomacy through initiatives such as the Asian Infrastructure Investment Bank.

Continued China–US engagement and cooperation is indispensable to security and prosperity in the Asia-Pacific region and beyond.

I am confident in our region's future. I have no doubt, along with China and the US, that we will continue work together to achieve our shared goals.

Foreword

Professor Grant Guilford

Vice-chancellor at Victoria University of Wellington, New Zealand

Based on an international conference at Victoria University of Wellington in October 2015, the New Zealand Contemporary China Research Centre now is publishing this volume on *China–US Relations in Global Perspective*.

Featuring world-class scholars and practitioners from China, the US and elsewhere, the conference was timely and significant. It was held merely two weeks after an historical meeting between the presidents of the two most powerful nations on earth. It was the first state visit by Chinese President Xi Jinping to the US. He and US President Barack Obama spent many hours in formal meetings and less formal settings, working through an agenda that touched on the most pressing issues facing the world today. There was a broad-ranging agenda of bilateral political, economic and security issues that they needed to manage. But more widely, their discussions held significance for countries well beyond their own borders, for peoples living in our Asia-Pacific region and far beyond.

How many millions—billions—of people have their livelihood and prosperity directly linked to the economic wellbeing of the world's two largest economies and their ability to provide leadership to the global economic system? How many countries have their security influenced by, if not dependent on, the ability of the world's two largest powers to exercise responsible leadership in times of tension and in areas of instability? How important is it for New Zealand's ongoing prosperity that there should be a constructive relationship between Beijing and Washington?

A relatively new institution, the Contemporary China Research Centre is the only nationwide research centre on contemporary China in the world, with seven member universities. Under the leadership of Professor Bo Zhiyue, the centre aims to be a think tank for the government, a consultancy for business, an academic leader on China research, and a provider of up-to-date information on a changing China for the benefit of New Zealand.

On behalf of Victoria University and the China Research Centre, I would like to thank our distinguished contributors to the conference and this volume. I would also like to acknowledge financial contributions from a range of partners. This includes two embassies—the Embassy of the People's Republic of China and the Embassy of the United States of America—and New Zealand government agencies, which do so much to support and promote dialogue and collaboration between government and the academic community in this capital city, including New Zealand Trade and Enterprise, the Ministry of Foreign Affairs and Trade, the Ministry of Business, Innovation and Employment, the Ministry of Defence, Treasury, and Education New Zealand. I also thank the Lee Foundation in Singapore and KVB Kunlun Limited, as well as an anonymous donor.

The conference and the publication of this volume are excellent illustrations of Victoria's commitment to providing a forum for discussion on issues that are important for New Zealand and for the world.

Notes on Contributors

Robert Ayson has been a professor of strategic studies at Victoria University since 2010 and works in close association with the Centre for Strategic Studies. He has also held academic positions with the Australian National University (ANU), Massey University and the University of Waikato, and official positions with the New Zealand government. Professor Ayson completed his MA as a Freyberg Scholar to the ANU and his PhD at King's College London as a Commonwealth Scholar to the UK. He is an adjunct professor with the ANU's Strategic and Defence Studies Centre, an honorary professor with the New Zealand Defence Force Command and Staff College, and a member of New Zealand's Public Advisory Committee on Disarmament and Arms Control.

Professor Ayson has a particular interest in strategic competition and cooperation, including in relation to the management of armed conflict. This work ranges from exploring the ideas of Hedley Bull and Thomas Schelling to evaluating New Zealand and Australian responses to the changing Asia-Pacific balance between China and the United States. It also includes his current book project on Asia's security and his long-standing interest in nuclear issues. He teaches and supervises on a range of related areas, and is a frequent media commentator.

Bo Zhiyue is director of the New Zealand Contemporary China Research Centre and a professor of political science at Victoria University of Wellington, New Zealand. He obtained his LLB and LLM in international politics from Peking University and his PhD in political science from the University of Chicago.

He has taught at Peking University, Roosevelt University, the University of Chicago, American University, St John Fisher College, Tarleton State University and the Chinese University of Hong Kong. He is a recipient of the Trustee Distinguished Scholar Award at St John Fisher College and was the inaugural holder of the Joe R. and Teresa Lozano Long Endowed Chair in Social Sciences at Tarleton State University. He has also been a visiting distinguished professor at Shanghai Jiao Tong University in China and chair professor at both National Chengchi University and National Taiwan University.

His research interests include China's elite politics, Chinese provincial leaders, central–local relations, cross-strait relations, Sino–US relations, international relations theories, and global governance. He has published more than 190 book chapters and articles and is the author of a trilogy on China's elite politics: *Chinese Provincial Leaders: Economic Performance and Political Mobility since 1949* (2002); *China's Elite Politics: Political Transition and Power Balancing* (2007); and *China's Elite Politics: Governance and Democratization* (2010). His most recent book is *China's Political Dynamics under Xi Jinping* (World Scientific, forthcoming).

Gerald Chan is professor of politics and international relations at the University of Auckland. He obtained his PhD in Chinese politics and history at Griffith University in Australia and his MA in international relations at the University of Kent, UK. Gerald has taught international relations and Asian politics for 15 years at Victoria University of Wellington. He has held visiting or short-term positions at many universities, including the Chinese University of Hong Kong, Cambridge University, the National University of Singapore, Nanyang Technological University, Singapore, and Kobe Gakuin University in Japan. He is a life member of Clare Hall, Cambridge. He has been an external examiner to the politics programme at the University of Hong Kong. He also holds the position of an external PhD examiner in Chinese international relations at the University of Malaya. He sits on the international editorial/advisory board of many academic journals, including *Global Society*, the *Journal of Asian Security and International Affairs*, the *Journal of Human Security*, and the *International Journal of China Studies*. Before he joined Auckland in 2009, he was professor of East Asian politics and director of the Centre for Contemporary Chinese Studies at Durham University.

Gerald's key research area is Chinese international relations. He has published a number of books and many articles in this area. He is currently working on several projects relating to China's New Silk Road plan; the social evolution of Chinese politics; China's ability to create norms and rules that change the behaviour of other states; and China's role in global financial governance.

Gerald's recent publications include 'China eyes ASEAN: Evolving Multilateralism', *Journal of Asian Security and International Relations*, 2015; 'For Better, for Worse: China Embraces Global Poverty Reduction', *Bandung Journal of the Global South*, 2015; 'China's Economic Power and the Global Financial Structure', *Harvard Asia Quarterly*, 16:1, 2014, pp. 13–18; 'Capturing China's International Identity: Social Evolution and Its Missing Links', *Chinese Journal of International Politics*, 7:2, 2014, pp. 261–81; 'China and Small States in Food Security Governance', *African and Asian Studies*, 13.1; 13:2, 2014, pp. 59–79.

Two of Gerald's co-authored articles won the Best Essay of the Year award: one entitled 'Rethinking global governance: a China model in the making?' in *Contemporary Politics*, 2008; and the other 'Japan, the West and the whaling issue', in *Japan Forum*, 2005.

Jaewoo Choo is professor of Chinese foreign policy in the Department of Chinese Studies at Kyung Hee University, Korea. He was a visiting fellow at the Center for East Asian Studies, the Brookings Institution (2014, Spring) and a visiting associate professor at the Georgia Institute of Technology (2011–12). He graduated from Wesleyan University (BA in government) and Peking University (MA and PhD in international relations). His research areas are Chinese foreign policy, multilateral security cooperation and China–North Korea relations. He was a contributor to *Asia Times* on the Korean peninsula affairs (2002–05).

Prior to teaching, Choo worked in a number of think tanks in Korea. He was a research fellow at the Northeast Asia Development Center, Institute East and West Studies, Yonsei University, Seoul (1997–1998); an associate research fellow at the International Affairs Office, National Security Policy Institute (1998–2000); a director and research fellow at the Northeast Asian Studies Program, Institute Strategy and International Affairs (2001–2002); and a research fellow at the Trade Research Institute, Korea International Trade Association (2002–2003).

Choo's prior fellowships also include visiting research fellowships at the Institute of International Relations, National Chengchi University, Taipei (2003); Pudong Institute for the United States Economy, Shanghai (2004); East Asian Institute, National University of Singapore (2005–2006, 2007–2008); Silk Road Studies Program, Uppsala University, Sweden (2006).

In addition to numerous contributions to edited volumes, his academic journal work includes 'China's Frustration over North Korea: Editorial Analysis (December 2012–April 2013', *Korea Journal of Security Analysis* (2014); 'Does China's Charm Offensive Pose a Dilemma for South Korea?', *China Brief* (2014); 'China's Dilemma on the Korean Peninsula: Not an Alliance but a Security Dilemma', *Korea Journal of Defense Analysis* (2013); 'Ideas Matter: China's Peaceful Rise', *Asia Europe Journal* (2009); 'East Asia Security Community Building', *Journal of Korean Political Science* (2009); 'Mirroring North Korea's Growing Economic Dependency on China: Political Ramifications', *Asian Survey* (2008); 'Energy Cooperation in Northeast Asia: Unfolding the Reality', *East Asia: An International Quarterly* (2006); 'Is Institutionalization of the Six-Party Talks Possible?' *East Asia: An International Quarterly* (2005). He is currently working on book manuscripts for *China's Diplomacy: Concepts, Strategies and Diplomacy* (London: Chandos Publishing, to be published in 2015), and *China and North Korea relations in Kim Jong-Il Era: From Party-to-Party Relations Perspectives* (publisher TBD).

Bei Gao holds a doctorate degree from Xi'an Jiao Tong University (China) in 2011. Dr Gao engaged in research work at Dagong Credit Rating from 2011–2013 and joined the Institute of World Economics and Politics, Chinese Academy of Social Sciences, as a post-doctoral fellow in 2013. During this period, Gao was seconded to the International Division, Ministry of Finance, China for the preparation of the AIIB. Now, she is a lecturer at the School of Finance and Economics, Xi'an Jiao Tong University. Her interests mainly focus on China's macro economy, China's monetary policy, RMB internationalisation and international development financing.

She has published over ten articles in Chinese journals and over ten columns in leading Chinese media. And one book has been published on the American subprime mortgage crises, titled *A Study of the US Sub-Prime Mortgage Crisis and Its Monetary Policy: Based on a Capital Flow Perspective*, China Social Science Press, 2015.

Crawford Falconer was appointed the Sir Graeme Harrison Professor of Global Value Chains and Trade at Lincoln University in late 2015. Prior to that, he has worked on international trade issues one way or another for the last 30 years. He has been the New Zealand government's deputy secretary for trade and economic affairs. He has been New Zealand's ambassador to the World Trade Organisation (WTO). He has been an independent chair for a number of international trade negotiating bodies including the WTO Agricultural Trade Negotiations, the WTO Cotton negotiations, the GATT Subsidies Committee and the OECD Trade Committee. He has worked for the Victoria University Institute for Governance and Policy Studies (where, with Sir Frank Holmes, he co-authored 'Open Regionalism?'), and has worked for several years at the Paris-based OECD where most recently, he led a path-breaking project on Trade in Services. He has also worked as an independent judge on large number of international trade disputes.

Mark Gilbert was nominated by President Barack Obama as the United States Ambassador to New Zealand and Samoa on 6 January 2014. The US Senate confirmed Ambassador Gilbert's appointment on 12 December 2014 and he was sworn in by Vice President Joe Biden on 7 January 2015. Ambassador Gilbert presented his credentials in New Zealand to Governor-General Sir Jerry Mateparae on 9 February 2015, and to Samoan Chief Justice Patū Sapolu on 12 May 2015.

Ambassador Gilbert formerly served as a managing director of UBS Group AG; the culmination of a distinguished career in finance, which included positions at Barclays, and the Goldman Sachs Group. From 2009–13 he served as the deputy national finance chair for the Democratic National Committee.

Prior to his banking career, Ambassador Gilbert played professional baseball for eight seasons, reaching the major leagues with the Chicago White Sox in 1985. Ambassador Gilbert is the first former major league player to become a United States ambassador.

Ambassador Gilbert served on the Development Committee and Utah Advisory Board of the Sundance Institute; as chairman of the Board of Trustees and Finance Committee at Pine Crest School (1992–2012); and as president and chairman of the Budget and Finance Committee of B'nai Torah Congregation (1994–2007).

Stephen Jacobi is the executive director of the New Zealand International Business Forum. The New Zealand International Business Forum (NZIBF) provides leadership to enable New Zealand businesses to exploit new opportunities in international markets. The NZIBF works with businesses and other business organisations to implement key projects, including working to develop New Zealand's key international business relationships.

The NZIBF is also responsible for providing policy advice to the three New Zealand members of the APEC Business Advisory Council (ABAC). Jacobi also serves as alternate ABAC member for New Zealand.

Stephen has a first class honours degree in French and German from the University of Auckland and is a graduate of the École Nationale d'Administration (ENA) in Paris, as well as of the Leadership Seminar of Georgetown University and the New Zealand Institute for Strategic Leadership. He was a Fulbright scholar and visiting researcher at Georgetown University in 2013.

Stephen has broad experience in industry and trade development. He was formerly chief executive of the New Zealand Forest Industries Council and executive director of the NZ US Council. Stephen is a frequent media commentator on industry and trade issues.

Stephen also has extensive diplomatic, trade and government experience including posts as deputy high commissioner in Ottawa; assistant trade commissioner in Paris; and adviser on trade and diplomatic issues with the Ministry of Foreign Affairs and Trade. He was formerly private secretary to the Minister for Trade Negotiations, Hon. Jim Sutton, advising on trade policy, international affairs and government-to-government negotiations.

Stephen is an accredited director, the chairman of the St John's College Trust Board in Auckland, one of the country's largest private trusts with diverse commercial property and financial investments, and the Te Aute Trust Board which is the proprietor for two Māori Anglican schools in the Hawke's Bay. The Te Aute Trust Board also operates two farms. Jacobi serves concurrently as managing director of Jacobi Consulting Ltd, a consultancy offering advice to public- and private-sector clients in the fields of international trade, government relations and industry development.

Dongmin Liu is a senior research fellow and the director of the Division of International Finance, Institute of World Economics and Politics (IWEP), Chinese Academy of Social Sciences. His research area focuses on reform of the international monetary system, internationalisation of RMB, development of the AIIB and NDB, shadow banking system, financial regulation and the construction of China's financial centre.

Liu graduated from Tsinghua University, getting his BA degree in Automation and MA in Management Science and Engineering. He got his PhD in Finance from the Institute of Finance and Trade, Chinese Academy of Social Sciences. Since he joined the IWEP in 2009, Liu has finished about 20 research projects sponsored by central and local governments, financial institutions and companies. Now he is the expert on the AIIB for the Ministry of Finance. He has participated in financial industry planning for the Qianhai free trade zone in the Guangdong Province. In order to facilitate the internationalisation of the RMB, he proposed to initiate a pilot program of cross-border RMB loans between Hong Kong and the Qianhai free trade zone. His proposal was approved by the central government in 2012 and is now the pilot programme of cross-border RMB loans has already successfully applied to all China's free trade zones (Shanghai City, Tianjin City,

Guangdong Province and Fujian Province) and Qingdao, a city in the Shandong Province.

Manjeet S. Pardesi is a lecturer in international relations and an Asia research fellow at the Centre for Strategic Studies at Victoria University of Wellington in New Zealand. He obtained his PhD in political science from Indiana University, Bloomington (IUB). His dissertation work focused on the initiation of strategic rivalries and their escalation to war. His research interests include causes of war, theories of foreign policymaking, the rise and fall of great powers, international relations in world history, Asian security and Indian foreign and security policies.

He was an editorial assistant with *International Studies Quarterly* from 2009–12. From 2006–08 he worked as a graduate assistant at the Center on American and Global Security at IUB. He has an MS in Strategic Studies from the Institute of Defence and Strategic Studies (IDSS), Nanyang Technological University, Singapore. After completing his MS, he worked as an associate research fellow at IDSS where he focused on the institute's projects on the Revolution in Military Affairs (RMA) and India. He has lectured, conducted tutorials and led discussion groups of the Tri-Service Staff Course and the Command and Staff Course at the SAFTI Military Institute, Singapore, and at the Advanced Command and Staff Course (Joint), New Zealand Defence Force Command and Staff College. He is a co-editor of *India's Military Modernization: Challenges and Prospects* (Oxford, 2014).

His articles have appeared in the *Air and Space Power Journal* (USAF), *The Fletcher Forum of World Affairs*, *World Policy Journal*, *India Review*, *Asian Security*, *Defense and Security Analysis*, and in several edited book volumes. He has also written commentaries on the RMA and India's foreign and security policies, which have appeared in the *Straits Times* (Singapore), the *Korea Herald* (South Korea), the *Indian Express* (India), *Daily News and Analysis* (India), the *Times of India* (India), and *Asia Times Online*.

Susan Park is an associate professor in international relations at the University of Sydney. She teaches classes on international organisations and global environmental politics. She has previously taught at the University of New South Wales and Deakin University. Her research focuses on how actors make the multilateral development banks green and accountable.

Susan has published in a wide range of journals including *The Pacific Review*, *Third World Quarterly*, *International Politics*, *Global Governance* and *Global Environmental Politics*. She is the author of *The World Bank Group and Environmentalists* (Manchester University Press, 2010) and has co-edited two volumes: *Owning Development: Creating Global Policy Norms in the IMF and the World Bank* with Antje Vetterlein (Cambridge University Press, 2010) and *Global Economic Governance and the Development Practices of the Multilateral Development Banks* with Jonathan Strand (Routledge, 2016).

Susan is currently working on a manuscript comparing the creation, reformulation and efficacy of the accountability mechanisms of the multilateral development banks. In addition, Susan is collaborating with Teresa Kramarz (University of Toronto) on a long-term research project titled 'Accountability in Global Environmental Governance'. The research project has three objectives. It creates a coherent theoretical framework to investigate accountability in global environmental governance (GEG); it documents whether accountability procedures in GEG work; and examines whether accountability procedures are linked to improving environmental outcomes. The aim of the research project is to yield a game-changing approach to understanding, investigating and evaluating accountability in GEG.

Robert G. Patman is the head of the Department of Politics at the University of Otago. He previously served as the founding director of the multidisciplinary Master of International Studies programme (2000, 2013); directed and co-directed the annual University of Otago Foreign Policy School on several occasions; and served as an editor for the scholarly journal *International Studies Perspectives* (2010–14). His research interests encompass US foreign policy, international relations, global security, great powers and the Horn of Africa. Robert is the author or editor of 11 books. Recent publications include *Strategic Shortfall: The 'Somalia Syndrome' and the March to 9/11* (Praeger, 2010) and three co-edited books titled *The Bush Leadership, the Power of Ideas, and the War on Terror* (Ashgate, 2012); *China and the International System: Becoming a World Power* (Routledge, 2013); and *Science Diplomacy: New Day or False Dawn?* (World Scientific Publishers, 2014). He is a Fulbright senior scholar, an honorary professor of the New Zealand Defence Command and Staff College, Trentham, and provides regular contributions to national and international media on global issues and events.

Shao Yuqun is a senior fellow and the executive director of the Center for American Studies, Shanghai Institute for International Studies (SIIS), which is one of the leading think tanks in China on international relations, China's foreign policy and international strategy.

Dr Shao obtained her BA in Chinese language and literature and MA in international Chinese studies from the East China Normal University, and her PhD in international relations from Fudan University, Shanghai.

Her main research area includes US global strategy and foreign policy, US policy towards central and south Asia and the Asia-Pacific in particular, US policy and cross-strait relations, China–US relations, and US domestic politics. She also teaches US foreign policy for the SIIS MA programme.

She has published various papers and articles on cross-strait relations, US Afpak strategy, Afghanistan reconstruction, US–India relations, the Shanghai Cooperation Organization and the regional security situation, China and the US' interaction in the Asia-Pacific region, US public diplomacy, US global strategy, and foreign policy in Chinese, US and European journals. She has participated in second-track dialogues with US, European and Southeast Asian counterparts on the Taiwan question, as well as with US and Indian counterparts on reconstruction and reconciliation in Afghanistan. She has joined Chinese government delegations to observe elections in several countries. She has also led several research projects for related government departments in Beijing.

She was a visiting fellow in the Freeman Chair in China Studies, Center for Security and International Studies in 2010, and a visiting fellow in the German Development Institute in 2008.

She is a regular commentator for Oriental TV in Shanghai, and also contributes articles and comments for newspapers and websites in China.

Laura Southgate is a PhD student in the Department of Politics, University of Otago. Her research interests include the Association of Southeast Asian Nations (ASEAN), state sovereignty and the international relations of Southeast Asia.

Robert Sutter has been professor of practice of international affairs at the Elliott School of International Affairs (ESIA), George Washington University, since 2011. He also directs the ESIA BA programme in international affairs, which involves over 1,000 students.

A PhD graduate in History and East Asian Languages from Harvard University, Sutter taught full-time at Georgetown University (2001–2011) and part-time for 30 years at Georgetown University, George Washington University, Johns Hopkins University and the University of Virginia. He has published 21 books, and hundreds of articles and government reports dealing with China, Asia and the US. His most recent books are *The United States and Asia* (Rowman and Littlefield, 2015) and *Chinese Foreign Relations: Power and Policy since the Cold War 4th ed.* (Rowman and Littlefield 2016).

Sutter's government career (1968–2001) involved work on Asian and Pacific affairs and US foreign policy. He was the senior specialist and director of the Foreign Affairs and National Defense Division of the Congressional Research Service. He also served as the National Intelligence Officer for East Asia and the Pacific at the US government's National Intelligence Council; the China division director at the Department of State's Bureau of Intelligence and Research; and a professional staff member of the Senate Foreign Relations Committee.

Akio Takahara is professor of contemporary Chinese politics at the Graduate School of Law and Politics, the University of Tokyo. He received his PhD in 1988 from the University of Sussex, and later spent several years as visiting scholar at the consulate-general of Japan in Hong Kong (1989–91); the Japanese Embassy in Beijing (1996–98); the Fairbank Center for East Asian Research, Harvard University (2005–06); and at the School of International Studies, Peking University

(2014–15). Before joining the University of Tokyo, he taught at the J.F. Oberlin University (1991–95) and Rikkyo University (1995–2005). He also served as a programme officer of the Sasakawa Peace Foundation USA (1988–89); a member of the governing body of the Institute of Development Studies, UK (1999–2003); president of the Japan Association for Asian Studies (2009–11); and secretary general of the New Japan–China Friendship for the 21st Century Committee (2009–14). He currently serves as senior fellow of the Tokyo Foundation, adjunct fellow of the Japan Institute of International Affairs and senior fellow of the Japan Forum on International Relations.

His publications include *The Politics of Wage Policy in Post-Revolutionary China*, (Macmillan, 1992); *New Developments in East Asian Security* (Akashi Shoten, 2005, co-editor, in Japanese); *Beyond the Borders: Contemporary Asian Studies Vol. 1* (Keio University Press, 2008, co-editor, in Japanese); *The History of Japan–China Relations 1972–2012, Vol. 1: Politics* (University of Tokyo Press, 2012, co-editor, in Japanese), *Modern History of Japan–China Relations* (Yuhikaku Publishing, 2013, co-author, in Japanese); and *To the Era of Developmentalism, 1972–2014, Series on China's Modern History, Vol. 5* (Iwanami Shoten, 2014, co-author, in Japanese).

Carlyle A. Thayer is emeritus professor at the University of New South Wales (UNSW) and the Australian Defence Force Academy (ADFA). Thayer studied political science at Brown University, was awarded an MA in Southeast Asian Studies from Yale (1971) and a PhD in international relations from the Australian National University (ANU, 1977). He served in Vietnam with the International Voluntary Services (1967–68). Thayer first taught at the Bendigo Institute of Technology/Bendigo College of Advanced Education in Victoria from 1975–78. He joined the UNSW in 1979 and taught first in the Faculty of Military Studies at The Royal Military College, Duntroon, before transferring to University College at the ADFA in 1985. He was head of the Department of Politics (1995–97), promoted to full professor in 1998 and formally retired in 2010.

Thayer was given 'leave in the national interest' to take up a senior appointment at the US Department of Defense's Asia-Pacific Center for Security Studies, Pacific Command, Hawaii (1999–2002). On return to Australia he was appointed Deakin University's on-site academic coordinator for the senior Defence and Strategic Studies Course at the Centre for Defence and Strategic Studies (CDSS), Australian Defence College (2002–04). He then directed Regional Security Studies at the Australian Command and Staff College (2006–07, 2010). In 2005 he was honoured by appointment as the C.V. Starr Distinguished Visiting Professor of Southeast Asian Studies at the School of Advanced International Studies, Johns Hopkins University, and in 2008 as the inaugural Frances M. and Stephen H. Fuller Distinguished Visiting Professor of Southeast Asian Studies at Ohio University.

Thayer has also held appointments at Harvard's Center for International Affairs; Yale University's Department of Political Science, Chulalongkorn University in

Bangkok, the Institute of Southeast Asian Studies in Singapore, the International Institute for Strategic Studies in London, the ANU's Department of Political and Social Change and Strategic and Defence Studies Centre. Thayer is a Southeast Asia regional specialist. He is currently the director of Thayer Consultancy, a small business registered in Australia that provides political analysis and research support on current regional security issues.

Thayer also writes a weekly column on Southeast Asian defence and security affairs for *The Diplomat*. He is the author of over 500 publications including: 'China and ASEAN', in Mahendra Gaur, ed., *Studies on China No. 3* (New Delhi: Foreign Policy Research Institute, January 2015), 208-215; 'China and Vietnam Eschew Megaphone Diplomacy', *The Diplomat*, 2 January 2015; 'Vietnam Mulling New Strategies to Deter China', *The Diplomat*, 28 May 2014; 'ASEAN and China Consultations on a Code of Conduct in the South China Sea: Prospects and Obstacles', in *Security and Cooperation in the South China Sea* (Moscow: Institute of Oriental Studies, Russian Academy of Sciences, 2014), pp. 34–49; 'China–ASEAN and the South China Sea: Chinese Assertiveness and Southeast Asian Responses', in Yann-Huei Song and Keyuan Zou, eds., *Major Law and Policy Issues in the South China Sea: European and American Perspectives* (Farnham: Ashgate Publishing Inc., 2014), pp. 25–53; and *Southeast Asia: Patterns of Security Cooperation* (Canberra: Australian Strategic Policy Institute, 2010).

Wang Gungwu is professor at the National University of Singapore, emeritus professor of the Australian National University and formerly director of the East Asian Institute, 1997–2007.

His recent books include *The Chinese Overseas: From Earthbound China to the Quest for Autonomy* (2000); *Don't Leave Home: Migration and the Chinese* (2001); *Anglo–Chinese Encounters since 1800: War, Trade, Science and Governance* (2003); *Diasporic Chinese Ventures: The Life and Work of Wang Gungwu*, Gregor Benton and Liu Hong, eds. (2004);《移民及兴起的中国》(2005);《离乡别土：境外看中华》(2005); *Wang Gungwu: Junzi: Scholar-Gentleman, In Conversation with Asad-ul Iqbal Latif* (2010); *Wang Gungwu: Educator and Scholar*, Zheng Yongnian and K.K. Phua, eds., (2012);《华人与中国：王赓武自选集》(2013); *Renewal: The Chinese State and the New Global History* (2013); *Another China Cycle: Committing to Reform* (2014); and《五代时期北方中国的权力结构》(2014); and《天下华人》(2016). His dialogues on world history were edited by Ooi Kee Beng and published as *The Eurasian Core and Its Edges* (2015).

He also edited *Global History and Migrations* (1997); *Nation-Building: Five Southeast Asian Histories* (2005); and (with Zheng Yongnian) *China and the New International Order* (2008).

He is a fellow and former president of the Australian Academy of the Humanities; Commander of the Order of the British Empire (CBE); foreign honorary member of the American Academy of Arts and Science; member, Academia Sinica; and honorary member of the Chinese Academy of Social Sciences. He was also awarded the Fukuoka Asian Culture Prize and the Nara Economic and Social Science Prize.

In Singapore, he is chairman of the Institute of Southeast Asian Studies; and chairman of East Asian Institute and Lee Kuan Yew School of Public Policy at the National University of Singapore. He has also been awarded the Public Service Star Award and the Meritorious Services Medal (Singapore).

Professor Wang received his BA with honours (1953) and MA (1955) from the University of Malaya in Singapore, and his PhD at the School of Oriental and African Studies, University of London (1957). He was professor of history at the University of Malaya, 1963–68; professor of Far Eastern history at the ANU (1968–86) and director of the ANU Research School of Pacific and Asian Studies, 1975–80. From 1986–95, he was vice-chancellor of the University of Hong Kong.

Wang Lutong started his tenure as the Ambassador Extraordinary and Plenipotentiary of the People's Republic of China to New Zealand, the Cook Islands and Niue in 2013. He worked as the staff member and attaché in the information department of Ministry of Foreign Affairs (MOFA, China) from 1992–96. From 1996–2000, he served as attaché and third secretary at the Chinese Embassy in the UK. From 2000–02, he worked in the information department of the MOFA as third secretary and deputy director. From 2002 to 2003, he worked in the Department of West Europe Affairs at the MOFA as second secretary and director. From 2003–05, he worked at the general office of the MOFA as first secretary and counsellor. From 2005–13, he worked successively as counsellor and director, associate counsel and counsel at the office of the Foreign Affairs Leading Group, CPC Central Committee.

Brantly Womack is professor of Foreign Affairs and holds the Miller Center's C.K. Yen Chair at the University of Virginia. He received his BA in politics and philosophy from the University of Dallas, studied Philosophy at the University of Munich and completed his PhD in political science from University of Chicago. After his post-doctoral research at the University of California, Berkeley, he taught at Northern Illinois University and at the School of Oriental and African Studies before coming to the University of Virginia.

Womack is the author of a number of books including *Asymmetry and International Relationships* (Cambridge University Press, 2016); *China Among Unequals: Asymmetric International Relationships in Asia* (World Scientific Press, 2010); and *China and Vietnam: The Politics of Asymmetry* (Cambridge University Press, 2006). He edited *China's Rise in Historical Perspective* (Rowman and Littlefield, 2010); and *Contemporary Chinese Politics in Historical Perspective* (Cambridge University Press, 1991). He has authored more than a hundred articles and book chapters, primarily on Asian politics.

In 2011 Womack received the China Friendship Award for his work with Chinese universities. He holds honorary positions at Jilin University, East China Normal

University and Zhongshan (Sun Yat-Sen) University. He recently completed a visiting research professorship at the East Asia Institute of the National University of Singapore and was visiting researcher at East China Normal University in Shanghai.

Wu Jianmin (1939–2016) was a member of the Foreign Policy Advisory Group of the Chinese Ministry of Foreign Affairs, special research fellow of counsellor's office of the State Council, member and vice president of the European Academy of Sciences and honorary president of the International Exhibitions Bureau (BIE).

From 2003–08, former ambassador Wu served as president of the China Foreign Affairs University, executive vice president of the China National Association for International Studies, vice chairman of the Foreign Affairs Committee of, and spokesperson for, the Chinese People's Political Consultative Conference (CPPCC). Earlier, he served as China's ambassador to France (1998–2003); to the United Nations office in Geneva, to other international organisations in Switzerland (1996–98) and to the Netherlands (1994–95). Before that, he was director general of the Information Department of, and spokesperson for, the Chinese Ministry of Foreign Affairs (1991–94), deputy chief at China's embassy in Belgium and its mission to the European Community in Brussels (1989–90) and counsellor for China's mission to the United Nations in New York (1985–89).

From 2003–07, former ambassador Wu served as president of International Bureau of Expositions (BIE), making him the first Asian to take up the post.

Former ambassador Wu was born in 1939. He graduated from the Beijing Foreign Studies University with a major in French, and from 1965–1971 interpreted many times for Chairman Mao Zedong and Premier Zhou Enlai. In 1971, he became a member of China's first delegation to the United Nations.

He was awarded the honour of Knight of the French Legion of Honour in 2003 by French President Jacques Chirac.

Former ambassador Wu tragically passed away on 18 June 2016.

Qiyuan Xu received his doctoral degree from Northeast Normal University in 2008. Xu has worked for the Institute of World Economics and Politics (IWEP), the Chinese Academy of Social Sciences (CASS) since 2008, and has been a senior research fellow since 2011.

In 2012 he also took up the role of adviser in the international collaboration department of China's Ministry of Finance. Xu also sits in the work team of China's External Economic Environment (CEEM) in IWEP. This work team issues a quarterly report on global macroeconomics, and he is responsible for the research on China and RMB issues.

He has published 45 articles issued in *China and World Economy* and other Chinese top academic journals, over a hundred columns published in the *Financial Times*, *Financial World* in English and in leading Chinese media. Three books have been published on the RMB: *The Study of Exchange Rates Variation during RMB's Internationalization* (with Liu Lizhen, China Financial Publishing House,

2009); *The Economic Analysis of China Yuan's Exchange Rate Regime* (with He Fan, Shanghai University of Finance and Economics Press, 2008); *A Study of China Yuan's Internationalization* (with Liu Lizhen, People's Publishing House, 2006).

Qiyuan has been a visiting fellow at the Centre for International Governance Innovation (CIGI, 2014), Universidad Autónoma de Madrid (2014), Bruegel (2013), Hitotsubashi University (2009), and the Institute of International Monetary Affairs (IIMA) at the Bank of Tokyo-Mitsubishi UFJ (2011).

Jingdong Yuan is associate professor at the Centre for International Security Studies and the Department of Government and International Relations at the University of Sydney, where he is also an academic member of the China Studies Centre. Professor Yuan specialises in Asia-Pacific security, Chinese defence and foreign policy, Sino–Indian relations, and global and regional arms control and nonproliferation issues. A graduate of the Xi'an Foreign Languages University, People's Republic of China (1982), he received his MA in international affairs from the Norman Paterson School of International Affairs, Carleton University in 1990; PhD in political science from Queen's University in 1995; and has had research and teaching appointments at Queen's University, York University, the University of Toronto, and the University of British Columbia, where he was a recipient of the prestigious Izaak Killam Postdoctoral Research Fellowship. He was also the recipient of the Canadian Department of National Defence R.B. Byres Postdoctoral Fellowship and the Chiang Ching-kuo Foundation/Canadian Asian Studies Association (CASA) Postdoctoral Fellowship.

Between 1999–2010, he held various appointments at the Middlebury Institute of International Studies at Monterey, including as director of the nonproliferation education programme and East Asia nonproliferation programme; the James Martin Center for Nonproliferation Studies; and associate professor of International Policy Studies. Professor Yuan has also held visiting appointments at the National University of Singapore, the University of Macau, East–West Center, and the National Chengchi University. He is co-author of *A Low-Visibility Force Multiplier: Assessing China's Cruise Missile Ambitions* (Washington, DC: National Defense University Press, 2014), co-editor of *Australia and China at 40* (Sydney: University of New South Wales Press, 2012) and co-author of *China and India: Cooperation or Conflict?* (Boulder, Co.: Lynne Rienner Publishers, 2003). His publications have appeared in *Asian Affairs, Asia Policy, Asian Survey, Asian Perspective, Far Eastern Economic Review, Contemporary Security Policy, The Hindu, International Herald Tribune, International Journal, International Politics, Jane's Intelligence Review, Japan Times, Journal of Contemporary China, Journal of International Affairs, Korean Journal of Defense Analysis, Los Angeles Times, Moscow Times, Nonproliferation Review, Security Challenges, The Washington Quarterly*, and in many edited volumes including, most recently, *The Oxford Handbook of the International Relations of Asia* (2014). He is currently working on a book-length manuscript on China's relations with South Asia since the end of the Cold War.

List of Tables

Table 7.1   Global infrastructure investments by China, the EU, and the US, 1992–2011 (January 2013)
Table 7.2   China-led international financial institutions (June 2015)
Table 7.3   The GDPs of the BRICS, 2014
Table 7.4   Comparing the AIIB, the ADB, and the World Bank, 2015 (June 2015)
Table 7.5   The international economic position of the US, 1945 vs 2013 (November 2014)
Table 8.1   G7 member states voting power as a per cent of total votes in the MDBs FY2011 (July 2012)
Table 11.1 China's and the US' visions of regional multilateral security cooperation architecture

List of Figures

Figure 6.1   The term *xinxing daguo guanxi* ('a new type of major-country relationship') mentioned in the *People's Daily* (January–September 2015)
Figure 7.1   A model of China's multilateral financial involvement
Figure 7.2   Economic growth, West vs East, 2011–2060
Figure 9.1   From globalisation to fragmentation: trade system
Figure 9.2   From globalisation to fragmentation: financial system
Figure 9.3   Structure of the infrastructure financing needs and gaps in 2020: divided by sovereign credit rating (October 2015)

Introduction

China and the US: A Tale of Two Civilisations

Wang Gungwu

University professor and chairman of the East Asian Institute at the National University of Singapore

The People's Republic of China and the United States are not only two powerful states in a globalised world but also the products of two ancient civilisations. How their respective civilisations brought them to this stage of modernisation from opposite ends of the huge landmass Eurasia is a tangled story of human endeavour and endurance. The two countries have had two totally different trajectories of development, but their peoples still trace the sources of their successes and failures to ideas and values that go back for millennia. These two states and civilisations have now reached an unexpected stage of interdependence and confrontation, and the paths they have taken to reach this new stage must therefore become a subject of increasing importance. The trajectories of their growth over millennia should throw light on the problems that their leaders face today. Without going too far back in history, this introduction offers a perspective on the subject through the prism of political leaders seeking to define what kind of world is needed to enable their peoples to attain their goals.

Civilisation and State
'Civilisation' and 'state' are terms in modern Western social sciences for which there are no exact Chinese equivalents. The closest word to civilisation in classical Chinese is *wenjiao* (literate moral teachings), and to state is *tianchao* (court [of the son] of

heaven). This points to the US representing the most powerful state, embodying a civilisation of universal values that came from ancient civilisations (the Tigris–Euphrates and the Nile) and other powerful Mediterranean states. As for the Chinese, their civilisation was a literacy-based system mandated by heaven that, over three millennia, had brought miscellaneous peoples together into a powerful state. Thus I shall use the word 'civilisation' as shorthand for civilisation-*wenjiao,* and 'state' for state-*tianchao,* on the understanding that the two concepts have been converging for the past century and a half. Coming from a considerable distance apart, there are deep differences between the two states and civilisations that still need time to be resolved. But there are signs that China is moving towards a common modernity with the US while also seeking to offer distinct contributions to it.

US Cultural Heritage

When the US became an independent country in 1776, it bore a large part of Britain's cultural heritage. Its people also saw Britain as the dominant maritime power in a progressive Euro-Mediterranean civilisation that was on the verge of two revolutions. Britain was leading the industrial revolution, which brought science and entrepreneurship into fruitful partnership. It was also leading the political revolution that was transforming the whole of Western Europe. That revolution moved in two directions: it introduced new ideals of freedom and equality to the peoples of Europe, and it established a system of nation-states that fostered both pride and imperial ambitions, and which ultimately provided new impetus for expansionist wars that confirmed Britain as the greatest global maritime power the world had ever seen.

Both these revolutions would eventually transform the world. The new US nation began by turning away from the entanglements in Europe. They valued their independence and concentrated on the vast lands on their own continent, free from the burdens of centuries of religious and dynastic conflicts. They were proud to have established a country in which church and state were separated and a unique mix of Christian communities were given the freedom to worship as they chose. They were aware that, in the Old World from which they kept a distance, there were other empires. Many were Islam-dominated empires and states that controlled their half of the Mediterranean Sea and still exerted pressures on parts of Eastern and central Europe. That Muslim conglomerate of states, however, could no longer block Western Europe from the riches of India and China. Since the 1500s the commercial revolution had further changed the terms of economic power by extending across three oceans. Situated in the New World, the former thirteen colonies, now united in a federal state, were free to find their own way to profit from that global opening and harness the new forces of scientific and economic revolutions to build a different kind of nation. Formerly British peoples who migrated across Atlantic could turn to the large raw continent with fresh political will and the newest technical and financial tools to help them chart their future.

The Chinese Historical Legacies

In contrast, the Qing Empire in China (1644–1912) was a powerful Old World empire on the Eurasian continent. Its rulers had marched south from Manchuria to conquer a vast bureaucratic state established by the Chinese rulers of the Ming dynasty. That state was founded on Confucian principles of governance, and prided itself for being the embodiment of an ancient and morally superior civilisation. The Manchus then incorporated this state into a continental Eurasian empire that expanded westwards into Mongol and Turkic lands. By the time the US became an independent country, Qing China under the emperor Qianlong was at the peak of its power and controlled the largest Asian empire since the death of Kublai Khan in 1294.

This was also a time of imperial hubris for the Qing dynasty. Its elites did not realise that their land empire was losing out to the new maritime forces battling for control of its coastal waters. When Lord Macartney sought to open direct trade with China in 1793, Qianlong dismissed the British as if they were members of a recalcitrant non-tributary state. He did not live to regret his haughty response to the British monarch, but his successors found themselves facing an enemy who quickly defeated them at sea. In addition, the British also sold them larger quantities of opium, a product that destroyed their people's moral will as well as the country's agrarian economy. When these intrusions were combined with dissensions within their borders, the Qing leaders found themselves unable to stop the empire's rapid decline and final destruction.

When the Americans followed the British into East Asia, they wasted no time reaching out to the China coasts for their share of the opium trade. Qing officials saw them as a minor branch of the European great powers and thought that their New World state was unthreatening. Unlike those of Britain and France, and later of Japan, US activities in China were not accompanied by threats of gunships and arrogant protests.

The Chinese thus saw the low-key missionary culture that the Americans brought to China as young offshoots of a powerful civilisation. While not always welcome, the successful missions were often recognised as having contributed much to modern education and public health. This was an asymmetric beginning. Qing mandarins were conscious of China's ancient roots as a civilisation, which Western empires saw as decadent and declining fast. Educated Americans were presenting their values as those of a truly modern civilisation, but many Confucian scholars saw them as the crude and somewhat benign products of an aggressive civilisation. In this way, the two countries managed to avoid direct conflict. In retrospect, the relationship may be described as having got off to a good start, and, despite the many twists and turns of war and diplomacy in East Asia, it remained so until the mid-20th century.

Barack Obama and Xi Jinping

When the leaders of China and the US, Xi Jinping and Barack Obama, met for the first time in history, reports of their meetings speculated on the possibility of either more or less trust emerging between their countries. I shall use their meetings to consider how the two states have things in common. The most interesting thing is that they have each tried to shake off the past mistakes of their stem civilisations. They have separately and under wholly different conditions discovered what it means to seek a common modernity. But they are not agreed whether the modernity should be one where universal values are widely shared or whether it could be based on different political and cultural priorities. As China and the US stand today, they face tough choices. Should they embark on a struggle for dominance; the US to protect its position as the global superpower and China to seek greater security within what it sees as its historical sphere of influence? Can they arrange their relations on the basis of mutual respect for what each believes? If that were possible, how can they together cooperate with other like-minded states to find ways to strengthen a world order that would be easier to defend?

Barack Obama and Xi Jinping represent distinct values and institutions that were shaped by centuries of history. For Obama, his country has long held fast to the American Dream, one based on a New World civilisation that has been using its own nation-state to project that dream to the Old World. For Xi Jinping, he has highlighted the pursuit of a China Dream in order to revive a distinctive heritage by rebuilding a powerful state. Both men have, on different occasions and in distinctive language, done their utmost to articulate what they believe their respective countries stand for.

In one aspect, the early lives of the two men are comparable. Both lived through turbulent times during their youths and emerged remarkably unscarred. But their adult political lives have been markedly different. For example, if we take the mixed migrant origins of Barack Obama, the contrast with Xi Jinping's princeling origins could not be greater. Barack Obama grew up moving between worlds spread far across the Atlantic, Pacific and Indian Oceans. Only in America could that background have led him to the White House. But it was his ability to embrace the country's rich mix of values that made his success possible. When he chose to focus his legal skills to improve the lives of the people of Chicago, he was also learning the best way he could to serve his country.

Xi Jinping, on the other hand, was sent from the privileged courtyards of Beijing to discover the peasant life of his ancestors in deep northwestern China, in the ancient heartland. After he finished his university studies, he had the choice of working in the world of state-supported enterprises, in jobs that would almost certainly have led him to wealth and comfort, or to serve the socialist revolution that his father had fought for. He chose the latter. He resumed his connections within the ruling communist party and the People's Liberation Army. He brought his experiences in China's continental interior to the coasts of China. For the next 20 years he served in the open maritime entrepreneurial provinces of Fujian, Zhejiang and Shanghai. When he was picked in 2007 to become his Party's future leader at the age of 54, he had spent half his life facing inwards and the other half looking out. No doubt this helped him to imagine the potential interplay of an overland Silk Road as an economic belt and the maritime routes of the Indian Ocean. Seeing the two roads meeting on the shores of the Mediterranean Sea is his way of recognising the continued relevance of Old Word certainties to his country's future.

Both Barack Obama and Xi Jinping came to office with heavy burdens left behind by their predecessors. In the US, it was a combination of futile wars in the Middle East and a finance system that needed restructuring. In China, the damage of the past decade was no less challenging. Accompanying what was achieved in 30 years of rapid economic development was pervasive corruption that undermined the credibility of the Chinese Communist Party (CCP). Both leaders responded vigorously to deal with the problems created and won broad support within their countries by employing language recalling the value systems that had made their respective civilisations great.

For Obama, the lofty ideals of the American Revolution can be traced back to Greco-Roman and Semitic Mediterranean roots, ideals that were uplifted and secularised during the Renaissance and Enlightenment periods in Western Europe. These ideals were reinforced when Obama received the best legal training available in the US and were further strengthened by his Christian faith. Xi Jinping, on the other hand, began with a more recent revolutionary and patriotic heritage exemplified by what Mao Zedong and Deng Xiaoping had won for China. But he too joined his predecessors in echoing the call for the renewal of an ancient civilisation cultivated on Chinese soil. That heritage had stressed the goal of unity, harmony and social cohesion that had been attained from time to time through the exercise of central control.

Differences between US and Chinese Presidents

There are further differences between US and Chinese leaders. Presidents of the US have learnt to address the world as governed by an international order of nation-states, the United Nations, which their country fought hard to establish and permanently lodge in its largest city, New York. They see their duty as one of preserving their country's global leadership position. The Chinese leaders are, on the whole, more defensive, concerned primarily with bringing stability and prosperity to the country's 1.3 billion people. Their effectiveness and credibility is based on meeting their people's expectations of social and economic betterment. At the same time, they share widespread hope for the restoration of the civilisation's past greatness and are keen to make the world understand their aim.

Of no less significance is the fact that the US reached the peak of global power in the 1990s at the end of the Cold War just when the Chinese economy was about to become the second largest in the world. Neither country was accustomed to such a dramatic change in their respective global position. Since then, political leaders and their advisers everywhere scrambled to find historical analogies to chart the future strategies the world now needs. For example, the US turned to Thucydides, Machiavelli and other similar thinkers of the Euro-Mediterranean world for guidance. There is the language of great power leaders like Metternich, Churchill and de Gaulle. China, for its part, has equally searched past ideas and experiences, from Sun Tzu, Confucius and the strategists of the Warring States to the statesmen of the Han, Tang and Qing dynasties, to assist its recalibration of the paths ahead. In addition to having to learn all they can about how the West thinks and acts, the Chinese had to do more. They looked to their classical writings to provide them with distinctive answers to meet the challenges ahead.

Observing the differences between the two presidents, I am reminded of some earlier leaders and the decisions they made in response to powerful changes their respective countries had to face. I have picked two sets of leaders as examples, to explore what lay behind the value systems that drove each country to action and to offer here some brief comparisons of the civilisational factors behind what they thought their states were trying to do.

Hong Xiuquan vs Abraham Lincoln

The first set of leaders is from the mid-19th century, when the Old World great powers, Britain and France, had forced open the doors of China and insisted on their extraterritorial rights in the treaty ports. At the same time, the elites of Qing China were threatened with destruction from within by a series of rebellions which eventually took decades to crush. On the other side of the Pacific Ocean, the Gold Rush brought a flood of settlers to California, known as 49-ers for their arrival in 1849, and the US, a rich continent between the Atlantic and the Pacific Oceans, was about to conquered. However, this expansion westwards also coincided with a growing divide within the country between two parallel economies: the slave-owning southern states and the industrialising capitalist states in the north, which largely opposed slavery. Beyond the 49-ers of California, the country was about to face its greatest test: the Civil War, which cost some 600,000 lives. Similarly, nothing in China prepared its mandarin classes for the rebellion in 1851 by a group of Hakka believers in Jesus Christ. This religious fervour had started in the southwestern province of Guangxi and spread right across the empire towards Beijing. It lasted over 14 years and inspired wars that cost the lives of an estimated 20 million people. There is no comparison between the Confederate rebels in the southern US and those who established the Taiping Heavenly Kingdom in Nanjing, even though their commitment to their respective causes might seem to have a similar ferocity.

Instead, let me look at the fallout that followed the death of Hong Xiuquan, the Taiping Heavenly King, aged 50, in 1864 and the assassination of Abraham Lincoln, aged 55, only a few months later.

Hong Xiuquan has been interpreted in different ways, all of those extreme. At one end, he was a madman who dreamt he was the brother of Jesus Christ. Inspired by his meeting with missionaries and the reading of a few Christian tracts, he led his Hakka faithful to a decade of glory, defeating the forces of at least ten provinces on the way to capturing the southern capital of the empire. There, his Heavenly Kingdom rejected all that was associated with Confucian ideals of governance. In the name of God, his armies killed everyone who had links with the Qing dynasty, notably the gentry and literati families whose Confucian loyalties supported the Manchu Banner garrisons that dominated China for 200 years. After his defeat, the Qing mandarins vilified Hong Xiuquan and had all records of the Taipings destroyed.

At the other end, Hong Xiuquan was the heroic precursor of revolution; China's first popular response to the challenge of the alternative civilisation as presented by the Christian West. Sun Yat-Sen, China's first modern political leader, admired him. A generation later, Mao Zedong recognised Hong Xiuquan's pride of place in history as the first leader radical enough to initiate something akin to class struggle in China.

In between these opposite interpretations are efforts to place the Taipings in the spectrum of traditional rebels, mostly of peasant origins, who were inspired by esoteric sects of Buddhism and Daoism and local popular beliefs. Perhaps the most telling judgment came from Protestant missionaries who visited them in Nanjing and concluded that Hong Xiuquan was no Christian and that the West should support the Qing government to crush them. The Western capitalists and financiers of the treaty ports were quick to respond, and offered their help to restore law and order.

The fall of the Taipings was followed by several other rebellions. Although they were disbanded, the dynasty was further weakened by the strenuous efforts to achieve that, and this attracted more interventions by the great powers. Some, like Britain in India and Tsarist Russia in Central Asia, were active among Muslims in the provinces of Xinjiang and Yunnan on China's western borders. The imperial court was alarmed and proclaimed the need for fundamental reforms. This was the Tongzhi Restoration (sometimes identified with the Self-Strengthening Movement), and began when the boy-emperor Tongzhi came under the tutelage of his mother, the Empress Dowager Cixi, who dominated the Qing government for the next 40 years. The Qing court agreed that China needed to make greater efforts to learn from the West. Initially, it concentrated on heavy industry, on new methods of military training and on the manufacture of modern armaments.

However, at the heart of the reforms were really reaffirmations of traditional Confucian values, and these became the essence of the restoration. The leaders concluded that the empire was weak because it had slackened its standards; what it needed most were dedicated officials well-trained by the best Confucian scholars. The rest was merely a question of mastering the latest technologies and updating military hardware. This included, for the first time in four centuries, an attempt to build a modern navy with French and British help. It is doubtful that the Manchu aristocrats knew what it meant to change their continental mindset to one that embraced naval power. It was not enough to have larger and better-armed warships and more men to arm them. New kinds of education were needed to meet the demands of modern strategic thinking. Throughout the restoration years, the only indication that some officials thought there was something lacking in Chinese methods of education was the decision to send 120 very young students to US schools in 1872. After a few years, the programme was ended when it was discovered how Americanised these students had become.

This Chinese version of restoration was nothing like the Meiji Restoration in Japan which overturned the Tokugawa Shogunate. The latter marked a wholesale learning from the West while Empress Dowager Cixi and her courtiers were more concerned with recovering their ancient confidence. In other words, the victory against the Taipings and other sets of rebels led Cixi and her most senior Manchu aristocrats and Confucian mandarins to choose the conservative course and bring back the values they felt had been seriously neglected. The reactionary steps taken were later recognised to have been totally inadequate and the main reason why the Chinese navy was so easily destroyed by the Japanese. That defeat in 1894 then led to xenophobic frustration; for example, the Boxer uprisings, which brought even greater humiliations to the empire. The defeat to Japan also thoroughly discredited the idea that Western learning was a body of new technologies that could be used to protect and reaffirm Chinese core values. After that approach failed, generations of Chinese concluded that nothing less than total westernisation could save China.

In comparison, Abraham Lincoln's death marked an expansive beginning for the US. Lincoln's achievements centred on the preservation of the Union. By keeping the country whole, he reaffirmed the promises established in the American Revolution; of freedom, manifest destiny and charity—'the city upon a hill'—to set an example for all. He had evoked the grand vision that kept the 13 states together after independence. Lincoln's soaring rhetoric recalled how three generations of leaders fought against their former British masters as well those frontiersmen who kept pushing westwards when new borders were drawn. The country was poised to develop vast new territories and acquire previously unimaginable resources. Union victory ensured that the US could become a single continental Western power in the New World, the first of its kind, something Christian Europe had dreamt of since the last centuries of the Roman Empire but had not found possible to build in the Old World. Thus Lincoln's assassination marked the moment when the US people could open up the continent to become the nation it is today.

The 13 colonies had fought desperately to survive against British power at a time when Britain was the most powerful maritime power in the world. They had to pool their respective state resources and form a federated union, inspired by the most progressive ideals that European civilisation had to offer. Significantly, they avoided what the Latin American states were to do shortly afterwards, which was to build separate 'nation-states' that replicated the state system in Europe. This was possible in the Spanish colonies because their imperial master was relatively weak. For the 13 colonies, however, their best decision was to unite against Britain.

Eighty years after independence, as the frontiers moved west and gold was found in California and the British and French imperial rivals were busy elsewhere, it was the age of opportunity in the US. But it was also when the southern states felt strong and self-sufficient enough to secede from the Union. The choice these states made marked a dangerous moment for the country. The political debates of the 1850s made it clear that disagreements over slavery and the future of the country's economic development were fundamental issues for discussion. New leaders arose to express righteous confidence and pride on both sides. But both also reaffirmed the ideals of the original act of rebellion in 1775 that made a clarion call for exceptionalism. Fortunately for the US, Lincoln's Yankees won and the Union was saved, paving the way for the industrial capitalism of the north to thrive.

Woodrow Wilson vs Sun Yat-Sen

The second set of leaders comes from the early 20th century, when the US and China moved again in opposite directions. This was when the US moved upwards towards overwhelming power while China moved downwards towards division and near helplessness. Two extraordinary leaders, Woodrow Wilson in Washington and Sun Yat-sen in Nanjing, reached the highest positions in their respective countries within months of each other. Both wanted to shape new visions of their respective countries' futures and both spoke strongly of what they hoped for in the world. But their terms in power vividly illustrate the extent of the US–China civilisational divide.

On 1 January 1912, to the astonishment of those who followed Chinese affairs closely, the outsider and rebel with a price on his head, Sun Yat-sen, was proclaimed provisional president of the new Republic of China. He was a southern Cantonese Christian who was educated in English schools in Hawaii and Hong Kong; a respected medical graduate turned revolutionary who embraced the notion of nationalism as well the ideals of freedom and equality. He was also someone who had spent most of his life outside his own country, learning from the West, not least with countrymen who worked and lived among modern European administrators and colonists in Asia as well as with North American and Australian settlers.

A few months after the appointment of Sun Yat-Sen, with considerable luck and against everybody's expectations, including his own, the academic-cum-politician Woodrow Wilson rose from being a disputed candidate of the minority Democratic Party to become the first southerner elected president since the Civil War. He was also one of the best-educated leaders the US ever had, and one who had great admiration for the classical origins of modern wealth, power and civilisation. As he sought to redefine the US' future as the leader of the New World, he must have wondered what could possibly have led the confident and all-powerful Europe to stagger blindly towards one of the most destructive wars the world had ever known.

The two men's paths diverted after 1912. Sun Yat-sen was soon pushed out of his position as provisional president of the newly proclaimed Republic of China and returned to his home province of Guangdong. From there he battled, until his early death in 1925, for his party's revival by changing political course several times. He found his republican ideals and hopes for democracy totally subverted: to restructure his nationalist party, the Kuomintang (KMT), he had to insist on dictatorial powers for his leadership. He set aside his national pride to seek foreign funds for his cause, turning away from reluctant Western backers to Japan and the Soviet Union. Inspired by Lenin's party-military apparatus, Sun Yat-sen accepted Soviet support to build a revolutionary army and accepted communist members into the KMT. He did not live long enough to see his army defeat the warlord regime in Beijing and give China a new start in Nanjing, but he came close to linking China to an international ideological civil war in the West between Marxist communism and capitalist imperialism.

Sun Yat-sen was a practical politician ready for any syncretic mix that could unite his people and restore China's independence. He had no difficulty adjusting his Christian faith to fit Chinese traditions. He was comfortable with the Buddho-Daoist practices behind the secret societies he recruited to his cause. He approached capitalist and progressive Japanese for help. He revived a range of Confucian concepts and attracted literati to his nationalist cause. Not least, he was open to Communist International rhetoric and employed Soviet advisers to train his soldiers.

In short, Sun Yat-sen represented a pluralist response to the impact of Western modernity. His unfinished set of lectures, entitled 'The Three Principles of the People', crystalised his ideas into a manifesto for change. This was adopted by the KMT to serve as the basis for a nationalist revolution. It was a mix of old and new political ideas that Sun Yat-sen thought could become achievable goals for the new Chinese nation. When the CCP won the civil war in 1949, the works of Lenin and Stalin and then Mao Zedong replaced all his writings. But 'The Three Principles' remains symbolic of early efforts to find an answer to China's division and decline. Sun Yat-Sen expected China to be open yet resilient, willing to learn from others but dedicated to restoring its great traditions.

Woodrow Wilson's New World heritage was drawn from another civilisation, with ancient origins in multiple cultures along the shores of the Mediterranean Sea. His father was a devout and learned Christian minister and Wilson himself was steeped in the Greek and Roman classics. His political education was founded on American Enlightenment principles, and as a political scientist he connected the country's constitution to its roots in British political traditions and European history. He had an admirable reputation as a scholar and ended his academic career as president of Princeton University.

When Wilson entered the political arena, the US had joined the world of powerful empires, having absorbed the Kingdom of Hawaii and taken the Philippines from the Spanish. When his immediate predecessors extended America's frontier further westwards across the Pacific Ocean, continuing the push seemed the most natural thing for for Wilson to do. At the continent's western edges, the call to 'Go West, young man!' drew them to global maritime challenges as the far West met the far East of older empires.

Woodrow Wilson became president when Europe was on the eve of World War I. The US' decision to enter the war brought the New World to bear on the stupidities of the Old. When the war ended, President Wilson saw it as his duty to help build a new order that would put an end to such wars. His support for the League of Nations was salvation in spirit, given to rescue Europe from future madness. He spoke with missionary zeal, and his message to the world set the tone for later American leaders, not least his successors from Roosevelt to Obama.

Sun Yat-Sen and Woodrow Wilson died within a few months of each other. Neither succeeded in their ambitions. China in 1925 was at its weakest point in modern history, neither a unified state nor a credible civilisation. The Japan that Sun Yat-sen had asked for help from had copied the Europeans and become another national empire poised to invade China. Wilson's hopes to convince Old World nations to create a system that would end all wars came to nothing. The US Congress failed to support his New World ideals which were offered to rescue Europe from its aggressive politics, and voted against joining the Leage of Nations. A decade later, another disastrous war enveloped the world.

This summary account of the two pairs of leaders brings me back to ideas about state and civilisation. On the one hand, we see the trajectory of a civilisation that was strengthened because it united to create a powerful state in the New World. Abraham Lincoln's Union army fought off the secessionists and consolidated America as a continental power. This enabled Woodrow Wilson to advise his European partners about how they might work together to create a future universal order. On the other hand, we observe how another civilisation almost died for lack of a strong and prosperous state. Hong Xiuquan and Cixi struggled to move China's *wangchao* state from its anchorage in deep traditions towards a foreign modernity. Sun Yat-Sen, however, understood that China needed a new kind of state if it wanted to save its civilisation. Yet he was not to know what tragedies the Chinese people would have to go through before they could achieve that.

In 1945 a new start was possible for both countries. The US won the war across both the Atlantic and the Pacific. It demonstrated that a country with its own continent could at the same time be the master of two oceans. It put the US in a position where they could consider becoming a global power for ensuring global peace. For China, its part in that victory over Japan showed that its civilisation had touched bottom and survived. The nationalist regime that led the fighting, however, did not survive and, after a short civil war, was replaced by another that claimed an internationalist outlook. Could a modern civilisation be built from what remained? Many Chinese were hopeful that modernity would now spring from what had been learnt during the past century of war and revolution. They even thought the new China under the CCP could lead to a distinct civilisation that embraced vital parts of their heritage.

At the end of the 18th century, an independent US rejected what the Old World stood for. Early in the 20th century, the US gained enough power for the New World, under its leadership, to redefine the maritime world order inherited from the British Empire. The country mounted the mission to fight the continental ideologies of Eurasia as represented at the time by Nazi Germany and the Soviet Union. By the end of the Cold War, the maritime global order began to represent the modern Euro-Mediterranean civilisation as it came to embody universal values. As the leader of this order, the US was effectively a New World superpower. While the Old World in Eurasia was tired, if not exhausted. The world order that the Euro-Mediterranean civilisation had promised finally found its home in America.

Replacing the League of Nations, the US led the victors of World War II to set up the United Nations organisation to project the ideals of freedom, justice and individual rights into all institutions of the new international order. This New World initiative was also ingrained in the nation-state system that the Europeans had invented in the 17th century. Thus US leaders like Barack Obama know they have to educate these Old World units to adopt universal values and, where necessary, the US established alliances with those that sought its help. But that Old World state framework is still able to draw the US itself back to its British and European past, to the idea that only a powerful state can control what the world does. Can the US get away from the nationalism that aims to make its civilisation as universal as possible?

China's Civilisational Challenges

Xi Jinping's China faces the opposite problem. It admires the modern achievements of Euro-Mediterranean civilisation and seeks to emulate them. It wants to learn all it can in order for the modern Chinese state to revive and enrich its own distinctive heritage. Its people have shown that they are capable of mastering everything they want to and only stop short when there is doubt that particular ideas and institutions would benefit the country. Nevertheless, a key goal is to build a strong state that will revive and modernise the best of its ancient civilisation.

That civilisation remains rooted in the Old World, in a continent that is still unsafe, if not as unstable as it had been in the past. In that world, China, Japan, India and the Association of Southeast Asian Nations (ASEAN) states all look for help to safeguard the maritime supply lines essential for their continued economic development. In China's case, having eyes on both continental and maritime interests fits well with its history. Chinese leaders know that the power balance between land and sea has been the secret of its civilisation's longevity. The difference is they now believe that a modern civilisation has to be embodied in a nation. They believe this was the lesson the past century of weakness taught them, and the only way China's future can be secured is by following the Old World model.

In the debate over the clash of civilisations launched by Samuel Huntington, I stand with those who believe that civilisations learn from one another and do not fight. It is the states who fought in the name of the civilisation that each believed should prevail. The Sinic and the Euro-Mediterranean civilisations had not really met before modern times. When they did, it was in the framework of nation-states, and it was the nation-states that emerged to overshadow the vitality of civilisation. The strongest among them thereafter expected to determine the conditions for the establishment of a future global order. It is not obvious that the world should be dominated by any one civilisation using the nation-state as its power instrument. It would be unfortunate if the most powerful nation-state that represents the peak of one civilisation needs to act as a super nation-state to achieve that end.

I cannot imagine what Abraham Lincoln and Empress Dowager Cixi would have talked about had they met 150 years ago. Fifty years later, Woodrow Wilson and Sun Yat-Sen could have conversed in English if they had met, even though their ideals were traceable to rhetoric that pulled in opposite directions. Fortunately, when Barack Obama and Xi Jinping met, conditions were more propitious for dialogue. They still spoke for two civilisations; Obama seeking to use a modern civilisation to build an community of nation-states, while Xi Jinping is adapting the nation-state model to modernise China's distinctive cultural heritage. Obama's New World strives to remain dominant and tries to curb the use of its firepower to impose world order. Xi Jinping, on the other hand, is counting on a unified multiethnic nation to renew its faith in an Old World civilisation. The world still hopes that the fear of mutual assured destruction and the rise in global interdependence will temper their respective national approaches and win a lasting peace. However, that may depend on whether these powerful leaders can learn to distinguish between what their states should and should not do and what their two civilisations could share in order to achieve the peace they both want.

I. THE CHINA–US BILATERAL RELATIONSHIP

The China–US Relationship Matters

Wang Lutong

Ambassador of the People's Republic of China to New Zealand, the Cook Islands and Niue

China–US Relations and World Peace and Development

The China–US relationship matters. It matters in relation to world peace and development. There is no doubt that China and the US are two of the most important countries in the 21st century and this relationship has an impact which extends far beyond their own borders.

Viewing the world today, China and US are working in virtually all major international arenas, acting as engines for global economic growth, counter-terrorism, cybersecurity, climate change, nuclear nonproliferation, and are safeguarding the fruits of victory of a global anti-fascist war and addressing regional hotspot issues. Together, we have a huge and exciting international agenda which I'm confident will bring peace and prosperity to the world.

The Bilateral Relationship between China and the United States

The China–US relationship matters. It matters in relation to its complexity and scope. For obvious reasons delineated along social, political and cultural lines, we have different views on some issues. But looking back at the past few decades, we find that despite the ups and downs, contradictions and reconciliations that exist side by side, this relationship has generally remained on the right track and achieved substantial developments.

Today, bilateral trade exceeds US$550 billion and there are more than 10,000 people traveling between China and US every day. We also have over 90 dialogue and consultation mechanisms in place between the two sides. There is growing interdependence between our two countries. Our partnership is formed on a broad range of mutual interests and shared responsibilities to the global community.

We should not be blindfolded by the differences and miss the broader picture where cooperation forms the mainstay of this relationship. Cooperation is far more prevalent than competition in the China–US relationship. If we continue to advance our common interests through cooperation, our people will benefit and the world will be better off. China and the US are in the same boat, so let us row together.

China–US Relations and the 'Thucydides trap'

The China–US relationship matters. It matters in relation to whether a new history can be created by the combined efforts of a rising power and an existing superpower. The belief that China and the US cannot escape the 'Thucydides trap' bears utility for some in the international community. In fact, the goal of China's development is to realise a national revival and ensure a better life for its people. The primary motivation is not for China to become a dominant country and to use that power to challenge or threaten others. There is a long way to go for China to develop. The heart of the Chinese, like the rest of the global world order, desires a long-term peaceful and stable international environment.

During President Xi's visit, President Obama made it clear that 'the United States does not agree with the "Thucydides trap" that an existing superpower and a rising power are bound for conflict. China and the United States are capable of controlling their differences.'

President Xi noted during his meetings with President Obama at the Annenberg Retreat in 2013 and in Beijing last year that constructing a new model of major-country relations with the United States that features non-conflict, non-confrontation, mutual respect and win–win cooperation is a key priority for China's foreign policy. The visit last month reaffirmed the direction for construction of a new model of a major-country relationship. As long as we continue to work towards building such a relationship, China and the US can avoid repeating the tragic old 'great power' path set by the international politics of the 20th century, and instead forge a new political trajectory for the 21st century.

The whole world shares an interest in greater cooperation between China and the US, and therefore should encourage and support the development of this relationship. Attempting to hijack China–US relations to serve one country or a particular interest group is shortsighted and irresponsible. It is not consistent with global and regional interests and certainly will not succeed.

China–US Relations and the New Zealand Model

New Zealand is a good model in this context. Pursuing an independent foreign policy, New Zealand is a leader among Western countries when it comes to building relations with China. It is the pioneer of promoting understanding between China and the West and exploring friendship and cooperation between different countries.

We are happy to have so many renowned scholars from New Zealand, China, the United States, Australia, Singapore, Japan and South Korea, to interpret China–US relations from different perspectives and to elaborate on the impact of this relationship to other countries and regions. I'm sure this book will be a catalyst for the creation of valuable ideas to promote a better understanding of China, the US and China–US relations.

As a passionate believer in China–US relations, I look at this relationship with enthusiasm and optimism. What we have achieved so far is just a beginning. The best is yet to come. The most important chapter of our shared history is the one we are about to write together.

The US–China Relationship

Mark Gilbert

United States Ambassador to New Zealand and Samoa

Under President Obama's leadership, we are deepening our engagement throughout the Asia-Pacific region, including with China. Despite our differences, US–China bilateral relations have grown remarkably in breadth. It is no secret that we have a complex relationship. Our differences and our concerns are real. But we speak frankly and stand up for our values.

It is important to recognise that we are building a productive and cooperative relationship—one that delivers benefits not just for the American and Chinese people, but also for our partners in the region. The US has demonstrated a commitment to work together with China.

President Xi's Washington visit (24–25 September 2015) was the most recent engagement. President Obama has held six bilateral meetings with President Xi, and Vice President Biden visited Beijing just a few years ago. The US and the world gain most when China is an active partner in efforts to resolve regional and global problems. Areas of US–China cooperation are vast and varied, ranging from climate change to cybersecurity, to educational exchanges.

Climate Change
Since President Obama took office, US exports to China have nearly doubled and now support nearly one million American jobs. China is now the third-largest market for goods made in the US, following Canada and Mexico. Over this same period, Chinese investment in the US has grown dramatically. We share with China

an interest in promoting a strong and open global economy, sustainable development and a healthy international financial system.

To reiterate, one of President Obama's comments during President Xi's visit emphasised that the US welcomed the rise of a China that is stable, prosperous and peaceful—because that benefits us all. Whether working together to promote international trade, preventing Iran from obtaining a nuclear weapon, or fighting climate change, our nations and the world become more prosperous, more secure.

President Obama and President Xi share the conviction that climate change is one of the greatest threats facing humanity and that we both have a critical role to play in addressing it. China and the US are the two largest consumers of energy and the two largest carbon emitters in the world. Working together on climate change is vital to global security and prosperity. To quote President Obama, 'We cannot condemn our children, and their children, to a future that is beyond their capacity to repair.' To that end, we share a determination with China to implement domestic climate policies, promote sustainable development and foster green, low-carbon, and climate-resilient economies.

Last year President Obama and President Xi made an historic announcement in Beijing—committing our countries to cut carbon emissions and meet ambitious post-2020 climate targets. This was the first time China had ever agreed to reduce its emissions. Both leaders share a common vision for a globally comprehensive climate agreement [Note: The agreement was successfully concluded in Paris, December 2015.]

Another major milestone occurred during President Xi's visit to Washington: the release of a US–China Joint Presidential Statement on Climate Change. To achieve the goals set last year, the US and China have recently made significant domestic policy announcements, including the US Clean Power Plan which will reduce emissions by 32% in the US power sector by 2030.

We are both taking steps to phase down super-polluting hydrofluorocarbons (HFCs). In addition the US and China are making climate finance commitments to help developing countries build low-carbon and climate-resilient societies. The US has pledged US$3 billion to the Green Climate Fund, and China just announced it would respond in kind, donating a similar amount to assist countries in combatting climate change. This is China's most significant commitment to climate finance to date. So you can see that we are working closely together to ensure developing countries have the tools they need for sustainable development and to prepare for the impacts of climate change.

On polar and ocean conservation, we will work together on the US–New Zealand joint proposal to establish a Marine Protected Area in Antarctica's Ross Sea. On a similar note, we are working with China on the monitoring of ocean acidification. Our partnership between the coastal cities of Xiamen and Weihai in China, and San Francisco and New York in the US, will enable us to share best practices to reduce the flow of trash into the ocean.

Another area where our goals align with China's is in the development of new, heavy duty-vehicle fuel efficiency standards to reduce carbon pollution. In 2012 the Obama administration finalised ground-breaking standards to increase fuel economy and reduce oil consumption and greenhouse gas emissions. This programme was the first meaningful update to US fuel efficiency standards in decades. Not only is this programme protecting the environment, but these changes have spurred innovation and economic growth. The result is cleaner and more fuel-efficient vehicles, which reduce pollution and save consumers money.

Cybersecurity

As I mentioned earlier, we do have differences of opinions. One of those concerns is an issue of increasing global importance—cybersecurity. In his many meetings with President Xi, President Obama has made it clear that state-sponsored, cyber-enabled economic espionage for commercial gain must stop. This puts an enormous strain on our bilateral relationship. The US has been very clear that state-sponsored, cyber-enabled theft of intellectual property and sensitive business information for commercial gain is not acceptable. It could undermine long-term economic cooperation between the countries, and is an economic and national security concern to every country.

There has been progress on this front thus far. During President Xi's visit, the countries agreed that neither government will conduct or knowingly support cyber-enabled theft of intellectual property, including trade secrets or other confidential business information, with the intent of providing competitive advantages to companies or commercial sectors. We also agreed to increase cooperation on cybercrime investigations and to provide timely responses to requests for assistance concerning malicious cyber activities. In addition, we will continue to urge China to join us in promoting responsible norms of state behavior in cyberspace.

Rebalancing to the Asia-Pacific

Deepening productive relations with China is a critical element of President Obama's strategy for the Asia-Pacific where, as a Pacific nation, we have vital interests and vital contributions to make.

A significant part of our foreign policy is focused on what we call our Asia-Pacific Rebalance, which entails increasing our engagement within the region. We are determined to create benefits for the region through expanding mutual prosperity, enhancing security cooperation, strengthening the sustainability of development and advancing human dignity.

Constructive engagement with China is a pillar of the rebalance and essential to sustained prosperity and stability in the region. Engagements like President Xi's state visit are an important part of this. Our cooperation with China and strong lines of communication are yielding measurable progress. From the joint climate change announcement to the Iran nuclear deal to progress made on a bilateral investment treaty, our cooperation contributes to a safer and more prosperous world.

We reject the idea that conflict between the US and China is inevitable. We do have differences, and because we address them candidly and regularly, we are able to manage these differences in robust discussions. Therefore, we welcome a China that upholds the rules-based order that serves both our nations and the region as well.

Our position on maritime disputes in the East and South China Seas is clear. The US takes no position on competing territorial claims, but we have a fundamental interest in preserving freedom of navigation and commerce through some of the world's busiest sea lanes. We want to ensure that ships and planes from all countries, even the smallest, are able to enjoy their navigational rights and freedoms without risk.

We seek to prevent territorial disputes from growing into larger conflicts that destabilise the region. We work with all our partners to establish a peaceful process based on international law for resolving maritime claims through diplomacy, not force or coercion. We call on all claimants to halt land reclamation, stop the construction of new facilities and to halt the militarisation of outposts on disputed areas. It is vital that China and ASEAN countries conclude work on a Code of Conduct and set clear, predictable and binding rules of the road in the South China Seas.

Socio-Cultural Exchanges

I began by mentioning our long-standing relationship and deepening engagement. We have a long and deep history of cultural and personal connections with China, dating back to the 1800s, when the first Chinese immigrants arrived on our shores, just as they did in New Zealand.

There are more connections between our cultures than ever. Our leaders declared 2016 the 'US–China Tourism Year', a cooperative tourism initiative to expand and develop travel between our countries. The program will support progress on market access, helping the US and China ensure a quality visitor experience for the greatly increasing numbers of travellers between our nations.

On the issue of education, President Obama announced his support for the 'One Million Strong' initiative, which aims to have one million American students studying Mandarin by 2020. This initiative, which China supports, also aims to double the number of Mandarin language teachers in the US, and will use technology to reach students in underserved and underrepresented communities. A number of US governors have committed to expanding Mandarin language-learning around the country.

We have exceeded President Obama's goal of sending 100,000 Americans to study in China. We continue to encourage more student exchanges with China, just as we do here in New Zealand. There are currently more than 300,000 Chinese students studying in the US, a figure that has increased three-fold since President Obama came to office. We have also increased the number of visas we issue to Chinese travellers (inclusive of business people, students and tourists) from less than half a million in 2009 to more than 1.7 million last year.

As you can see from this long list, China and the US do great things together. A stable and prosperous and peaceful China that upholds international law benefits everyone. We cannot ignore the points of friction between us, and we will continue to candidly address our differences and stand up for our values. But we can and do work together to meet global challenges.

Our relationship is expansive. It is stable, productive and durable, and it will remain at the centre of our foreign policy for years to come.

China–US Relations after President Xi Jinping's State Visit to US

Wu Jianmin

Former member of the Foreign Policy Advisory Group of the Chinese Foreign Ministry, special research fellow of Counselors' Office of the State Council, member and vice president of the European Academy of Sciences and honorary president of the International Bureau of Exhibitions (BIE)[1]

Abstract

President Xi Jinping's state visit to the US in September 2015 was the most challenging of his overseas visits. Recently, international press has focused on the differences and frictions between the US and China. Some even predicted the failure of this visit. I disagreed, though I didn't underestimate the differences between our two countries. However, I believed the fundamentals of the US–China relationship remained unchanged: the two countries' economies were highly interdependent, and the common interests between China and the US far outweighed their differences. In 2013, President Xi and President Obama reached an important consensus in Sunnylands, California, to build new type of major-country relationship, which is characterised by 'no conflict, no confrontation, mutual respect and win–win cooperation'. This consensus indicated the path forwards for the development of their relationship. And lastly, the international community expects China and US to improve relations, as it is in the best interests of world peace and development.

---

1   Wu Jianmin tragically passed away on 18 June 2016. The editor wishes to acknowledge his memory and his valued contributon to this conference.

Earlier in 2015, President Xi Jinping's state visit to the US from 22–25 September was expected to be the most challenging among his foreign visits. Before the visit, the international press focused on the differences and frictions between the US and China regarding the South China Sea, cyber security and human rights. Between April and June 2015, I travelled twice to the US and met with a few American friends. They told me that sentiment surrounding the US–China relationship was bad. They feared this kind of atmosphere would cast a shadow on President Xi's forthcoming state visit to the US.

President Xi's Successful State Visit to the US
Early in September, I was interviewed by both international press and Chinese press about President Xi's state visit to the US. I disagreed with their pessimistic views. I expressed my conviction that the visit would be successful.

On 26 September 2015, the Chinese Foreign Ministry published the fact sheet of President Xi's visit to the US, which contained 49 topics of discussion, by far exceeding the 27 topics achieved in November 2014 during President Obama's visit to China. The success was received by the international community with a sigh of relief. A growing China–US cooperation is good news not only for the two countries, but also for the rest of the world.

Fundamentals of the China–US Relationship
Why did I believe that President Xi's visit to US would be a success, amidst widespread pessimistic views? Because the fundamentals of the China–US relationship remain unchanged. What are the fundamentals?

1. The new type of major-country relationship points in the right direction for the China–US relationship to follow
In June 2013 in Sunnyland, California, President Xi and President Obama reached an historic consensus to build a new type of major-country relationship, characterised by 'no conflict, no confrontation, mutual respect and win-win cooperation.' This consensus has a huge impact on the China–US relationship. 'No conflict, no confrontation' means that the two leaders are determined not to let the relationship fall into a Thucydides trap. This is the political will expressed by the two leaders on behalf of their respective governments.

'Mutual respect'. This is the precondition for developing cooperation. 'Win–win cooperation' is the roadmap to building this new type of major-country relationship. For the China–US relationship, the right orientation is crucial because it outlines a clear path along which they can develop their relationship constructively.

2. Interdependence
Since Dr Henry Kissinger's visit to China in July 1971, the China–US relationship has grown tremendously, to the great satisfaction of our two peoples. In 1971 China–

US bilateral trade amounted to only US$5 million dollars. In 2014 it increased to US$550 billion. Such figures are illustrative of the deep interdependent ties that have been built between China and the US.

Interdependence is not only at an economic level; it has a human dimension as well. People-to-people exchanges between China and the US have been growing steadily in the past 44 years. Today, five million people travel across the Pacific between China and the US every year. The number is still increasing. When people meet each other face to face, it makes a big difference.

On 25 October 1971 the UN General Assembly adopted a resolution to restore the lawful rights of the People's Republic of China at the UN. That was a milestone not only for Chinese diplomacy, but also for international relations.

At the invitation of the UN secretary-general, the Chinese government formed a delegation headed by Vice Minister Qiao Guanhua to go to New York to attend the 26th session of the UN General Assembly.

On 8 November 1971 Chairman Mao Zedong met with Qiao Guanhua, chairman of the Chinese delegation and his associates. Mao said: 'As the saying goes, how can you catch tiger cubs without entering the tiger's lair? You must remember, a refusal to venture forth means that nothing is gained.'

A day later, the Chinese delegation left Beijing for New York. I was a junior member of the delegation. We were seen off at Beijing Capital Airport by Premier Zhou Enlai, members of the cabinet and 5000 people representing different quarters of the Chinese society. We waved to people coming to see us off. They were very happy. I can still recall how some people at the far back of the airport bore a huge slogan: 'People of the world, unite and defeat US imperialism and its running dogs'.

On 11 Novemeber 1971 we arrived at JFK International Airport, New York. About 500 journalists were waiting for us there. I had never seen so many journalists. The return of the Chinese delegation to the UN was very newsworthy. Wherever we went, we were pursued by journalists. One weekend, my wife and I went to Central Park to take a walk. At the time, we were all wearing Maoist suits, and were easily identified. I remembered we met an elderly American lady.

She looked at us and asked, 'Are you from Red China?'

I said, 'Yes, but we don't say Red China. We say People's Republic of China.'

She answered, 'Well, whatever! You're most welcome. It is long overdue that you should be here.' My wife and I were deeply moved by these simple words. Since then, so much water has passed under the bridge.

In September 2014 former US president Jimmy Carter and his wife Rosalynn went to China. The daughter of Deng Xiaoping and her husband hosted a private dinner for them at Beijing Hotel. My wife and I were invited. We chatted with Carter and his wife. Back in the day, my wife was the Chinese interpreter responsible for negotiating the establishment of diplomatic ties between China and the US. She recalled to former president Carter what happened at the negotiating table. He was very interested in that conversation.

At dinner, Carter and Rosalynn, following Chinese practice, toured from table to table to toast everyone. At our table, a man in his 50s said to Mr Carter: 'Mr President, when China and the US established diplomatic ties, I was in the countryside. With diplomatic ties between our two countries, I got the opportunity to go to the US for my studies. That changed my life.' Former president Carter and Rosalynn listened to these words with satisfaction. Indeed, China–US diplomatic ties have changed many Chinese and Americans for the better. The bonds between human beings are everlasting and have a positive impact on a bilateral relationship.

3. The common interests between China and the US far outweigh their differences
Five generations of Chinese leaders, from Deng Xiaoping to Xi Jinping, all say that the common interests between China and US by far outweigh their differences. This is not merely rhetoric, but a factual statement. The past 44 years have seen us witness tremendous growth of common interests between China and the US.

On the other hand, when Chinese leaders keep emphasising the common interests between China and the US, it means that they put common interests above other issues. This is an important approach. Common interests determine the quality of a bilateral relationship. As China focuses on growing common interests vis-á-vis the US, one can be reassured that the foundation of the China–US relationship will grow stronger and stronger. This would allow for us to address our differences in a more effective and constructive manner.

Beyond Hegemony: The US–China Relationship in a Multi-Nodal World

Brantly Womack

Professor of foreign affairs at the University of Virginia, US

Abstract
With one-third of the world's productivity split in equal masses between the two great powers, the China–US relationship will remain the focus of global politics for the foreseeable future. However, neither the US nor China—nor the two together—can enjoy the kind of hegemonic control that existed in earlier bipolar and unipolar eras. The diffuse interdependence created by globalisation gives every state broader alternatives and raises the cost of hostility. Cold War camps are unlikely to form. Despite apparent parity, the US and China do not face each other as hegemon and challenger, but rather as the largest players in a world that neither controls. As the primary nodes of a world order that they cannot dominate, the US and China are likely to restrain their rivalry. If not, they will isolate themselves.

What does it mean that the US and China are entering a situation of parity without symmetry in a globalised, multi-nodal world? By the end of this chapter I hope that the terms of the question will be clear, if not the answer. Since 2008 the global political economy and the relationship of its two principal powers have entered a qualitatively new stage. The presumption of unipolar hegemony that characterised the post-Cold War era is gone. All are confronting a situation in which the US remains the central global power but is not dominant, China is the principal power of Asia and of the global manufacturing economy, and global state interactions have become more diffuse.

It is possible that the slowdown of the Chinese economy, highlighted by the volatility in the Chinese stock markets in June 2015, marks the 'end of the beginning' of China's rise. China is no longer frightening its neighbours (and stabilising the world economy) by marching along at 10% growth despite the global financial crisis, as it had done since 2008.[1] Instead, resource-supplying states such as Australia are now worried about dwindling markets. But China's slower pace is more likely to be the 'new normal' rather than the beginning of the end of its development. And the new normal includes continued asymmetric parity with the US at the top of the world economy, each state's economy greater than the combined economies of India, Japan and Germany; the next three largest.[2]

It is especially difficult for the US to accustom itself to the change in the global situation. It has been in a dominant role for the past 70 years. Before becoming the unipolar superpower after the collapse of the Soviet Union it was the hegemon of its extensive Cold War camp, and the alliances of that era remain in place. It is therefore tempting to see the retention or restoration of hegemony as its primary diplomatic challenge, and to see China as the challenger. China is less inclined to the Cold War perspective, since it started the Cold War on the Soviet side (1949–60), became hostile to both (1960–71), then leaned to the American side (1972–82) and finally slipped in between (1983–91). China's own comforting frame of reference is the pre-modern imperial 'all under heaven' (*tianxia* 天下), remembered as a central place of honour and order amid neighbours who were grateful and accepting. President Xi Jinping considers China's dream to be a 'rejuvenation' emerging from a century of deprivation.[3] The rest of the world tends to be more realistic than either of the principal powers since it has to cope with both the economic presence of China and the global political and security preeminence of the US.

There are innumerable issues and small crises in the US–China bilateral relationship that have global reverberations, and in turn almost any perturbation in the global political web is felt at the centre. Moreover, the domestic political underpinnings of diplomacy are volatile—the US presidential elections are the most prominent example—and third-party diplomacy often entangles interactions. All these factors make the course of US–China relations impossible to predict. Nevertheless, underneath the diplomatic zigzag there will be a more stable structural terrain that affects the feasibility of any course of action. The likelihood of choices is affected by their prospective feasibility, and, more importantly, so is their outcome. While structure itself does not remain unaffected by choices—thermonuclear war would be a graphic example—a choice cannot predict its consequences. Reality changes, but reality testing remains.

This essay addresses the general structural constraints on Sino–American rivalry. It begins with its bilateral structure, including differences from the Cold War, the bilateral factors encouraging rivalry, and those constraining it. It then focuses on the difference between parity as understood by power transition theory and the asymmetric parity that has emerged in US–China relations. Attention then shifts to the global context of the Sino-American relationship, and it concludes with reflections on strategic consequences.

The Structure of Sino–American Rivalry
Beyond Cold War thinking

The IMF estimated that China's economy reached the size of that of the US by the end of 2014, measured in terms of purchasing power parity (PPP). While the market and currency gyrations of 2015 are a sobering reminder that timetables are uncertain, the two basic reasons for expecting China's continued relative growth, urbanisation and technology diffusion, remain unchanged.[4] Thus we can assume that the American and Chinese economies have entered a phase in which they will be roughly the same size, and much larger than other national economies.

The fact that China has risen and is not likely to recede, while the US remains a global power, immediately conjures images of the bipolar Cold War. But there are huge differences. The Soviet Union was not the economic powerhouse that China is. In 1990 its gross national income (GNI) was 27% of that of the US; a percentage that China achieved in 1994.[5] If the Soviet economy were the size of the US economy, the US strategy of exhausting it by an arms race would have been impossible. On the other hand, Russian per capita GNI was slightly more than one-third of US per capita income in 1990, while currently China's is less than one-quarter. China has come far—in 1990 its per capita income was only 4% of that of the US—but raising the productivity of 1.3 billion people is difficult.

A more important difference is that from 1947 the US and Soviet Union saw each other as symmetric global competitors. There was the race for the bomb, followed by the missile race, followed by the race for the moon. Differences of capacity were considered 'gaps' that must be overcome. The rivalry was a contest about getting ahead. By contrast, the 'China Dream' is more introverted and more modest. The goal is to attain moderate prosperity in a context of open international relationships based on mutual respect. The gaps are all on China's side, though China's security aim is not to be the equal of the US, but to reduce the vulnerability of its core interests. China aims at adequate defence rather than symmetric parity, but this still conflicts with the post-Cold War US equation of its own security with global invulnerability and the resulting US mission to become the omnipresent decisive power.

Meanwhile the US response to China's rise has combined openness and general approval of reform with increasing concern about China playing by the rules (as the US imagines them). As President Obama put it recently, 'the United States welcomes the rise of a China that is stable, prosperous and peaceful—because that benefits us all.'[6] While the Soviet economic recovery in the 1950s was attributed to the success of a competing economic model that promised to 'bury' capitalism, China's economic success is seen as a confirmation of US capitalist values despite the presence of 'Chinese characteristics'. To be sure, China is a communist country, which remains profoundly alienating to US political sensibilities. But the ideological pressure has reversed direction since the Cold War. Now China worries about peaceful evolution and a democrat under every bed, while the US is more concerned about China's power and potential than about its persuasiveness.

The most important difference between US–Soviet relations during the Cold War and US–China relations now is the disappearance of distinct camps. Despite the preeminence of the US and China, bipolarity requires a global division which no longer exists. China is the top trading partner of all US allies in Asia,[7] and its multilateral initiatives tend to be open-ended, unlike the former Council for Mutual Economic Assistance (COMECON) or Warsaw Pact. It is clear from China's current tensions with Japan that economic integration does not create political affinities. Nevertheless, economic enmeshment creates a situation in which each has more to lose from hostility and faces a less certain future. American alliances are heritage of the Cold War never formally retargeted at China, and the US policy disasters in the Middle East would not encourage other states to bear real costs and risks in a new Cold War alignment.

The reality of rivalry

International rivalry is usually conceptualised as a zero-sum relationship of mutual hostility and the grounds for armed conflict, with the Middle East providing many prominent examples.[8] Clearly the US–China relationship is more complex. Although neither side formally pictures the other as threatening, each views the other as its major concern. They have many interests in common, many that are oblique, and only a few in direct conflict.

Thus we need a softer and thicker idea of rivalry if we are to use it for the US and China. First, the relationship is asymmetric, but for each the bilateral relationship is the most significant exposure to the actions of another state. Each can harm the other's interests. While a war would be asymmetric, no one would consider it a 'small war'. China cannot do to the US what the US can do to China, but in economics, politics and security its options are more extensive than mere resistance.

Second, China's ambitions as a regional power are in oblique conflict with US claims as a global power. Since any region is a subsystem of global politics, there is an inherent antinomy between the situation of a global power and that of a regional power.[9] To the extent that their interests differ, the overarching concerns of the global power are pitted against the autonomous leadership of the regional power. Moreover, smaller regional states have the option of either global or regional alignment. In part because of the rapidity of China's rise since 2008, US concerns about China's regional rise resonate with the concerns of China's neighbours, and to some extent with their ambitions. If a regional power is decisive in its region, the global power is no longer completely global.

Third, China's global presence and activities are unsettling for the US global status quo. China's advances beyond Asia mean a proportional decrease in American presence and they hold no direct advantage for the US. If China's development efforts such as One Belt, One Road or the Asian Infrastructure Investment Bank (AIIB) succeed, the model and institutions of the Washington Consensus are diminished, if not challenged. If they fail, then early criticism will appear farsighted. These new initiatives are complementary to existing institutions and responsive to shortages of development funding, but Xi Jinping clearly intends to participate in the reform of existing political and economic structures.[10] As Kevin Rudd points out, however, Xi does not intend an antagonistic challenge.[11] In any case, China's presence in Africa, South America, central Asia, and even Europe is adding a dimension to global changes that is outside the US sphere.

Finally, the difference in regimes and values creates a gulf of otherness that provides fertile soil for suspicions and misinterpretations. On the US side, there is the axiom that democracy and limited government are the only legitimate goals of political development and that a communist party-state is bound to fail. Moreover, there is the conviction articulated by democratic peace theory that war is the product of authoritarianism. Of course, Americans wish the Chinese people long life and happiness, but they don't expect this from the communist regime despite its accomplishments thus far. On the Chinese side, a special great-power relationship based on mutual respect is desired but not expected. Rather, China sees US strategic interest as to isolate, contain, diminish and divide China, and to sabotage the Chinese leadership.[12] Clearly this is a summary of China's concerns about the US rather than a comprehensive analysis of policy, but they are real concerns.

The limits of rivalry

US–China rivalry is limited in incentives and in confrontational options. At a fundamental level, neither state's grand strategy requires the removal of the other. Neither controls a resource that the other requires. Both compete for external resources, but so does the rest of the world, and neither is resource-poor. Both depend on commerce and therefore on trade routes, but only for pirates is the deliberate interference with trade an end in itself. As the largest developing and developed countries respectively, China and the US are on opposite sides of the intellectual property fence, but China is decreasing the technological have/have not gap, and in any case the theft of intellectual property discourages both voluntary transfer and indigenous innovation. Both have incentives for cooperation and collaboration in many areas. Even in areas where interests are competitive, both have incentives to reduce uncertainty by respecting structures of competition. Both have interests and commitments related to third parties that might entangle them in confrontation, but both have reasons to limit the extent of entanglement.

Although rivalry can become imprudently hostile, it cannot escape the consequences of imprudence. The first and most obvious limit is economic interdependence. More important than the scale of trade is its complementarity. China exchanges its manufactures for US capital, services and technology. As China's production becomes more sophisticated it will become more directly competitive, but it is a long way from the qualitative levels of Canada or Europe. While the contact and displacement involved in trade inevitably produce friction, bilateral economic interdependence provides a material foundation for a continuing and mutually beneficial relationship.

Beyond bilateral interdependence—and perhaps more important in terms of policy alternatives—is the diffuse economic linkage created by global value chains (GVC). Trade in products is increasingly displaced by trade in parts, often organised by vertically integrated multinational firms. To take a famous example, each iPhone assembled in China adds US$179 to China's total exports but includes US$172 in imported components—and it is assembled by a Taiwanese firm for a US brand.[13] Domestic producers who are dependent on imported inputs are less likely to be protectionist[14] and despite the increase in economic anxieties since 2008, global value chains have not been domesticated.[15] Besides removing some of the teeth of domestic protectionism, GVCs make the protectionist bite less country-specific. If the US decided to restrict iPhones made in China, the biggest losers would be in Taiwan, Japan and the US. The rapidity of the trend away from final product trade and toward GVC since the 1990s makes obsolete the usual ideas of trade interdependence. The reality now is trade enmeshment.

Lastly, the costs and risks of security competition are enormous. The China spectre inspires enthusiasm in the most expensive parts of the American military-industrial and military-electronic complexes and their congressional supporters.[16] Similarly, the US threat distorts Chinese military development toward high-technology counter measures. In both cases military expenditures exert pressure on resources. The US spends almost twice China's percentage of GNI on military, thus risking repeating the Soviet fate of militarising itself at the cost of relative economic progress.[17] Then there are the risks of actual military contact, beginning with accidental encounters and running all the way to thermonuclear war. The levels of risk can easily be linked by escalating the theatre and scale of conflict.

If, for example, we imagine a Taiwan military crisis, China would face the risk of US involvement and the certainty of lingering US hostility as well as the alienation of neighbours and the probable militarisation of Japan. The US would be faced with the unwelcome choice of either backing off from the commitment of the Taiwan Relations Act or risking significant losses. If conflict escalated along the lines of the AirSea Battle concept, the US could easily become involved in a comprehensive war with China, and the only obstacle to the war going nuclear would be China's commitment to no first use of nuclear weapons. Neither side can be decisively eliminated without eliminating both—and the neighbours as well. Stopping short of the hell of Armageddon, any level of military conflict will start a long purgatory of embedded hostility. Thus the security dilemma should be seen in absolute as well as relative terms.

Presumably any government on either side would find these limits sobering. When sobriety prevails, differences will be negotiated, competition will be peaceful and collaboration will be pursued for mutual benefit. Even when leaders are not fully sober, the prospect of the increasing costs of confrontation should function as an increasing marginal cost of expanding confrontation. To the extent that confrontation is not avoided or restrained, adding up the lose–lose outcomes should lead to more prudence in the future (assuming an outcome short of thermonuclear war, where there is no future). Thus interactions within the rivalry are neither in a virtuous circle of constant improvement nor a vicious circle of escalating conflict, but rather they are in a bowl in which increasing escalation raises costs and thus encourages leaders to slide back into negotiation. The reality of rivalry will keep the bowl lively, but the reality of limits will increasingly discourage climbing to the edge.

Asymmetric Parity vs Power Transition

The idea of China reaching parity with the US presents the spectre of the 'Thucydides Trap'; an inevitable conflict between the incumbent hegemon and a rising challenger.[18] Graham Allison notes the grim fact that of the 15 cases in which a rising power has emerged to challenge a ruling power, 11 have resulted in war.[19] But what of asymmetric parity in a post-hegemonic context?

All realist international relations theorists would be gloomy about the prospects of approaching parity. Power transition theory, originating from A.F.K. Organski's general theory of world politics, has devoted itself to the study of such transitions.[20] Defining power parity as equal economic mass plus or minus 20%, war is not necessary at power transition but it is the most likely point of major conflict.[21] But there are two fundamental problems with the prospects for a grand confrontation. The first is the problem of parity, and the second is that of hegemony. This section discusses asymmetric parity, while the next deals with the post-hegemonic world order.

Is China already within the parity moment, and how long will it remain in it? Using World Bank estimates of purchasing power parity (PPP), China reached 80% of American GNI in 2010 and, using conservative projections of China's continued relative growth[22]—5% per year for China and 3% for the US—China will pass beyond parity at 120% in 2023. Using the World Bank's Atlas method[23] of adjusted nominal GNI and the same China 5%/US 3% assumptions, China doesn't reach the 80% threshold until 2032, and would not reach 120% of US GNI until 2053. Needless to say, a 32-year gap between the estimates—highlighted by the nine-year gap between their 40% windows of parity!—raises questions about what to believe. Neither estimate is perfect,[24] and extrapolation into the future magnifies their imperfections into fantasies. However, the magnitude of the gap is due to asymmetry rather than inaccuracy.

The PPP and Atlas estimates agree that, combined, the US and China are roughly one-third of the global economy in 2014, although PPP figures their shares to be equal while Atlas estimates them at 22% and 13% respectively. In terms of population, together they are 23% of global, with China at 19% and the US at 4%. By 2050 the UN estimates that their respective shares at 14% and 4%.[25] China is by both PPP and Atlas counts the second largest economy. According to Atlas, it passed Japan in 2009 and now is almost twice the Japanese economy (or almost four times by PPP). Last is that the US–Japan comparison is relatively unaffected by the method of estimate. Japan is 30% of the US economy by both measures. The last fact is perhaps the most interesting because it underlines the economic asymmetry between China and the US. Japan and the US are both developed economies, so their PPP market baskets and their tradable productivity are similar. China is another story. If Chinese productivity is equal in terms of domestic purchasing power, that is, in terms of consumable material goods, but has only 57% of US productivity in terms of international value, then China has a different kind of economy from the US (or Japan). Reversing the dialectic of Friedrich Engels, quality has transformed into quantity.[26]

China has four times the US population, but Americans do not work four (or six) times harder or longer. Rather, the capitalisation and technological levels of US production are significantly higher, and the Atlas estimates suggest that the difference is not likely to be overcome in the foreseeable future. Chinese work harder to feed and clothe themselves. The PPP magnitude of the economies is not an illusion, and even in Atlas terms China is by far the second largest economy. But China's economy has many short legs, while the US economy has fewer but longer ones.

Combining the estimates of the relative economies of the US and China, we can conclude that they are currently in a situation of asymmetric parity and that the situation is likely to last for the next generation. The reality of asymmetry is underlined if we add differences in population and geopolitical location. The US and China are not about to trade places. Symmetry implies transposability, and the relationship is not symmetric.[27] However, parity is not simply a numerical artifact. For each the bilateral relationship is the one of greatest exposure and complexity. As China's PPP productivity exceeds that of the US and it approaches tradable parity, the constraints on American policy options will grow. China will not be able to do to the US what the US can do to China in areas that presuppose capital concentration and technology, but the reverse is also true in other areas. Their interaction will have a sort of disjunctive reflexivity. Each will be able to help or hurt the other, but not in the same manner. This is not power transition, however. China will be a confronter but not a challenger. There is no mace of ultimate power to fight over, and the option of decisively defeating the other entails mutual destruction.

Asymmetry has important implications for rivalry. Although it is becoming more innovative, technological diffusion is still China's best hope for qualitative progress, and a hostile relationship with the leading technological power would be a handicap. And a larger (and aging) population means more pressure on the welfare side of the national budget. Although the burden of this limitation falls directly on China, US measures that exploit its capital and technological superiority run the risk of alienating other developing countries that share China's situation, if not its scale. Attempts to embargo technological innovation have a historical record of failure, and restricting the current global architecture of scientific innovation would have costs for US progress.

In sum, asymmetric parity implies long-term rivalry rather than hegemonic confrontation. If China cannot become the US, then its relative gain may be inconvenient and distressing to the United States, but not threatening. Similarly American prosperity will not cause it to re-cross some threshold of power transition, so continued US growth should not bother China. With the prospect of victory or defeat removed, win–win becomes possible.

Beyond Hegemony

The second major problem with anticipating a power transition rather than sustained rivalry is that a post-hegemonic situation is fundamentally new. This is recognised, to some extent, by power transition theorists. Tammen and Kugler write: 'The United States, though the single largest military superpower, is not a global hegemon. In maintains dominance only by assembling and managing a coalition of nations with congruent preferences.'[28]

However, the key word here is 'dominance', and that requires a dominator. To quote Tammen and Kugler again: 'Global peace is maintained when there is one overwhelmingly powerful dominant country... The basic argument of power parity is that key contenders in the international system challenge one another for dominance when they anticipate that the prospects of overtaking the regime leader are credible.'[29]

Hence, 'the United States and China are locked in a long-term competition for economic primacy', and the question deciding war or peace will be whether China considers itself a 'satisfied nation' in the current status quo.[30]

While parity defines the capacity to challenge, hegemony gives its rationale: one controls, the other wants to. But the global financial crisis of 2008 began a transition to an era in which globalisation has created a situation of inequality but not dominance, a multi-nodal world rather than a multipolar one.[31] The diversification of each country's significant relationships means that there are no natural camps of followers. Moreover, China's role in global development is not that of replacement for the US but rather as first among the unequals of the developing world.

As the earlier discussion of global value chains (GVC) would suggest, globalisation has created an enmeshed matrix in which power still matters, but the more powerful find it difficult to unilaterally impose their preferences on the less powerful. While the problems of domination are not new, globalisation has displaced the hegemonic world order with one based on asymmetric negotiation. Economic enmeshment is supplemented by informational enmeshment, and while interests remain localised and divergent, isolation is impossible.

Exposure is not uniform. States with greater capabilities are less exposed than their lesser counterparts, creating a multi-nodal asymmetric pattern. The US and China are the primary nodes, of major importance to all other actors. Secondary nodes such as Brazil, Germany, Russia, India and South Africa are key actors in their regions, and there are tertiary nodes as well. But the nodes function primarily as centres and sub-centres of attention and concern rather than as hierarchical levels of control. Brazil does not control Argentina, nor do the US and/or China control Brazil. But, unless a crisis distorts normal attention patterns, Argentina is more concerned about Brazil than it is about Paraguay.

Uncertainty, rather than domination, is the key characteristic of international life since 2008. Each state is more exposed in its external relationships, and the connectivity revolution has amplified the public's awareness and anxiety about external events. The general growth in nationalist sentiment is not due to some primordial upwelling of tribal identity but rather to the greater challenge to identity and interests presented by a more pressing world. Publics tend to absolutise national interests and to demand resolution of crises, but their governments face tangled situations in which compromise is necessary and closure is impossible. Enmeshment prevents radical, clean-cut solutions, so the multi-nodal matrix tends to be one of noisy but stable disorder. In their attempts to reduce uncertainty governments diversify their relationships and try to buffer their exposure by commitments to regional and global regimes.

A choice between being in a US camp or in a Chinese camp would limit options and increase uncertainty. As the primary nodes compete for influence, smaller states enjoy increased bargaining leverage, but if one or the other primary node demands an exclusive relationship then the smaller state faces a loss of some of its current options and a new dependence on its patron. A diplomatic romance can be rewarding, but marriage is not. Even if the suitor provides enough concessions to induce commitment there is the possibility of post-nuptial remorse. Thus if one primary node demanded exclusivity the main effect would probably be self-isolation.

If the US and China attempt a replay of the Cold War and both demand exclusive partners, the situation becomes more tense for other states. However, a decisive conflict is unlikely, and therefore it would be foolish to guess which side might prevail and to bandwagon with that side. It would be more prudent to maintain neutrality to the extent possible. Moreover, given the costs to the primary nodes of zero-sum conflict, it would be prudent for others to develop their relationships with other non-primary states, who after all are two-thirds of the global economy. Thus if both primary nodes issue calls for camps, they would likely be unsuccessful and they might reduce the global significance of the primary nodes.

Moving to the larger global picture, the asymmetric parity of the US and China is the most prominent part of a general convergence between middle-income and high-income countries. As with China, the principal drivers are urbanisation and technological diffusion. In 2010 China was 49.2% urban compared to the US 80.8%, and middle income countries stood at 48.1% compared to high-income countries at 79.3%—almost identical ratios.[32] By 2050 the UN expects China to be at 74% urban and the middle-income countries to be at 65%. Urbanisation drives higher productivity, though within a generation it also lowers birthrates and increases dependency ratios. The most prominent effect over the next 20 years will be fundamental changes in the global balance of wealth and productivity. Neither China nor the other middle-income countries are likely to leapfrog the wealthy in terms of per capita productivity, but reducing the gap in per capita productivity increases the salience of population size. Thus Price Waterhouse expects the ranked five largest economies in 2050 to be: China, India, United States, Indonesia and Brazil, while the five wealthiest major countries will be from among the usual suspects: United States, Australia, Germany, South Korea and Canada.[33] The great divide that defined the modern world between wealth/productivity on the one side and population on the other—between the West and the rest—has become a diminishing divide between wealth on the one side and population/productivity—size in all dimensions—on the other. Demographic power has overtaken the power of wealth and technology in its aggregate output, with China in the lead. In this situation global hegemony is not possible, and imagining global order becomes a challenge.

While asymmetric parity, global enmeshment and the emergence of demographic power create problems for contemporary expectations of power transition, it is a tribute to the theory's originator, A.F.K. Organski, that in 1958 he anticipated the broad sweep of socioeconomic development that we are now experiencing. He saw his own moment as 'living between two eras',[34] one of recent wars and a distant one of global industrialisation. Industrialisation would bring demography—and therefore China—to the fore:

> The question is not whether China will become the most powerful nation on earth, but rather, how long it will take her to achieve this status . . . If we can slide through the dangerous years with Russia without a war, a later war with China is not likely. From China's point of view, it would be pointless, from ours—hopeless . . . It is the certainty of her power that may prevent a war, for if America understands that she cannot stop the rise of China, she may resign herself to the inevitable and let her pass in peace.[35]

Strategic Corollaries of Sustainable Rivalry

What Organski envisioned as the peaceful passing of the hegemonic torch is considerably more complicated in a situation of asymmetric parity in a multi-nodal world. There is no moment of parity but rather decades of juxtaposition of primary nodes. Moreover, the asymmetry of the US–China relationship is only the major part of a larger asymmetric parity between middle- and high-income countries. It is a world in which the management of uncertainty is the key strategic concern of all. Indeed, the only certainties over the next 30 years are that the median age of populations will increase, especially for countries in the second generation after urbanisation, and that international cooperation will be necessary for the effective handling of global problems such as global warming.

If uncertainty must be contained by sustained management rather than eliminated by enforced hierarchical structure, several major strategic corollaries follow. First, security does not lie in invulnerability, but rather in negotiation predicated on stalemate. Second, attempts to convert asymmetric relationships into relationships of domination are likely to produce self-isolation. Third, multilateral agreements and institutions play a crucial role in managing uncertainty, but are most effective as implicitly inclusive partnerships rather than implicitly exclusive alliances. Fourth, cooperation is necessary in sustainable rivalry, and therefore it is necessary to maintain an overarching posture of mutual respect. Each of these corollaries will be discussed in turn.

Invulnerability is not an option
During the Cold War both sides initially sought invulnerability through a preponderance of power, but the Cuban missile crisis was the most prominent of a number of reminders that the pursuit of invulnerability increases the risk of mutually assured destruction. Not only were desperate actions and misunderstandings possible, but one's own weapons posed a real risk of accidental detonation.[36] Security required US–Soviet agreements to control risk. The most profound departure from the security-is-invulnerability mindset was the Anti-Ballistic Missile Treaty of 1972. It created security by leaving both superpowers exposed to one another's ballistic missiles. But with the end of the Cold War and the US success in the Persian Gulf War, invulnerability appeared to have been achieved, at least for the US. It was no longer nose-to-nose with the Soviets, and its conventional superiority was such that the military could do whatever it wanted, whenever it wanted, wherever it wanted, with no significant risk of loss or of failure. Invulnerability was demonstrated in the Persian Gulf War and in the initial occupations of Afghanistan and Iraq. The assumptions of invulnerability were shaken by 9/11 and by the elusiveness of victory in the Middle East, but these led to tactics of attempting to eliminate terrorism rather than to a rethinking of security.

China faces the US with the necessity of returning to a model of negotiated security, but the necessity is more subtle than the grand threat of mutually assured destruction. China's increasing military capabilities in its near waters face the US military with the prospect of significant losses or even failure in a conflict close to China. Moreover, China's growing capabilities in the areas of cyber warfare and space weaponisation raise spectres of US vulnerability.

The US military rose to the challenge of improved Chinese capabilities in its near waters by devising the AirSea Battle concept, which attempted to reclaim invulnerability by devising joint air and naval operations that would eliminate sources of threat before they could be launched. Since many of the sources of threat were missile bases and mobile launchers scattered on the mainland of China, the concept implied extensive pre-emptive attacks on mainland China. In effect, AirSea Battle solved the problem of limited vulnerability by escalating to general war.

The immediate problem with AirSea Battle was put succinctly in the title of one review article: 'Kick the Door Down With AirSea Battle—Then What?'[37] Although China could not respond with a similar conventional attack on the US, the prospect of a pre-emptive attack could lead to pre-pre-emptive surprises against US interests in the Pacific, and ultimately there is the rough equality of the nuclear option. In any case, what would the US accomplish beyond creating an implacable enemy intent on winning the next time? Experiences in the Middle East do not augur well for occupying China. It might be the case that one can cure the flu by catching the plague, but it is not a good solution.[38]

Vulnerability in the western Pacific is mutual. Indeed, the only novelty is that now the US is vulnerable as well. American vulnerability (uncorrected by AirSea Battle) does not make China invulnerable. In effect, a zone of stalemate is created in which both are vulnerable in the event of conflict. Neither rules China's near waters. Stalemate is a lose–lose situation in which time is on no one's side. Therefore, both have an interest in negotiated protocols of conduct and in avoiding crises. These reduce the likelihood of conflict, and therefore they increase security.

Similar scenarios of mutually assured loss that should lead to negotiated security could be described for space weaponisation and cyber security, but these concerns are not limited to the Asia-Pacific. Especially in the case of cyber security a global protocol is necessary. The US is reluctant to negotiate limits in these areas because it is the technological leader, but it is already vulnerable, and it will be increasingly vulnerable. If invulnerability is no longer an option and domination is also impossible, security must be negotiated.

Containment and self-containment

In a multi-nodal world the attempt to contain another country is an expensive and uncertain enterprise. Unless the client in containment felt an equal aversion to the target, its compliance would have to be forced or purchased. If forced, the containing country becomes the immediate threat, creating the possibility of the client siding with the target. If purchased, the fidelity of the client might last no longer than the attractiveness of the bargain. In the case of one primary node trying to create a military perimeter around the other, these difficulties are magnified. A client would put at risk its beneficial relations with the target and it would become the presumptive front line in the great power struggle. Moreover, its foreign policy would be subordinate to the patron's.

The containment of the Soviet Union in the Cold War is the exception that proves the rule. By consolidating its domination of Eastern Europe in 1947, the Soviets proved to Europe that they were an alien threat. By contrast, the Marshall Plan not only aided Western European recovery, it respected the autonomy of its governments. NATO institutionalised a common sense of risk. And thanks to the autarky of command economics, there was little to be lost in dividing Europe. The success of the containment of European communism depended on the gulf between the autarkic domination of the Soviet Union and the inclusive policies of the US. From the beginning with Yugoslavia and continuing with Romania and Poland (to name only the successful outliers), the Soviets had problems policing their domination, while NATO became so accepted that it outlasted its enemy.

Implicit in the Soviet experience is the other lesson of containment. The attempt to force or purchase exclusive deference is likely to backfire. While it is difficult to contain an enemy, it is not so difficult to surround oneself with alienated and insecure neighbours. To the extent that a powerful state demonstrates that it will use its power to impose its interest on its neighbours, it creates an incentive in its reluctant neighbours to hedge or even to balance against. To be sure, smaller states are always anxious about their larger neighbours because they are more exposed in the interactions and have less control. Therefore they prefer to buffer their dependence on a specific neighbour by diversifying their external relations, joining multilateral associations, and supporting international regimes. These actions do not limit their contact with a large neighbour, but rather reduce their proportional exposure. They take the worry out of being close. However, if the large neighbour reacts negatively and attempts to build an exclusive fence around its neighbourhood then it is demonstrating the difference between its interests and those of the neighbours. Then begins the soft self-containment of hedging and evasion, and possibly the hard self-containment of balancing against.

Partnerships, not alliances
It follows from the above discussion that joining an alliance targeted at an enemy is a bad idea for both the patron and the client. For the patron, a targeted alliance is an expensive and unreliable arrangement. Meanwhile the client obtains the favours of the patron, but with them the loss of opportunities with the target and the loss of autonomy in foreign policy. On the other hand, bonding together with other states is an important method of reducing external uncertainty. Although partnerships are between specific partners, they are not targeted and therefore do not exclude the possibility of each partner engaging in further partnerships. Even the most ambiguous partnerships affirm the abstract commitment of both parties to mutual benefit and non-threatening behavior. They provide a diplomatic platform that is useful both for pursuing collaborative projects and for minimising the damage of conflicts of interest. Partnerships of all sorts are more important for smaller states because of their implicit acknowledgement of the normalcy and mutual benefit of the relationship. More comprehensive and intense partnerships might be exclusive in the sense that other states would not be in a position to enjoy a relationship of such density. But in principle any partner can establish relationships with others, and these other connections can buffer the exposure of the partner in its more intense relationships.

Multilateral organisations such as Association of Southeast Asian Nations (ASEAN) or the Shanghai Cooperation Organisation (SCO) can work as regional partnerships, in contrast to NATO's alliance structure. Even though its membership is limited to states in the region, ASEAN is a paragon of inclusive partnership. It is a leader in broader transregional connections of all sorts. The expansion of its Treaty of

Amity in 2002 to non-members was an imaginative move, and broader institutions such as the Asia Regional Forum (ARF) and the East Asia Summit have contributed to large-scale tension reduction and cooperation. It is an impressive accomplishment for a region that was once a cockpit of domestic and regional violence. Similarly, the SCO began from modest efforts to control cross-border terrorism (the Shanghai Five) and has become a group with an ever-expanding membership and agenda.

In the US–China relationship there is the problem of the existing US alliance structure. The Asian alliance system originated as hub-and-spoke arrangements centred on the US and originating in various relationships of domination—post-colonialism in the Philippines, occupation in Japan and South Korea—as well as Cold War alignments with Australia and Thailand. Memories of domination interleave layers of resentment with thicker and more apparent layers of familiarity and contact. In all cases the benefits of a special relationship to the US were appreciated and formed core parts of diplomatic national identities. One of the core strengths of the US alliance system is that its inclusiveness allowed the contents of client relationships in Asia to change as the regional political economy transformed. The form and mentality of alliance remains, and anxieties about China resonate with earlier Cold War habits. However, as long as China is also inclusive and non-threatening, the US alliances function more as a special kind of partnership than a structure of reliable submission to US strategy. Moreover, US problems with China at the global level are different from Asian problems with China at the neighbour level, and the overlap of concerns should not be mistaken for complete agreement.

The protocol of sustainable rivalry
If the US and China are to face each other as the primary nodes of world politics for the next generation, the modality of their interaction should be a central strategic concern. The future is unknown, but the major partner is known. It is therefore important that the relationship be managed by both sides in such a way that the pursuit of opportunities and appropriate solutions to unknown future crises are facilitated. The *sine qua non* of sustainable rivalry is mutual respect.

Perhaps the best illustration of the ill effects of a lack of respect is the US–Iranian relationship. Long-term suspicion and hostility, grounded on the Iranian side by US support for the Shah and on the US side by the 1980 hostage crisis, prevented significant cooperation in dealing with the Taliban in Afghanistan despite shared interests, and has hampered cooperation against ISIS in Iraq. The lack of diplomatic recognition underlined the suspicion that neither accepted the legitimacy of the other's government as well as inconveniencing negotiations concerning common problems. From the time of Henry Kissinger's visit in 1971 the US–China relationship has been more fortunate.

The optimum protocol for sustainable rivalry would maintain mechanisms and avenues for future cooperation while at the same time allowing the articulation and negotiation of differences of interest. It begins at the top, with state visits such as

President Xi's to the US. The most important dimension of such visits is their ritual re-enactment of mutual respect. Negotiations and deliverables are secondary. In a relationship as important as the US–China one, the utility of official exchanges cascades down the governmental systems, and exchanges at each level and specialty have the additional advantage of putting cognate officials in personal contact with each other. In the same direction, official encouragement of educational exchange and tourism both enhances individual connections and is evidence of mutual openness.

Kevin Rudd's proposal of interaction on the basis of 'constructive realism and common purpose' could provide useful positive framing of the relationship.[39] It does not preclude open differences of interest, and it provides a forward-looking common posture that is in line with existing formal positions of both sides.

A significant risk in long-term US–China rivalry is that the two primary nodes become fixated with one another to such an extent that their policies toward other countries are simply derivative—what might be called the 'G-2 syndrome'. The talk of 'proxy wars' during the Cold War is an extreme example, but in any case other countries do not want to be treated as third parties that are significant only in how they relate to a 'great game'. In East Asia there is an almost inevitable triangularity in relationships of any state with China and the US, and it is important to make clear that the autonomy and interests of all are respected. Otherwise the G-2 syndrome will induce other states to hedge against dependence on the primary nodes.

Conclusion

As the Chinese economy slows to a 'new normal', general anxieties about China's meteoric trajectory should subside. But three basic truths remain from the contrast between global confusion since 2008 and China's continued growth. The first is that globalisation is no longer a threat; it is a fact. In the 1990s globalisation appeared to be the economic and cultural dimension of US omnipotence, and a threat to the individuality and identity of other cultures. Since 2008 the image of US omnipotence has been shaken, but the reality of global interconnectedness has been demonstrated.

The second basic truth is that China has now risen. It is not only one of the world's two largest economies, it now shares with the US the exalted rank of primary node in the global political economy. The parity is asymmetric, but real. Given its asymmetry, the relationship is not approaching—or passing—a point of equality. Rather, its current situation can be expected to last a generation. Moreover, as the generation moves along, it will prove to be part of an even larger convergence of middle-income demographic power and higher-income capital and technology.

The third basic truth is that the management of uncertainty through negotiation has become the primary diplomatic task of all states. The US is and will remain the only global military power, but it is no longer the 'hyperpower' enforcing world order. The contrast between the 'coalition of the willing' dragged along in the invasion of

Iraq and role of the five powers involved in negotiating the Joint Comprehensive Plan of Action on nuclear weapons with Iran is instructive. The 'coalition of the willing' weren't significant and weren't willing. France, United Kingdom, Germany, Russia and China were not only important players in the negotiation, but their agreement meant that if the US backed out, its sanctions would not be effective. This coalition was both willing and able.

The world is thus beyond hegemony but not beyond power. The general exposure of peoples to each other is greater than it has ever been. Capabilities differ, and they matter. The US and China, in their own ways, are the most powerful states, but neither controls the world, thus there is no need for a hegemonic struggle. Together they do not control the world, but they are in the default position of leadership for addressing common challenges, including the construction of regional and global regimes based on consent rather than on imposition.

The implications of these three truths are different for the US and China, and for the rest of the world. For the US, China is a challenge, but it is not the challenger to an otherwise unproblematic US hegemony. Re-fighting the last cold war would a mistake; not because China is a friend, but because the context and structure of global power has changed. The US remains the strongest political and military power, and it can use its advantages for constructive leadership.

Also for China a change of perspective is necessary. Because the US was the hegemonic global power and remains the pre-eminent technological power, it appears to be the primary obstacle to China's wealth and power. But self-isolation is a greater threat than US containment. If other states see reassurance and mutual benefit in their relationships with China they will not side against it. If China's regional and global initiatives, such as the AIIB and One Belt, One Road plan, are inclusive, then the United States would be foolish to oppose.

For the rest of the world, the US and China, individually and in their bilateral relationship, will be at the centre of world attention for the foreseeable future. They are already the primary nodes of a post-hegemonic world order. Thanks to globalisation, interdependence is more vivid. But it is a post-hegemonic world order—the US and China are the biggest players, but they are not in control. Again thanks to globalisation, states have choices. If China and the US compete for control, the rest will hedge against the global centre. If one tries to contain or force out the other, other states will avoid the risk of conflict and the state issuing the ultimatum will end up isolating itself. The US and China will be centrestage, but the rest of the world will vote either with their hands or with their feet.

Notes

1. Brantly Womack, 'China and the Future Status Quo', *Chinese Journal of International Politics* 8:2 (Summer 2015), pp. 115–137.
2. These and following figures are calculated from World Bank, *World Development Indicators 2015*, purchasing power parity (PPP) data, accessed at http://data.worldbank.org/.

3. 'Full Transcript: Interview With Chinese President Xi Jinping', *Wall Street Journal*, September 22, 2015.
4. *China 2030: Building a Modern, Harmonious, and Creative High-Income Society* (Washington, DC: World Bank, 2012).
5. Soviet figures are calculated by aggregating the former Soviet component economies. The Russian Federation is used for per capita calculations.
6. 'Remarks by President Obama and President Xi of the People's Republic Of China at Arrival Ceremony', 25 September 2015. http://www.newsroomamerica.com/story/520428/remarks_by_president_obama_and_president_xi_of_the_peoples_republic_of_china_at_arrival_ceremony.html. Accessed 25 September 2015.
7. The semi-exception is the Philippines, but if exports to Hong Kong are combined with China then China is its largest export and import partner. CIA Factbook https://www.cia.gov/library/publications/the-world-factbook/geos/rp.html Accessed 25 August 2015.
8. Zeev Maoz and Ben Mor, *Bound by Struggle: The Strategic Evolution of Enduring International Rivalries* (Ann Arbor: University of Michigan Press, 2002).
9. Brantly Womack, *Asymmetry and International Relationships* (New York: Cambridge University Press, 2016), pp. 125–146.
10. Timothy Heath, 'Xi's Visit Exposes Mismatch in US and Chinese Expectations', *World Politics Review*, September 2015. http://www.worldpoliticsreview.com/articles/16748/xi-s-visit-exposes-mismatch-in-u-s-and-chinese-expectations. Accessed 24 September 2015.
11. Kevin Rudd, *US–China 21: The Future of US–China Relations under Xi Jinping, Summary Report* (Cambridge: Belfer Center, Harvard, April 2015).
12. As summarised in a 2014 Chinese internal document cited in Kevin Rudd, *US–China 21*, p. 14.
13. Claire Jones and Chris Giles, 'WTO and OECD Add Value to Trade Debate', *Financial Times* 16 January 2013.
14. Yildirim Aydin, 'Value Added Trade, Global Value Chains, and Trade Policy: Renewed Push for Trade Liberalisation', Background paper for WTO's 'Made in the World Initiative', 19 January 2015, https://www.wto.org/english/res_e/statis_e/miwi_e/paper_january15_e.htm. Accessed 1 September 2015.
15. Marcel P. Timmer, et al., 'An Illustrated User Guide to the World Input–Output Database: the Case of Global Automotive Production', *Review of International Economics*, 23.3 (2015), pp. 575–605.
16. William Overholt, 'The Enemy is Us', *The International Economy* (Summer 2015), pp. 8–12.
17. There are technological spinoffs derived from military investments, but presumably they could be obtained more efficiently if pursued directly.
18. Graham Allison, 'Avoiding Thucydides's Trap', Op-Ed, *Financial Times* 22 August 2012.
19. Ibid.
20. A.F.K. Organski, *World Politics* (New York: Knopf, 1958).
21. Ronald Tammen and Jacek Kugler, 'Power Transition and China–US Conflicts', *Chinese Journal of International Politics* 1:1 (2006), pp. 35–55, here p. 43.
22. These projections reflect a certain amount of pessimism about Chinese statistics and perhaps some optimism about American growth. See Josh Noble, 'Doubts Rise about China's Official GDP Growth Rate', *Financial Times* 16 September 2015.
23. The World Bank's Atlas method uses a three-year moving average of exchange rates as well as an inflation estimator to estimate productivity in tradable terms rather than the PPP's estimate of productivity in terms of domestic consumption.
24. A recent, careful recalculation of China's GDP would put it 13–16% higher than official estimates. See Daniel Rosen and Beibei Bao, *Broken Abacus? A More Accurate Gauge of China's Economy* (Washington, DC: CSIS, September 2015). http://rhg.com/books/broken-abacus-a-more-accurate-gauge-of-chinas-economy?utm_

     source=The+Sinocism+China+Newsletter&utm_campaign=905735d6a9-
     Sinocism09_22_159_21_2015&utm_medium=email&utm_term=0_171f237867-
     905735d6a9-29617753&mc_cid=905735d6a9&mc_eid=4894df43ce
25   United Nations, Department of Economic and Social Affairs, Population Division, World
     Population Prospects, 2014 revision. http://esa.un.org/unpd/wup/CD-ROM/ Accessed 25
     September 2015.
26   Frederick Engels, *Anti-Dühring. Herr Eugen Dühring's Revolution in Science* (New York:
     Progress Publishers, 1947), chapter 12.
27   Hermann Weyl, Symmetry (Princeton: Princeton University Press, 1952), p. 4. Weyl quotes
     Leibnitz to the effect that symmetry exists when two things are indiscernible when considered
     by themselves (p. 127).
28   Tammen and Kugler, 'Power Transition', p. 36.
29   Ibid, pp. 39–40.
30   Ibid, pp. 45–46.
31   Brantly Womack, 'China's Future in a Multi-Nodal World Order', *Pacific Affairs* 87:2 (June
     2014), pp. 265–284.
32   United Nations, World Population Prospects, 2014 revision.
33   Price Waterhouse, 'The World in 2050', February 2015, https://www.pwc.com/gx/en/issues/
     economy/future-economy.html. Accessed 19 September 2015.
34   Organski, World Politics, p. 4.
35   Ibid, p. 446; p. 449.
36   Eric Schlosser, Command and Control (New York: Penguin, 2014).
37   Martin Murphy, 'Kick the Door Down with AirSea Battle—Then What?' Parameters 45:2
     (Summer 2015), pp. 97–107.
38   AirSea Battle has now been subsumed into the 'Joint Concept for Access and Maneuver in
     the Global Commons', but essentially this keeps the old content and brings in the Army and
     the Marines. Paul McLeary, 'New US Concept Melds Air, Sea and Land', *Defense News*, 24
     January 2015.
39   Kevin Rudd, *US–China 21*.

Top: Part of the audience in the Council Chamber of the Victoria University Hunter Building at conference proceedings.

Bottom: Dr Jian Yang (left), Member of Parliament, National Party, New Zealand, chairing a panel.

Two Roads, but One Destination?

Shao Yuqun

Senior fellow and executive director of the Center for American Studies, Shanghai Institute for International Studies, China

Abstract

A stable and peaceful China–US relationship is in the interest of both countries and the world. The critical question now is how to solve the problem of mutual strategic trust deficit between them. Since neither country has a solution so far, the best way is to effectively manage the differences while creating more opportunities for cooperation. The New Silk Road initiative (or the One Belt, One Road strategy), raised by the Chinese government three years ago, offers a great opportunity for the two countries to have practical cooperation in the economic and development sectors, especially in central and South Asia, where China and the US have many common interests, such as regional security, stability and sustainable economic development of the regional countries.

When visiting India in July 2011, then US Secretary of State Hillary Clinton proposed the 'New Silk Road' initiative, an idea conceived to promote regional economic cooperation in central and South Asia. During his visit to Kazakhstan in September 2013, Chinese President Xi Jinping suggested creation of a 'Silk Road Economic Belt', a new concept used to encourage innovative cooperation between relevant countries.

Historically, the Silk Road refers to the pathway that connected business and trade flows between Asian, African and European countries. It also bridged political, economic and cultural exchanges between the East and West. Interestingly enough, during this new decade of the 21st century, both China and the US have headlined their ideas about regional economic cooperation under the same name. While the name is the same, the strategic intents and specific contents covered therein are widely different.

Then, what are these differences? And will they lead to the same one destination? Beyond a doubt, the strategic intents of the US and Chinese Silk Road initiatives are totally different from one another. Immediately after the disintegration of the Soviet Union and the subsequent end of the Cold War, the US came up with a Silk Road initiative designed to free the newly independent central Asian countries from Russian and Iranian influences, and bring them onto the path of freedom and democracy. At the same time, the US hoped to serve its own interests: diversification of its energy imports by making good use of the oil and gas resources newly discovered in the Caspian Sea region.

To facilitate its military withdrawal from Afghanistan and to prevent its strategic interests in central and South Asia from being jeopardised by deterioration of the security situation in Afghanistan, the US came up with an updated version of the Silk Road initiative in 2011, hoping to turn Afghanistan into the pivot of closer economic cooperation between central and South Asian countries. According to estimates, from the start of the war in Afghanistan until 2011, the US offered Afghanistan a total of US$18.8 billion in aid, an amount bigger than its aid to any other country during the same period. Heavy consumption and massive aid from the US and its allies created a 'war economy' in Afghanistan, and distorted the country's economic growth model, with 97% of Afghanistan's GDP coming from international consumption.

According to the World Bank's calculations, Afghanistan will hardly be able to keep its current economic growth after 2016, because the withdrawal of US and NATO forces will directly cut its annual economic growth rate by 2–3%. After 2016 consumption by US forces in Afghanistan will contract drastically, and the US and international aid to Afghanistan will also plummet sharply, exposing its economy to the risk of collapse. Given the lack of endogenous power in the Afghanistan economy, and the uncertainties from its political and security situation, the US hopes to form a trade gateway connecting central Asia and South Asia via Afghanistan through implementation of its New Silk Road initiative, thus helping Afghanistan secure energy supplies, create more job opportunities and open new markets for its products.

Apart from this core strategic intent, the US is also attempting to strengthen its strategic partnership with India, prevent monopoly of central Asian affairs by Russia and China, and guard against Iran's intervention in Afghanistan through its New Silk Road initiative.

Meanwhile, the Silk Road Economic Belt, proposed by President Xi Jinping, has a strategic goal with both domestic and international significance. From an international perspective, the Silk Road Economic Belt along with the new Maritime Silk Road, constitute a part of China's general intent to fortify periphery diplomacy and strengthen friendly ties, particularly with its western neighbours. China needs a peaceful and stable neighbouring environment for its all-round economic and social development. But due to the sheer number of countries along its borders, and the development of a complicated strategic environment, China has run into unprecedented challenges in its periphery diplomacy as its national strength grows rapidly.

At its first national conference on periphery diplomacy in October 2013, President Xi Jinping highlighted China's basic principles, which encompass good-neighbourliness, peace and security, and mutual prosperity, stressing that China would remain close, sincere, kind-hearted and tolerant to all its neighbours. Through implementation and development of the Silk Road Economic Belt, China can share its economic achievements with its neighbours and promote mutual benefit and common prosperity through close and honest cooperation, thus fulfilling its responsibility and performing its duty as a leading regional power.

Also, the security situation in central and South Asia will become highly uncertain after the US withdrawal from Afghanistan in 2016. This will give the three forces new soil to grow, adversely affect regional economic development, jeopardise political and social stability in western China and pose new challenges to the economic 'go-out' strategy being pursued by western Chinese regions. Given these factors, the Silk Road Economic Belt initiative's promotion of regional economic cooperation is great news to all countries in this region. Since economic development also helps to improve the regional security situation, implementation of the initiative will be of positive significance to stabilisation of the regional security situation.

From a domestic perspective, the initiative is an obvious part of the strategic blueprint drawn up by China's new leadership for opening the Chinese economy to the outside world. Over the past three decades since it started the drive of reform and opening-up, China favoured an eastward thrust of its economic opening-up, focusing efforts on development of economic and trade ties mainly with the US and European countries. However, with the contraction of the US and the European markets resulting from the global economic crisis, the tightening of its economic and trade relations, and energy cooperation with Middle East, central and South Asian countries, and the pressing need for economic development in its western part, China has come to escalate westward opening-up of its economy on its agenda. For instance, the New Eurasian Land Bridge from Lianyungang Port to Amsterdam runs through 47 cities in 17 countries, with rich resources lying all over the route. If this bridge is turned into a passageway that is less costly in logistics and much greater in efficiency than marine routes, Chinese enterprises will enjoy a smoother sailing during their 'Go Global' voyage, and the country's western regions will get a new gateway with new acting point for its westward economic opening-up. Since Xi's proposal of the Silk Road Economic Belt, Xinjiang, Shaanxi, Qinghai and some other provinces and regions have all rushed into action, following each other to work out strategic programmes and action plans.

On 14 December 2013, the State Development and Reform Commission and the Ministry of Foreign Affairs co-sponsored a forum on the development of the Silk Road Economic Belt and the Maritime Silk Road. It was decided at the forum that the Silk Road Economic Belt would cover Shaanxi Province, Gansu Province, Qinghai Province, Ningxia Hui Autonomous Region, Xinjiang Uyghur Autonomous Region, Chongqing Municipality, Sichuan Province, Yunnan Province and Guangxi Zhuang Autonomous Region. Finalising the geographical coverage of the Silk Road Economic Belt has once again confirmed China's goal to promote the opening-up of its western regions.

The items of regional economic cooperation covered in the New Silk Road initiative include four parts: first, acceleration of infrastructure development (including mainly road construction in Afghanistan, railway network development in Afghanistan and its neighbouring countries, and regional power grids development); second, lowering of trade barriers and promotion of regional trade contacts; third, construction of the Turkmenistan–Afghanistan–Pakistan–India natural gas pipeline; fourth, promotion of water resource sharing.

Currently there has been encouraging progress in the construction of transnational railways, but no significant headway has been made in other fields of infrastructural development. A lot of factors are to blame for the slow progress, particularly making Afghanistan the pivot of the drive. Due to the instability of the security situation in this central Asian country, no substantial progress can be achieved in many projects. Also, the US is essentially concerned with facilitating its military withdrawal from Afghanistan instead of promoting regional economic cooperation in central or South Asia. Few high-ranking officials from the Obama administration have visited central Asia since his re-election, a phenomenon that has incurred criticism even from US scholars.

The Silk Road Economic Belt initiative, meanwhile, is still at the stage of finalisation. Viewed from its current evolution, the chief measures under contemplation mainly include creation of an extensive transportation and logistics passageway, promotion of trade and investment facilitation by removing bottlenecks strangling regional economic development, acceleration of financial cooperation, establishment of an energy club and installation of a grain cooperation mechanism. According to its design by the Chinese Academy of Social Sciences, the Silk Road Economic Belt will run along three lines: the northern line dominated by the Eurasian Bridge, the middle line composed mainly of oil and gas pipelines, and the southern line featuring mainly transnational highways.

A comparison of the New Silk Road initiative and the Silk Road Economic Belt reveals that for all the differences of their geographical coverage, the two do meet each other somewhere—namely, in central Asia. They differ from each other in terms of strategic targets, but still they share some similar goals, such as improvement of the regional security situation by economic means, including acceleration of infrastructure development and subsequent promotion of economic cooperation and trade contact. Specifically speaking, the two initiatives opt for different projects; but generally speaking, they go in the same and one direction: acceleration of regional economic cooperation. Under such circumstances, the two countries should include their respective initiatives in their policy dialogues on South and central Asian strategies, and continue communicating their policy to find a new point of cooperation and pool efforts for the development of the regional economy.

Xi Jinping's US Policy: Building a 'New Type of Major-Country Relationship'

Bo Zhiyue

Director of the New Zealand Contemporary China Research Centre and professor of political science at Victoria University of Wellington, New Zealand.

Abstract

Nine months before taking over as the top leader of the Chinese Communist Party, Vice President Xi Jinping proposed a new policy to the US. Instead of confrontation and competition, he suggested that China and the US build a 'new type of major-country relationship' characterised by mutual respect, mutual benefit and win–win cooperation. Since becoming general-secretary of the CCP in November 2012, however, the 'new type of major-country relationship' has remained only diplomatic rhetoric. Although China and the US have continued their economic cooperation, their security and political relations have deteriorated significantly. In particular, the US has taken a clear stand over the issue of the Senkaku (Diaoyu) Islands both rhetorically and legally. Evidently, President Xi's state visit to Washington in September 2015 failed to reverse the situation.

A relationship with the US has been one of China's top priorities since the early 1970s. In the recent past, a visit to the US has become an important preparatory course for the forthcoming leader of the Chinese Communist Party (CCP). In his official visit to the US in February 2012, Vice President Xi Jinping articulated his policy toward the US as the would-be president of China: to build a 'new type of major-country relationship.' Since he took over as the head of the CCP in November 2012, however, the bilateral relationship has not made any significant progress along the lines of 'mutual respect, mutual benefit, and win–win cooperation.' In some areas of security, the relationship has deteriorated significantly. In particular, the US has taken a clear stand over the issue of Senkaku (Diaoyu) Islands both rhetorically and legally. During his recent state visit in September 2015, President Xi continued to emphasise the importance of establishing a new type of major-country relationship with the US, but his host—President Obama of the US—dropped all references to this concept this time.

Hu Jintao's Legacies

In retrospect, the decade from 2002 to 2012 under the leadership of Hu Jintao was probably the best period in the history of China–US relations. The US cooperated with China against Taiwanese independence forces under President Chen Shuibian of Taiwan; China and the US worked on their differences through institutionalised channels; and both sides were willing to collaborate over matters of fundamental interests.

In contrast to his immediate predecessor, President Jiang Zemin, President Hu Jintao paid more attention to the institutionalisation of bilateral dialogues. He worked with President George W. Bush of the US in establishing two major dialogues: the US–China Senior Dialogue and the China–US Strategic Economic Dialogue (SED).

The US–China Senior Dialogue was conceived at an APEC meeting in November 2004 after a suggestion made by Chinese President Hu Jintao to US President George W. Bush to create a forum where the global superpower and emerging global player could come together and discuss issues of mutual concern. Typically, each meeting went for one or two days, and there were six meetings altogether between August 2005 and December 2008. In the process, the US urged China to become a 'responsible stakeholder' and China responded to the call favourably.

The China–US Strategic Economic Dialogue (SED) was initiated by President Hu Jintao and President George W. Bush in 2006 as a framework for the two countries to discuss bilateral economic issues. There were five meetings altogether between 2006 and 2008, each running for two days with alternating locations between China and the US. The two sides discussed various issues of mutual concerns and reached a number of agreements.

After President Barack Obama took office, President Hu worked with him to combine the two dialogues into one: the China–US Strategic and Economic Dialogue (S&ED). The dialogue has two tracks: a strategic track and an economic track. By the end of May 2012, the two countries had gone through four rounds of dialogue. Through these dialogues, Hu Jintao managed to depoliticise issues between China and the US, and reached some basic understanding between the two countries.

Although Hu Jintao's 2006 visit had some awkward moments, both President George W. Bush and President Barak Obama were willing to cooperate with him over some politically sensitive issues for China. During Premier Wen Jiabao's visit to the US in December 2003, President Bush made it clear that the US government opposed the independence of the Taiwanese leader. In his words,

> Let me tell you what I've just told the Premier on this issue. The US government's policy is one China, based upon the three communiqués and the Taiwan Relations Act. We oppose any unilateral decision by either China or Taiwan to change the status quo. And the comments and actions made by the leader of Taiwan indicate that he may be willing to make decisions unilaterally to change the status quo, which we oppose.[1]

Moreover, in order to support Hu's Beijing Olympics, President Bush made a decision not to meet with the Dalai Lama in 2008. Similarly, President Obama decided not to meet with Dalai Lama in 2009 before his Beijing visit.[2]

It was also under Hu Jintao that China proposed to establish 'a new type of major-country relationship' with the US. The concept, *xinxing daguo guanxi*, was first mentioned in the *People's Daily* on 3 January 2001. An editorial on China's foreign policy noted that Jiang Zemin's leadership in the aftermath of the end of the Cold War made efforts to build a new type of major-country relationship with major countries such as the US, Russia, Japan and Europe, and that these relations feature 'no alliance, no confrontation, and not against any third party'.[3]

In his opening remarks at the first China–US S&ED in Washington, DC on 27 July 2009, State Councillor Dai Bingguo of China made a statement that by coming together for the dialogue, China and the US were creating a history of establishing a new type of major-country relations of mutual respect, harmonious coexistence and win–win cooperation in the globalised 21st century. He ended his remarks by saying 'Yes, we can' in English to the 'new type of major-country relations' between China and the US.[4]

Xi Jinping's US Policy

Although the concept of a 'new type of major-country relationship' had been introduced under Jiang Zemin and applied to the China–US relations in particular under Hu Jintao, Xi Jinping decided to use this concept as his US policy.

During his visit to the US in February 2012 as vice president of China, Xi proposed to establish a new type of major-country relations with the US through joint efforts in four areas. First, two countries should improve mutual understanding and strategic trust. Second, both sides should show mutual respect for each other's core interests and major concerns. Third, the two powers should develop win–win cooperation. Fourth, they should cooperate and coordinate with each other over international and global issues such as the Korean peninsular and Iranian nuclear issues. As for China's core interests, Xi mentioned Taiwanese affairs, Tibetan affairs and their differences over human rights issues.[5]

During his first visit to the US in June 2013 as president of China, Xi spent two days with President Obama in Sunnylands, California. They spent more than eight hours together discussing a wide range of issues of mutual interest.[6] Apparently, the two presidents were both interested in establishing a new type of relationship between China and the US. For Xi, it was a 'new type of major-country relationship'. For Obama, it was a 'new model of cooperation'[7] or 'this new model of relations' between the US and China.[8]

Although Obama did not use the same wording as Xi in reference to the new type of major-country relationship, he did respond favourably to the concept. It thus is not farfetched for State Councillor Yang Jiechi to have concluded that the two presidents agreed to work together to build a new type of major-country relationship of mutual respect and win–win cooperation.[9] Unlike 'core interests', Hu Jintao's favourite term, which has been officially incorporated in the joint statement issued on 17 November 2009,[10] the Xi–Obama agreement has no official documentation because of the nature of their informal meeting.

Evolution of China–US Relations

In the subsequent developments, however, China and the US did not find a way to build a new type of relationship with each other over security issues. Due to a strategic trust deficit, the bilateral security relationship has in fact deteriorated.

With the new type of major-country relationship, for instance, China wished to put pressure on Japan through the US. Initially, the US appeared to have valued its relationship with China more than its relationship with Japan. During Japanese Prime Minister Abe's visit in February 2013, President Obama met with him only once for one hour and forty-five minutes.[11] During their meeting, Obama did not mention the issue of the Senkaku (Diaoyu) Islands at all.[12] But Obama devoted more than eight hours to meetings with Xi Jinping in June. During their meetings, Xi and Obama spent about 40 minutes over the issues of Japan and the Senkaku (Diaoyu) Islands.[13]

Five months later, however, China disappointed the US. On 23 November 2013, China's Ministry of Defense unilaterally declared an Air Defence Identification Zone (ADIZ) over the East China Sea that included the Senkaku (Diaoyu) Islands without any prior communications with the US. The US reacted very strongly against the declaration and on 25 November flew two B-52 bombers over the zone in defiance of China's declaration.

From the Chinese point of view, this was not unprecedented, and China had every right to declare an ADIZ on its own. From the point of view of the US, this was a big surprise. The US did not challenge China's right to declare an ADIZ, but was not happy about the way it was done. The main problem, according to the then US Secretary of Defense Chuck Hagel, was not the ADIZ itself. It was China's failure to consult prior to imposing it.[14]

Consequently, the US began to clarify its policy over Senkaku (Diaoyu) Islands. Hagel reaffirmed the military alliance between the US and Japan, and reminded Beijing that the Senkaku (Diaoyu) Islands are covered by the 1952 US–Japan

Security Treaty. In his call to Japanese Defence Minister Itsunori Onodera on 27 November 2013, Hagel criticised Beijing's establishment of the East China Sea ADIZ as 'a potentially destabilising action designed to change the status quo in the region' that raises 'the risk of misunderstanding and miscalculation'. He reaffirmed the 'longstanding US policy that article five of the Japan–US mutual defence treaty applies to the Senkaku Islands' and pledged to 'consult closely with Japan on efforts to avoid unintended incidents.'[15]

During his trip to Japan in April 2014, President Obama made it clear that the US–Japan Security Treaty applies to the Senkaku (Diaoyu) Islands. At a joint press conference with Prime Minister Abe on 24 April 2014, Obama stated that the US treaty commitment to Japan's security 'is absolute' and that 'article five covers all territories under Japan's administration, including the Senkaku Islands.'[16]

This is in stark contrast to the position of the Obama administration since 2009. According to a report from the *Japan Times* on 17 August 2010, the Obama administration embellished Senkaku security pact status. According to the report,

> When Tokyo sought confirmation of the US position in March 2009, the Obama administration said the islands have been under Japanese administrative control since the 1972 reversion and the Japan–US security pact applies to territories under Japanese administration, but it did not directly state that the Senkakus are subject to the pact, the sources said.[17]

Now, in April 2014, to the pleasure of the Japanese and the displeasure of the Chinese, President Obama made a clear statement that the US–Japan security pact applies to the Senkaku Islands as well.

In the meantime, China and the US have made substantial progress on the climate change issues. During his state visit to China in November 2014, President Obama reached an historic agreement with President Xi Jinping over climate change. In their joint announcement on 12 November 2014, the two presidents recognised the critical role that the two largest emitters of CO_2 in the world could play in combating global climate change and agreed to work together and with other countries to adopt a protocol at the United Nations Climate Conference in Paris in 2015.[18] They also set specific goals for their countries. The US aims to reduce its emissions by 26–28% below its 2005 level in 2025, and China intends to achieve its peak CO_2 emissions around 2030.

Xi Jinping's US State Visit

During his most recent state visit to the US in late September 2015, President Xi Jinping exchanged views with President Barack Obama on a range of global, regional and bilateral subjects. The two presidents agreed to work together to manage their differences, such as those of cybersecurity, and decided to expand their cooperation on a number of mutually concerning global and regional issues such as Afghanistan, peacekeeping, wildlife trafficking and ocean conservation.[19] They declared 2016 a US–China Tourism Year and endorsed a 'One Million Strong' initiative that aims to have one million American students studying Mandarin by 2020.

The two leaders reaffirmed their commitment to global climate change targets and issued a joint presidential statement on climate change.[20] According to this statement, the US took a major step forward in August 2015 to finalise the Clean Power Plan, which will reduce CO_2 emissions from the power sector to 32% below 2005 levels by 2030.

In the meantime, China will lower carbon dioxide emissions per unit of GDP by 60–65% from the 2005 level by 2030 and increase forest stock volume by around 4.5 billion m³ from the 2005 level by 2030. In 2017 China also plans to start its national emissions trading system, covering key industry sectors such as iron and steel, power generation, chemicals, building materials, paper-making and non-ferrous metals.

Unfortunately, the timing of Xi's state visit was not perfect. His visit coincided with that of Pope Francis to the US. A country 70.6% Christian and 20.8% Catholics, the papal visit was the focus of the media. Xi arrived in Washington, DC at 5.16 pm local time on 24 September,[21] less than two hours after Pope Francis left the US capital for New York.[22] Xi left for New York at 11.25 pm on 25 September.[23]

Xi spent altogether 30 hours in the capital. During these hours, the two presidents met for about 10 hours. Most of these hours were spent on the rituals of a state visit, though their dinner on 24 September is reportedly to have been longer than expected, for 2.5 hours.[24] However, Xi was not the focus of the US media. At a joint press conference for President Xi Jinping and President Obama, American reporters asked a lot of questions about the sudden resignation of the house speaker, John Boehner.[25] Furthermore, American media was stunned by Michelle Obama's Vera Wang dress at the state dinner for the Chinese president.[26]

Of course, this lack of attention in Western media was more than offset by the Chinese media attention on every move of the Chinese president during his entire visit to the US. In the *People's Daily*, the phrase '*xinxing daguo guanxi*' ('a new type of major-country relationship') was mentioned 396 times between 3 January 2001 and 30 September 2015, and between 1 January 2015 and 30 September 2015, it was mentioned 110 times. In the month of September alone, the phrase was mentioned 60 times (Figure 6.1).

Unfortunately, President Obama, who had been sympathetic to the phrase 'a new type of major-country relationship' between the US and China previously, dropped any reference to any type of new model of cooperation between the two countries.

The Future of China–US Relations

Apparently, Chinese President Xi Jinping is very keen to build a new type of major-country relationship with the US. In his first two speeches delivered in Washington state before his visit to Washington, DC, he mentioned the term seven times.

In his speech at the welcome dinner in Seattle on 22 September, he told the

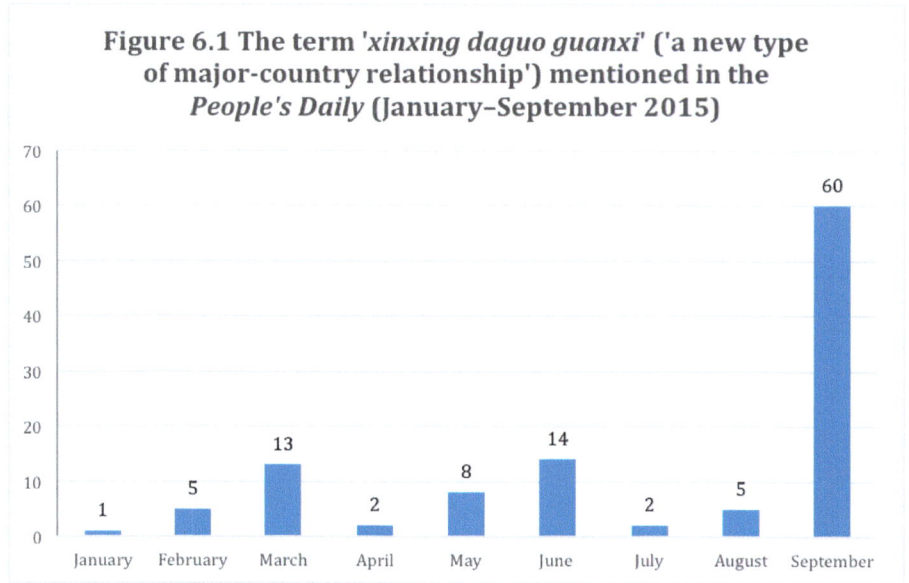

Figure 6.1 The term 'xinxing daguo guanxi' ('a new type of major-country relationship') mentioned in the *People's Daily* (January–September 2015)

audience that he and President Obama had reached a consensus at their meeting in Sunnylands in 2013 to build a new type of major-country relationship and proposed to deepen the relationship through joint efforts in four areas.

First, both sides should have a correct assessment of the other side's strategic intentions. They should learn to avoid strategic misunderstandings and misjudgements. They should not create a 'Thucydides Trap' for themselves because of misjudgement. Second, the two countries should promote win–win cooperation, because cooperation is the only correct way for mutual benefits. China and the US should respect each other's interests and concerns. Third, the two countries should manage their differences effectively. It is very natural that China and the US have different views on some issues, but the key is to expand common understanding. Fourth, the two countries should develop people-to-people friendship. The Chinese government will support exchange programmes through which 50,000 Chinese students will study in the US and 50,000 American students will study in China.[27]

Xi reiterated these remarks during his meetings with President Obama. During their joint press conference at the White House, Xi once again expressed his wishes to establish a new type of major-country relationship with the US. But Obama did not echo in kind. In contrast to his enthusiastic concurrence with Xi's proposal in 2013, Obama did not mention any similar phrases at all.[28]

Given the US concerns over the South China Sea and the East China Sea and their frustration with China's cyber attacks, the US president is not prepared to endorse China's proposal on the new type of major-country relationship. As in any relationship, it takes two to tango. It is difficult to see a bright future for this new concept if the US side is not ready to take it. In contrast to President Hu Jintao's state visit in 2011, when the two presidents issued a joint statement elaborating various areas of cooperation, there was no joint statement this time, except for a joint presidential statement on climate change.

However, this does not mean the end of cooperative relationship between the US and China. On the contrary, the US is willing to cooperate with China over a broad range of bilateral, regional and global issues.

Notes

1 'President Bush and Premier Wen Jiabao Remarks to the Press', 9 December 2003, http://2001-2009.state.gov/p/eap/rls/rm/2003/27184.htm. Accessed on 24 May 2016.
2 For details, see Bo Zhiyue, 'Obama's China Policy', in Sujian Guo and Baogang Guo, eds., *Thirty Years of China–US Relations: Analytical Approaches and Contemporary Issues* (Lanham, MD: Lexington Book, 2010), pp. 253–279.
3 Shi Xiaohui and Liu Shuiming, 'Dongfang julong yili shijie—shengli maixiang xinshiji shuping zhiwu' ('Rising Dragon in the World: A Commentary on China's March Toward the New Century [5]'), *Renmin Ribao*, 3 January 2001, p. 1.
4 For his remarks in Chinese, see Liu Hongke, '有感于奥巴马和戴秉国在演讲中引用的话' ('A comment on quotes by President Obama and State Councilor Dai in their speeches') 30 July 2009. Accessed on 24 May 2016.
5 Speech by Xi Jinping, Xinhuanet, '习近平在美国友好团体欢迎午宴上的演讲' ('Xi Jinping's Speech at an American Gala Lunch'), http://news.xinhuanet.com/world/2012-02/16/c_111532782.htm. Accessed on 24 May 2016.
6 Xie Huanchi, '记习近平同美国总统奥巴马安纳伯格庄园会晤' ('An Account of Xi Jinping's meeting with US President Barack Obama at Sunnylands'), http://www.gov.cn/ldhd/2013-06/11/content_2424357.htm. Accessed on 24 May 2016.
7 Office of the Press Secretary, The White House, 'Remarks by President Obama and President Xi Jinping of the People's Republic of China Before Bilateral Meeting', https://www.whitehouse.gov/the-press-office/2013/06/07/remarks-president-obama-and-president-xi-jinping-peoples-republic-china-. Accessed on 24 May 2016.
8 Office of the Press Secretary, The White House, 'Remarks by President Obama and President Xi Jinping of the People's Republic of China After Bilateral Meeting', https://www.whitehouse.gov/the-press-office/2013/06/08/remarks-president-obama-and-president-xi-jinping-peoples-republic-china-. Accessed on 24 May 2016.
9 Chen Zhi and Xue Ying, '杨洁篪谈习近平主席与奥巴马总统安纳伯格庄园会晤成果' ('Yan Jiechi's Discussion About The Positive Outcomes of Chairman Xi Jinping's meeting with President Obama in Sunnylands'), http://news.xinhuanet.com/world/2013-06/09/c_116102752.htm. Accessed on 24 May 2016.
10 Office of the Press Secretary, The White House, 'US–China Joint Statement', https://www.whitehouse.gov/the-press-office/us-china-joint-statement. Accessed on 24 May 2016.
11 Takanori Hashimoto, '奧巴馬隻給安倍15分鐘說明什麼' ('What is the significance of Abe's fifteen minute speech given by Obama'), http://opinion.haiwainet.cn/BIG5/n/2013/0701/c232601-18977381.html. Accessed on 24 May 2016.
12 Li Boya and Tian Wang, '安倍访美受冷遇 钓鱼岛问题奥巴马只字未提' ('Abe's visit received coldly by America, No mention of the Diaoyu Islands issue by Obama'), http://japan.people.com.cn/35469/8141187.html. Accessed on 24 May 2016.
13 Qian Tong, '奥巴马安倍电话讨论奥会内容' ('Obama and Abe's Phone Call to Discuss Issues from Xi-Obama's Summit'), http://www.bbc.com/zhongwen/simp/world/2013/06/130613_japan_us_china. Accessed on 24 May 2016.
14 Bill Gertz, 'Pentagon: China Failed to Consult Before Imposing Air Defense Zone', http://

freebeacon.com/national-security/pentagon-china-failed-to-consult-before-imposing-air-defense-zone/. Accessed on 24 May 2016.
15 James Rosen, 'Hagel: US–Japan Mutual Defense Treaty Covers Islands China Also Claims', http://www.mcclatchydc.com/news/nation-world/world/article24759682.html. Accessed on 24 May 2016.
16 Office of the Press Secretary, The White House, 'Joint Press Conference with President Obama and Prime Minister Abe of Japan', https://www.whitehouse.gov/the-press-office/2014/04/24/joint-press-conference-president-obama-and-prime-minister-abe-japan. Accessed on 24 May 2016.
17 *The Japan Times*, 'US Fudges Senkaku Security Pact Status', http://www.japantimes.co.jp/news/2010/08/17/national/u-s-fudges-senkaku-security-pact-status/. Accessed on 24 May 2016.
18 Office of the Press Secretary, The White House, 'US–China Joint Announcement on Climate Change', https://www.whitehouse.gov/the-press-office/2014/11/11/us-china-joint-announcement-climate-change. Accessed on 24 May 2016.
19 Office of the Press Secretary, The White House, 'Fact Sheet: President Xi Jinping's State Visit to the United States', https://www.whitehouse.gov/the-press-office/2015/09/25/fact-sheet-president-xi-jinpings-state-visit-united-states. Accessed on 24 May 2016.
20 Office of the Press Secretary, The White House, 'US–China Joint Presidential Statement on Climate Change',https://www.whitehouse.gov/the-press-office/2015/09/25/us-china-joint-presidential-statement-climate-change. Accessed on 24 May 2016.
21 Lei Xuan, '习近平抵达华盛顿 拜登亲自迎接' ('Biden receives Xi Jinping's visit in Washington'), http://www.bbc.com/zhongwen/simp/world/2015/09/150925_china_xi_washington_arrival. Accessed on 24 May 2016
22 Catholic to the Max, 'Official Schedule for Pope Francis' Visit to US', http://www.popefrancisvisit.com/official-final-schedule-of-pope-francis-u-s-visit-2015/. Accessed on 24 May 2016.
23 Wenxue City, '习近平离开华盛顿前往纽约 将在联合国演讲' ('Xi Jinping departing Washington for a presentation at the United Nations, New York'), http://www.wenxuecity.com/news/2015/09/26/4592313.html. Accessed on 24 May 2016.
24 Li Chen, '奥巴马习近平私人晚宴时间长于预期' ('Obama and Xi's Private Dinner Longer than Expected'), http://www.epochtimes.com/gb/15/9/25/n4535750.htm, Accessed on 24 May 2016.
25 Office of the Press Secretary, The White House, 'Remarks by President Obama and President Xi of the People's Republic of China in Joint Press Conference', https://www.whitehouse.gov/the-press-office/2015/09/25/remarks-president-obama-and-president-xi-peoples-republic-china-joint. Accessed on 24 May 2016.
26 Barnali Pal Sinha, 'Michelle Obama stuns in Vera Wang Dress at Chinese State Dinner', http://www.ibtimes.com.au/michelle-obama-stuns-vera-wang-dress-chinese-state-dinner-1470057. Accessed on 24 May 2016
27 Speech by Xi Jinping, Xinhuanet, '习近平在华盛顿州当地政府和美国友好团体联合欢迎宴会上的演讲' ('Xi Jinping's Speech at the US–China Business Council Welcoming Banquet'), http://news.xinhuanet.com/world/2015-09/23/c_1116656143.htm. Accessed on 24 May 2016.
28 Zhang Shuo, '习近平白宫致辞谈中美关系：随时而动 顺势而为' ('Xi Jinping and the White House to talk about Sino-US relations: Adapting to the Changing Times'), http://news.qq.com/a/20150926/001550.htm. Accessed on 24 May 2016.

2. CHINA–US ECONOMIC RELATIONS AND THE NEW WORLD ECONOMIC ORDER

China's New Silk Roads: A New Global Financial Order in the Making?

Gerald Chan

Professor of politics and international relations in the School of Social Sciences at the University of Auckland, New Zealand

Abstract

China's initiation of the New Silk Road plan in late 2013 has a potentially huge impact on global development. How is China going to finance the various infrastructural projects that it has so far proposed under the plan? What are the impacts of such development on the existing global financial system? Is a new international financial order in the making? I argue in this chapter that the extent of change so far in global developmental financing as a result of implementing the plan does suggest that a new global financial order is in the making. The basic reason is that China has reached a consensus with international financial institutions and other countries that there is a need for infrastructural development in many places around the world as a way to sustain growth based on a formula of win-win cooperation. China is able to show to other stakeholders that it has the financial and human resources as well as the political will to enter into such cooperation. To make this argument, I will focus on China's high-speed rail investment around the world and examine available evidence to make a case for a paradigm change in global development from the existing US-dominated Bretton Woods system to a relatively new financial architecture.

Introduction

In late 2013 China's President Xi Jinping initiated a New Silk Road plan, in two separate speeches made in Kazakhstan and Indonesia. The plan has two major components, one on land and the other by sea. The land-based Silk Road is officially called the 'Silk Road Economic Belt' and the maritime one, the '21st-Century

Maritime Silk Road', or in short 'One Belt, One Road' (*yidai yilu*).[1] The One Belt on land will link up 47 countries, including 6 in central Asia, 18 in West Asia, 16 in the Middle East, 4 in the Independent Russian Federation, in addition to Mongolia, Egypt and Kenya. The One Road by sea will link up 18 countries: 11 in Southeast Asia and 7 in South Asia. The connections will therefore link up a total of 65 countries with 4.4 billion people,[2] some 60% of the world's population,[3] and roughly 30% of its GDP. China becomes the engine of growth in this network of countries. Other neighbouring countries close to these 65 countries can join in to form a vast network of trade flows and exchanges of people across Asia, Europe, Africa and various regions in between. This new Silk Road initiative has become the centrepiece of China's foreign policy. At the core of this foreign policy is the development of infrastructure facilities around the world, and at the inner core of this infrastructure diplomacy is China's high-speed rail investment. Financing the development of the One Belt, One Road has become China's new financial diplomacy.

This chapter shows the heavy demand for infrastructure development around the world. It then assesses China's contributions towards meeting those demands, through the country's recent establishment of several major financial institutions such as the New Development Bank (NDB), the Asian Infrastructure Investment Bank (AIIB), and the Silk Road Fund (SRF). By comparing China's contributions with that of the World Bank and the Asian Development Bank, the chapter argues that a new global financial architecture is gradually taking shape. Theoretically, the main features of this new structure can best be captured by a new term, called 'geo-neo-functionalism' or 'neo-functionalism with Chinese characteristics', or even 'geo-developmentalism'.

Demands for Infrastructure Development

According to the Asian Development Bank (ADB), Asia needs new investments worth $8 trillion for infrastructure development from 2010 to 2020,[4] or $800 billion per year. (All dollar signs referred to in this chapter are US$.) Indonesia alone will need $230 billion; the Greater Mekong Sub-region, linking Vietnam, Laos, Cambodia and Thailand, is estimated to need $50 billion.[5] But the ADB can only lend about $10 billion per year for infrastructure building,[6] meeting only 1.25% of the estimated demands. In 2014 the bank's total lending was $13.7 billion,[7] catering mainly for new projects. Southeast Asia plans to spend an estimated $7 trillion from 2015 to 2030 to upgrade its infrastructures.[8] In 2013 the ASEAN Infrastructure Fund, established by the ADB and the ten ASEAN states, came into operation, but it has only $485.3 million at its disposal,[9] a relatively small amount in contrast to the huge demand. India alone needs $1 trillion infrastructure investments for five years through to 2017.[10]

The World Bank too has pointed out that developing countries at present spend $1 trillion for infrastructure development per year but they need another $1 trillion investment until 2020 to maintain growth:[11] South Asia needs to invest up to $2.5

billion to bridge the region's infrastructure gap in the next ten years from 2015 to 2025;[12] and Africa needs to spend about $93 billion annually until 2020 for similar constructions.[13] Developed countries like the UK and the US too would require hefty sums of money to repair or upgrade their infrastructures.[14] Investments from the non-state sector can only account for less than $150 billion per year.[15] So overall there is a huge shortage of investments to maintain adequate infrastructures for sustainable growth around the world. China's proposed New Silk Road initiative is likely to cost $232 billion, according to the HSBC, a global commercial bank.[16] Infrastructure development is particularly acute in Asia, considering the mismatch between its rising economic activities and the huge gap in its overall infrastructure spending. Asia now takes up 27% of the global GDP, whereas fifty years ago, it took up less than 5%.[17]

Table 7.1 shows that, among the major countries, China has overtaken the United States and the European Union to become the world's largest investor in infrastructure development.

Table 7.1 Global infrastructure investments by China, the EU and the US, 1992–2011 (January 2013)

	China	EU	US
Weighted average spend applied to 2010 GDP (US$ billion)	503	403	374
Weighted average % of GDP	8.5	2.6	2.6

Source: Author's compilation based on McKinsey Global Institute, 'Infrastructure Productivity: How to Save US$1 trillion a Year', (January 2013) p. 12.

Financial Supplies to Meet the Demands

This section first looks at the work of the World Bank at the global level and then China's contribution to meet the demands. The World Bank launched the Global Infrastructure Facility (GIF) in 2014. The GIF became fully operational in April 2015. Under it, the World Bank Group mobilised $24 billion to finance infrastructure development.[18] The launching of this initiative might have been goaded by China's aggressive move to mount its infrastructure diplomacy. The amount that the World Bank could harness, however, seems to have been dwarfed by China's massive investments in the field.

To help finance various ongoing and projected infrastructure programmes, China has recently taken the lead to establish several major financial mechanisms. These include the NDB, the AIIB and the SRF (see Table 7.2), apart from other multilateral, bilateral, and local arrangements including corporate arrangements. In addition, China makes good use of the resources amassed by its state-owned banks.

Table 7.2 China-led international financial institutions (June 2015)

	NDB	AIIB	SRF
No. of members	5 (Brazil, Russia, India, China, South Africa)	57 (founding)	1 (China)
Capital	$50 billion ($10 billion from each member; $100 billion long-term)	$50 billion (mostly from China); $100 billion long-term	$40 billion (all from China)
Targets	Infrastructure projects in BRICS countries as priority	Infrastructure projects of developing countries in Asia	Infrastructure projects of countries along the One Belt, One Road
China's influence in comparative terms	Medium	Small	Big

Source: Author's revision from Tyler Durden, '"One Belt, One Road" May Be China's "One Chance" to Save Collapsing Economy' 8 June 2015, Zero Hedge, www.zerohedge.com/news/2015-06-08/one-belt-one-road-may-be-chinas-one-chance-save-collapsing-economy. Accessed 10 June 2015.

The New Development Bank

The NDB was first proposed in 2012. The five heads of states of the BRICS countries signed an agreement to set it up at their summit in Fortaleza, Brazil, in mid-2014. The bank is scheduled to become operational by the end of 2015 and to begin lending in 2016. It will be open to member states of the UN General Assembly to join, but the BRICS share of the bank will be maintained at no less than 55% to ensure control.[19]

Because of the internal differences within its five members, the NDB may encounter some difficulties in its operation. The need to strike a balance of interests among the members may slow down the decision-making process. Some balance has already been struck. For example, the members contribute on an equal footing at $10 billion each to the $50 billion subscribed capital. In terms of the distribution of power and control, a consensus has been reached so that the headquarters of the NDB is based in Shanghai, the first president is an Indian, K. V. Kamath (for a five-year term on rotation basis among the five member states), the first chair of the board of governors is a Russian, the first chair of the board of directors is a Brazilian, and the first African regional office is based in South Africa.

As of 2014, the BRICS countries have a combined population of nearly 3 billion people (41.6% of the world's total), a combined GDP of about $15.8 trillion (or 19.8% of the global total, which is slightly less than that of the US), and a combined total of export and import trade amounting to $6.14 trillion (16.9%).[20] Table 7.3 shows a breakdown of the figures among the BRICS countries. These figures are somewhat different from the figure quoted above, due to different sources and the rounding up of numbers.)

Table 7.3 The GDPs of the BRICS, 2014

	GDP (nominal in billion US$)	GDP (% of global total)	GDP growth rates (%)
China	10,380	13.43	7.4
Russia	1,857	2.40	0.5
Brazil	2,353	3.04	0.3
India	2,050	2.65	7.4
South Africa	350	0.45	1.4
Total	16,990	21.97	—

Sources: Nominal amounts and percentages of global total are taken from the IMF; growth rates from *The World Factbook 2014–15*, Washington, DC: Central Intelligence Agency, 2015.

Note: In 2015 China's stock market suffered a heavy fall in August; Brazil had its credit rating downgraded to junk status by Standard & Poor in September; and Russia suffered a slowdown in its economy.

The Asian Infrastructure Investment Bank

In his speech to the Indonesian Parliament on 3 October 2013, President Xi announced the One Belt, One Road initiative and proposed the setting up of the AIIB to help finance the initiative. On 24 October 2014 finance ministers or their representatives from 21 countries signed a memorandum of understanding in Beijing to set up the bank. By 31 March 2015 57 countries had applied to become founding members. These are mostly countries in Asia, Europe, and the Middle East, with two in Africa (Egypt and South Africa) and one in South America (Brazil). The fact that there are more countries joining than originally anticipated shows that many countries agree with China on the need to boost infrastructure investments in Asia and that reasonable returns from such investments can be expected. Conspicuously absent from the group of founding members are the US and Japan. The US is obviously worried about the erosion of its influence over international development finance,[21] and Japan, being a staunch ally of the US and having politico-economic conflicts with China, is hesitant to join. Japan has turned from being the arch enemy of the US in the Pacific War in the 1940s to now a close ally and avid burden-sharer to support the American-led global politico-economic order. However, the US can, without being an official member, work with the AIIB within the framework of the G20 or other multilateral or bilateral arrangements, in which the US and China have ample opportunities to discuss and coordinate their policies.

The AIIB is scheduled to start operation by the end of 2015. It provides China with an opportunity to play a leading role in infrastructure diplomacy, in collaboration with other countries. The AIIB is arguably the most important intergovernmental organisation set up by China so far. China's shareholding in the bank is around 30%, making China by far the largest shareholder and theoretically a veto power.[22] The AIIB's servicing scope will cover 4.4 billion people (63% of the world's total), representing an economic size of US$21 trillion (29% of the world), and 23.9% of the world's import and export trade and services.[23]

Apparently, to counter China's fast increasing influence in infrastructure diplomacy, Prime Minister Shinzo Abe of Japan pledged, at the seventh Pacific Islands Leaders Meeting in May 2015, a contribution of $110 billion to support Asian countries to develop infrastructure projects over five years. Half of the fund will be channelled through Japan's aid agencies and half through the ADB,[24] where Japan has a strong hold. Japanese companies take up around 40% to 50% of the ADB's procurement of commercial products and services.

To what extent will the work of the AIIB replace that of the ADB or the World Bank? In terms of finance, the role of the World Bank is difficult to replace, as it still has substantive development funds and potentials. Since its operation in the 1960s, it has accumulated a large pool of experience, knowledge, management skills, and 'good practices'. The reason why China needs to establish the Silk Road Fund and to deploy its state-owned banks to help invest in global infrastructure building shows indirectly the likely inertia of the AIIB. The fact that Japan proposes to fund Asian infrastructure development by itself (as indicated above) shows that Japan fears that the ADB could be overshadowed by the AIIB. In terms of staffing, Natalie Lichtenstein, a US attorney who has over 30 years of working experience in the World Bank,[25] has been appointed as a general counsel to the AIIB.[26] This bodes well for the standardisation of the operation procedures of the AIIB. David Dollar of the Brookings Institution, a former US Treasury official and a former World Bank country-director for China and Mongolia, has served as an unpaid consultant to the AIIB. Jin Liqun, the president-elect of the AIIB, has served before as a vice-president of the ADB and as an alternative executive director of China in the World Bank. In a visit to Beijing in July 2015, the president of the World Bank, Jim Yong Kim, met with Jin. The two heads discussed cooperation and co-financing of future projects to help Third World development.[27] China is poised to become the third largest shareholder of the World Bank. It has contributed financially to the International Development Corporation and the Global Infrastructure Facility of the World Bank. In 2015 China helped to launch the first World Bank Trust Fund to promote development and reduce global poverty. All these working connections show that some continuity of influence coming from the ADB and the World Bank to the AIIB exists. In terms of policy work, because of the wide membership composition and the relative voting powers, transparency and democracy of policy formulation and implementation can largely be assured in the AIIB. The fact that China has made it clear that it does not want to have veto power in the AIIB has reassured other members of the bank and other stakeholders that proper procedure could have a better chance of being followed. By and large, the AIIB is likely to play a complementary role to the ADB and the World Bank. Developing countries naturally welcome the AIIB as an additional or alternative source of funding to finance their development.

The Silk Road Fund

On 29 December 2014 China set up a company in Beijing called the China Silk Road Fund Limited Liability Company to manage the Silk Road Fund, with a registered capital of $10 billion. The company's shareholders include the China Investment Corporation—the country's sovereign-wealth fund under the control of the Ministry of Finance (with $1.5 billion contribution, or 15% stake), the China Development Bank ($1.5 billion, 15%), the Export Import Bank of China ($500 million, 5%), and the State Administration of Foreign Exchange ($6.5 billion, 65%).[28] The Fund is expected to increase its capital to $40 billion. Under the control of the People's Bank of China (PBC), it started to operate in February 2015, headed by Jin Qi, an assistant governor of the PBC. She said in March 2015 that the Fund will invest in projects with reasonable mid- to long-term returns; it is not an aid agency that does not consider returns. The Fund will seek to cooperate with other financial institutions when investing in projects.[29] The PBC governor, Zhou Xiaochuan, indicated that the SRF will adopt at least a 15-year time horizon for investments, rather than the 7–10 year horizon adopted by many private equity firms.[30] This is to account for the slower return on infrastructure investment in developing countries. Also, the Fund aims to achieve a faster approval time for project applications than traditional development agencies.

Compared with the NDB and the AIIB, the SRF will allow China a greater control over as well as a greater flexibility in planning and implementing its investment strategies. According to the *21st-Century Business Herald*, the China Development Bank, established in 1994 as one of the country's policy banks, would invest more than $890 billion in over 900 projects involving 60 countries, as part of the bank's efforts to bolster the One Belt, One Road initiative.[31] This bank is the fifth largest in China and one of the fifteenth biggest globally, with assets of 10.3 trillion yuan ($1.7 trillion) at the end of 2014.[32] Its foreign-currency loans at the end of 2014 totalled $267 billion.[33] It invests heavily in oil-producing countries, including Venezuela, which has received $37 billion since 2008,[34] as well as Russia, Turkmenistan, Ecuador and Brazil. Since 2012, the China Development Bank (CDB) has overtaken both the World Bank and the ADB as the world's largest lender of overseas loans. The size of its outstanding loans reached $220 billion by March 2012, compared with $71.4 billion of the ADB as of June 2011 and $136.3 billion of the World Bank as of 2012 fiscal year.[35] In 2011 its assets reached more than $1 trillion, about three times the total assets of the World Bank in the same year.[36] It came to prominence as a result of the 2008 global financial crisis: while big banks in the West such as the Citigroup of the US and the London-based HSBC were forced to limit their lending due to pressure on their capital base and risk controls, the CDB took the opportunity to diversify its businesses and to expand its overseas lending, making it the hope for many resource-rich but capital-poor nations. So did China's other big banks, such as the Industrial and Commercial Bank of China, the world's largest bank by market value, which vastly expanded its international business.

Apparently, China uses multiple financial vehicles and goes through multiple channels to advance its infrastructure diplomacy in order to enhance its geo-economic interests. This new development allows China to make use of a full array of tools to maximise its interests through taking different degrees of investment risks, in terms of returns of different resources over different time periods as a result of balancing various economic and political demands. China can afford to take a long-term view on investments, thanks to its hefty reserves and comparatively little or no pressure from private shareholders.

The first project financed by the Silk Road Fund is in Pakistan.[37] In President Xi Jinping's state visit to the country in April 2015, China forged the largest Silk Road programme so far, amounting to $28 billion initially. The programme could eventually reach a target of $46 billion,[38] of which $4 billion would be used to upgrade Pakistan's railway network.[39] According to the BBC,[40] this amount of $46 billion is more than double the amount of foreign assistance Pakistan has received since 2008 and is considerably more than the US assistance to Pakistan since 2002. In its Marshall Plan, the US extended $12 billion ($120 billion in current rates) to help several European countries to reconstruct and develop after the Second World War.[41] Known as the China–Pakistan Economic Corridor, the programme covers developments in rail, roads, power plants, and trade over a 15-year period. The project is expected to increase Pakistan's GDP by 15%. Of great strategic significance is the linking of China's western Xinjiang province to the deep-sea port of Gwadar in Pakistan. The port is being built with the help of China. When completed, the China Overseas Port Holdings will have operation rights for 40 years. This China–Pakistan land connection will shorten, by at least 10,000 km,[42] the traditional trade route between China and the Arabian and Mediterranean Seas via the Malacca Strait at the southern tip of the Malaysian peninsula, a possible choke point in case of political and military conflicts.[43] Nearly 20% of the world's oil passes through the Strait of Hormuz, where Gwadar is just 400 km away. Neighbouring countries like India and Iran are expected to benefit from the new trade routes in future.

This economic corridor serves in part a similar purpose as the twin pipelines that run through the whole length of Myanmar bringing oil and gas from the Middle East to China. China and Myanmar agreed to build the pipelines in 2008 and 2009 at a total cost of $2.5 billion. Work started in 2010 and was completed in 2014. Gas started to flow through Myanmar to China in late 2014 and oil in early 2015. The length of the pipelines measures 771 km in Myanmar and a further 1631 km in China,[44] bringing energy supplies to industrial cities in western China, like Kunming, Chengdu, and Chongqing. The transport time has been substantially slashed, as normal shipping from Saudi Arabia to Shanghai via the Malacca Strait takes up to two weeks.[45] This new route changes the global oil market as well as the strategic importance of the Malacca Strait,[46] and hence the politico-economic calculations of Southeast Asian countries and other stakeholders. In terms of geo-strategic considerations, the China–Pakistan Economic Corridor can serve as a balance or an alternative to the twin pipelines running through Myanmar, and vice versa, giving China enhanced strategic security and greater bargaining power and negotiation flexibility in the resources market and transportation market.

China's Financial Contributions in Comparative Perspectives
Apart from the Chinese-led financial institutions and major Chinese banks, China's state-owned enterprises, too, have been active in participating in the One Belt, One Road initiative. In July 2015, the State-owned Assets Supervision and Administration Commission of the State Council released a report which showed that, by the end of 2014, 107 out of 110 state-owned enterprises had set up 8,515 branches overseas. Over 80 Chinese state-owned companies had set up branches in countries and regions along the 'Belt and Road'.[47]

Both the heads of the ADB and the World Bank have expressed their welcome to the establishment of the AIIB. The financial fatigue of the West subsequent to the 2008 US financial crisis and the 2010 Eurozone crisis has opened up a space for the AIIB to play a rather unique role. Although China is not happy with the Bretton Woods system which bestows the West, and the US in particular, with overwhelming voting power, it has moved beyond making public complaints about the uneven power representations in the World Bank and the IMF to the setting up new multilateral financial institutions of its own to project its preferences in global development.

Table 7.4 Comparing the AIIB, the ADB and the World Bank (June 2015)

	AIIB	ADB	World Bank
Founding year	2015	1966	1945
Leading member state	China	Japan	US
Largest funding country	China (about 50%)	Japan (15.7%); US (15.6%)	US (16.5%)
Share: US	0	12.8% (voting)	15.85%
Share: China	30% (estimate)	5.5%	2.77%
Share: Japan	0	12.8% (voting)	7.62%
Subscribed capital	US$100 billion	US$175 billion	US$10 billion (in 1945) US$223 billion (2015) Loan amount available (2015): $150 billion +
Aim	To finance infrastructure construction in Asia	To eradicate poverty in Asia and to promote economic development	To provide loans to combat poverty in developing countries
Members	57 (founding)	67	188
HQs	Beijing	Manila	Washington, DC
President	Jin Liqun (elect) (Chinese)	Takehiko Nakao (Japanese)	Jim Yong Kim (US citizen, ethnic Korean)
Veto power	China?	No	US

Sources: Adapted and updated from Ho Lok-Sang in *Economic Herald* 9 (biweekly, Chinese), Hong Kong, (4 May 2015), p. 17; Stephen S. Roach, 'China's global governance challenge,' YaleGlobal Online, 9 June 2015; Internet materials.

Implications of China's Contributions for Global Order

China's recent diplomatic moves and monetary contributions to the setting up of new global financial institutions have nurtured the growth of a new structure in which China plays an increasingly greater role in global development than before. Figure 7.1 captures the essential features of such a structure from a Chinese perspective.

The significance of this China-centric financial structure depends largely on the extent of power shift between the US and China. China is now the biggest trade partner to 124 countries, while the US is the biggest trade partner to 76.[48] The *relative* decline of the US can be seen partially from Table 7.5, while the *relative* rise of China and India can be seen from Figure 7.2.

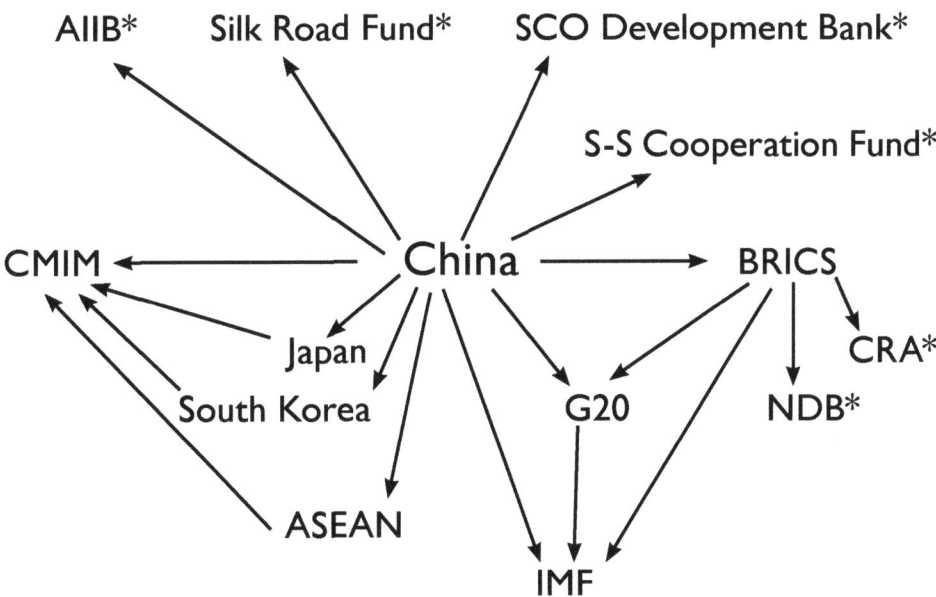

Figure 7.1 A Model of China's Multilateral Financial Involvement
Direction of China's desired flow of its influence: ⟶

* These are new initiatives taken by China since 2013

AIIB: Asian Infrastructure Investment Bank
CMIM: Chiang Mai Initiative Multilateralisation
CRA: Contingency Reserve Arrangement
SCO (Shanghai Cooperation Organisation) Development Bank
Source: Author's own drawing

Note 1: The G20 holds 65.8% of the quotas and 64.7% of the votes in the IMF.
Note 2: The establishment of the South–South Cooperation Fund was announced by President Xi Jinping in his first address to the UN General Assembly on 28 September 2015.
Note 3: China has formed more than a dozen or so bilateral financial arrangements with individual countries or groups of countries. It has also exercised its loan extension through such big state-owned banks as the China Development Bank.

Table 7.5 The International Economic Position of the US, 1945 vs 2013 (November 2014)

	Gold reserves (nominal in tons)	Gold reserves (% of global total)	GDP (nominal in billion US$)	GDP (% of global total)
1945	21,770.0	59.00	223.0	45.00
2013	8,133.5	25.48	16,799.7	22.69

Source: *Economic Outlook Bimonthly* (in Chinese), 12 November 2014, p. 100, quoting from the IMF and the World Gold Council.

The evidence derived from Table 7.5, Figure 7.2, and many other similar statistics are by their very nature selective and to a certain extent biased, but they point to a general trend in which China rises in power capabilities relative to the US.

From ASEAN's perspective, the establishment of the AIIB, the NDB and the SRF is part of a larger financial scheme that begins to change the regional architecture, currently populated by organisations such as ASEAN, the ASEAN Regional Forum, and the East Asian Community.[49] This means that ASEAN countries need to strike a fine balance between allying with the US strategically and connecting with China economically. A similar sort of situation challenges many countries, including Japan and South Korea, Australia and New Zealand, although in different degrees and under different sets of circumstances.

Concluding Thoughts

China's One Belt, One Road initiative has just started in practice. Many mega projects in the initiative will take many years, even decades, to complete.[50] Future success is not fully assured. There are potentially numerous kinds of risks. However, based on the current situation, several observations can be made. First, a new globalisation process is gathering pace, as there is a general consensus around the world, especially among developing countries, on the urgent need for infrastructure developments, as China is willing to co-finance many projects, and as most, if not all, developing countries welcome China's initiation and extend their cooperation to mount various projects. A new model of development is gradually taking shape, one that is based on mutual, mainly economic, benefits and focused on infrastructure

Figure 7.2 Economic Growth, West vs East, 2011–2060

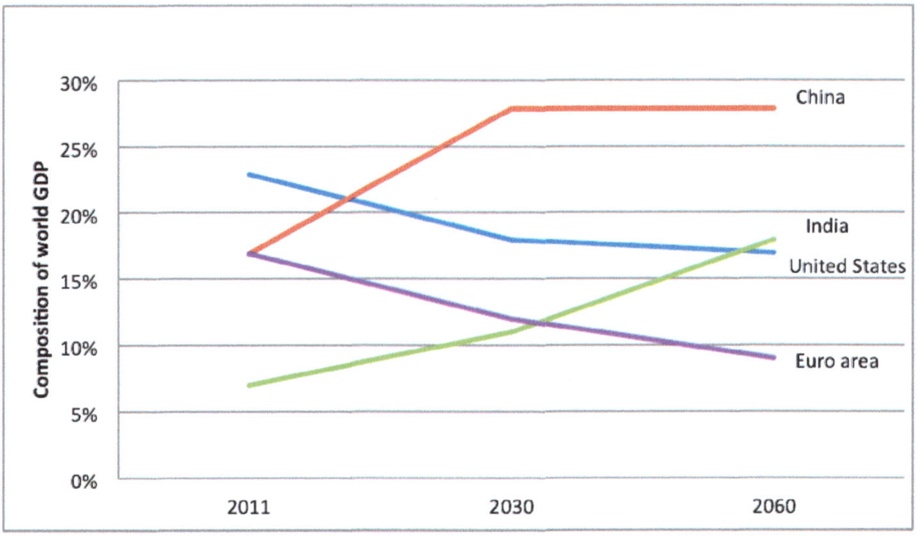

Source: Author's own drawing based on OECD, 'Looking to 2060: Long-Term Growth Prospects for the World', www.oecd.org/eco/lookingto2060.htm

development. The simple philosophy of a win–win solution for all participants is not a Chinese language alone, but also gradually a US one as well.

Second, a new term, coined here as geo-neo-functionalism, captures well the essence and spirit of this new development model. It is functional, as the overall approach aims to promote economic and social wellbeing in an incremental way over a relatively long period of time—a piece-by-piece process of building peace.[51] It is prefixed 'neo-' because the whole enterprise is led mainly by states and governments, with China as the initiator and the leader, and with host governments giving their consent to co-manage and co-finance projects in most cases, although private, commercial sectors are also involved. It is prefixed 'geo-' as the initiative involves geopolitics and geo-economics. This new form of development is an integration process, and can be alternatively called neo-functionalism with Chinese characteristics or, for want of a better word, geo-developmentalism. From a Chinese perspective, it is a new phase of China going global, after the initial reform and open policy that the country has adopted since the late 1970s. China is now ready to provide some global public goods, as a contribution befitting a rising peaceful power shouldering greater international responsibility. In a way, China is showing its new-found soft power.

In global infrastructure investment, China is not without competition coming from other countries and international institutions. Officially China says it is not replacing the existing well-established development agencies such as the World Bank, the IMF and the ADB. Its initiation in the area of global development and finance is, however, likely to goad these existing institutions to take greater measures to become leaner and more efficient. In addition, working together in collaboration among them would increase the amount of material resources, to the overall benefits of donors as well as recipients of development aid. Mutual support, mutual learning and mutual accommodation would strengthen functionalism as a theory and as a practice, thus nurturing an evolving system with a fairer distribution of financial powers and a more pluralist world order.

Third, by its ability to finance infrastructure developments in the developing world and beyond, China is able to help shape the economic and political landscapes of Asia, Eurasia, Africa and further afield. It is able to link up advanced technology from the West with natural resources from the Global South to form new global production chains by massively investing overseas. China's FDI overseas reached $116 billion in 2014, almost twenty times the amount ten years ago.[52] In the same year, China's outward FDI has surpassed for the first time its inward FDI.

In the end, China's infrastructure diplomacy, and its accompanying financial diplomacy, aims to promote China's national interests:[53] to benefit China's economy, to increase its power and influence; to 'democratise' international (financial) relations; to diversify China's investments, to promote its trade, and to raise the country's profile and prestige.

Acknowledgements

This chapter is a revised and updated version of a paper that I presented at an international conference on China–US relations held at Victoria University of Wellington on 8–9 October 2015. I have benefited from the organisers and participants of the conference. I am grateful to Dr Pak K. Lee of the University of Kent, UK, and Dr Lai-Ha Chan of the University of Technology Sydney for reading an early draft and offering comments and criticisms.

Notes

1. On 28 March 2015 the China National Development and Reform Commission issued an official document entitled 'Vision and Actions on Jointly Building Silk Road Economic Belt and 21st-Century Maritime Silk Road', detailing China's plan in the One Belt, One Road. Available at http://en.ndrc.gov.cn/newsrelease/201503/t20150330_669367.html. Accessed 22 August 2015.
2. The presentation on China's sister-cities links with other countries along the *yidai yilu* by Li Xinyu at the Shanghai Forum, 24 May 2015.
3. 'US$40b Silk Road Fund will follow private equity route', *South China Morning Post*, Hong Kong, 17 February 2015, p. 1.
4. 'Public private partnerships key to meeting Asia's $8 trillion infrastructure needs—study', ADB, 30 May 2012, http://www.adb.org/news/public-private-partnerships-key-meeting-asias-8-trillion-infrastructure-needs-study Accessed 5 May 2015.
5. *China Pictorial*, December 2014, p. 67.
6. *Economic Herald* (*Jingji daobao*) 24 (1 December 2014), p. 7; 'China expands plans for World Bank rival', *Financial Times*, 24 June 2014.
7. 'ADB to partner with AIIB in joint financing and boost its own lending by 50%', http://ajw.

asahi.com/article/behind_news/social_affairs/AJ201505030020 Accessed 22 August 2015.
8. 'Infrastructure fails to bridge gap in SE Asia', *South China Morning Post*, Hong Kong, 5 December 2014, p. B8.
9. Asian Development Bank, www.adb.org/print/site/aif/overview Accessed 12 June 2015.
10. 'Yashwant Sinha or Arun Shourie? PM Narendra Modi to decide first president of BRICS bank', *Financial Express*, New Delhi, 7 April 2015.
11. 'World Bank group launches Global Infrastructure Facility', World Bank Press Release, 9 October 2014, http://www.worldbank.org/en/news/press-release/2014/10/09/world-bank-group-launches-new-global-infrastructure-facility Accessed 15 May 2015.
12. Graham Crouch, 'South Asia's $2.5 Trillion Infrastructure Gap', World Bank, 2 April 2014, http://www.worldbank.org/en/news/feature/2014/04/02/south-asia-trillion-infrastructure-gap Accessed 5 May 2015.
13. 'Bridging the Gap: Ensuring Execution on Large Infrastructure Projects in Africa', http://www.ey.com/Publication/vwLUAssets/EY-Bridging-the-Gap/$FILE/EY-Bridging-the-Gap.pdf Accessed 5 May 2015.
14. *Economic Daily (Jingji ribao)*, 9 January 2015, p. 9.
15. 'Asia Infrastructure Investment Bank and Korea–China relations', in *Sungkyun China Observer* 4 (Seoul: Sungkyunkwan University, 2014), p. 9.
16. 'The AIIB and global governance', Project Syndicate, 27 April 2015, http://www.project-syndicate.org/commentary/aiib-china-global-leadership-by-andrew-sheng-and-geng-xiao-2015-04 Accessed 25 August 2015.
17. *Economic Herald* (weekly in Chinese), Hong Kong, 4 May 2015, p. 5.
18. Global Infrastructure Facility, World Bank website Accessed 22 June 2015.
19. 'Putin signs law on ratification of $100 billion BRICS New Development Bank deal', 9 March 2015, http://rt.com/news/238981-putin-signs-brics-bank Accessed 10 April 2015.
20. Ibid. The NDB website, however, says that the combined GDP of its five member states account for more than 25% of the global GDP. See http://ndbbrics.org Accessed 15 August 2015.
21. Paola Subacchi, 'The AIIB is a threat to global economic governance', *Foreign Policy*, 31 March 2015, http://foreignpolicy.com/2015/03/31/the-aiib-is-a-threat-to-global-economic-governance-china/ Accessed 25 August 2015.
22. According to the Articles of Agreement, AIIB (p. 29): China's percentage share of the total is 29.7804%.
23. Ibid., p. 6.
24. 'Japan unveils $110 billion plan to fund Asia infrastructure, eye on AIIB', http://www.reuters.com/article/2015/05/21/us-japan-asia-investment-idUSKBN0O617G20150521 Accessed 19 July 2015.
25. 'The leaderboard: Natalie Lichtenstein', *cogitASIA*, CSIS, April 2015, http://cogitASIA.com/the-leaderboard-natalie-lichtenstein/ Accessed 25 August 2015.
26. Stephen S. Roach, 'China's global governance challenge', YaleGlobal Online, 9 June 2015.
27. 'China launches first World Bank Trust Fund to end poverty and promote development', 16 July 2015, http://www.worldbank.org/en/news/press-release/2015/07/16/china-launches-first-world-bank-trust-fund-to-end-poverty-and-promote-development Accessed 19 August 2015.
28. Elvin Chuanye Ouyang, 'The opportunities of China's "One Belt, One Road",' 23 March 2015, http://globalriskinsights.com/2015/03/the-opportunities-of-china-one-belt-one-road/ Accessed 17 June 2015.
29. Tyler Durden, '"One Belt, One Road" May Be China's "One Chance" to Save Collapsing Economy' 8 June 2015, Zero Hedge, www.zerohedge.com/news/2015-06-08/one-belt-one-road-may-be-chinas-one-chance-save-collapsing-economy, Accessed 10 June 2015.
30. 'Development finance with Chinese characteristics?' Project Syndicate, 20 May 2015, http://

www.project-syndicate.org/commentary/china-silk-road-fund-development-financing-by-richard-kozul-wright-and-daniel-poon-2015-05 Accessed 25 August 2015.
31. As reported by China Daily, http://usa.chinadaily.com.cn/business/2015-05/28/content_20845678.htm Accessed 10 June 2015.
32. Based on data from S&P Capital IQ. See also 'Venezuela oil loans go awry for China', *Wall Street Journal*, 18 June 2015, http://www.wsj.com/articles/venezuela-oil-loans-go-awry-for-china-1434656360 Accessed 25 August 2015.
33. According to the company's annual report, Ibid. See also 'Performance highlights' of the China Development Bank, http://www.cdb.com.cn/english/Column.asp?ColumnId=100 Accessed 25 August 2015.
34. 'Venezuela oil loans go awry for China', *Wall Street Journal*, 18 June 2015.
35. 'China Development Bank grabs chance for aggressive global loan expansion', *South China Morning Post*, Internet ed., 13 March 2013.
36. According to Brookings Institution fellow Erica Downs, in Ibid.
37. 'Why Pakistan gets Silk Road Fund's first investment?' Beijing Review, 21 April 2015, http://www.bjreview.com.cn/quotes/txt/2015-04/21/content_684220.htm Accessed 26 April 2015.
38. 'China's Xi Jinping launches investment deal in Pakistan', *Wall Street Journal*, 20 April 2015.
39. 'Pakistan–China railway to extend Beijing's influence, says scholar', Want China Times, 26 April 2015, http://www.wantchinatimes.com/news-subclass-cnt.aspx?cid=1101&MainCatID=11&id=20150426000082 Accessed 26 April 2015.
40. Quoted in Sajjad Ashraf, 'China link-up an opportunity and a challenge for Pakistan', East Asia Forum, 2 June 2015, http://www.eastasiaforum.org/2015/06/02/china-link-up-an-opportunity-and-a-challenge-for-pakistan/ Accessed 25 August 2015.
41. Sajjad Ashraf, 'India's dual dilemmas', China-India Brief 53, Centre on Asia and Globalisation, Lee Kuan Yew School of Public Policy, 9-23 June 2015.
42. Ashraf, 'India's dual dilemmas'.
43. It has been reported that Thailand is considering building a canal which cuts across the narrowest strip of the Malay Peninsula in south Thailand called the Kra Isthmus. The Kra canal could then connect the Gulf of Thailand to the Andaman Sea of the Indian Ocean, bypassing the increasingly crowded Malacca Strait and speeding up substantially the shipping route between East Asia and South Asia. See 'New Viet port a clue to Kra Canal?' http://www.straitstimes.com/opinion/new-viet-port-a-clue-to-kra-canal Accessed 22 August 2015.
44. 'This new project changes the global oil market', Oilprice.com, 4 February 2015, http://oilprice.com/Finance/investing-and-trading-reports/This-New-Project-Changes-The-Global-Oil-Market.html Accessed 6 May 2015.
45. 'New China-Myanmar oil pipeline bypasses Malacca trap', *The Hindu*, 30 January 2015, http://www.thehindu.com/news/international/world/new-chinamyanmar-oil-pipeline-bypasses-malacca-trap/article6839352.ece Accessed 6 May 2015).
46. See 'New Viet port a clue to Kra Canal?'.
47. 'The roadmap of SOE's presence in "Belt and Road"', http://www.newsgd.com/news/2015-07/16/content_128580279.htm Accessed 19 July 2015.
48. 'OBOR should be strongly considered: TAITRA head', *The China Post*, Taipei, Internet ed., 24 July 2015.
49. The view of Mr Ong Keng Yong, executive deputy chairman and director of the Institute of Defence and Strategic Studies, S. Rajaratnam School of International Studies, Singapore, in a roundtable speech on ASEAN given at the University of Auckland, 26 June 2015. Mr Ong was a former secretary-general of ASEAN and a Singaporean ambassador.
50. Estimates of completion time range from one to two decades to even more. Professor Zhang Yunling, director of International Studies, Chinese Academy of Social Sciences, told me that it might take a hundred years to complete, in a conversation at a TEDx talk in Seoul, organised by the Korean Foundation of Advanced Studies, 6 August 2015.

51 Both the Philippines and Vietnam are founding members of the AIIB. Both have acute territorial disputes with China over the islands in the South China Sea. Whether or not cooperation in infrastructure development and trade can ameliorate the conflict situation and to what extent have yet to be tested. The implication of political practice for the theory of functionalism would be interesting. A similar situation applies to Taiwan, which wants to become a member of the AIIB, despite China's political reservations.
52 About 90% of such investments are from SOEs. See *The Mirror* (monthly in Chinese), Hong Kong, May 2015, p. 50.
53 I share Yun Sun's view in 'China's AIIB challenges', *PacNet* 16, Pacific Forum CSIS, Honolulu, 11 March 2015.

The Multilateral Development Banks: Innovation or Stagnation?

Susan Park

Associate professor in international relations at the University of Sydney, Australia

Abstract

The multilateral development banks (MDBs) are similar international organisations in the international system. Sharing many of the same shareholders, occupying the same development policy space, and built on the same borrowing and lending model, the MDBs vary little in their arrangements and operations of governance. For the first time since the end of the Cold War, new MDBs are being created, such as the Chinese-driven Asian Infrastructure Investment Bank (AIIB) and the New Development Bank (NDB). As rules are being established for governing these institutions, the changes made across the other MDBs reveal the challenges of complementarity. Change across the old MDBs currently tends to follow 'coercive isomorphism', with powerful member states such as the US demanding the MDBs reform in order to accord with shifting ideas about how best to encourage development. Usually beginning with the World Bank, change is isomorphic because the US is a dominant shareholder in all of these institutions, and shared agreement for change in one bank is quickly followed by the others. China's entry into leading MDBs provides a clear distinction between old MDBs and new ones, with the new banks potentially driving more innovation. This paper explores the extent to which coercive isomorphism among the old MDBs is likely to continue in light of changed dynamics in the institutional environment, or whether other isomorphic processes and the prospect of innovation or stagnation will spread among the MDBs and in what direction.

The Multilateral Development Banks: Innovation or Stagnation?

Introduction

The multilateral development banks (MDBs) are similar international organisations in the international system. Sharing many of the same shareholders, occupying the same development policy space, and built on the same borrowing and lending model, the MDBs vary little in their arrangements and operations of governance. For the first time since the end of the Cold War, new MDBs are being created, such as the Chinese-driven Asian Infrastructure Investment Bank (AIIB) and the New Development Bank (NDB). As rules are being established for governing these institutions, the changes made across the other MDBs reveal the challenges of complementarity. Change across the old MDBs currently tends to follow 'coercive isomorphism', with powerful member states such as the US demanding the MDBs reform in order to accord with shifting ideas about how best to encourage development. Usually beginning with the World Bank, change is isomorphic because the US is a dominant shareholder in all of these institutions, and shared agreement for change in one bank is quickly followed by the others. China's entry into leading MDBs provides a clear distinction between old MDBs and new ones, with the new banks potentially driving more innovation. This paper explores the extent to which coercive isomorphism among the old MDBs is likely to continue in light of changed dynamics in the institutional environment, or whether other isomorphic processes and the prospect of innovation or stagnation will spread among the MDBs and in what direction.

The chapter proceeds as follows. First, the similarities in the structures and functions of the MDBs are detailed before looking at the procedures of new MDBs. Second, the process of change within the old MDBs is articulated, focusing on the concept of coercive isomorphism. This is then examined in light of changes to operating procedures of MDBs across safeguards and accountability. Section three then analyses how the new MDBs, the AIIB and the NDB seek to complement the old MDBs, but demonstrates through policy statements how this might prove challenging considering how change is articulated in the old MDBs. The chapter concludes by assessing the likelihood of innovation among MDBs and from which direction that change will come.

The Function and Structure of the Old MDBs

The old MDBs include the African Development Bank (AfDB), Asian Development Bank (ADB), European Bank for Reconstruction and Development (EBRD), Inter-American Development Bank (IDB) and the World Bank, and are similar in their objectives and arrangements of governance. This section details their mandates and functions before unpacking their arrangements of governance. Designed as conservative, primarily Western financial institutions by states and for states,[1] they aim to provide loans, grants, technical assistance and other financial products to their borrowing member shareholders. These multilateral institutions are vehicles for injecting much needed capital to developing states for economic growth and development. Articulating the view that it was a lack of capital preventing growth in developing countries, the MDBs are charged with providing additional financing beyond bilateral official development assistance and where private capital is absent.[2] They do so through the provision of ordinary capital resource lending (OCR) which is the most common form of lending to borrower member states at or near market rates, with longer maturities. All of the banks except the EBRD also provide soft loans (offered at low or zero interest) and grants from their concessional lending facilities for their poorest member states. These include the World Bank's International Development Association (IDA; established in 1960); the IDB's Fund for Special Operations (FSO; created in 1959); ADB's Asian Development Facility (ADF; established in 1973); the AfDB's African Development Fund (AfDF; established in 1973). In 2017 the ADB will integrate its OCR and concessional lending funds. Beyond the ordinary and concessional lending, the MDBs all have special funds which allow member states to direct funding for specific issues, ranging from climate change to agriculture. They may also be country-specific: In the AfDB Nigeria established a special trust fund in 1976; Japan has its own fund in the ADB and the IDB, and there has been a proliferation of such funds in the World Bank. These funds are dispersed generally without board approval and do not affect member states' voting allocation.[3]

Primarily project-based lending for development has been offset to varying degrees among the banks with programme-based lending, from structural and sectoral adjustment beginning in the 1980s to lending to financial intermediaries today. The MDBs are similar in how they structure their loans and how they operate according to a project or programme cycle. In the early 1980s the World Bank moved towards providing structural adjustment loans to borrowers, emphasising the shift from an engineer's bank to an economist's one. While still maintaining project lending for infrastructure, structural adjustment lending sought to provide states with the funds and technical assistance for macro-economic restructuring to drive innovation and economic growth. The rest of the MDBs would follow suit, although not to the same extent. In the 1990s all of the MDBs would also broaden and deepen their lending to other sectors such as health and education.[4]

Despite many of the MDBs being regionally oriented with provisions for supporting regional integration, the MDBs tend not to deviate substantially from each other in the development ideas they articulate.[5] Indeed, the regional flavour of the banks is more apparent in management and staffing than in the development ideas they promote,[6] despite their unique cultures.[7] Even where the MDBs seek to differentiate themselves, they nonetheless face the same pressures from their shareholders, who tend to replicate the same power structures. As detailed in the next section, the banks tend to support the same development policy approaches, owing to having overlapping member states with donor member states providing significant resources for the banks and therefore having weighted votes in their favour. This means that policy is often driven by powerful states. For example, the ADB may have been the first MDB to have a policy on good governance. It differs from the World Bank in how it interprets this concept but it was nevertheless pressured to have such a policy from its donor member states.[8] This strengthens viewing the MDBs as a coherent class of international organisations that operate similarly, have similar objectives and view development in broadly similar ways. How they are governed is also structurally the same.

Governance of the old MDBs
While the World Bank took some of the ideas proposed for a bank for Latin America, in 1944 it was nonetheless the first MDB to be established. All of the subsequent banks were modelled on it. World Bank membership is open to all states but is determined by prior membership in the IMF. The regional banks allow membership if states are members of the United Nations or regional organisations such as the Organization of American States. All MDBs are structured similarly. To become a member, states must provide both 'paid-in' and 'callable' capital to underpin the banks' operations. The banks also raise money from interest and loan repayments as well as floating bonds and borrowing on international capital markets. The banks may differentiate membership between regional and non-regional members, with a specified allocation of capital and therefore votes for regional members (at approximately 60%). Voting is determined by the capital subscribed to the organisation according to a formula of basic and proportional votes. All of the banks thus have weighted voting systems (one dollar, one vote) compared to the one state, one vote formula of the United Nations.

Organisationally the banks are the same. Member states are represented on the boards of governors, comprised of ministers of finance or central bank governors who meet once or twice annually. The boards of governors are responsible for the overall policy direction of the banks. The governors delegate to a resident board of executive directors to oversee the general running of the MDBs, including activities such as approving the budget and lending. The numbers of executive directors vary across the banks but are apportioned to member states according to the subscribed capital and regional allocations. The US is the only state to have its own executive director for each of the banks. The rest may be represented by an executive director for their own country in one bank but share an executive director in a constituency of a group of states in other banks (as determined by their voting allocation).[9] For example, Japan has its own executive director in the ADB, the EBRD and the World Bank, but shares an executive director in a constituency with other member states in the AfDB and the IDB (although Japan is the director of its constituency on both of these banks' boards). China has its own executive director in the World Bank and ADB, but shares an executive director in the IDB and in the AfDB, and it is not a member of the EBRD. From 2014 China was the director of its constituency for the AfDB for the first time.[10]

Despite the rapid changes to the global economic fortunes of the BRICS countries (Brazil, Russia, India, China and South Africa), there has not been a dramatic change in the representation of these rising powers in the MDBs. The G7 states retain significant voting power across the old MDBs, and the US has the largest vote in them all except for the AfDB, where it is second (see Table 1).[11] While considerable attention has been paid to efforts of non-G7 states to change the weighted voting of the World Bank and the IMF, leading to minor changes in 2008 and 2010, less attention has been focused on the other MDBs. Modest changes to the World Bank's voting allocations have occurred, but the US remains resistant to fundamentally reallocating votes for the Bretton Woods institutions.[12] For example, China has increased its vote within the World Bank from 2.8% to 4.2% despite shifting from a poor state to the second largest economy in the world in 2010. For the regional development banks it is not clear whether there has been little change in voting and representation because of US and European resistance to a reallocation (although it would be unsurprising if this were the case) or because there has been little effort to do so on behalf of the BRICS countries.[13]

In terms of the daily running of the banks, this is done by the bank president, who is elected by the board (through different processes across the banks). The bank president is traditionally American for the World Bank and Japanese for the ADB, with presidents elected from the regions for the other banks. The president is chair of the board as well as head of the organisation, with control over management and staffing. Staff assist states with preparing project or programme proposals that are then vetted by management and taken to the board of executive directors for approval. Once a loan has been approved then the first loan tranche can flow. In sum, the banks all operate in the same way; they tend to have similar development policy approaches and are governed in the same manner.

Coercive Isomorphism and Change in the Old MDBs

The US uses its power within the banks to achieve its policy preferences through coercive isomorphism. Taken from organisational sociology, coercive isomorphism is defined as 'both formal and informal pressure exerted on organisations by other organisations upon which they are dependent and by cultural expectations in the society within which organisations function'.[14] DiMaggio and Powell argue that coercive isomorphism may result from government regulation or from the way regulatory agencies engage with organisations. While the formal power of the US has been identified through its voting strength in the banks, it also has informal power. The banks often have an informal quota of staff from the major shareholders and allocate them with high profile managerial positions (for example, in the IDB the executive vice president is always from the US, and in the ADB one of the five vice presidents is from the US. Staffing, professional training of economists, location and the dependence of the banks on US shares and concessional replenishments have led many scholars to suggest that the US has shaped the organisational culture of the World Bank.[15] The other banks do not have such a constellation of factors and are not therefore viewed as reflecting US influence. Nonetheless, all of the banks routinely seek to ascertain the position of the most powerful shareholders before bringing important policy changes to the board for approval. Informal influence is therefore intimately tied to its formal power in shaping the policy direction of the banks. The process is isomorphic because of the banks' financial dependence on the US. In both cases on the environment and accountability described below, US Congress stipulated that change had to take place otherwise they would block any replenishment of soft-loan financing. The ability of the US to do so rests on its dominance in the banks.

It is clear from the governance of the old MDBs that they are dominated by donor states, particularly the G7 countries. The outcome of this dominance is two-fold: first, in terms of influencing who the MDBs lend to, and second, in terms of the policy direction of the banks or what they lend for, and how they conceive the banks should meet their economic growth mandates. Research suggests there is a correlation between those who who receive loans in the World Bank and state support of US strategic interests through core votes in the United Nations General Assembly as well as to borrowing states' needs.[16] It is also clear that lending through the ADB tends to benefit those borrowers with strong ties to Japan and the US.[17] On the other hand, big borrowers in Latin America are the greatest recipients of loans from the IDB, reflecting both their capacity to absorb capital as well as their significant shareholding in the IDB. Meanwhile the US tends to push its agenda less in the AfDB, owing to its smaller status.[18] While evidence therefore supports the theory of US influence in channelling loans to its allies through the World Bank and the ADB, it does not always have the power to determine which project are approved in the MDBs. Project approval remains with the board of executive directors, and recent research demonstrates that 64% of projects the US voted against were still approved, signalling the limits of the US voting for specific projects.[19]

Second, the influence of the US is evident in the policy direction of the banks. The US is considered an 'activist shareholder' championing a number of different policies often in conjunction with other G7 states.[20] Formal influence provides states with the platform to determine changes to the banks. The formal voting power of the US determines its ability to vote, to form voting coalitions and even to affect blocking majorities in the banks.[21] The US uses its formal power to propose policies for the banks through negotiations of their OCR during general capital increases (GCI) and through periodic soft loan replenishments (for the concessional funds, which are granted approximately every three years). GCI occur relatively infrequently and are used to maintain the banks' capital to lending ratio. All of the MDBs sought GCI in 2009 in order to be able to provide lending to states affected by the Global Financial Crisis of 2008. For example, the US has the largest formal voting share in the IDB, with approximately 30% of the vote. While borrower member states can override US votes through coalition voting, the US could always decide to walk away from the IDB should it not have its policy preferences accepted, which Babb states is 'enough to keep the banks in check'.[22]

Donor member states have been successful in pushing the banks to establish a number of non-economic policy prescriptions addressing gender, poverty alleviation, human rights, good governance, environmental and social standards, and accountability. This has therefore expanded the concept of development from merely providing capital to spur economic growth to providing detailed policy prescriptions for development. Many of these non-economic concerns have emerged over vitriolic debates beginning in the 1980s over the impact of multilateral finance lending, as donors were increasingly questioning the quality of project lending and the effectiveness of lending by the multilaterals.[23] The rest of this section looks specifically at the coercive isomorphism the US has used to drive its policy preference within the MDBs, particularly in its demand for accountability and environmental and social safeguards.

Coercive Isomorphism and Environmental Policy Change in the Old MDBs

All of the old MDBs have social and environmental safeguard policies. Designed to protect communities and the natural environment from irreparable harm, the policies aim to identify what impact a proposed project will have on communities and the environment. This then determines the extent to which the project needs oversight and evaluation in order to minimise harm. The environmental and social safeguards of the banks vary in terms of their robustness and the extent to which they are incorporated into the project cycle and monitored and evaluated for their impact. Nonetheless, the banks all incorporated these into their operations within a relatively short timeframe. The World Bank had piecemeal policies from the 1970s, but it was not until the mass environmental campaigns against World Bank projects in the 1980s that the US intervened to demand the bank have policies for protecting the environment.

This occurred when US Congress prepared to pass a law to ensure that all MDBs adopt environmental assessment principles and guidelines while considering requests for IDA 9 contributions (the ninth round of replenishing the bank's soft loan window for the poorest borrowing states).[24]

> In contrast to the general policy demands the United States had made in previous replenishment talks [on other issues], its environmental demands included specific policy and operational reforms: environmental impact assessments of proposed projects, environmental action plans for borrower countries, and disclosure of assessments and plans to local non-governmental organisations and other concerned groups in advance of loan approvals by the bank board.[25]

The World Bank complied with establishing a policy Operational Directive (OD) 4.00 on environment assessment (later revised to OD4.01) which would set out the procedures and conditions of environmental assessment (EA) throughout the bank.

In 1991 the revised OD made it compulsory that borrower information be circulated to communities and local NGOs prior to consultations regarding the project and again after an EA had been undertaken, and to release the EA to the executive directors.[26] All of the MDBs then followed the World Bank's lead in establishing a classificatory system for determining the anticipated effect on the environment.[27]

Coercive Isomorphism and Accountability in the Old MDBs

The old MDBs all created independent accountability mechanisms between 1994 and 2004. The first MDB to do so was the World Bank, which was reacting to an internal report (the Wapenhans Report) outlining the bank's high level of project failures, as well as a wave of environmental and social campaigns against large-scale bank projects in the late 1980s and early 1990s, which culminated with the Sardar Sarovar dam project in India. The Sardar Sarovar dam was in part funded by two World Bank loans, and activists demanded the bank address the environmental and social fall-out of the project. This lead the bank to establish an independent investigation into the effects of the dam,[28] which eventually upheld many of the activists' claims.

Member states on the board, particularly the Dutch, became increasingly determined that some form of redress mechanism be established by the bank to ensure such damage be prevented in the future. The US put forward a proposal for an independent accountability mechanism for the World Bank, opening it up to hear project-affected people's claims, even though the focus for the board of executive directors was how to improve bank compliance with its own policies. The US then threatened the World Bank for withholding funding to the IDA 10 until the bank created such a mechanism. This was crucial to the establishment of what would become known as the Inspection Panel, rather than the creation of an in-house compliance mechanism to improve the bank's project performance.[29]

After the World Bank created its Inspection Panel the other banks followed suit. All MDBs were perceived to be non-transparent, ineffective and unaccountable and donors, particularly the G7 states, made it clear that greater MDB accountability was needed.[30] The World Bank's Inspection Panel created a 'ripple effect on the global decision-making process' because the MDBs had the same major shareholders.[31] To that end, the IDB created its mechanism in 1994, the ADB in 1995 and the rest of the World Bank Group in 1999. The EBRD and the AfDB would then create their inspection panels in 2003 and 2004 respectively.

Rise of the New MDBs

The MDBs were established in waves. The majority of MDBs were created in the post-World War Two period through to the 1960s (World Bank, AfDB, ADB and the IDB). The end of the Cold War led to the creation of the EBRD in 1991. While the EBRD differs slightly in having a mandate to emphasise lending to aid central and eastern European states transition to democracy and free markets, it has tended to revert its practices to align with the other MDBs, which have apolitical technical lending mandates for economic growth and development.[32] We are currently in a third wave of establishing multilateral development lenders. Not since the end of the Cold War has there been such debate over the creation of new lenders in multilateral development and what this means for the international order. Driven by rising powers, the entrance of the AIIB and the NDB reorders the multilateral development landscape but may not necessarily lead to innovation.

The Asian Infrastructure Investment Bank

The creation of the AIIB has followed the same process as the old MDBs (especially the ADB).[33] This time, China's President Xi Jinping and Premier Li Keqiang outlined such an initiative during state visits to Southeast Asia in 2013. The idea behind the bank is to provide 'financial support for infrastructure development and regional connectivity in Asia'.[34] It is widely recognised that there is a one-trillion dollar gap in meeting the infrastructure needs of developing states, and that the existing MDBs, the World Bank and the ADB are unable to meet such a demand. On October 2014, 22 states signed a memorandum of understanding to create the AIIB, determine its location in Beijing and create a Multilateral Interim Secretariat (MIS) for the bank.[35]

These 'prospective founding members' agreed to establish chief negotiators meetings to further identify the rules or articles of agreement for the AIIB. Beginning in November 2014, there have now been six chief negotiators meetings, with the draft articles of agreement being circulated from the second meeting in Mumbai in January 2015. The deadline for becoming a prospective founding member (PFM) of the AIIB was 31 March 2015. Fifty-seven states signed by that date, including states from Asia and the Pacific, Africa, the Middle East, western and eastern Europe, and Latin America. The US was notably absent, as was Japan and Canada, all strong supporters of the older MDBs. Like the provision in older MDBs, to become a member of the AIIB states must first be either a member of the World Bank or the ADB.

The final articles of agreement document was adopted on 22 May 2015 in Singapore at the fifth chief negotiators meeting. In August Mr Jin Liqun, a former Chinese deputy finance minister, vice president of the ADB and former World Bank manager, was appointed to be the president of the AIIB. Jin is the secretary-general of the MIS while the bank is being established. The MIS is located in the Chinese Ministry of Finance, a connection not dissimilar to that between the ADB and Japan's Ministry of Finance.[36] Jin must be voted in by the board of governors upon the bank's establishment. The articles of agreement were opened for signature on 29 June 2015; PFM have until 31 December 2015 to sign and ratify the articles of agreement and deposit their subscriptions to become permanent founding members. By early November 54 of the 57 PFM had signed the articles of agreement (AIIB 2015b).[37] On 4 November 2015 China ratified its membership.

Like the other MDBs, the AIIB follows a weighted voting system based on the amount of capital subscribed. From the beginning China has offered to place a huge injection of capital into the bank—half of the proposed US$100 billion capital of the bank. The weighted voting structure of the older banks has been replicated within the AIIB, with China followed by India, Russia, South Korea and Germany as the top five donors.[38] However, China has signalled that it will not have a veto over the AIIB's governance arrangements and capital, unlike the US in the World Bank.[39]

Also like the older MDBs, the mandate of the AIIB is to provide financing for economic development (specifically identifying infrastructure as its primary aim) and regional cooperation (or 'connectivity' in AIIB parlance). Like the ADB and EBRD, lending will be for both sovereign and non-sovereign to states and entities in the region (with language including 'international and regional agencies'). While the ADB and the EBRD have expanded their conceptions of the region significantly since their inceptions the AIIB signals that it is open to lending outside Asia and Oceania if it 'contributes to the economic development of the Asia region'. The AIIB will have US$100 billion in authorised capital stock, 20% of which will be paid-in. The bank's financial instruments include loans, equity investments, guarantees and 'other types of financing' recognising the advance of capital markets since the EBRD was created in 1991.[40] In seeking to reassure prospective members that this is not a bank dominated by China that only benefits China, the AIIB has incorporated the provision that procurement of goods and services from its loans will not be tied to financing from any particular member states.[41] Nonetheless the bank retains the ability to establish trusts, and special funds for members to channel loans through the bank for specific interests.

In terms of governance the AIIB mimics the older MDBs, with a board of governors, board of executive directors, president, vice president and staff. Power is vested with the bank's board of governors, who meet annually and delegate decision-making to their representatives on the board of executive directors. Also like the older regional banks, the AIIB ensures regional allocation determines the executive directors, with three of the twelve executive director seats to be filled by non-regional members. The AIIB will reserve a voting allocation for regional members as per the other regional development banks, but at a 75% threshold compared with the approximately 60% of the other banks. This is much higher than the other banks and speaks to the desire to have a bank by the region and for the region, challenging the ADB's pre-eminence in this regard. Voting in the AIIB will be determined by a formula of basic and proportional votes as well as a foundational member vote, introducing a distinction to an otherwise tried model. The implications of this are not yet clear but indicate the desire by China and AIIB-backers to gain sufficient founding members. Additionally, the US and Japan could still become members but this would need to increase the bank's capital as shares of the US$100 billion have already been taken by PFM who have signed the bank's articles of agreement.[42]

Departing from the older banks is the decision to have a non-resident board.

This replicates borrower-dominated multilateral lenders like the Development Bank for Latin America (the CAF in its Spanish acronym), although the EBRD allows its president to approve loans under a low ceiling without requiring board approval). This will allow the AIIB to approve loans much faster than the MDBs that require loans to go to the board for approval, and gives significant power to the president. The president must be from the region and will be elected by the board of governors. The position of the president as the chief of staff as well as chairman of the board emulates the older MDB model. In a visiting to the Brookings Institute in Washington, DC, President-designate Jin has stated that his is 'a new development bank with 21st century governance' that combines 'the merits of the existing multilateral development banks and those of the successful private sector companies'. This will enable the bank to be 'lean, green and clean', reflecting concerns by the US and others that the bank will skimp on the high transparency, environmental, social and anticorruption standards set by the World Bank, in an effort to disburse loans more quickly.[43]

One area that stands out for further scrutiny: the bank's provisions in relation to oversight. It is indicative of the AIIB's position that the board of executive directors will:

> ensure that each of its operations complies with the bank's operational and financial policies. These policies would be based on international best practices and would include, among others, environmental and social frameworks, disclosure, procurement, debt sustainability and operations in disputed areas. The draft environmental and social policy framework is being developed through an ongoing consultative process with AIIB's Prospective Founding Members and other stakeholders.

In addition,

> The board of directors will supervise the management and the operation of the bank on a regular basis and will establish an oversight mechanism for that purpose in line with the principles of transparency, openness, independence and accountability. The mechanism is expected to address such areas as audit, evaluation, fraud and corruption, project complaints and staff grievances.[44]

Taken together, it would seem as though the AIIB is following the hard-won changes in the old MDBs in relation to environmental and social safeguard policies, as well as policies on corruption, transparency and accountability. This has led *The Economist* to suggest that the AIIB is 'reverting to the mean' in undertaking development lending, with little uniqueness in its lending or policy objectives.[45] Of course, the devil is in the details, so emulation may be in the broad brushstrokes only.

It is the intended aim of the bank to be leaner and faster than the older MDBs.

This speaks to the hassle factor felt by many borrowing states in relation to the World Bank described earlier and the position of the AIIB to serve its regional borrowers without the same degree of red tape as the pre-existing MDBs. In this regard, procurement rules the AIIB may follow from the other older MDBs, though they themselves are not driving the agenda here but responding to it. As I suggest below, this is coming from powerful borrowers, suggesting that change is still taking place through a process of isomorphism.

The New Development Bank
In contrast the NDB is a different sort of bank. It has deliberately chosen to have equal voting among the five original BRICS members: Brazil, China, India, Russia and South Africa. These members control the bank with 55% of the vote, which is linked to their subscribed capital. The NDB articles of agreement, which were agreed upon by the five founding members in 2014, ensure that non-borrowers cannot have a combined vote exceeding 20% of the bank, and that a non-founding member cannot exceed its voting power above 7% of the bank's total voting power. Voting will be by simple majority, with qualified and special majority voting required for decisions substantially changing the nature of the bank's operations.[46] Ensuring the equality of its members has meant that all five have contributed the same amount of capital, meaning it has a much smaller capital base than that of the AIIB.[47] The NDB has an authorised capital of US$100 billion and a subscribed capital of US$50 billion, with the latter comprised of both paid in and callable capital. Thus, the amount China has sunk into the AIIB (US$50 billion) is approximately the same amount provided by all five of the founding members of the NDB. This means that the AIIB has the potential to 'scale up' with input from an expanding number of members over time (while drawing down on China's percent of the overall subscription and vote), while the NDB places limits on how the bank can grow. Moreover, the AIIB is likely to achieve a much higher credit rating, owing to the involvement of industrialised economies compared with the NDB, with the likelihood of attracting more borrowers with sound projects to the former.[48]

Based in Shanghai, with an Indian president, K.V. Kamath, and one local office in Johannesburg, the NDB is open to all members of the UN and is structurally similar to the older MDBs in terms of having a board of governors, board of executive directors, a president (who is also chair of the board) and vice president. Organisationally, the NDB has emulated older MDBs, although it too has chosen not to have a resident board. Where it differs is in its intention to rotate the presidency among the founding members. It has also followed the older banks in its purpose to 'mobilise resources for infrastructure and sustainable development projects in BRICS and other emerging market economies and developing countries'.[49] It will provide loans, guarantees, equity investment and other financial products to borrowers, using public and private sources for infrastructure and sustainable development projects (like the AIIB, ADB and EBRD) as well as for projects in more than one country.⁵⁰ This replicates the regional development banks' provisions for inter-state projects to facilitate regional integration in addition to national lending, although there has been little success in achieving inter-state loans in the past.⁵¹

In sum, the NDB is a curious mix of old and new. New in the sense that it is a collective agreement among rising powers to create a bank they control equally, but old in the sense that it is a bank with an unequal voting and power structure for prospective borrowers. Moreover it has borrowed the same general aims and structures of the older banks with similar modifications as the AIIB (such as not having a resident board). As a result, the main debates over the creation of the new MDBs have not focused on the NDB, with attention being paid to the AIIB's drive to attract members and its attempts to emphasise that China will not have the same amount of entrenched power (particularly in relation to procurement) that the US has in the other MDBs. As the next section argues, the new MDBs replicate many of the stagnant procedures of the older MDBs, but innovation may yet come from isomorphism among the banks—just not coercively from the US.

Stagnation and Innovation Among the MDBs

Like the ADB, the AIIB will not compete for projects with the other MDBs in the same way that corporations compete for projects in an open market. The MDBs tend to co-finance many of the large infrastructure projects with each other and it is widely recognised that the MDBs cannot meet demand. Indeed, the AIIB has already signalled that its first projects will be co-financed with the World Bank and the ADB.⁵² However, borrowers do consider both financial and non-financial lending criteria when choosing projects for MDB loans. This section focuses specifically on environmental and social safeguards to reveal how isomorphism may still be at work in the MDBs, including the AIIB, even when not driven by the US. Again we begin with the World Bank, demonstrating how it has revised its guidelines, less with US interests, but to reflect borrower demands.

In the late 1990s many began to argue that the 'hassle factor' associated with the World Bank's safeguard policy, along with the lengthy wait and cost of bank loans, made the bank increasingly unattractive to.⁵³ This led the bank to streamline its operations to make its policies more user-friendly.

Revising safeguards

From 2012 the World Bank has been revising the whole suite of its environmental and social safeguards, with keen attention being paid by other MDBs. The process has been protracted, controversial and incomplete. Driving the revision is the argument that the World Bank's environmental and social safeguards have been viewed as compliance driven such that borrowers have to meet formal policies and loan requirements.⁵⁴ However, rising powers or middle-income countries (MICs in World Bank parlance) led the bank to curtail its use of safeguards in the mid-2000s, raising questions as to how strongly they would remain. Borrowers viewed the safeguards as some of the many onerous obligations they had to contend with in order to borrow from the World Bank. Moreover, borrowers were concerned with the costs of compliance. All shareholders were at the same time recognising the need for borrower ownership for development to be sustainable. This led the World Bank's board of executive directors to request greater flexibility in the safeguard policy.[55]

Therefore, the bank's revision of the safeguard policy is part of its effort to become more 'client-focused'. Rising powers' concerns over the safeguards triggered the bank's safeguard policy revision, first by delimiting the policy to include low-income borrowers as well as MICs and then by opening up the policy to a country systems framework. Thus, environmental and social safeguards are applied to IDA loans for low-income states and a new country systems approach (CSA) is applied to OCR loans for MICs. The CSA applies to the World Bank's operational policies for procurement, other fiduciary areas and the safeguards. The policy enables MICs to use their own national policies while 'streamlining policy conditionality in bank lending operations'. The CSA is open to countries that have policies equivalent to the bank's policy framework applicable to the operation, and where the relevant country's implementation practices, capacity, and track record are acceptable.[56] This would further enhance a borrower's capacity and ownership of their development while reducing bank lending costs. This introduced greater flexibility into the safeguards, prior to opening up all of the policies for revision. In sum, the World Bank is revising its rules on safeguards, after concerns of key stakeholders such as NGOs and affected people that the latter undermines the ability of the World Bank to undertake sustainable development projects.

This is important because of the isomorphic process; what the World Bank does, the other banks usually follow. Yet the World Bank has the most stringent of standards among the MDBs, and newer, more regionally oriented development lenders may choose to operate differently. An example of this is the Development Bank for Latin America (CAF). Although it has been in operation since 1970, it has not been until recently that this regional development bank has dramatically increased its lending within the region. This is because the CAF does not have any of the traditional donors as its members. The CAF is comprised of its regional members, who are borrowers as well as private sector entities. Unlike the World Bank's detailed safeguards, the CAF has only a few paragraphs on its environmental and social requirements and states quite specifically that the onus is on the borrower to meet its own environmental legislation. This has led one scholar to describe the CAF as 'several orders of magnitude more lax, leaving almost complete flexibility [for borrowers] to assess each project as it chooses'.[57] Of course, the scrutiny facing the AIIB may mean that it will be forced to mimic the World Bank more so than the CAF, reinforcing the isomorphism of the MDBs but not reflecting their coercion from the US.

Conclusion

The creation of new MDBs by China creates significant room for a reevaluation of how and why the old MDBs change. This chapter has examined the extent to which the old MDBs, dominated over by the US, have innovated. As similar international organisations in the international system, I contend that these MDBs have effectively changed to meet the interests of the US as the largest shareholder according to what is considered best international development practice. This has led to innovations in accountability and environmental and social safeguards. Usually beginning with the World Bank, change follows coercive isomorphism because the US is a dominant shareholder in all of these institutions and shared agreement for change in one bank is quickly followed by the others. This chapter questions whether the AIIB and NDB will innovate in ways that diverge from the old MDBs through prioritising different development needs or whether it will, by default, mimic the policies and practices of the old MDBs. Ultimately this means that introducing new MDBs with different dominant shareholders may lead to stagnation across the entire class of MDBs rather than providing new and innovative ways to do development.

Table 8.1

G7 Member States Voting Power as a % of Total Votes in the MDBs for the Financial Year 2011 (July 2012)

G7 Voting Power in the MDBs FY2010–2011	World Bank	IFC	MIGA	EBRD	ADB	AfDB	IDB
United States	15.55	22.7	14.99	10.32	12.82	6.87	30
Japan	9.16	5.65	4.21	8.76	12.82	5.69	5
Germany	4.58	5.16	4.19	8.76	3.77	4.27	1.89
France	4.1	4.85	4.02	8.76	2.17	3.89	1.89
United Kingdom	4.1	4.85	4.02	8.76	1.95	1.75	0.96
Italy	2.62	3.43	2.81	8.76	1.75	2.5	1.89
Canada	3.08	3.43	2.95	3.51	4.5	3.94	4
G7 Total	43.19	50.07	37.19	57.63	39.78	28.91	45.63

Sources:
World Bank, IFC and MIFA. Accessed: 18 September 2012. Last Updated: 6 July 2012
AfDB figures from AfDB: Accessed: 18 Septeber 2012.
ADB figures from ADB 2012 Annual Report 2011. Accessed: 18 September 2012.
EBRD Figures from: CEE Watch 1999 Accessed: 18 September 2012; Babb 2009: 25, 40; Bronstone 1999: 27. IDB figures from: IDB, 2011 Annual Report 2010: Accessed 18 September 2012.

Notes

1. N. Dutt, 'The US and the Asian Development Bank: Origins, structure and lending operations', *Journal of Contemporary Asia* 3:2 (2001) pp. 241–61; E.S. Mason and R.E. Asher, *The World Bank Since Bretton Woods* (Washington, D.C: The Brookings Institution, 1973).
2. S. Park and J. Strand, eds., 'Global Economic Governance and the Development Practices of the Multilateral Development Banks', in *Global Economic Governance and the Development Practices of the Multilateral Development Banks* (London: Routledge, 2016), pp. 3–20.
3. J. Strand and M. Trevathan, 'Implications of Accommodating Rising Powers for the Regional Development Banks', in *Global Economic Governance and the Development Practices of the Multilateral Development Banks* eds. Susan Park and Jonathan R. Strand, (London: Routledge, 2016), pp. 121–142.
4. R. Culpeper, *Titans or Behemoths? The Multilateral Development Banks* (London: Intermediate Technology Publishing, 1997), pp. 35–38.
5. Park and Strand, pp. 3–20.
6. K. Mingst, *Politics and the African Development Bank*. (Lexington, Kentucky: University Press of Kentucky, 1990)
7. C. Wright, 'From "Safeguards" to "Sustainability": The Evolution of Environmental Discourse within the International Finance Corporation' in D. Stone and C. Wright, eds., *World Bank and Governance: A Decade of Reform and Reaction* (London and New York: Routledge, 2016), pp. 67–87.
8. Morten Boas, 'Governance as multilateral development bank policy: the cases of the African Development Bank and the Asian Development Bank', *The European Journal of Development Research* 10:2 (1998), pp. 117–34; Janne Jokinen, 'Balancing between East and West: the Asian Development Bank's policy on good governance', in Morton Boas and Desmond McNeill, eds., *Global Institutions and Development*, (London and New York: Routledge, 2004),pp. 137–50.
9. J. Strand, 'State Power in a Multilateral Context: Voting Strength in the Asian Development Bank', *International Interactions* 25:3 (1999), pp. 53–74; J. Strand, 'Institutional Design and Power Relations in the African Development Bank', *Journal of African and Asian States* 36:2 (2001), pp. 203–223; J. Strand, 'Measuring Voting Power in an International Institution: The United States and the Inter-American Development Bank', *Economics of Governance* 4:1 (2003), pp. 19–36.
10. J. Strand and M. Trevathan, 2016, p. 133.
11. Sarah Babb, *Behind the Development Banks* (Chicago: Chicago University Press, 2009), pp. 24–25, 39–40
12. R. Wade, and J. Vestergaard, 'Protecting Power: How Western States Retain the Dominant Voice in the World Bank's Governance', World Development, 46 (2013), pp. 153–164.
13. J. Strand and M. Trevathan, 2016, p. 133.
14. Paul DiMaggio and Walter Powell, 'The Iron Cage Revisited: Institutional Isomorphism and Collective Rationality in Organisational Fields', *American Sociological Review* 48:2 (1983), p. 150.
15. R. Wade, 'Greening the Bank: The Struggle over the Environment 1970–1995,' in D. Kapur, J. Lewis and R.C Webb, eds., *The World Bank: Its First Half Century*, (Washington, DC, Brookings Institute), 1997, pp. 611–734
16. A. Dreher and N. Jensen, 'Independent actor or agent? An empirical analysis of the impact of US interests on IMF conditions', *The Journal of Law and Economics* 50:1 (2007), pp. 105–124; Dreher, A., Sturm, J., and J. Vreeland, 'Development Aid and International Politics: does membership on the UN Security Council influence World Bank decisions?' *Journal of Development Economics* 88 (2009), pp. 1–18; Kilby, C., 'An Empirical Assessment of Informal Influence in the World Bank', Villanova School of Business Department of Economics and

Statistics Working Paper #9. 2010. Cited: http://repec.library.villanova.edu/workingpapers/VSBEcon9.pdf Accessed: 15 May 2013.
17. Christopher Kilby, 'Informal Influence in the Asian Development Bank', Review of *International Organisations* 6 (2011), pp. 223–267.
18. Less research has been conducted on US' role in the EBRD; Mingst, p. 17
19. J. Strand and T. Zappile, 'Always Vote for Principle, Though You May Vote Alone: Explaining United States political support for multilateral development loans', *World Development* 72 (2015), pp. 224–239.
20. Babb, p. 37.
21. Bronstone, A., *The European Bank for Reconstruction and Development* (Manchester: Manchester University Press, 1999).
22. Babb, 37; DeWitt, R.P., 'Policy Directions in International Lending, 1961–1984: The Case of the Inter-American Development Bank', *Journal of Developing Areas* 21 (1987), pp. 277–284.
23. Culpeper, p. 2.
24. I. Bowles and C. Kormos, 'The American Campaign for Environmental Reforms at the World Bank,' *The Fletcher Forum of World Affairs* 23:1 (1999), pp. 217.
25. C. Gwin, 'US Relations with the World Bank 1945–92', Washington D.C., Brookings Institution: Brookings Occasional Papers, 1994, p. 49.
26. Wade, pp. 682, 686–7; Park, 2010, p. 84.
27. D. Kohn, 'Setting a Standard: Environmental Impact Assessment Policies of Multilateral Development Banks and Export Credit Agencies,' *Environmental Law* 9 (2002), pp. 288–89.
28. B. Morse and T. Berger, *The Independent Review of the Sardar Sarovar Projects* (Ottawa: Resource Futures International), 1992.
29. Park, 2010, p. 26.
30. R. Bissell and S. Nanwani, 'Multilateral Development Bank Accountability Mechanisms: Developments and Challenges', *Central and European Journal of International and Security Studies* 3:2 (2009), p. 8; E. Suzuki and S. Nanwani 'Responsibility of International Organisations: The Accountability Mechanisms of Multilateral Development Banks', *Michigan Journal of International Law* 27 (2006), p. 187.
31. Suzuki and Nanwani, p. 177.
32. In addition the EBRD must lend over 60% of its lending to the private sector, compared with the sovereign lending of the other MDBs (excepting the ADB, which lends to both public and private). The World Bank and the IDB have separate private sector lending instruments: the International Finance Corporate (IFC) for the World Bank Group and the Inter-American Investment Corporation (IIC) and the Multilateral Investment Fund (MIF) as part of the IDB Group; M. Stein, 'Conflict Prevention in Transition Economies: A Role for the European Bank for Reconstruction and Development?' in Abraham and Antonia Chayes, eds., *Preventing Conflict in the Post-Communist World: Mobilising International and Regional Organisations* (Washington, D.C: Brookings Institution, 1996), pp. 339–378.
33. Watanabe, Takeshi, Towards a New Asia (Singapore: Times Printers, 1977); Mason and Ascher; Bronstone.
34. AIIB, 2015, 'About Us,' Accessed 2 October 2015. http://www.aiibank.org/html/pagefaq/Background/
35. Ibid.
36. Dennis Yasutomo. *Japan and the Asian Development Bank* (New York: Praeger, 1983), p. 148.
37. AIIB, 2015b, 'The 8th AIIB Chief Negotiators', Meeting convened in Jakarta, Indonesia on 3–4 November 2015'. Accessed: 15 November 2015, http://www.aiib.org/html/2015/NEWS_1104/28.html
38. Ina Parlina, 'AIIB Ready to Help Finance Infrastructure Projects', Business Jakarta Post, 5 November 2015. Accessed: 16 November 2015. http://www.thejakartapost.com/

39 C. Humprheys, 'China's AIIB bank set to become major player while new BRICS bank lags behind' Comment, 30 April 2015, Overseas Development Institute. Cited: 16 November 2015. Accessed http://www.odi.org/comment/9524-chinas-aiib-bank-set-become-major-player-while-new-brics-bank-lags-behind
40 AIIB, 2015.
41 Ibid.
42 S Donnan, and D. Sevastopulo, 'AIIB head vows to be clean, lean and green—and fast' The Economist, Asia Pacific Economy, 25 October 2015, Accessed 16 November 2015. http://www.ft.com/intl/cms/s/0/b6f95846-7b0d-11e5-a1fe-567b37f80b64.html#axzz3rbVUH0X4
43 Xinhuanet, 'Spotlight: AIIB to be run with highest standards of "21st century governance" English News China, 22 October 2015. Accessed 16 November 2015. http://news.xinhuanet.com/english/2015-10/22/c_134740305.htm
44 AIIB, 2015.
45 *The Economist*, 'Reversion to the Mean', Banyan, 26 September 2015, Accessed: 3 October 2015. http://www.economist.com/news/asia/21667964-chinas-new-infrastructure-bank-has-gained-wide-support-lending-will-be-tougher-reversion
46 NDB, 2015 'Articles of Agreement of the New Development Bank,' Accessed 16 November 2015 http://ndbbrics.org/agreement.html
47 C. Humphreys, 'Developmental revolution or Bretton Woods revisited? The prospects of the BRICS New Development Bank and the Asian Infrastructure Investment Bank', Overseas Development Institute Working Paper 418, 2015b, Accessed 16 November 2015. http://www.odi.org/sites/odi.org.uk/files/odi-assets/publications-opinion-files/9615.pdf
48 Ibid.
49 NDB, 2015.
50 Ibid.
51 D. Tussie, *The Inter-American Development Bank* (Boulder, Colorado: Lynne Rienner Publishers, 1995) p.146.
52 Donnan and Sevastopulo.
53 Nancy Birdsall, ed., *Rescuing the World Bank: A Centre for Global Development Working Report and Selected Essays* (Washington D.C.: Centre for Global Development, 2006), p. 124; C. Humphreys, 'The "hassle factor" of MDB lending and borrower demand in Latin America', in Susan Park and Jonathan Strand, eds., *Global Economic Governance and the Development Practices of the Multilateral Development Banks* (London and New York: Routledge, 2016), pp. 143–166.
54 Wright, p. 79.
55 World Bank, 'Safeguard Policies: Framework for Improving Development Effectiveness, A Discussion Note', ESSD and OPCS, 7 October 2002, p. 1.
56 World Bank, 'Enhancing World Bank Support to Middle Income Countries: Management Actions Plan Progress Memorandum', Washington DC, February 1 2005, pp. 1–2.
57 Humphreys, p. 10.

What the AIIB Means for the Development Finance System? A View of China–US Relations

Qiyuan Xu, Bei Gao, Dongmin Liu

Research fellows at the Institute of World Economics and Politics, Chinese Academy of Social Sciences, China

Abstract

The Asian Infrastructure Investment Bank (AIIB) is going to be formally founded by the end of 2015, and is neither a shaper nor a shaker to the existing development finance system, but rather a supplement. We will introduce the conception of the AIIB both from the views of China and the international development finance system, and clarify the relationships between the AIIB and the One Belt, One Road initiative. Although the US has missed the opportunity to join the AIIB as a permanent founding member mainly due to domestic political dilemmas, the door for the US and China to cooperate in the development finance system is still open. In this paper, the potential ways for China and the US to collaborate in the development finance system will be elaborated on as follows: (1) to jointly push forwards the reforms of the existing multilateral development banks (MDBs); (2) in the near future to facilitate collaborations between experienced and new MDBs; (3) to establish an MDB coordination mechanism/platform, so as to integrate the lending standards, potential projects and financing, and to avoid the fragmentation of MDBs.

Introduction

The AIIB, which was proposed by China, was formally established and put into operation by the end of 2015. As the new MDB led by the emerging economies, the establishment of the AIIB has drawn great attention in the world. It received support from a large number of countries both inside and outside Asia, enhancing China's influence in the world. As well, it was the first time China had led the establishment of a new MDB, representing China's new attempt to take responsibility in international society.

The establishment of the AIIB is considered to challenge to the existing development finance systems overseen by the US. The US not only rejected China's offer to get into AIIB, but also got angry at Britain joining the Chinese-led AIIB.[1] To express their skepticism, on 28 April 2015, US President Obama and Prime Minister Abe of Japan remarked in a joint press conference on AIIB that '. . . a fair governance . . . sustainability, and the environment and society and the impact of this should be considered.'[2]

As we know, when President Xi Jinping visited the US in September 2015, the two sides reached an understanding on the issue, but to be sure, there is still a long way to go in development finance system cooperation for both sides in the future.

In addition, it is significant for the AIIB to promote economic development and regional economic integration in Asia. Moreover, the establishment of the AIIB brought fresh blood into the international monetary system and development financial system.

First, the establishment of the AIIB expanded the overall strength of the development of the financial system, and helped to make up for the gap between the size of the MDB loans and real money demand. Second, the establishment of AIIB brought about the reform of the governance concept. Prior to this, developed countries mainly dominated the MDBs. Led by emerging economies, the AIIB will give more consideration to the recipient of the actual situation in the loan payment process, and AIIB will not insist on the policy of a free market economy as proposed by the World Bank, which requires the borrower to make exchanges for loans through the privatisation or deregulation. Finally, the innovative solutions of the AIIB will force a reform of the existing institutions. For example, the AIIB will do global sourcing in its loan projects, and will not limit procurement for member states. For the effective reduction of operating costs in the AIIB, a permanent executive board will not be implemented. The investment model will take bank loans and equity investment, and guarantee business operations at the same time. These will hugely impact the existing MDBs, forcing a revision of current conservative practices.

However, the existing development finance system has not formed a united mechanism for collaboration. The multilateral mechanism is to some extent fragmented. Although the establishment of the AIIB will force the existing development finance system to start reforms, the reform path remains long and requires a lot of effort, and such effort naturally requires close cooperation between

China and US. The development finance system mechanism will be in line with the interests of both sides, but also contribute to the recovery and development of the global economy.

In the second section of this chapter, we will explain what is new for the AIIB. The relations between AIIB and the One Belt, One Road (OBOR) initiative will be discussed. At the same time, relations between AIIB and the existing MBDs are also a pressing topic. Are they competitive or complementary? In the fourth section, we will check their relationships with new estimation. Based on this analysis, we will conclude on how China and the US could collaborate with each other in the development finance systems.

What's New in the AIIB?

What is the distinction between the AIIB and the existing MDBs? Some believe that the World Bank and the Asian Development Bank (ADB) look at poverty reduction, whereas the AIIB targets infrastructure investment to support the Asian economic and social development. In fact, infrastructure is also an important business for almost all multilateral financing institutions that are involved in development, especially for those aimed at less-developed countries. For example, the ADB focuses 60% of its loans on infrastructure, including transportation, communication, energy and water conservancy. The World Bank designates almost 50% of its loans for such projects. Considering that these institutions have more abundant capital overall, the AIIB has nothing unique in its function and orientation.

At the same time, the AIIB and the implementation of the OBOR initiative have created concerns among the international community about China's exporting of backward manufacturing industries and, along with them, environmental pollution. Such headlines as 'China's Plan to Export Pollution' appear in foreign media from time to time.[3]

In late May 2015, Japanese Prime Minister Abe announced a US$110 billion investment plan for Asian infrastructure over the next five years. The Japanese highlighted the concept of 'high-quality infrastructure' and proposed international standards for the advancement of 'high-quality infrastructure investment.' What development concepts should the AIIB and the OBOR initiative adopt in response to these challenges? The AIIB must address these concerns through the orientation of its own business.

The issue of quality pertains not only to infrastructure but also to all commodities. Infrastructure is also about networks and externality. It has a fundamental status in the global value chain. On this basis, how should these emerging multilateral financing institutions shape concepts for development financing?

The ginger industry in Nepal provides an interesting starting point for analysis. In 2013, Nepal's ginger production accounted for 12% of global production, coming in third after that of India and China. Nepal also ranked third in the world in ginger exports. However, Nepal's ginger has not sold at a good price. According to data from the United Nations Food and Agriculture Organisation, which an ADB report also quotes, the unit price of the ginger exported by China was US$833 per ton. In comparison, a ton of ginger from India sold for US$1,173 and US$1,407 from the Netherlands, whereas it sold for only US$195 from Nepal.[4] Therefore, the price of ginger from Nepal was just 23% of that for China and less than 14% of that for the Netherlands. Selling at such a low prices makes it difficult for Nepal to reap any tangible benefits from its ginger industry.

Why is the ginger exported by Nepal unable to be sold at a good price?
Nepalese ginger does not command a higher price in part because of its quality. In many major ginger-producing areas in Nepal, ginger varieties have not been improved genetically. Therefore, they are fibrous and have a hard texture. At harvest time, local farmers pack dozens of kilograms of ginger in big bags and carry them to the agro-product markets kilometres away for sale. Owing to a lack of automatic cleaning and sorting equipment, Nepal exports most of their ginger without processing it.

The second reason is an absence of high value-added industries downstream. As a Chinese saying goes, turnip in winter and ginger in summer can keep doctors away. Indeed, ginger has many high value-added uses. For example, ginger has medicinal values, such as inhibiting tumours and migraines, promoting digestion, and preventing carsickness. Ginger is also used as a hangover cure. Cosmetic companies use it to produce acne treatments. Ginger has many culinary uses. These processed ginger products have a high added value. They also command a high price in unit weight, which makes their export economical, even if transportation costs are great.

However, these industries cannot survive in Nepal, not only because of problems in connection with market demands but also because of backward infrastructure. The ginger industry of Nepal confronts serious restrictions in infrastructure and trans-shipment trade. India, which borders on Nepal, also is well-known for its deficient infrastructure. In Indian author Chetan Bhagat's novel *Half Girlfriend*, published in 2014, the hero, Madhav, complains about terrible road conditions on a bus trip. In response, the bus driver responds, 'Dude, there is no road at all here!'[5] The infrastructure in Nepal is even worse than it is in India. According to the 2012 World Development Indicators, the length of road per 100 km² in India equaled 2,226 km. Nepal had only 121 km, less than one-tenth of what existed in India.[6] Moreover, half of these roads are unpaved. The mileage of the Nepal railway system is negligible. Related to these challenges, Nepal also has a serious energy shortage. Even where energy can be imported, Nepal's degree of electrification is only 60% of that of India.

Serious lags in infrastructure construction, including water conservancy, energy and transportation, make it impossible for high value-added downstream industries to survive in Nepal. According to the Davos World Economic Forum's Global Competitiveness Report, Nepal is ranked 132nd in infrastructure quality amongst

148 economies. It had an economic indicator score of 2.1 out of a full score of 7. In comparison, India had an indicator score of 3.6.[7]

The price of electricity in Nepal reflects the shortage of infrastructure. Nepal has one of the highest electricity prices among all South Asian nations. For example, Nepal's population pays 18% more for electricity than the people of Sri Lanka do. They pay 43% more than people in Pakistan and 115% more than the populations of India or Bangladesh.

Lags in infrastructure development not only create a bottleneck for the deep processing of ginger but also make it difficult to use modern modes of production to grow, irrigate, store and transport ginger. These circumstances affect product quality and crop yields. For example, on average, Nepalese producers take one-and-a half months to complete only one of the processes necessary for product export. In comparison, in India and other South Asian countries they take an average of one month to complete one of these processes. In ASEAN countries, they need only two weeks. However, Nepal's geographic position poses serious limitations. Landlocked and sandwiched between China and India, Nepal has to sell most of its ginger to India. The Himalayas form a barrier to trade in the north. Therefore, India presents the only option for a comparatively unimpeded exchange of goods to the south. Consequently, Nepal's foreign trade relies heavily on India. Even with transit trade to a third country, more than 60% of its ginger exports can be sold only to India. Owing to a lack of other competitive export channels, the market easily forces down Nepal's ginger prices.[8]

Indeed, India has often found it easy to take advantage of this situation. In 1989 India imposed a trade blockade on Nepal for a time. Although India's trade with Nepal has normalised since then, Nepal constantly faces the possibility of being sanctioned. Trade in Nepal, therefore, always involves uncertainty. Even if Nepal carries out transit trade via India at ordinary times, it still faces many problems. The three Indian states that neighbour Nepal all have prescribed minimum standards for Nepal's freight rates. Thus, these Indian states have reached a tacit agreement about rates. The sensitivity of certain commodities has been used by India as an excuse, therefore India's official agencies have monopolised some insurance services for Nepal's foreign commodity trade. Moreover, the export of merchandise through transit trade to a third country via India requires Nepalese traders to go through customs-clearance procedures twice. Delays on the Indian side often cause merchandise to be stranded.[9]

How will Nepal be integrated into the global value chain?

Under such conditions, the export of primary products and import of final goods characterises the nature of trade between Nepal and India, its most important trade partner. This trade structure signifies Nepal's marginalised status in the global value chain.

The problems of the ginger industry in Nepal provide enlightenment for future investment in such economies. Lack of infrastructure in water conservancy, electricity and transportation will make it unfeasible to invest only in high value-added downstream ginger industries, such as medicine, cosmetics and candy. However, direct investment in infrastructure may cause problems, as well. Investment in infrastructures that have positive externalities is bound to benefit high value-added downstream industries but, with relatively low returns, may still be of little interest to investors. Furthermore, infrastructure investment usually requires large amounts of capital, and the construction cycle for infrastructure is often long. Therefore, from any perspective, investment in infrastructure and investment in other high value-added downstream industries should be planned together as a whole, rather than separately. Last, even if Nepal perfects its infrastructure and extends its domestic ginger value chain, it will still encounter many difficulties because of its position as a landlocked nation.

Therefore, strategies for investment cooperation with Nepal should highlight two points. First, to bring more jobs, tax revenues and other spillover effects for Nepal, a package of plans for investment both in infrastructure and in high value-added industries such as ginger should be put in place to extend its domestic industry. Second, construction of international, especially Sino–Nepalese, transportation infrastructure would promote integration of Nepal's ginger industry into the global value chain.

Many aspects of the situation in Nepal are representative of economic problems of other nations. For example in Indonesia, marine fisheries face similar challenges, including a short domestic value chain, and a low added value. The industry has a weakening effect on economic development. Therefore, to solve these problems, similar strategies for development should be followed to extend Indonesia's marine fishery value chain and connect it to the international value chain.

The AIIB will not be directly involved in high value-added downstream industries, but the institution can still be part of the large-scale planning of the whole value chain. Instead, the AIIB primarily focuses on the development of infrastructure. Nevertheless, as this essay demonstrates, plans for a country's infrastructure can be separated neither from the development of its domestic high value-added downstream industries nor from the global value chain. Without high value-added downstream industries, the AIIB's infrastructure investment would make no sense, and its projects-repayment capacities would be compromised. Without comprehensive planning and policy guidance regarding preliminary infrastructure and high value-added downstream industries, it would take more time to construct the whole value chain, and the earnings cycle of infrastructure investment would be extended even further. Therefore, in an era of increasingly integrated global value chains, new international multilateral financing institutions such as the AIIB need to formulate development concepts that transcend the vision of a single project and evolve into a package of investment models for the integration of upstream and downstream industries.

The Relationship between the AIIB and the One Belt, One Road Initiative

The One Belt, One Road (OBOR) initiative is an important measure to take in an open economic system and is conducive to the realisation of shared opportunities, common development and prosperity between China and other countries and regions. The establishment of the AIIB is in the context of this background, demonstrating a close relationship between AIIB and the OBOR initiative. But there are a lot of misunderstandings of this relationship as well.

The spokesman of twelfth National People's Congress Fu Ying pointed out, when asked on their relationship by the media, that the AIIB and the Silk Road Fund should support the OBOR initiative.[10] But some foreign media think the AIIB is just a tool that serves the OBOR. Even some native scholars regard the AIIB as the core or pillar of the initiative, and so on.

Although AIIB should support the OBOR, this does not mean the AIIB is just a tool to serve the initiative. When the minister of finance, Lou Jiwei, accepted an interview, he mentioned that the AIIB and the OBOR initiative do have overlapping areas but are also different to each other.[11]

The OBOR initiative is proposed based on the perspective of a full opening-up in line with the tenets that established the AIIB, but that does not mean that the AIIB must primarily serve the initiative. As with all the existing MDBs, the AIIB is an international organisation as well as having links to the Chinese OBOR initiative. The AIIB will operate according to its own agreement, drafted by its 57 member countries. Therefore, as an international institution, the AIIB maintains its independence. Only if the OBOR and AIIB have overlapping interests can the AIIB support the OBOR. So, are there any overlapping interests?

The answer is affirmative. The OBOR initiative is a great concept of China's, based on the development of a vast hinterland, and it coincides with initiatives launched by other countries, such as India's Project Mausam, Mongolia's Steppe Road and Indonesia's Global Maritime Axis. Although these regional plans have different focuses, there is a common ground between them that seeks to promote regional integration and interconnection, subsequently driving the economic recovery and development of these regions. With the current stagnate state of the global economy, these initiatives create new drivers in the growing the world economy. In such cases, the initiatives of these countries are well matched. With this in mind, the AIIB could justifiably support the OBOR initiative.

Finally, with a reverse trend from globalisation to fragmentation, explained below, China has the same motivation to push forwards both the AIIB and OBOR to better integrate China into the global economy.

China's economy has mainly been driven by two engines; exports and investments. They have benefited from China's entrance into the WTO and foreign direct investment. From a broader perspective, the development of China over the past few decades has benefited greatly from globalisation as well as an effective international trade system (organised by the WTO) and a relatively stable international financial system (organised by the IMF). Or we can call this benefit a globalisation dividend to China, comparing with domestic demographic dividend.

Nevertheless, there shows a reverse trend from globalisation to fragmentation. Since the failure of the Doha Development Round multilateral negotiations at the WTO, many mega-regional free trade agreements (FTAs) are being developed. In October 2015, TPP member countries arrived at an agreement. At the same time, the TTIP, RCEP, Japan–EU FTA and some other mega-FTAs are in negotiations. All of these mega-FTAs are exclusive to non-member countries. In this way, the mechanism of the WTO has been weakened. The international trade system is being fragmented (Figure 9.1).

Figure 9.1 From Globalisation to Fragmentation: the International Trade System

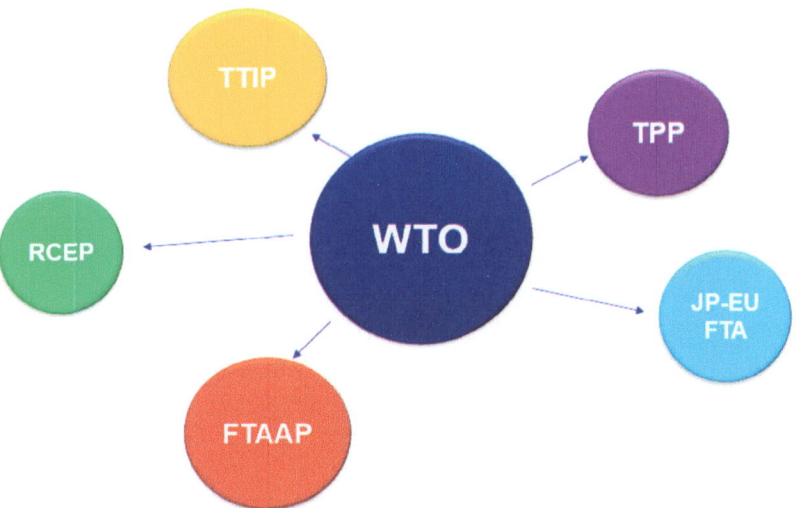

In the international financial system, the role of IMF has been considerably weakened. In 2010 the IMF started to make substantial reforms and plans to increase capital. But these were delayed by the US, who only approved these plans with some preconditions in late 2015. At the same time, six major central banks have assigned three-year currency swap arrangements[12]. These swap arrangements have been extended into permanent agreement,[13] which ensures the central banks' ability to stabilise the foreign exchange market if the increases in interest rates by the Federal Reserve Board cause some tension in liquidity. For the emerging and developing countries outside the permanent swap arrangements, they must find other solutions to realise self-insurance (Figure 9.2). For the ten ASEAN countries and China, Korea and Japan, this 10+3 framework has launched the Chiang Mai Initiative (CMI) in 2010 and aims to expand the foreign exchange reserve pool to a scale of US$240 billion. In 2015 the agreement on the NDB's US$100 billion currency reserve pool also came into force. Moreover, all of the BRICS countries accumulate official reserves independently. A fragmented international financial system blocked direct international investment and led to over-savings in these emerging and developing countries. From this perspective, the AIIB can make better use of these over-savings and facilitate more international investment.

Figure 9.2 From Globalisation to Fragmentation: the International Financial System

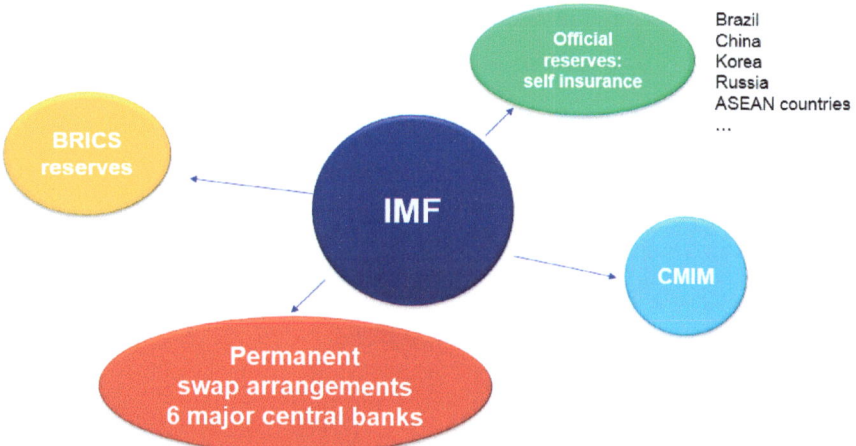

In short, China launched the initiatives of the AIIB and OBOR in order to connect itself to the global economy, especially given the context of the reverse trend of globalisation to fragmentation. And these limitations will not only benefit of China, but many other economies.

Competitive or Complementary: The Relation between the AIIB and the Existing MDBs

Some observers regard the new MDBs, such as the NDB and the AIIB, as a challenge to the existing international economic order, and the AIIB has positioned itself to specifically challenge the ADB.[14] On the other hand, the ADB shows different data and a different perspective for this concern. According to the estimates of the ADB, the annual demand of infrastructure investment in Asia will be around US$730 billion by 2020.[15] Meanwhile, the ADB only offered US$21 billion for infrastructure loans in 2013, of which $US6.6 billion was joint financing.[16] Obviously, there is a huge gap between the demand and supply of funds. So the AIIB came into being, its mission to improve infrastructure interconnection through investments in infrastructure and other productive sectors. Therefore, the relationships between the AIIB and the existing MDBs are more complementary than competitive.

According to Bhattacharya and Romani,[17] an estimated US$0.9 trillion is currently invested annually in infrastructure in emerging and developing countries, which

What the AIIB Means for the Development Finance System

equates to a gap of approximately US$1 trillion annually in meeting infrastructure needs by 2020. They also argued that the existing global development financing architecture does not provide finance at a sufficient scale to meet infrastructure development needs.

Although there is a large financing gap from an overall perspective, we will find more structural information if we analyse the needs and gaps divided by sovereign credit ratings.

Figure 9.3 Structure of the Infrastructure Financing Needs and Gaps in 2020: Divided by Sovereign Credit Ratings (October 2015)

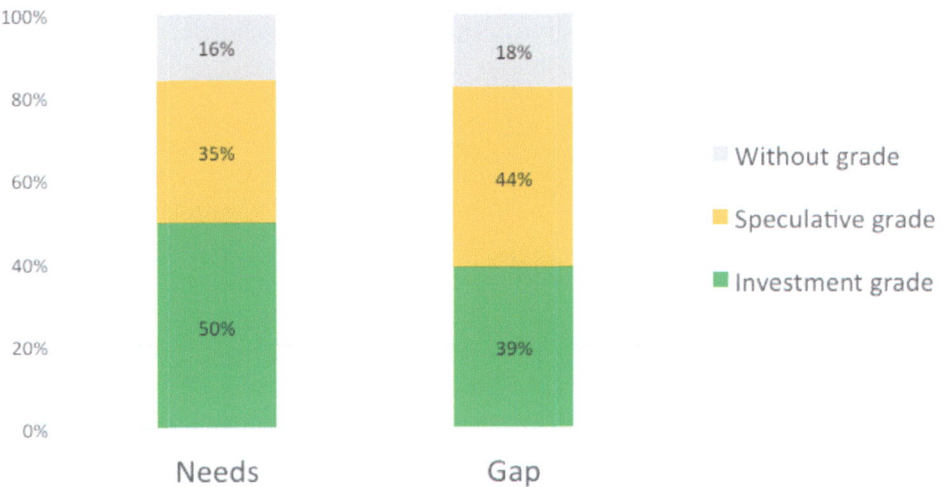

Source: 161 countries, authors' estimation based on Bhattacharya & Romani,[18] Fay et al.,[19] with data from the World Bank and the IMF. For methodology, we refer to Fay et al. to estimate the needs and gaps for each country, and then match each country's credit rating with their needs and gaps. The credit rating for each country is based on the Fitch Ratings from 12 October 2015.

Figure 9.3 shows the infrastructure financing needs and gaps in 2020. For infrastructure financing, 50% will be from investment-grade countries, 35% from speculative-trade countries and 16% from countries without grade. For the gaps in infrastructure financing, the situation is even worse. Only 39% of the gaps come from investment-grade countries, while 44% and 18% come from speculative-grade countries and countries without grade respectively. From this figure, we know that although the needs and gaps for infrastructure financing are large, the structural distributions show great risks, especially for the financing gap, more than 60% of which is from speculative-grade countries or countries without grade. With such risky needs and gaps of infrastructure financing, the AIIB and existing MDBs could to some extent compete more on the projects in high-grade countries.

Even if it was assumed that competition exists between the AIIB and other

MDBs, this should be good news for the international developing finance markets. In the commodity market, the Washington Consensus defends a free market, with free competition and free entrance. Therefore, why is there not room for one more MDB? If the introduction of the AIIB increases the competition among MDBs, it could not only help make up the gap of infrastructure financing, but also force the existing MDBs to make their own reforms. For these considerations, the World Bank should be more welcoming to the AIIB.

However, if the new MDB creates excessive competition in the international infrastructure financing system, the result could be negative. For example, without essential collaborations among MDBs, the competition order could be in a mess, and the non-performing loans could destroy the MDBs' sustainability. The potential contradictions demand the establishment of an effective collaboration mechanism among the MDBs, which we will elaborate in the next section.

The Collaboration between China and the US
The cooperation between the existing MDBs and the new MDBs
In the future, there will be cooperation and competition at the same time between existing MDBs and new MDBs. But cooperation, including capital cooperation and project cooperation, could and should be the main focus. As a new MDB, the AIIB has the advantage of capital adequacy, but lacks corresponding pipeline projects and operational experience. Therefore, in its early stages, the AIIB can choose to participate in well-established projects of the existing institutions. In the future, the AIIB's subsequent independence should not keep it from supporting large and inter-regional projects in the form of syndicated loans.

In addition, China and the US need to cooperate on global developmental economics. In the future, there will be a huge gap in global infrastructure financing, and since the middle-income countries still face challenges in reducing poverty, the MDBs can play an important role in response to these specific needs. However, as the financing capacity of MDBs such as the World Bank and the ADB remain insufficient to meet demand, their lending capacity needs to be increased in order to strengthen the role of the MDBs. The main way to do this is to increase funding for the existing MDBs. China will not only serve as a shareholder and borrower, but also enhance its role as the donor country in all MDBs. And the US needs to reform the equity distribution for MDBs such as the World Bank, with emphasis on the design of the equity allocation formula and the corresponding capital needs.

China can also cooperate with the US and existing MDBs through increasing grants and setting up trust funds. For example, China announced the set up of the first trust fund in World Bank in 2015. At the same time, the US also needs to accept the establishment of new MDBs proposed by China.

Besides that, China and US can also strengthen cooperation through the IMF, and continue to improve its share and governance structure. The US should implement the 2010 IMF reform programme about share and governance as soon as possible and reconfirm that the allocation of shares should continue to transfer to the dynamic emerging markets and developing countries, better reflecting the relative weight of IMF member countries in the world economy. Increasing the share of the IMF for China would allow it to take on more international responsibility and obligations relative to its economic size.

Finally, China and the US can cooperate in the development financing of third parties through MDBs. For example, China and the US can finance energy sectors under the OBOR initiative by establishing a specialised multilateral energy bank. Such cooperation based on a joint investment will mobilise advantages for both China and the US respectively and ensure the sovereignty of the borrower country is respected.

Establishment of the coordinated development mechanism for MDBs
As mentioned above, the cooperation between China and the US in the development of the financial sector is to further promote cooperation between new and existing MDBs, but when this cooperation is mainly based on temporary bilateral cooperation, there is the problem of fragmentation. With an increase in the number of MDBs in the future, how to effectively promote the coordination among them remains a problem waiting to be solved.

Presently, many countries have realised the importance of strengthening the cooperation of the MDBs. On 15 November 2014 the rotating president of the G20, then Australia, and the World Bank met at a conference and discussed the strengthening of MDB cooperation. Multilateral development agencies also participated in the conference, including the African Development Bank, the Asian Development Bank, the Islamic Development Bank and the World Development Bank. The multilateral development agencies shared their problems and successes in infrastructure investment and financing. Australia has suggested that a new agency is needed to carry out the relevant procedures and standards for harmony, so as to reduce the cost of private investors and multilateral development agencies. In addition, Australia has proposed the establishment of a Global Infrastructure Hub as a platform to promote the successes of various development banks and share relevant data. The World Bank is preparing to establish a global infrastructure platform (the Global Infrastructure Facility [GIF]) and it has been widely supported by participating members. The GIF is a comprehensive platform that aims to integrate various resources, experiences and financing instruments. It has entered the stage of trial operations, and its members include not only various MDBs, but also a number of institutional investors.

In general, the international community has reached a consensus that existing multilateral development banks must coordinate development through the integration of resources, introducing private sector funds to expand the scale of investment. It is also important to improve investment efficiency, and promote the role of MDBs in global economic growth. Presently, although there have been a number of coordination platforms for MDBs, there remains a lack of specific and effective coordination mechanisms across them. For these mechanisms to play a key role in the future, they must include the US and the US must recognise all major countries. Therefore, in addition to the establishment of an MDB, China and the US can strengthen cooperation in this area.

It is important to emphasise that the role of China in this quartet of cooperation with the United States, multilateral development agencies and developing countries, needs to be expanded. There is still a lack of effective coordination mechanisms between existing international multilateral development agencies, and their coordination remains insufficient as well. As a result, it is suggested that in the US–China Strategic and Economic Dialogue there is a need to integrate multilateral development agencies in the overall coordination mechanism. This mechanism is not only aimed at strengthening the substantive cooperation of the multilateral development agencies in the world, but also at responding to the financing needs and claims of developing countries.

For the US, new institutions such as Asian investment banks and the AIIB will be included in the existing international financial system framework, to ensure that they are inclusive, foster continuous improvement and meet current and future challenges. On the other hand, the establishment of MDB coordination development mechanisms ensures that new institutions comply with the highest international governance standards, to prevent them from challenging and damaging the existing order. For China, the maintenance, further strengthening and promotion of modernisation in international financial institutions can only be beneficial.

An MDB-coordinated development mechanism can be carried out in the following ways. First, there needs to be an established sharing platform, facilitating investment and financing cooperation through a promotion of the global MDBs (including the World Bank, ADB, AIIB, NDB, EIB and so on). This can be achieved through in-depth development of cooperation in the fields of syndicated loans, mutual guarantees, co-financing and joint research.

Second, the establishment of an MDB anti-corruption and coordination mechanism. The 2014 G20 summit culminated in the adoption of an anti-corruption action plan. If China and the US can cooperate successfully and launch an MDB anti-corruption coordination mechanism, it will benefit the world.

Third, the establishment of MDB environmental standards in the field of sustainable development, where the global MDBs assume common but differentiated responsibilities, is consistent with the global development of ecological civilisation, but also helps provoke much thought from the international community on the issue of environmental standards.

Finally, the establishment of MDB lending standards, especially the public-private partnership (PPP) model in the introduction of private capital, needs to be standardised to avoid creating vicious competition between institutions.

The establishment of an MDB coordination mechanism could have two modes:

weak coordination and strong coordination. A weak coordination model would be a simple coordination mechanism; an intangible mechanism without offices. The strong coordination model would be to establish the International Development Association (IDA), which could be an entity with offices and staff. It can also be built in Hong Kong, Washington or other cities. This will further enhance the MDBs in the field of global economic governance and innovation. In fact, in the field of international economic cooperation, coordination between the MDBs and state action is not just a pressing need, but also could have a significant impact on the global economic governance. So far there is no coordination mechanism for MDBs, but if the two countries can cooperate to launch the IDA, it will contribute to the global economic governance.

China and the US in north–south cooperation

Infrastructure is characterised by positive external effects and network effects. Therefore infrastructure is to some extent a public good and this is also the case for infrastructure financing. Developed countries such as the US have the capacity and resources to provide public goods at a global level.

In order to push the global sustainable development agenda, China needs to strengthen its cooperation with developed economies, encouraging them to share their resources, experiences and knowledge with developing countries. At present there are more international platforms than ever to carry out North–South cooperation, such as through the G20, APEC or the S&ED. China can take advantage of these platforms so as to strengthen cooperation with developed countries. On the other hand, China needs to unite with international society to supervise and urge the developed countries to fulfil their promises, such as on official development assistance (ODA), debt relief and technology transfer.

South–South cooperation is a necessary and useful supplement to North–South cooperation, and also requires reinforcing. In order to support the developing countries to implement the post-2015 agenda, China has made commitments at the UN General Assembly to provide financing by establishing the South–South Climate Cooperation Fund, and will offer the development knowledge by founding an international development knowledge centre. These commitments indicate that China has taken a remarkable step in the area of South–South cooperation. For the next step, China needs to earnestly implement these commitments and ensure that all states efficiently receive the effects of such cooperation. In this regard, China would enhance the collaborations with developing and emerging economies, and assist the developing economies with working in unity and seeking mutual development. As the largest developing economy, China is responsible for negotiating with the north, shaping the international development financing system in a way that is more favourable to developing countries.

Now, China is also considering the possibility of cooperating with the US or other developed countries, so as to build a cooperative mechanism of three sides that does not only include China and a developing economy, but a third, developed party like the US, to build a new global partnership for development.

In keeping with the basic principles of doing business, this new partnership should, first of all, see all the participants benefit from a three-sided win–win–win scenario, including the partnered developed country. Only in this way can a new global partnership for development be sustainable.

The second key point is that each of the three participants' comparative advantages should be fully utilised: the comparative advantages of the US are in financing and technology and China's is in development as an emerging country, which resonates with the experiences of other developing countries and offers specific knowledge that can be both used by MDBs and applied effectively to states. Therefore, it is possible for China to promote this cooperative mechanism of three sides. It would not be confined to just the US and other MDBs, but also to other private sectors, social groups and other non-governmental organisations.

The new global partnership for development could be applied to a specific, compact model of three sides. Considering the case of AIIB, the following triangle partnership could work:

(1) official developmental assistance (ODA) by the US
(2) production capacity cooperation by China through the platform of AIIB
(3) developing countries as the recipients

The US is the largest ODA country in the world. The departments responsible for the US ODA could share project information, including their pipelines, with the AIIB, and find a third partner with vested interests. From there they could shape a package of programs to arrange ODA and development financing. The ODA in improving education, hygienic environment and peace, will definitely facilitate the development of financing from the AIIB and other MDBs, and make the latter more effective. At the same time, the effects of US ODA could be consolidated and reinforced by subsequent development financing.

Notes

1. A US statement says of UK membership in the AIIB that it is 'worried about a trend of constant accommodation' of China, in a rare public breach of the special relationship. *The Guardian*. 'US anger at Britain joining Chinese-led investment bank AIIB', 13 March 2015. http://www.theguardian.com/us-news/2015/mar/13/white-house-pointedly-asks-uk-to-use-its-voice-as-part-of-chinese-led-bank
2. Rose Garden, Remarks by President Obama and Prime Minister Abe of Japan in Joint Press Conference, the White House Office of the Press Secretary, 28 April 2015.
3. Dexter Robert, 'China's Plan to Export Pollution', *Bloomberg*, 27 November 2014, Accessed 19 May 2016 http://www.bloomberg.com/bw/articles/2014-11-27/chinas-pollution-solution-move-factories-abroad
4. Yurendra Basnett and Posh Raj Pandey, 'Industrialisation and Global Value Chain Participation: an examination of Constraints faced by the Private Sector in Nepal', *ADB Economics Working Paper Series* 410 (October 2014).
5. Chetan Bhagat, *Half Girlfriend* (Kolkata, India:Rupa Publications, 2014).

6. World Bank, World Development Indicators, World Bank online, 2012.
7. Klaus Schwab, World Economic Forum, 'Global Competitiveness Report 2014–2015',World Economic Forum, Thursday 21 August 2014.
8. United Nations, Economic and Social Commission for Asia and the Pacific, 'Enabling Environment for the Successful Integration of Small and Medium sized enterprises in Global Value Chains,' *Studies in Trade and Investment* 70 (2011).
9. Basnett and Pandey (October 2014).
10. Fu Ying, at a press conference in Beijing, as a spokeswoman at third session of the 12th National People's Congress (NPC), March 4, 2015. Source: http://lianghui.people.com.cn/2015npc/GB/394035/394252/
11. Lou Jiwei, An interview with journalists to introduce the preparation of AIIB, 20 March 2015. http://www.mof.gov.cn/zhengwuxinxi/caizhengxinwen/201503/t20150320_1205011.html
12. A currency swap agreement is a commitment between two countries to exchange the principal and interest payments of a loan in one currency for equivalent amounts, in the other currency.
13. The Federal Reserve Board of US; Bank of England; European Central Bank; Bank of Switzerland; Bank of Canada; Bank of Japan.
14. Sebastian Heilmann, et al., 'China's Shadow Foreign Policy: Parallel Structures Challenge the Established International Order', China Monitor, Mercator Institute for China Studies, Berlin, 18 November 2014. pp. 2–4.
15. 'Asia Infrastructure Bank', Legislative Council of the Hong Kong Special Administrative Region of the People's Republic of China, Accessed 16 June 2016, http://www.legco.gov.hk/research-publications/english/essentials-1415ise13-asian-infrastructure-investment-bank.htm
16. 'ADB loans US$50 million for tourism infrastructure', *Vietmaz*, 24 November 2015, Accessed 16 June 2016, https://www.vietmaz.com/2014/11/adb-loans-50m-for-tourism-infrastructure/
17. Amar Bhattacharya, Mattia Romani and Nicholas Stern, 'Infrastructure for development: meeting the challenge', Policy paper, Centre for Climate Change Economics and Policy, Grantham Research Institute on Climate Change and the Environment in collaboration with Intergovernmental Group of Twenty Four, June 2012
18. Ibid.
19. Marianne Fay et al., 'Infrastructure and Sustainable Development', in *Postcrisis Growth and Development: A Development Agenda for the G-20*, S. Fardoust, Y. Kim and C. Sepúlveda, eds., (Washington: World Bank Publications, 9 November 2010), pp. 329–382.

Top: Professors (from left) Wang Gungwu, Brantly Womack and Carlyle A. Thayer, chatting between sessions

Bottom: The Hon. Jim Sutton, CNZM, former minister of agriculture and trade negotiations, New Zealand, chairing a panel.

3. PERSPECTIVES OF ASIAN COUNTRIES (I)

The American Factor in Japan–China Relations

Akio Takahara

Professor of contemporary Chinese politics at the Graduate School of Law and Politics, the University of Tokyo, Japan

Abstract

The rise in China's military strength and its assertive actions increases the importance of the Japan–US alliance in the relationship between Japan and China. In the realm of economics, the US–Japan-led Trans-Pacific Partnership (TPP) and the China-led Silk Road initiative appear to be at loggerheads with each other. However, China is learning fast that the Asian Infrastructure Investment Bank (AIIB) must operate according to international standards to survive and thrive. For all countries in East Asia, including Japan, it is vitally important to maintain a relationship with the US and develop ties with China at the same time. Attempts at maintaining this delicate balance will continue for the foreseeable future.

Introduction

The late Shigeharu Matsumoto, journalist and founder of the International House of Japan, had an insight that the core issue in Japan–US relations was China.[1] In fact he was referring to the trilateral relationship in the 1920s. Even today, however, it is hard to deny the importance of the third country in all the bilateral relations between these three largest economies in the world.

For all the countries in East Asia, including Japan, it is important to maintain their good relationship with the US and develop ties with China at the same time. This difficult balancing act is a function of the development of Sino–American relations, which is increasingly complex as the two powers face simultaneous intensification of strategic competition and economic interdependence.

This paper will focus on Japan–China relations and analyse the American factor in it. First, I shall briefly review the bilateral relations since 2010, a year when the size of China's GDP surpassed that of Japan's and when the Chinese trawler rammed into two Japanese coastguard vessels. The political tension between Japan and China greatly intensified in 2012 when China decided to react forcefully to the decision by the Japanese government to purchase three of the Senkaku (Diaoyu) Islands in order to prevent the then Governor of Tokyo from buying them. In 2014, however, President Xi Jinping decided to meet Prime Minister Shinzō Abe and seek rapprochement. Upon analysing the factors in this policy shift, I shall discuss the US factor in the realms of security and economics.

Tension Mounts: 2010, 2012 and beyond

As China increased its national power and surpassed Japan in terms of its economic size in 2010, more Chinese seemed to adopt the view that there is no need to deal with Japan as its foreign policy is immutable from that of the US. The idea to dismiss Japan as a negligible factor in its international strategy perhaps played a role when China attacked Japan to have the government release the captain of a Chinese trawler that rammed into Japanese coastguard vessels.[2] This happened in the territorial waters around the Senkaku (Diaoyu) Islands in September 2010. In adopting economic sanctions against Japan, some argued that they would be effective because the Japanese economy is more dependent on the Chinese economy than the other way round.[3]

After the Japanese purchase of three of the five major Senkaku islands from a private landlord in September 2012, the Chinese government stepped up efforts to change the status quo by physical force and began to frequently send their patrol boats into the territorial waters.[4] This added to China's assertive actions in the South China Sea as factors in the US strengthening policy towards rebalancing Asia, and the President of the US was invited to announce the applicability of the Japan–US Security Treaty in the Senkaku (Diaoyu) Islands dispute.

There are signs that President Xi Jinping has changed his mind and his approach towards Japan since 2014. After gradually increasing the number of meetings between ministers of the two governments, Xi finally decided to meet Prime Minister Shinzō Abe on the sidelines of an APEC meeting in Beijing that November. They then met again in April 2015 at the 60th anniversary of the Bandung Conference in Indonesia, this time more amicably, with broad smiles on their faces. In May Xi Jinping spoke to a gathering of over 3000 Japanese delegates engaged in tourism, saying that, 'Through you I send my sincere greetings and good will to the Japanese public at large!'[5]

What brought about this new phase in Japan–China relations? There was no basic change of position on the Japanese side: first, any change in the status quo by physical force was unacceptable, and as long as China continued its maritime advancement Japan had no choice but to adopt some hedging measures; second, the two sides should not let the question of the Senkaku (Diaoyu) Islands and the Yasukuni Shrine disrupt the entire relationship; and third, the two powers were responsible to the region and the world for improving and developing their relations, and the leaders should meet without any conditions. In fact it was always the Japanese political heavyweights that visited China in an attempt to crack an opening in the gridlock. Such visits included those by the New Komeito Party leader Natsuo Yamaguchi in January 2013 and by the former Prime Minister Yasuo Fukuda in July 2014. Thus, this time it was primarily the Chinese side that changed its position towards the China–Japan relationship and sought for rapprochement.

Shift in China's Japan Policy, 2014

The factors in China's policy shift seem to include the following events. First, there was increased tension in the military and in security. Two air-miss incidents between Chinese and Japanese military aircraft took place consecutively in May and June 2014. Once an accident occurred, it was highly likely that the conflict would escalate badly, though Xi Jinping wanted to avoid war no less than Shinzō Abe. After Secretary of State Hillary Clinton did so during President Barak Obama's administration, Obama also stated in April 2014 that the Senkaku (Diaoyu) Islands were covered by the Japan–US Security Treaty.[6] Perhaps the PLA was reacting to that. Xi Jinping may have perceived the urgent need to resume political contact at the top level to create a favourable atmosphere so that the authorities could negotiate and operationalise mechanisms for maritime and airborne communication and crisis management.

Second, economic slowdown became a source of increasing concern for CCP leadership. In addition to the serious fiscal debt that had emerged in many localities, what was worrisome was the impact of the slowdown on social stability. According to the Institute of Sociology at the Chinese Academy of Social Sciences, there was a resurgence of social contradictions in 2014 and hot incidents of social contradiction/conflict that attracted nationwide attention, amounting to around 400 cases.[7] Specifically, there was a large increase in labour strife. The Chinese leadership eventually recognised that political confrontation with Japan was affecting the economic aspect of their relationship. The amount of Japanese investment in China from January–September 2014 decreased by 42.9% compared to the previous year.[8] In September commerce minister Gao Hucheng told a high-level economic delegation from Japan in September that cooling in politics leading to a downturn in economics was something they did not want to see.[9] China has been acting pragmatically in attempting to secure economic benefits, and did not discontinue talks over the Japan–China–South Korea trilateral free trade agreement (FTA) even when it refused all ministerial-level contact with Japan. The Japanese strategy has been to conclude the TPP deal with the US and other countries first, so they would be in a better position to negotiate for a high-standard FTA with East Asia.

Third, on a global level, China found it increasingly difficult to promote a new type of major-power relations with the US. This was because strategic competition with the US was intensifying, due to rows over cybersecurity and China's continuous maritime advancement and their different interpretation of the legality of military action in the exclusive economic zones, among other factors. There was also recognition in Beijing that hardline policy against neighbours including Japan, the Philippines and Vietnam had not benefited China, but rather it had promoted a united front against China in international forums such as the ASEAN Regional Forum or the Shangri-La Dialogue. These contributed to China's emphasis on its Silk Road initiative and neighbourhood diplomacy, resulting in a 'rebalance' with Japan.

Finally, in terms of domestic politics, rapprochement with Japan proceeded while Xi Jinping consolidated his power base by making significant progress in his anti-corruption campaign. That is, at the end of June 2014, he expelled Xu Caihou, the former vice chairman of the Central Military Commission (CMC) from the Party, and a month later he formally announced that Zhou Yongkang, a former member of the Politburo Standing Committee was under investigation. Zhou was eventually expelled from the CCP in early December. It was widely rumoured that Xu and Zhou supported Bo Xilai, the disgraced former party secretary of Chongqing, in his struggle for power and challenge to Xi Jinping. Because patriotic education was reinforced in the 1990s, and especially as a result of the fierce anti-Japanese propaganda campaign launched after the Japanese government purchased the Senkaku (Diaoyu) Islands in September 2012, there is now a social atmosphere in which it is politically incorrect to show understanding towards Japan. However, with established power and authority, Xi was able to adopt a friendly policy towards Japan without much fear of being criticised as a weak leader.

Another aspect of Chinese domestic politics relates to the possibility of social instability that I mentioned as a result of the economic slowdown. Of course, if social and party unity is seriously disturbed, the CCP leadership could be tempted to reverse their direction and start stirring up nationalistic sentiments as they did in 2012. Unless the situation deteriorates to that level, however, the leadership would rather strive to temper nationalism so that anti-Japanese sentiments in society would not explode and pose a threat to their rule. As the economy slows down further and political rivalry intensifies among the leaders in the months leading up to the 19th Party Congress in 2017, some observers in Japan and China share a growing concern about their possible impact on Japan–China relations.

Thus, except for China's domestic politics, we find that other factors in the rapprochement of the relationship were related to the US in one way or another. In the following section, I shall elaborate on the US factor in Japan–China relations and discuss it under two topics; namely, security and economics.

The US Factor in Security

Because of the US–Japan Security Treaty of 1952, the US is automatically involved in issues of security between Japan and China. The superpower is also an important player in regional security issues that affect both Japan and China, such as the development of nuclear weapons by North Korea and China's advancement into the South China Sea. In this chapter we shall focus mainly on the bilateral issues between Japan and China.

The conflict over the Senkaku (Diaoyu) Islands has been at the forefront of security issues between Japan and China since 2010. The Chinese blame Japan for tension in recent years, arguing that China could not avoid responding to the provocations. That is, when the Chinese trawler collided with the Japanese coastguard vessels in 2010, Japan attempted to prosecute the captain of the trawler under Japanese domestic law.[10] In 2012 the right-wing Governor of Tokyo, Shintaro Ishihara, announced that his local government would purchase the Senkaku (Diaoyu) Islands to protect them from China.[11] The central government under the premiership of Yoshihiko Noda then decided to buy them instead, which, to the Chinese, was a direct provocation and serious challenge to China's sovereignty.[12] In addition, after returning to power in late 2012, the Liberal Democratic Party government led by Shinzō Abe has adopted new defence policies that expand the activities of the self-defence forces. Thus the Chinese side argues that Japan has changed and become more assertive, and China has responded to this with fortitude.

However, the picture looks very different from the Japanese perspective. Incidents in 2010 and 2012 are merely a part of a trend in China's maritime advancement. For example, in 1992 China promulgated the Law of the Territorial Sea and the Contiguous Zone, which included the name 'Diaoyudao' (another name for the Senkaku Islands), and this meant that China had breached their promise and started to touch on the question of Senkaku (Diaoyu) Islands.[13]

In 1996 a Chinese research vessel intruded Japanese territorial waters for the first time. In 2001 the two governments reached an agreement on mutual notification of their research vessels sailing to designated areas, but the Chinese side has since often breached the agreement. In 2003 the China Federation for Defending the Diaoyu Islands was set up on the 110th anniversary of Mao Zedong's birth, and in 2004 its activists forcefully landed on Uotsuri-jima, the largest of the Senkaku (Diaoyu) Islands. It was also that year that a Chinese nuclear submarine unlawfully entered Japanese territorial waters without surfacing. In 2006 China's State Oceanic Administration introduced a system for regular patrols in 'China's territory' in the East China Sea. In 2008 Chinese patrol boats intruded into Japanese territorial waters for the first time with the aim to claim sovereignty, and in 2010 they stepped up their activities following the trawler collision incident. Thus, the Japanese argue that China has changed and become more assertive, trying to change the status quo by physical force, and that Japan has responded to hedge any risks.

In hedging risks, a central measure for Japan has been to strengthen its alliance with the US. In the context of intensified strategic competition between the US and China, leaders in Washington have clearly stated that the US–Japan Security Treaty will apply to the Senkaku (Diaoyu) Islands. Although the provocative intrusion of Chinese patrol boats into territorial waters continues, the Japanese side appreciates that such US commitment has deterred the Chinese from taking further adventurous actions. The major purpose of the new security legislations that passed the Japanese Diet in September 2015 is to reinforce the alliance with the US. However, the legislations impose tight restrictions on the use of force. Because of the constitution and pacifist public opinion, Japan will not be a 'normal state' that wields its military power without constraint for the foreseeable future.

The US Factor in Economics

In the Chinese market, Japanese and US firms are competitors with each other. However, both countries, perhaps together with all the other countries, have common interests in promoting marketisation, transparency and fair treatment of foreign companies in China. One way of achieving these shared goals would be to negotiate and conclude FTAs or economic partnership agreements (EPAs). It has long been the wish of many big Japanese businesses to have an FTA with China in a bilateral, plurilateral or multilateral framework.[14]

However, the negotiations are stalled for the Japan–China–South Korea trilateral FTA or a regional comprehensive economic partnership (RCEP) that involves East Asia and India. When East Asian regionalism culminated in the establishment of the East Asia Summit in 2005, the US held grave concerns that they might be excluded from the dynamic of development in Asia. That anxiety was revived momentarily when the new Democratic Party of Japan prime minister, Yukio Hatoyama, advocated the East Asian community and pronounced that Japan had been inclined to be overly dependent on the US.[15] In 2010 however, it was Southeast Asia that became worried about China's active advancement into the South China Sea, and extended an invitation to the US to join the East Asia Summit.[16]

That was the year when the US and Australia joined the TPP. Japan joined in 2013, hoping that it would promote much-needed structural reforms in its economy and also that it would set a high standard for regional FTAs that were in the process of negotiation. Japan hopes the agreement on the TPP in October 2015 will provide them with an advantage in the negotiations and an impetus to facilitate Japan–China–South Korea trilateral and RCEP agreements, which both include China as an important partner.

Some Japanese see the TPP as an important pillar in the US rebalancing of Asia. However, it should not be seen as a fortress that excludes and encircles China. Rather, it is the framework for a rule-based community, in which China would be much welcomed as a partner and contributor to our common regional interests.

Concluding Remarks

In viewing Japan–China relations from the Japanese perspective, we find the US factor increasing in importance along with the rise in China's national power. This is rather obvious in the realm of security: Japan needs to take hedging measures and reinforce its alliance with the US in the face of China's intensifying maritime advancement. In the economic realm, the US–Japan-led TPP should provide a regional framework in which rules and norms constitute the reliable basis for economic exchange.

What is important to note is the fact that the US factor in Japan–China relations is not necessarily confrontational in character. This is related to the next two final important points to note. First, many of the issues that Japan faces in dealing with its neighbour are related to power-based and not rule-based approaches taken by China in solving many international issues. But there are internationalists and a development of epistemic communities that involve enlightened Chinese experts dealing with many common issues. In China, contradictory things often happen at the same time: in this case there is growth in open-minded internationalism as well as exclusive nationalism. We should engage in public diplomacy and do our best to support the former, while be very careful and critical about the latter. As a third party, for example, US scholars can take part in Japan–China joint history studies and relativise the viewpoints of the two parties.

And second, although the role played by the US in Japan–China relations is by far larger than the role of other countries, other smaller countries of East Asia are also very important, especially for Japan. This is because Japan, ASEAN nations and the Republic of Korea are all in the same boat that is sandwiched by the sole superpower and the sole superpower candidate. For these countries, there is no other way than to seek for coexistence with the US and China. Actually it is the same for the two powers as well. Xi Jinping is correct when he says that we are a community that share one destiny. Perhaps angry waves lie ahead, but the socio-economic trend indicates that this community eventually will extend to the other side of the Pacific.

Notes

1. Shigeharu Matsumoto, Shanhai Jidai (Days in Shanghai), *Chūōkōron*, 1974.
2. See the video of the collision taken by the Japanese coastguards: http://www.youtube.com/watch?v=sVVM2AmvD5U.
3. For a discussion on the 2010 trawler collision incident, see Akio Takahara, 'The Senkaku Trawler Collision Incident, September 2010', collected in Akikazu Hashimoto, Mike Mochizuki and Kurayoshi Takara, eds., *The Okinawa Question vol 3: Futenma, the US–Japan Alliance, and Regional Security*, (Sigur Center for Asian Studies, 2013), pp. 91–102.
4. On the purchase and China's reaction, see Akio Takahara, 'The Development of Japan–China Relations in the Period of Stability in Cross-Strait Relations', *The Journal of Contemporary China Studies* 4:2 (2015), pp. 119–143.
5. Xi Jinping, 'Zai ZhongRi Youhao Jiaoliu Dahui Shang de Jianghua' (Speech at the Sino-Japanese Friendship Exchange Convention), http://news.xinhuanet.com/politics/2015-05/23/c_1115384379.htm.

6. Mizuho Aoki, 'Obama assures Abe on Sekakus', *Japan Times*, 24 April 2014. http://www.japantimes.co.jp/news/2014/04/24/national/obama-tells-abe-security-treaty-covers-senkakus/#.V1bViuRztOZ.
7. Li Peilin et al., eds., Shehui Lanpi Shu 2015nian Zhongguo Shehui Xingshi Fenxi yu Yuce (Blue Book of Chinese Society Society of China Analysis and Forecast 2015), Social Sciences Academic Press (China), 2014, p.13.
8. Statistics of direct foreign investment in China are available on the Chinese Ministry of Commerce Website 'Invest in China', http://english.mofcom.gov.cn
9. '"Concerns about the direct investment decrease of Japan", Chinese Commerce Minister is meeting with business executives', *Reuters*, 9 May 2014. http://jp.reuters.com/article/china-japan-idJPKCN0HI1OF20140923.
10. See footnote 3.
11. The video footage of the speech can be seen at the following website: http://www.heritage.org/events/2012/04/shintaro-ishihara. He implies the central government is not doing enough to defend the islands.
12. In fact, there were not only hardline views but also moderate ones in China. Just before the Chinese leadership decided to embark on a series of harsh countermeasures against the purchase of the Senkaku (Diaoyu) Islands by the Japanese government, one general of the PLA had an interview with China's official media and stated that in Beijing there were two divergent interpretations of the purchase. On the one hand there were those who argued that this was a provocation and challenge to China; on the other hand, others argued that this was a measure to quell the situation by preventing the right-wing Governor of Tokyo from purchasing the islands, and that he was inclined towards the latter view. ('Zhu Chenghu: Japanese Government's Nationalisation of Diaoyudao May be For Calming Down the Disturbance' (in Chinese), http://bbs1.people.com.cn/post/7/0/0/122254985.html. This article was originally posted on 5 September 2012 on the Military channel of the *People's Daily Online*.)
13. For further information on the drafting of this law, see the reference in footnote 3.
14. As early as 2004, for example, a survey conducted by the *Nihon Keizai Shimbun* indicated that 70% of Japanese business leaders wanted a trilateral free trade agreement with China and South Korea (*Nihon Keizai Shimbun*, 24 March 2004).
15. His remarks at the Japan–China–Republic of Korea trilateral summit meeting, 10 October 2009 (*Nihon Keizai Shimbun*, 3 January 2010).
16. See the chairman's statement of the East Asia Summit Foreign Ministers Informal Consultations, Ha Noi, 21 July 2010, in which the process of the invitation is described http://asean.org/?static_post=chairman-s-statement-of-the-east-asia-summit-foreign-ministers-informal-consultations-ha-noi-21-july-2010.

Top: Professor the Hon. Bob Carr, Australia, chairing a panel.

Bottom: Professor Jaewoo Choo, Kyung Hee University, South Korea, listening to a presentation.

What does the US–China Relationship Present to South Korea?

Jaewoo Choo

Professor of Chinese Foreign Policy in the Department of Chinese Studies at Kyung Hee University, South Korea

Abstract

The US and China are obviously playing with what their peripheral states consider 'unfinished business' from the 1950s. The US failed to build an intra-alliance system between its allies in East Asia earlier, only to learn a much-valued lesson now. That is, that a more flexible military in Japan is a critical requisite to the success of US–East Asia relations because the US wants Japan and Australia to anchor the intra-alliance system. China's so-called New Asian Security Concept (NASC) is derived from Mao Zedong's strategic thinking that Asia's matters should be left for Asian peoples with the implication that China could help other regional players to meet this end should they need help, not dissimilar to the Nixon Doctrine. How will the contrasting strategies pursued by the two regional giants play out? Diplomatic gambit will be well underway sooner than expected. As one of the most highly dependent states on both countries, a South Korean perspective on the strategic implications of this diplomatic gambit will be shared on this occasion.

Introduction

The recent strategic behaviour by the US and China in East Asia has been contrary to their much-heralded diplomatic rhetoric. That is, the two countries want to rely on dialogue, cooperation and engagement in pursuit of constructive partnership for the years ahead.[1] Since 2010 however, the signs of a downward spiral have been more vivid across a wide spectrum of the bilateral relationship, from territorial dispute issues to climate change negotiation, the construct of regional financial institutions and regional free trade areas. Beijing and Washington seem unable to put themselves on the same starting line for negotiation. Where did it all begin? Why can't they be on the same page when dealing with common issue? Is it simply because of the mutual mistrust built up over the years? Where did these seeds of mistrust originate?

Instead of dissecting the mistrust embedded in the bilateral relationship, this article argues that the root cause of their contradictory behaviour to rhetoric lies in the different goals they hold for each other. These different goals are not necessarily shaped by differences in their perception of each other; it is largely because their perception to one another is built on the same ground. Both Washington and Beijing acknowledge each other as a great power; the US has, since the foundation of People's Republic of China (PRC), recognised China both as a regional power and an expansionist state, and the PRC recognises the US as a hegemonic power and an expansionist (imperial) state. Such mutual perception has converged only to deny any room for disagreement or even misperception. On this perceptional premise, this article assumes that it is more of a national goal that sets them apart at the start of their relationship than the ideological differences which many would like to attribute to them, as when explaining Cold War international relations.

Foreign behaviour of great powers like the US and China is driven by national goals, and great-power politics follows accordingly. Their foreign policy aims to achieve national goals set by the forefathers of their respective nations. Since their national goals are founded on their forefathers' conceptions of the state's geographical and materialistic standing in the world and its surrounding nature, the goals will be inherited by their successors indefinitely until they are realised. In this vein, foreign policy and behaviour of great powers is principled, guided and dictated by a realist school of thought. Ideology has little room for justification and rationalisation.[2] Institutionalism and functionalism are often utilised as a means of justification if and when realism's extreme mode of behaviour—unilateralism or exceptionalism—is left unchecked by their domestic and/or foreign constraints.

It all started out in the 1950s. For China, it was with its foundation in 1949. National goals set by Mao Zedong are still upheld. Domestically, they are to build a nation-state that is sound in economy for all the proletariat, and to achieve prosperity to enable China and its people to recover its pride and self-esteem. Externally, they are to preserve the nation's sovereignty and independence, and to create an international environment conducive to its domestic national goals and interests. As for the US, their goals were set out following the Korean War of 1950–1953. The primary goal since its rise to hegemonic stature following World War II and in the aftermath of the Korean War has remained unchanged: domestically, fostering bipartisan support for the spreading of US values (democracy, freedom, liberty and a free market economy); and externally, preserving US interests that conform to its values.

Given the respective goals of the two great powers based on their own convictions and beliefs, their behaviour can only vary in the pursuit of their respective national interests and therefore in the conduct of their foreign policies. If such behaviour, accorded with their own goals and therefore strategies, continue to prevail, constructive development in the bilateral relationship will be a foregone conclusion. Without conceding to each other, at least at the regional level, realism will remain a ideology behind the power politics between the US and China, and give rise to security dilemmas for themselves, alliance dilemmas to allies and dilemmas of strategic choice to other states.

From this perspective, this article will first examine the goals of the US in pursuit of its rebalancing strategy. Then it will argue how persistent and consistent China has been with its strategic goal of displacing US alliances in the region. To substantiate this argument from a realist perspective, the article utilises China's argument on the South Korea–US alliance over the years and will make a case from China's stance on the so-called 'peace treaty' for the Korean peninsula. The next section will present a comparative study of visions of future regional order by two regional powers, based on empirical studies of regional policy announced in recent years. It will then conclude with some thoughts as to what needs to be taken for consideration for future academic studies on this particular question.

US Goals in East Asia and the Truth about the 'Rebalancing Strategy'

When one is confronted with the question of the true intentions of the US and the goals behind its rebalancing strategy in East Asia, one cannot but ask why the US is so obsessed with such a strategy, let alone East Asia? Why is it that the US does not concede that non-political means can help it achieve and secure the goals laid out in its rebalancing strategy? Why does it have to first rely on political and military measures before economic and non-political ones? Why does the US seem to give prioritise the strengthening of the alliance over economically integrating the and thereby institutionalising regionalism under its leadership?

The US has, since the end of the World War II, been obsessed with establishing its primacy in three regions—Asia, Europe and Oceania. Although it has risen to invincible superpower status, two obstructing states have emerged. One was the Soviet Union in Europe and the other is China in Asia. Both were perceived as expansionist states that were willing to challenge US supremacy and leadership in the regions under their influence. Both communist regimes proactively pursued expansionist policies under communist internationalism and the liberation of nations under imperialism. Their anti-imperialist activities with expansionist motives were major threats to US strategic interests in the regions. America's strategic interests not only included the wellbeing of the regional states that wanted to embrace US values but also were peace and stability in the regions. The US was therefore compelled to act as a deterrent against anti-imperialist insurgencies and the expansion of communism.

The new predicaments raised by the growth of communism and international liberation movements led by the Soviet Union and China consequently led the US to adopt a policy of containment against the spread of communism. As geographically apart as the US is from these two regions, its containment strategy was to structure the regional balance of power by redistributing material power though alliances. The tactical means employed were military alliances formed by ratifying defence treaties, and economic assistance to facilitate their material power and thereby redistribute the balance to favour its allies.[3]

The end of the Cold War, coupled with normalisation of its relationship with China a decade before, has added a new dimension to US containment policy: engagement. In the age of information, technology and globalisation, no one country can survive in isolation and international issues cannot be solved without cooperation from others, especially those of great-power status. Global issues are now transnational in nature and multiplex in character. Hence, the economic cost of solving such global and regional challenges is too overwhelming for one state to bear alone. Furthermore, deepening interdependence and the subsequent process of globalisation have also undermined the role of ideology in the pursuit of relationships with ideologically different countries.

However paradoxical it may sound, US containment policy against China was simultaneously accompanied by policy of engagement.[4] Such a shift in the orientation of policy towards China reveals that US interests in China are now beyond political and military ones. Economic and related interests need to be protected by peaceful measures and this is now perceived to be though engagement. Engagement is expected to effectively safeguard the US non-political and non-military interests in China on the premise of its full embrace and effective practice of norms, rules and institutions fundamentally founded on Western values and a free market economy.[5]

The new policy strategy, however, has not altered the US original national goal to contain China. Given the US definition of China as an expansionist state and its geopolitical disadvantage of the absence of its physical presence in East Asia, the US adamantly upholds its national goal against China that was set out at the start of the Cold War and now requires greater commitment as a result of China's rise. The reasons behind US goals have not changed, either. They are: to secure US regional interests; to preserve the regional order and US leadership; to maintain open and free sea lanes of communication; and to protect the security of allies that are vulnerable to Chinese influence due to their relatively smaller power status.[6]

The strategic orientation and approach of the US towards China remains unchanged. Defending US national goals against China requires material power and a system that can articulate the merits of the US and the needs of its allies. The system is what is now known as a 'hub-and-spoke' alliance. However, because of vastness of East Asia's waters and land, such a structure has long been regarded as insufficient and ineffective, with too many gateways open to Chinese expansion. Hence, the US first successfully concluded a series of bilateral security alliance treaties with Taiwan and the Philippines in 1951, Japan in 1952 and South Korea in 1953.

The US once attempted to build a collective security system or intra-alliance system based on the 'hub-and-spoke' structure. In 1955 the first kind of collective security system was introduced to East Asia in the form of SEATO (the Southeast

Asia Treaty Organisation), signing the treaty in 1954. Also in 1954, the US articulated another collective security arrangement with the UK at the core, as well as Australia, New Zealand, the Philippines and Thailand. Washington wanted to connect SEATO to ANZUS (the Australia–New Zealand–US alliance, founded in 1951) and essentially tried to cover the vast water areas of East Asia. SEATO was dissolved in 1977 largely because member states lost interest and withdrew themselves after they each normalised relations with China.

The US rebalancing strategy is an emulation of past strategy and approach but with rhetorical emphasis on a different foundation for collective alliance aspiration. That is, multilateralism. In 2009 when 'Pivot to Asia' defined the core strategies and principles of US policy towards Asia, multilateralism was proclaimed the foundation of the policy. It recognised the value of relationships with partner states as well as the emerging powers in the region—China, Russia and India.[7] It alluded to a fundamental change in the paradigm of US Asia policy. However, the core of the policy, if analysed carefully, was not a complete detachment from bilateralism and a bilateral alliance system. Instead, bilateralism and a bilateral alliance system was given much greater value to US strategy in Asia, while multilateralism was emphatically defined as complementary, auxiliary and only in support of bilateralism.[8]

The US has undertaken an approach to, first, strengthen bilateral alliances as the in Asia; second, to build an intra-alliance system whereby all its alliances will be connected to each other, with the US as the pivot; and third, to expand to a multilateralism in which only those sharing values with the US will be included, as in the TPP.

Empirical arguments for strengthening bilateral alliances are discussed below in detail. Since 2010 the US has been moving forwards in its efforts to build an intra-alliance system with all its allies, with much success in some states, but little with South Korea.[9] The Trilateral Strategic Dialogue (TSD) that was designed to reconnect Japan and Australia was launched in 2002. At the start, the dialogue was convened at a senior-official level but in 2005 it was upgraded to ministerial level. The US' stated purpose was for allies to help facilitate the evolution of US global strategy, fighting against wars on terrorism and nuclear proliferation. Soon after that, the US was able to rally states in setting up the Quadrilateral Security Dialogue (QSD) in 2007, adding a member from India to the original members of TSD. The dialogue was matched by a series of joint military exercises, known as Exercise Malabar, at an unprecedented scale. Both endeavours were interpreted as a response that aimed at countering increased Chinese economic and military power in the Asia-Pacfic.

The endeavours were credited to former Japanese Prime Minister Shinzō Abe during his first stint as prime minister in 2006. The defence arrangement to incorporate the US, Japan, Australia and India was based on the Japanese notion of an 'arc of freedom and prosperity' and was first introduced in a speech by Abe's cabinet member Taro Aso in 2006.[10] The QSD would further envision the arc of Asia stretching from Mongolia, the Korean peninsula to other Southeast Asian states;

virtually all of China's peripheral states but China itself. The idea was not without criticism from the US audience, such as that from former US State Department Officer Morton Abramowitz, who defined it as 'an anti-China move.'[11] Proponents of the idea called it a 'democratic challenge' to the projected Asia-Pacific century, which must be realised in coordination with the US leadership. Others like Daniel Twining of the Center for a New American Security (CNAS) see it as eventually having a dual outcome: an Asian version of NATO based on democratic values of military coalition could either lead to eventual military conflict with China, or succeed in laying an enduring foundation for peace by converting China into a democratic leader in Asia through the means of 'peaceful evolution'.[12]

On the multilateralism front, the US has clearly defined eligibility requirements for potential member candidates. Eligibility is exclusively granted on full acceptance of US values. That is, democracy, liberty, freedom and a free market economy. Thus, in most of the multilateral arrangements that are currently being pursued and promoted by the US, those with differing values are not included, and they include Russia and China. The TPP is one salient example.

Continuity in China's Obsession with a US Alliance System and Long-Term Goal

Since the foundation of the PRC in 1949, one predominant diplomatic theme has dictated its relationship with the US. That is, to overcome US containment policy. Simultaneously, the US seems to have only one goal in its China policy: to effectively contain China and keep its influence under control. Against this background, China's overall strategic goal of the post-Korean War period was to 'thwart any marked extension of hostile power in the immediate vicinity of China by diplomatic means.'[13] China's aspiration for such a peripheral environment was manifested by its diplomatic efforts in promoting 'neutralism' in Asia and building 'zones of peace' around the region. Since then, China has long upheld one implicit goal in its peripheral security policy: to expel foreign influence in Asia. This dream of ridding all foreign influence is evidenced China's persistent advocacy of the same idea across generations of leaders.

China's strategic goal of expelling all foreign influence in Asia continues to live on in today's China. It is proved to have remained in the strategic thinking of Chinese leadership, as demonstrated in recent introduction of Chinese President Xi Jinping's 'New Asian Security Concept' in 2014.[14] The whole idea of the concept may sound as fresh and new, however, it is not. It existed in the Mao's era and was emphasised on numerous occasions by then Premier Zhou. What it all points to is that China has never given up on the idea of realising a foreign influence-free Asia, and this is the foundation of the regional order it envisions in the 21st century.

On 28 June 1950, at the advent of a US-led intervention in the Korean War and the deployment of the 7th Fleet in to the Taiwan Strait, Mao Zedong issued a statement that for the first time publicly declared the idea that 'Asian people must handle their own affairs and not . . . the US'.[15] It was later reiterated by Premier Zhou Enlai on numerous occasions. One of the most prominent declarations was delivered at the opening session of the Geneva Conference on 26 April 1954. Premier Zhou defined the US as an aggressor and demanded it, with other Western powers, exclude itself from far-Eastern affairs. It was then when he also introduced to the world Mao's notion that 'the countries of Asia should consult among themselves . . . seeking common measures to safeguard peace and security in Asia.'[16]

To achieve this end, China has persistently relied not only on bilateral ties but also a multilateral approach. At the bilateral level, China has demonstrated persistent efforts in conveying and persuading its idea of how Asia should be free of foreign influence, and in today's terms, it may be best described as a displacement of the US alliance system. China's distaste for alliances in the region has long remained. During the Cold War, Mao saw it as a source of divides, confrontations, conflicts, instability and war. In the post-Cold War period, Xi and other leaders also share the same perception in that it is a product of Cold War mentality that can be defined by Mao's words.

On the multilateral front, China has been persistent in seeking the foundation of a multilateral arrangement that excludes the US, as was the case with Asian–African Conference in 1954 and its attempt with the East Asian Summit in 2005. Both arrangements wanted to exclude the West as much as possible. China's failure to sustain these efforts can only be attributed to its insufficient power, which is critical in engendering leadership requisite to the institutionalisation of these arrangements. From this perspective, the Chinese dream is a necessary evil to achieve. It is a national goal that can facilitate China's long-held vision of regional order.

As early as the 1950s, Mao set out a goal to recover China's status as a global and major power, recover its self-esteem and reattain its status and rise again as a major power. This goal is now being reintroduced by Xi in the concept of 'China Dream'. It is, in short, to revive China, reassert China's rights and reinvigorate China's pride, thereby achieving the level of power and influence that is sufficient to achieve the so-called 'Community of Common Destiny'.[17] China's search for a multilateral institution in Asia that can displace the Western alliance system seems to stipulate one condition and that is to be of only Asian origin. It is under this precondition that China may only be willing to found an institution that might be more effective than those based on so-called 'open regionalism' or institutionalisation of the 'ASEAN Way'. It is largely because China wants to use the institution as a springboard that will enhance its presence in the region and China's status as a regional and emerging power.

Against this background, China obviously has much skepticism and criticism towards the US' return to Asia policy. Many in China have substantiated such ill-feelings and ill-attitudes towards it, as they widely perceive it as a policy with potential for conflict with China's strategic interests in the region. It is partly because its underlying effort is to contain China.[18] There is a wide consensus in China that President Obama is geopolitically more attached to the region than his predecessor was.[19] China's concerns were reinforced by US Secretary of State Hillary Clinton's address in July 2010 at ASEAN's 17th meeting of foreign ministers in Hanoi. She reiterated the US' trans-Pacific status and emphasised the value of its partnership with ASEAN member states.[20] She took the opportunity to make known the US position on rights to free navigation in the South China Sea while being explicit about its opposition to the use or threat of force by any claimants on disputed territories in the region.[21] Her remarks did not go without contention from the Chinese counterpart at the meeting. Chinese Foreign Minister Yang Jiechi criticised them as ill-intentioned; internationalising what was already a resolved issue.[22] Since China claims sovereignty rights to the entire South China Sea, it naturally sees the US as being strategic with its approach to China–ASEAN relations and desiring to be the interlocutor to potential maritime rivalry in the region.[23]

Prior to the meeting, the US' position was defined by a series of national strategic publications, starting with the Quadrennial Defense Review report (QDR) published 1 February 2010, followed by Nuclear Posture Review report (NPR) on 6 April and the National Security Strategy (NSS) on 27 May. These reports all emphasise a fundamental shift from unilateralism to bilateralism with importance on multilateral engagement, maintaining 'strategic ambiguity' by broadening the scope and type of traditional threats, avoiding unnecessary conflict with enemy states, and the regaining of leadership.[24] On the China front, however, they all share a propensity to define China as a double-edged sword; while cooperation with China is highly valued, however, it is perceived also as a potential threat to US interests because of its clandestine defence spending and the offensiveness of its military development programmes.[25] Consequently, the publications laid grounds for China to misconstrue US intentions and goals with its own interpretation.

The intentions of the US strategy reflected in these reports are not taken at face value. They are perceived to aim at curbing China's influence through the reinforcement of military and security cooperation with its allies in Asia. Furthermore, China explicitly related the QDR's ill intent as an offence to sovereignty; its 'analysis of China's military modernisation and transparency problems are a direct interference in domestic affairs of China.'[26] Some Chinese observers went a step further in criticising the QDR's intentions as hypocritical on the notion of embracing new partners and multilateralism. Although the US is 'ostensibly embracing new emerging powers such as China and India,' they argue, 'its underlying intention is to unite with India and contain China.' The observers also construed the US' intentions behind pursuit of enhanced cooperative relations with the regional states as such.[27] Moreover, they challenged the NPR for being self-centric: 'While there is a shift in US policy of prohibiting offensive use of nuclear weapons in armed confrontation, it fails to address prohibition of the use *per se*. Since the Nuclear Summit is scheduled to convene next year, the release of NPR is designed to only serve enhancement of US leadership at the Nuclear Security Summit.'[28]

China's smoldering discontent with the NSS is in line with their feelings towards the QDR. Beijing claims that the US' China policy is characterised by a 'hedging strategy between engagement and containment'.[29] Former Chinese ambassador to the United Arab Emirates and Jordan, Liu Baocai, also articulated Beijing's view that

> US leadership in Asia is connected by bilateral alliances (e.g. US–Japan and US–South Korea alliances) and multilateral alliances (e.g. US–Japan–Australia–Philippines–Thailand and US–Japan–Australia–India alliances), along with emphasised cooperation with ASEAN and Vietnam. It heightens the prospect for the foundation of an eastern model of NATO, designed to deter China's geopolitical and economic expansion.[30]

Furthermore, Beijing is getting more obsessed with the possibility of South Korea being incorporated into the US–Japan alliance. From Beijing's perspective, what all these strategic reports have in common is US goodwill tainted in hypocrisy. Although the US official stance is to accommodate China through cooperation, it will strive to secure its vital interests in Asia through containment of China.[31]

Chinese Discourse on the Withdrawal of the United States Forces Korea

To Chinese experts, the issues surrounding the United States Forces Korea (USFK) include the disestablishment of the United Nations Command, the role of the South Korea–US alliance, the scope of US–Japan cooperation, the diplomatic relationship with the North Korea, and the maintaining the trilateral alliance of South Korea–US–Japan.[32] These issues will be heavily subject to the outcomes of the US–North Korea relationship: if there is a drastic improvement in the bilateral relationship, the prospect for these issues becoming reality will greatly diminish. To establish this prerequisite to solve other issues that are concerning China, the Chinese government has constantly emphasised that all concerned parties should have mutual respect and work in cooperation. However, as there are huge interpretative gaps between the US, China and North Korea on the role of USFK, mutual understanding is difficult to be achieve, as witnessed in the series of northeast Asian multilateral discussions and cooperative ventures towards bringing peace to the Korean peninsula.

The US wishes to establish peace while maintaining the foundation of the South Korea–US alliance following unification. To Washington, the question is not about whether to maintain its forces in a unified Korea but rather 'the form it takes'.[33] To Beijing, regardless of the form, the presence of the alliance itself is nothing more than the continuation of the Cold War-era strategy of exploiting the third world.[34] It could ultimately dismiss the whole idea of a peace treaty and system, which everybody has assumed to be the perfect foundation to replace the alliance, even after the unification.[5] The solution should be that every actor involved in this issue should be able to establish a peaceful and cooperative bilateral relationship while not being hostile to the third nation. To this end, it has been emphasised that respective relationships of the US, Japan and South Korea with those other regional states outside of the alliance should be strengthened in order to realise a peace system based on peace treaty.[36]

Chinese experts have explained the biggest obstacles to a working peace treaty and system are the following. First of all, each side has a different understanding of what a peace treaty and system are. As nations are interpreting this based on their geological location, capability and strategic objectives, the basis of their stances are inevitable. Especially when it comes down to the opposing interests of the US and North Korea, the differences in their strategic interests will be the biggest obstacle for both sides.[37] The strategic confrontation between the US and North Korea has made this even more difficult to be achieved. According to the understanding of a Chinese analyst, the principal stance of the US is that it will only be able to agree to the treaty when North Korea surrenders its nuclear ambition.[38] In conclusion, this directly opposes the stance coming from North Korea.

Second, the instability of the inter-Korean relationship and its development is also a serious challenge. As North Korea takes the paradoxical stances of wishing to maintain the regime while also demanding guaranteed stability; allowing civilian interaction while refraining from government-to-government dialogue; and demanding economic support while evading political discussion, cooperation is far from being achieved.[39] The third factor working as a restraint is the condition to establish a peace system. North Korea is simultaneously demanding a peace treaty with the US to establish a legal framework and the withdrawal of the United Nations Command (UNC). All the arguments and demands coming from North Korea end up targeting the withdrawal of the USFK. Although the Chinese government understands such a stance coming from the North Korea, they also understand that it is a difficult short-term goal considering the long-term strategic implication for the US. Yet, Chinese experts hope the USFK will stay in the Korean peninsula rather than expanding as far as to Taiwan.[40]

Even so, Chinese experts acknowledge the fact that the UN does not legally bind the USFK to the UNC, although they were initially deployed upon UN intervention. Instead, they are focusing on the fact that US forces in Korea are the result of a South Korea–US alliance treaty, and claim that the concerned parties need in-depth discussion of the USFK, which is directly targeting North Korea, in order to discuss issues related to the peace treaty. For instance, if both Koreas agree to allow the USFK to remain on the peninsula, the Chinese argue the role and the status of US forces will have to be redefined. The first issue to be solved is the fact that the US forces in Korea use the title of the UN, even today.

The legal status of the forces staying within the Korean peninsula, including US forces and other foreign forces under the title of the UNC, is no longer valid, as all the titles that the UN used during the Korean War have lost their legal status.[41] Hence, according to the Chinese and North Koreans, the legal status of the USFK is claimed to have already been lost. Chinese experts further argue that such a claim was attested when South Korea's progressive governments, under the leadership of

Kim Dae-Jung and Roh Moo-Hyun had constantly demanded the US to negotiate for a possible change in role and status of the USFK following the changes in US global strategy.[42]

Chinese believe that although the gap between the interests of Korean government and the US government has been reduced with the Lee Myong-Bak administration (2008–12), this is still an issue for further discussion if a peace system based on a peace treaty were to be founded in the future.

Last, the North Korean stance is crucial when it comes to the continued deployment and the complete withdrawal of the USFK. From the point of view of a Chinese analyst, the North Koreans claim that it is legally justifiable for them to demand withdrawal of the US forces to achieve permanent peace in the peninsula under a new security relationship.[43] Resolving debate on the USFK will not only be crucial to establishing and ensuring security for North Korea, but also important to adjusting the function and role of the USFK under a new security structure. It also means that a new legal framework should work as the guiding principle for the USFK to resolve the potential role of the South Korea–US alliance in the northeast Asian region by coordinating with neighbouring nations.[44]

China has a principled understanding that establishing peace in the Korean Peninsula is consistent with the interests of Han Chinese and brings regional peace, stability and development. It has also constantly claimed that, as an influential actor in northeast Asia, it supports the establishment of a peace system in the Korean. As a mediator who has participated in the signing of an armistice treaty, China wishes to take constructive, active and crucial role in the process. It wishes to replace the armistice treaty with a peace treaty and contribute to the establishment of a peace system within the Korean peninsula.[45]

China's constructive role and responsibility has its historical and geographical location as background. First, historically, the importance of the role of China has been witnessed during the Korean War, as its participation changed the course of warfare, and this made China take an active role in resolving resultant issues. Second, the peace and security concerns of the Korean Peninsula can never be separated from those of China. Under this context, signing a peace treaty for the Korean peninsula and establishing a peace system is an integral part of Chinese diplomatic strategy to influence neighbouring states to improve the security environment of China. Such benefits have made it important for China to engage and participate in this resolution.[46] Last, the establishment of a peace system in the peninsula will enable more trade to take place, with both Koreas having win–win circumstances to maximise economic benefit and contribute to the modernisation of the Chinese economy.[47]

China has shown its constructive role as a key player in the region during the North Korean nuclear crisis. China has constantly argued that it has played a pivotal role in this crisis, as it has special diplomatic relationships and uses these to justify it taking responsibility and having a constructive role in the region. Chinese analysts believe that, as China can make positive interactions with both Koreas, this position will greatly contribute to the establishment of a peace system in the Korean peninsula.[48]

China gives two North Korean nuclear crises as evidence for their successful and constructive role in the region. First of all, the assessment coming from China is that its active involvement to bring peaceful resolution has led to peaceful conclusion of the case. Although Westerners would have a different opinion on this claim, Chinese experts have praised themselves, as China has quoted from leaders Jiang Zemin and Li Peng and argued that constant demand from the Chinese government to bring peaceful resolution has made a great contribution to ending the first nuclear crisis.[49] In regards to the second nuclear crisis, China emphasised its contribution in hosting the six-party talks and tried to emphasise the expected benefits for the peace system.[50]

Different Grounds, Different Architecture

With its growing influence and power status, China has been pursuing and advocating regional multilateralism on its own terms. The combined effects have resulted in China's own vision of regional multilateral security cooperation architecture. The impetus behind China's architecture is the foundation it has built with the success of its 'good neighbour' policy.[51] The synergy of the policy, with its growing regional influence and power status, has enabled Beijing to develop and pursue an unorthodox regional multilateralism. Its theoretical foundation does not derive from a fundamental framework, i.e. multilateralism based on regionalism or multilateral cooperation. Nevertheless, the key components to China's regional multilateral security cooperation architecture are stark in contrast to the frameworks of the US and its allies, as shown in Table 11.1.

China's vision of regional multilateral security cooperation architecture significantly differs from that of the US, which gives rise to a totally different paradigm foundation. First, in terms of goals and objectives, while China strives to achieve development and create a 'harmonious world', the US aims to preserve its primacy and create a value-based system. China's vision thus projects an impression that its pursuit of multilateral security cooperation is also for the legitimacy of the CCP rule and the priority of national development. It can be externally justified as working towards sustainable development of the world, while conforming to its proclaimed role as the world's economic benefactor and growth engine. China simultaneously seems to view the future world in horizontal terms, in contrast to the hierarchical vision of the US. The defining divergence in the foundation of their envisioned paradigm for multilateral security cooperation architecture lies in the other goal that the US pursues, that is, constructing a value-based security cooperation order. It functions as the foundation which characterises the fundamentals of US architecture.

Table 11.1 China's and the US' visions of regional multilateral security cooperation architecture

	China	US
Goals	– common development – harmonious world	– preserve primacy – constructing a value-based order
Values	– peace, development, and cooperation	– democracy, freedom, and a free market economy
Mechanical principles	– respect for diversity of the international community – democracy of international relations	– shared homogenous values and ideology – unwavering commitment abide by international laws
Premises of mechanical principles	– international laws and norms – rules of international relations	– international laws and norms
Order system	multilateral, cooperative	alliance (bilateral)
Framework	open regionalism	alliance-based regionalism
Vehicle	ASEAN+3	alliance network
Center of the order	ASEAN	allies
Members	inclusive	exclusive
Degree of openness	maintain and expand open regionalism	closed and exclusiveness strong
Binding power	– loose and open regionalism – non-legally or institutionally binding	– legal institutions and system – compliance matters

Sources of stability	common interest and new security concept	US leadership, primacy, positive influence and network alliances
Institutions	non-binding, voluntarism and consensus-building decision-making	legally binding, rule of law, and law enforcement

Second, the values that China and the US pursue for their respective envisioned architecture are not compatible, nor do they allow for compromise. While China claims that values should be 'peace, development and cooperation' (Table 11.1), the US does not deviate from its traditional ones—freedom, democracy and a free market economy. It is highly debatable if China's proclaimed 'values' are compatible with the normative definition of value. Reinforced by domestic scholarly debates in China, skeptics would even argue if there are any values to China's foreign policy. Values are critical to the shaping and evolution of architecture largely because they will impact the final form of the architecture. Principles, structure, architecture, membership character and binding force will be influenced and founded by the values in place. Thus, the value-based security order and system as pursued by the US would have constraining effects on the eligibility of the membership (value-sharing and exclusive), the structure of the architecture (alliance-based), the binding force (legally binding institutions and commitment) and the function of the structure (bilateralism within multilateralism).

Last, different visions and values naturally engender a difference in strategy. Both China and the US emphasise multilateralism as their founding strategy in building their envisioned multilateral cooperative security architectures. However, they fundamentally differ in strategic approach and therefore in its utility. While China emphasises 'open regionalism' in its multilateralism strategy, the US prefers multilateralism to supplement its alliance-based security cooperation. As great powers, both countries prefer bilateral approaches rather than multilateralism.[42] The difference is in the way they strategically utilise multilateralism to their own advantage, thereby serving their respective regional interests. China is seemingly more accommodating of the multilateralism claimed by its neighbours, especially by those whom China regards as in 'states in its backyard'.[53] It is largely because Beijing sees ASEAN as the focus of its good neighbour policy.[54] The US, on the other hand, relies more on a bilateral alliance structure than an all-out and indiscriminate multilateral approach; this is despite its recognition of the importance of cooperating with other partner countries and newly rising regional powers in the multilateral context. China's open regionalism has led to the inception of a set of mechanical principles called the 'Democracy of International Relations', which take into consideration the diversity of the countries in the region to develop the core mechanics of its multilateral security cooperation architecture. It advocates a peaceful resolution to regional conflicts through dialogues.

Concluding Remarks

The source of strategic mistrust between the US and China will persist as long as the two countries fail to compromise on the long-sought dream of creating a regional order that fits their appetite, and they will continue to take opposite and contrasting paths. It does not seem, at least for now, that there will be a merging point in their outlook of regional order in the short term. Their vision has been long-pursued and long-aspired to, and has simply been emulated generation after generation in different political rhetoric.

South Korea is obviously stuck in between them. It is the one of the US' largest hosting alliance states, second only to Japan. Yet, it is economically the largest dependent state on China in Asia. It therefore falls easily into a dilemma of strategic choice in various areas when in pursuit of relationships with the two regional powers. The only way for South Korea to avoid getting trapped in this dilemma is to pursue a policy that best serves its national interest. Unfortunately that seems to be the only viable choice that South Korea is left with. In order to effectively achieve this, South Korea must equip itself with a firm and concrete set of diplomatic principles and national strategy, which it truly lacks today.

There seems to be no force that can bind the two regional powers on any basis, and the discrepancies in their outlook for regional order is ever widening. The tug of war between the US and China will centre on their respective desires for intra-alliance and the displacement of the alliance system in Asia. As long as this aspiration is upheld, security cooperation based on multilateralism and cooperation in an institutional context will be a foregone conclusion. Only power transition theory with a more peaceful dimension, as in a peaceful transition, might constitute an alternative foundation for the regional transaction.

Notes

1. Aaron L. Friedberg, 'The Debate over US China Strategy,' *Survival* 57:3, (June–July 2015), pp. 89–110; and Biwu Zhang, 'Chinese Perceptions of US Return to Southeast Asia and the Prospect of China's Peaceful Rise', *Journal of Contemporary China* 24:91 (2015), pp. 176–195.
2. The ideological nature of some issues is still visible as a source of conflict over such notions as national sovereignty, human rights and a free market economy. Niu Xinchun, 'Sino–US Relations: Ideological Clashes and Competitions', *China International Studies* (May/June 2012), pp. 61–78.
3. Russell D. Buhite, 'Major Interests: American Policy toward China, Taiwan and Korea, 1945–1950', *Pacific Historical Review* 47:3 (August 1978), pp. 425–451.
4. Suisheng Zhao, 'Shaping the Regional Context of China's Rise: how the Obama administration brought back hedge in its engagement with China', *Journal of Contemporary China* 21:75 (May 2012), pp. 369–389.
5. Ashley J. Tellis, 'Balanceing without Containment: A US Strategy for Confronting China's

Rise', *The Washington Quarterly* 36:4 (Autumn 2013), pp. 109–124.
6   Hillary Clinton, 'Remarks on Regional Architecture in Asia: Principles and Priorities', 12 January 2010, http://www.state.gov/ secretary/rm/2010/01/ 135090.htm.
7   Phillipp Saunders, 'China's Rising Power, the US Rebalance to Asia, and Implications for US–China Relations', *Issues and Studies* 50:3 (September, 2014), pp. 19–55.
8   Remarks by President Barack Obama at Suntory Hall, Tokyo, Japan, 14 November 2009, http://www.whitehouse.gov/the-press-office/remarks-president-barack-obama-suntory-hall; Hillary Rodham Clinton, 'US–Asia Relations: Indispensable to Our Future', at Asia Society in New York, 13 February 2009, http://www.state.gov/secretary/rm/2009a/02/117333.htm; Hillary Rodham Clinton, 'Remarks at the Inaugural Richard C. Holbrooke Lecture on Broad Vision of US–China Relations in the 21st Century', 14 January 2011, Transcript available at http://seoul.usembassy.gov/p_gov_011411.html; Hillary Rodham Clinton, 'New Beginnings: Foreign Policy Priorities in the Obama Administration', Opening Remarks Before the House Foreign Affairs Committee, Washington, DC, 22 April 2009; Hillary Rodham Clinton, 'Foreign Policy Address at the Council on Foreign Relations', Washington, DC, 15 July 2009, http://seoul.usembassy.gov/rok_07509.html.
9   Lanxin Xiang, 'China and the Pivot', *Survival* 54:5 (October–November 2012), pp. 113–128.
10 Speech by Mr Taro Aso, Minister for Foreign Affairs on the Occasion of the Japan Institute of International Affairs Seminar 'Arc of Freedom and Prosperity: Japan's Expanding Diplomatic Horizons', 30 November 2006, http://www.mofa.go.jp/announce/fm/aso/speech0611.html.
11 Frank Ching, 'Asian Arc of Democracy', *Korea Times*, 24 February 2008.
12 Daniel, Twining, 'Asia's challenge to China', *Financial Times*, 25 September 2007, http://www.ft.com/intl/cms/s/0/87e194aa-6b95-11dc-863b-0000779fd2ac.html#axzz4BYw9w8sR.
13 Kuo-Kang Shao, 'Chou En-lai's Diplomatic Approach to Non-Aligned States in Asia: 1953–60,' *The China Quarterly* 78 (June 1979), pp. 327.
14 Xi Jinping, 'New Asian Security Concept for New Progress in Security Concept', Remarks at the Fourth Summit of the Conference on Interaction and Confidence Building Measures in Asia, 21 May 2014, http://www.fmprc.gov.cn/mfa_eng/zxxx_662805/t1159951.shtml.
15 'Dabai meidiguozhuyi de renhe tiaoxie (Defeat all kinds of challenges by US imperialist), in *Mao Zedong waijiao wenxuan (Selected Diplomatic Writings of Mao Zedong)*, PRC Ministry of Foreign Affairs and CPC Central Document Research Office, ed., (Beijing: Central Document Publisher, 1994), p. 137.
16 *China and the US Far East Policy, 1945–1966* (Washington: Congressional Quarterly Service, 1967), p. 68.
17 The idea of 'Community of Common Destiny' was first introduced in 2007 by President Hu Jintao at the 17th National Congress of Communist Party in his Working Report. http://www.china.org.cn/english/congress/229611.htm. It was reiterated at the 18th Party Congress in 2012 in the Work Report, http://news.xinhuanet.com/english/special/18cpcnc/2012-11/17/c_131981259_12.htm. It was reemphasised at the Boao Forum in 2013, 'Full text of Xi Jinping's speech at the opening ceremony of the Boao Forum for Asia AC 2013', http://english.boaoforum.org/mtzxxwzxen/7379.jhtml.
18 Xin Benjian, 'Hunaqiu liaowang: Meiguo xin yazhou zhanlue huzhiyuchu' ('Global Outlook: US New Asia Strategy Vividly Portrayed'), *Renmin wang (People's Daily Online)*, 17 March 2009, http://world.people.com.cn/GB/1030/8977911.html.
19 'Meiguo yinxian xin yazhou zhengce' ('Looming America's New Asia Strategy'), *Nanfang zhoumo (Southern Weekend)*, 4 November 2010, p. 11.
20 Hillary Rodham Clinton, 'Remarks at the ASEAN–US Ministerial Meeting, National Convention Center, Hanoi, Vietnam', 22 July 2010, http://www.state.gov/secretary/rm/2010/07/145046.htm.
21 Hillary Rodham Clinton, 'Remarks at Press Availability, National Convention Center, Hanoi,

Vietnam', 23 July 2010, http://www.state.gov/secretary/rm/2010/07/145095.htm.
22. 'Meiguo guowuqing xilali guzao nanhai wenti "guojihua"' ('Secretary Clinton Behind "Internationalization" of South China Sea Problems'), *Fuzhou wanbao* (*Fuzhou Evening News*), 26 July 2010, p. 19.
23. 'Sheping: Mei nanhai biaotai zujie zhongguo lanshu haijun' ('Editorial: US Blocking up PLA Blue Water Navy in South China Sea'), *Zhongguo Pinglun Nxinwen Wang* ('*China Review News*'), 30 July 2010, http://gb.chinareviewnews.com/crn-webapp/doc/docDetailCNML.jsp?coluid=137&kindid=5291&docid=101395795.
24. Lee Sang Hyun, 'Obama Administration's National Security Strategy', *Current Issues and Policy* (Seoul: Sejong Institute, July 2010), pp. 13–14.
25. Department of Defense, *Quadrennial Defense Review Report* (Washington, DC: Department of Defense, February 2010), p. 7, 31, 60; Department of Defense, *Nuclear Posture Review Report* (Washington, DC: Department of Defense, April 2010), pp. v–vi, x–vi; and The White House, *National Security Strategy* (Washington, DC: The White House, May 2010), p. 3, 8, 11, 43.
26. Chinese Ministry of Foreign Affairs Spokesperson's Press Briefing, 2 February 2010, http://www.fmprc.gov.cn/chn/gxh/tyb/fyrbt/jzhsl/t655470.htm.
27. Yang Qingchuan, 'Meiguo xin fangwu baogao dui zhong yin qubie duidai jianyi weidu zhongguo' ('New American Defense Report Suggests China–India Area to Surround China'), *Huanqiu* (*Global*), 16 February 2010, http://mil.huanqiu.com/Observation/2010-02/721372.html.
28. 'Meiguo xin de he zhanlue jiang gei guoji he anquan dailai zhongyao yingxiang' ('US New Nuclear Strategy to Have Important Effect on International Nuclear Security'), *Xinhuawang* (*Xinhua Net*), 7 April 2010, http://news.xinhuanet.com/world/2010-04/07/c_1221589.htm; 'He anquan fenghui zai ji, meiguo zuixin he taishi baogao xinyi he yongyi' ('Nuclear Summit Imminent, Latest on US New Nuclear Report and New Meanings and Intentions'), *Zhongguo jinrong wang* (*China Finance Net*), 8 April 2010, http://www.zgjrw.com/News/201048/index/628072461400.shtml.
29. 'Meiguo xinban guojia anquan zhanlue baogao shi ci tiji zhongguo' ('US New National Security Strategy Report Mentions China 10 Times'), *Renmin wang* (*People's Daily Online*), 30 May 2010, http://military.people.com.cn/GB/11730353.html.
30. Liu Baocai, 'Quzhe dongdang de yi nian: 2010 nian guoji xingshi huimou' ('A Distorted and Rocky Year: Reflection on the Developments in International Relations in 2010'), *Hongqi Wengao* (*Beijing: Qiushi Journal*) 1 (January 2011), http://www.qstheory.cn/hqwg/2011/201101/201101/t20110111_61809.htm.
31. Dong Wang and Chengzhi Yin, 'Mainland China Debates US Pivot/Rebalancing to Asia', *Issues and Studies* 50:3 (September 2014), pp. 57–101.
32. He Ping and Wu Zhengang, '*Hanmei tongmeng: Lengzhan hou chaoxian bandao anquan jizhi goujian de zhang'ai yinsu*' ('Korea–US alliance: Obstacles to building security system on the Korean peninsula in the post-Cold War era'), *Ha'erbin shifan daxue shehui kexue xuebao* (*Ha'erbin Normal University Social Sciences Paper*) 2 (2013), p. 19.
33. Richard Parker, 'US Military Presence in a Unified Korea', *USAWC Straegy Research Project* (Carlisle Barracks, P.A.: US Army War College, 4 July 2003), p. 15.
34. Ibid.
35. Russia has also argued for complete withdrawal of USFK as one of the most basic preconditions of Korea unification. Tien Mu, '*Zhuhan meijun: Xianru dongbeiya de heishou*' ('USFK: Falling into the trap of Northeast Asia's black hand'), *Jiandai wuqi* (*Shipborne Weapons*) (June 2003), p. 23. On sharing a similar views on the value of peace treaty and system as an effective alternative to alliance in a post-unified Korea, Guo Xuetang, '*Chaoxian bandao tongyi: Wenti yu qianjing*' ('Korean peninsula unification: Problems and prospects'), *Guoji guancha* (*International Observation*) 5 (1996) p. 29.

36 Shi Yuanhua, *'Lun zhongguo dui chaoxian bandao heping jizhi wenti de jiben lichang'* ('Debating China's basic position on the construct of peace system problem on the Korean peninsula'), *Tongji daxue (shehui kexue ban) (Tongji University (Social Sciences Edition)* 17:3, p. 77.
37 He Zhigong, and An Xiaoping, *'Chaoxian bandao heping xieding yu heping jizhi'* ('Korean peninsula peace treaty and peace system'), *Dongbeiya luntan (Northeast Asia Forum)*, 17:2, p. 33.
38 'Bush Considers Peace Treaty with North Korea', *Reuters*, 5 September 2007.
39 He Zhigong, and An Xiaoping, *'Chaoxian bandao heping xieding yu heping jizhi'* ('Korean peninsula peace treaty and peace system'), *Dongbeiya luntan (Northeast Asia Forum)*, p. 33.
40 Ibid.
41 Yang Xiyu, *'Guanyu jianli chaoxian bandao heping jizhi de jige falv wenti'* ('A few legal issues regarding the construct of peace system on the Korean peninsula'), *Guoji wenti yanjiu (International Studies)* 4 (2009), p. 34.
42 Ibid.
43 Furthermore, China at the fifth round of the four-party talks (5–10 August 1999), for the first time in public, made it known of its stance to be 'consistently' with the North on such issues as the withdrawal of the US forces, the eradication of the Armistice and the ratification of peace treaty between North Korea and the US. In addition, it also proposed for the first time that the demarcation of the so-called 'Northern Limitation Line (NLL)' be confirmed. Li Fuxing, *'Sifang huitan weihe nanyi qude jinzhan'* ('Why is four-party talks difficult to make progress'), *Guoji zhanwang (International Prospects)* 17 (1999) pp. 7–9.
44 Some Chinese experts have claimed that the peace treaty might undermine the legitimacy of the US forces in Korea remaining in the peninsular afterwards. If there were to be a simultaneous bilateral peace treaty signed between the US and North Korea, under the circumstances, Chinese believe the US factor in the inter-Korean conflict can hardly be accounted for largely because US support to the south in such conflict will violate all the intentions and purposes of the treaties. Zhang Liankwei, *'Heping xieding ying yu qihe tongbu'* ('Peace treaty must be accompanied by denuclearisation'), *Zhongguo xinwen zhoukan (China News Weekly)*, 26, 2007. pp. 46–47.
45 Liu Ming, *'Chaoxian bandao yu dongbeiya heping anquan jizhi: Gouxiang yu wenti'* ('Korean Peninsula and Northeast Asia's peaceful security system: Planning and challenges'), *Dongbeiya luntan (Northeast Asia Forum)*, 18:4, p. 4.
46 Shi, *'Lun zhongguo dui chaoxian bandao heping jizhi wenti de jiben lichang'* ('Debating China's basic position on the construct of peace system problem on the Korean peninsula'); Ibid., p. 73.
47 Ibid., p. 74.
48 China's such first high hopes were expressed at the idea of so-called 'four-party talks' that were initiated in 1997. Ding Shizhuan and Li Qiang, *'Chaoxianbandao heping jizhi jiqi qianjing'* ('Prospects for a peace structure on the Korean peninsula'), *Xiandai guoji guanxi (Contemporary International Relations)* (April 1999) pp. 42–44; and Lu Dasheng, *'Sifang huitan qude jinzhan'* ('Four-party talks shows progress'), *Liaowang xinwen zhoukan (Liaowang News Weekly)* 44 (2 November 1998), p. 56.
49 Shi, p. 76.
50 Such a hope was raised at the establishment of the working group on Northeast Asia Peace Treaty and System at the last six-party talks that were held on 13 February 2008. It was only further heightened by the actual meetings that were held twice thereafter. Wang Xiaobo and Chen Bin, *'Lengzhanhou meirihan lianmeng tixi yu zhongguo'* ('US–Japan–South Korea Alliance and China's Security Policy after the Cold War'), *Yanbian daxue xuebao (Shehuikexue ban) (Journal of Yanbian Unviersity [Social Science])*, 44:4 (August 2011) p. 44.
51 Lee Lai To, 'Domestic Changes in China since the 4 June Incident and Their Implications for Southeast Asia', *Contemporary Southeast Asia* 13:1 (June 1991), pp. 35–42; and Chen Jie,

'Major Concerns in China's ASEAN Policy', in Chandran Jeshurun, ed., *China, India, Japan and the Security of Southeast Asia* (Singapore: Institute of Southeast Asian Studies, 1993), pp. 144–180.
52 America's preference for bilateralism and even unilateralism over multilateralism is still at work, culminating during the Bush administration (2001–2008). Mark Beeson, 'Multilateralism, American Power, and East Asian Regionalism', *Working Paper Series* (Hong Kong: City University of Hong Kong, 2004).
53 Jie, pp. 147–148.
54 China Institute of Contemporary International Relations, '*Zhongguo dui dongmeng zhengce yanjiu*' ('A Research on China's ASEAN Policy'), *Xiandai guoji guanxi* (*Contemporary International Relations*) 10:1 (2002), pp. 1–10; and Wang Yi, '*Yulin weishan, Yulin weiban* (Friendliness and Companionship to Neighbors),' *Qiushi* (*Seeking Truth*) 4 (2003), pp. 19–22.

Managing the Hermit Kingdom: China, North Korea and the Art of Strategic Patience

Jingdong Yuan

Associate professor at the Centre for International Security Studies and the Department of Government and International Relations at the University of Sydney, Australia

Abstract

By any measure, North Korea would be considered the master survivor in international relations. Ever since the end of the Cold War, Pyongyang's perennial challenge has been regime preservation in a much-changed security environment. Gone are the days when the Democratic People's Republic of Korea (DPRK) took advantage of China–Soviet competition to get the maximum benefits from its two feuding patrons while maintaining a semblance of autonomy and independence. It now has to deal with two powers whose policies have significant impacts on its security. The US continues to pose the most serious threat; China, on the other hand, is no longer a trusted ally that North Korea can rely on for its economic wellbeing and security protection. These external variables inform Pyongyang's perspective of the China–US relationship, especially where their cooperation or difference in turn affect the former's national interests. For North Korea, understanding the divergent US and Chinese objectives and approaches is essential in formulating its own strategy for survival in an increasingly deteriorating environment.

Analysts have often described North Korea's provocative behaviour as at once irrational and dangerous. 'Irrational' because such behaviours, from launching ballistic missiles to conducting nuclear tests against strong and explicit warnings from its patron, China, deeply irritate as well as embarrass Beijing, resulting in the latter's endorsement of UN sanctions and cutting down of economic assistance. At the same time, North Korean provocations strengthen the US–South Korean alliance and further undermine its own security. 'Dangerous' because these actions heighten tensions, and could escalate to major military confrontation. While both are true to some extent, they ignore the fact that North Korea, since the early 1990s, has had to sustain regime survival (to be more precise, continue the Kim family rule) against perilous economic, diplomatic and security situations. That it has defied many premature predictions of its imminent collapse point to calculative, rational and occasional brinkmanship-style policy at work. It has been able to take advantage of the differences between major powers, notably the US and China, and has survived leadership successions, famines, international sanctions and diplomatic isolation over the past two decades. Its latest nuclear and missile tests have drawn swift condemnations from the international community; the United Nations Security Council (UNSC) has adopted new resolutions and imposed more stringent sanctions after major powers, China and the US in particular, have resolved their differences over the scope and severity of the proposed sanction measures. Clearly, the case of North Korea deserves careful reevaluation, and this paper will seek to make a preliminary analysis.

The Hermit Kingdom: Seeking Security, Prosperity and Prestige

Pyongyang has since 1998 publicly articulated a slogan of building North Korea into a 'strong and prosperous great nation', a goal that has seen the country pursue a military-first policy through the development of nuclear weapons while introducing limited reform, and following a policy of *juche*, or self-reliance to maintain its identity as a great and proud nation. While the last often refers to inter-Korea relations, security and prosperity in recent years have inevitably been impeded or facilitated as a result of its complex relationships with the US and China. North Korea, always the weaker party, has to operate in environments not of its own choosing but which could fundamentally affect its security, prosperity and prestige. Granted, its erratic behaviour has not helped alleviate this but make it worse. The crucial point is that North Korea, like any other state, responds to external environments in ways based on careful cost–benefit analyses and seeks to maximise national interests given the constraints as well as opportunities. Its perspectives on US–China relations and how the latter could affect its interests must be seen in this context.[1]

'The premise on which an analysis of DPRK perspectives on US–China rests is that North Korea's security, prosperity and its very identity have been closely related to the policies and attitudes of these two powers towards the hermit kingdom as much as to relations between them. The US has remained an arch-enemy of North Korea since the Korean War while China, an erstwhile ally, has adopted policies detested by the Kim regime even as the DPRK continues to depend on Beijing for occasional diplomatic cover as well as economic assistance. North Korea has always had to navigate between its powerful patrons and outsmart and survive its enemies, all the while fiercely guarding its political autonomy. Kim Il-Sung managed to get Stalin on board for his military assault on South Korea in a bid to unify the country;

beaten by the US-led UN forces he turned to China for assistance. Chairman Mao Zedong overruled most of his close advisers and top generals and dispatched the People's Volunteer Army across the Yalu River in support of Kim Il-Sung, even losing his own son in the three-year war.[2] For decades, the bilateral relationship was termed as 'sealed in blood and flesh'. The close ties between the two communist countries appeared to have been bound in ideologies, personal friendships, the common security interests they shared, and the threats they both faced.[3] As the Soviet Union and China fell out over ideological debates and boundary disputes, Beijing and Moscow both sought to secure Pyongyang's allegiance, further enhancing Pyongyang's position in Chinese strategic calculations in the 1960s and 1970s. In 1961 China and North Korea signed the Sino–North Korean Mutual Aid and Cooperation Friendship Treaty, committing both sides to the assistance of each in case of military attacks by a third country.[4]

However, even in the heyday of China–North Korea friendship and solidarity, bilateral ties had not always been smooth, and indeed at times became tense and strained. Recent archival revelations from declassified former Soviet and eastern European documents suggest that even at the height of the Korean War, and certainly during the Cold War, China–North Korea relations were experiencing periods of both stability and disputes. Kim Il-Sung was always worried about Beijing's dominance and sought to maintain a degree of autonomy by playing off the Soviet Union against China. Kim also was able to purge the DPRK leadership of the so-called 'Yan'an faction'—top officials having close affiliation with the Chinese revolution and who were therefore considered as a threat to Kim's own power.[5] Likewise, Pyongyang also was keen on purging the Soviet influence, especially after the 20th conference of the Communist Party of the Soviet Union in 1956, where Stalin was denounced for his personal cult.[6]

The rapprochement between China and the US in the early 1970s shocked North Korea and led to Pyongyang's brief scrambling for inter-Korean reconciliation, a sentiment shared by Seoul, who was also deeply concerned over Washington's détente with a communist enemy.[7] By the end of the Cold War, North Korea had effectively lost its former patrons, with significantly reduced economic assistance from both China and the Soviet Union/Russia. In August 1992, against Pyongyang's entreaty, Beijing formally established diplomatic relations with Seoul.[8] While the Chinese leadership had taken great care to ease the 'shock', Pyongyang still felt betrayed and the China–North Korea bilateral relationship entered a period of uncertainty, distance and occasional alienation.[9] Indeed, the Soviet and Chinese establishment of diplomatic relations with Seoul without corresponding diplomatic normalisations between North Korea and most Western countries, the US and Japan in particular, incurred added fear of insecurity and isolation, prompting Pyongyang to seek nuclear weapons as security insurance.[10]

With such titanic shift in the international geostrategic landscape and increasingly incompatible national interests, the old 'lip-and-teeth' relationship based on shared strategic interests and the need for mutual assistance was then replaced with a more or less ad hoc, utilitarian patron-client relationship, with growing asymmetry in responsibilities and interdependence.[11] For Beijing, managing the Korea policy has become a delicate balancing act to reconcile different interests: an economic tilt towards South Korea; a security imperative to keep the political and military relationship with North Korea intact, with North Korea serving as a buffer for China; promoting developments that will diminish the presence of external power or at least harm China's interests; and using its unique position to both promote peace and stability and enhance its own bargaining position vis-à-vis other powers.[12] For Pyongyang, on the other hand, views the rise of China with deep ambivalence and even disquiet. Beijing has become increasingly and openly critical of such North Korean behaviour as nuclear and missile tests, which in turn have been driven by its survival instinct. At the same time, China becomes less willing to provide Pyongyang with unconditional economic assistance and North Korea views Chinese calls for reform as carrying significant risks as well as rewards.

The strains and restoration of China–North Korea political ties

First, China–North Korea relations displayed noticeable signs of growing strain in the 1990s. Between 1992 and 1999, and in particular since the death of Kim Il-Sung in 1994, high-level bilateral exchanges registered a patent decline. Indeed, since Kim Il-Sung's last visit to China in 1991 (apparently to persuade Beijing not to recognise Seoul), no visits by either country's top leaders to the other took place until 2000—a sharp contrast to the previously frequent exchanges between top Chinese and North Korean leaders. Between 1958 and 1991, the two countries held 40 summit meetings to exchange views on various issues. Kim Il-Sung had close personal ties with Zhou Enlai.[13] It was not until 1999 that Kim Yong-Nan, president of the Presidium of the Supreme People's Assembly, visited Beijing. Modest improvement followed with Kim Jong-Il's two visits in 2000 and 2001, and upon the Chinese Communist Party (CCP) General-Secretary and State President Jiang Zemin's official state visit to Pyongyang in September 2001, where the two leaders pledged to develop bilateral relations according to the principles of 'carrying on the traditions, looking forward to the future, developing neighbourliness and friendship, and strengthening cooperation'.[14] However, even some of these limited exchanges were necessitated by the need to address emerging issues (such as the nuclear crisis, famine, refugees) rather than motivated by the drive to promote and cement the traditional friendship. Meanwhile, this same period witnessed many exchange visits between Chinese and South Korean leaders. A month after the establishment of diplomatic relations between Beijing and Seoul, South Korean President Roh Tae-Woo visited China. Since then all sitting South Korean presidents, from Kim Young-Sam (1994), Kim Dae-Jung (1998), Roh Moo-Hyun (2003) and Lee Myung-Bak (2012), to Park Geun-Hye (2013; 2015) have visited China. Chinese Presidents Jiang Zemin (1995), Hu Jintao

(2005), Xi Jinping (2014) and other top leaders also have visited South Korea.[15]

Ties between Kim Jong-Il and China's fourth-generation leadership headed by Hu Jintao were built upon the four guiding principles proposed by Jiang Zemin for China–North Korea relations. While a member of the Politburo Standing Committee, Hu led a delegation to North Korea in July 1993 to mark the 40th anniversary of the ceasefire of the Korean War. In April 2004, Kim Jong-Il made his third unofficial visit to China, and met with all the newly minted 40th-generation Chinese leaders. Kim also sought to secure more economic assistance as well as to renew North Korea's commitment to the process of the six-party talks.[16] In welcoming Kim Yong-Nam, president of the presidium of the Supreme People's Assembly, during his October 2004 visit to China, Wu Bangguo, chairman of the Standing Committee of the National People's Congress (NPC), put forth a four-point proposal to further bilateral relations. They are: mutual respect and equality based on the Five Principles of Peaceful Co-Existence; maintaining high-level contacts for timely exchange of views on majors issues; promoting cooperation for the benefit of the two countries and peoples; and enhancing coordination in international and regional affairs to create a peaceful environment.[17]

However, it took Hu almost three years after he became party general-secretary (November 2002) to finally make his trip to the hermit kingdom in late October 2005. Reportedly, the visit was originally scheduled to have taken place in April 2005, but Beijing postponed the visit due to lack of progress in Pyongyang's fulfilling its commitment to the six-party talks. North Korean leader Kim Jong-Il showered Hu with lavish ceremonies and the two leaders extolled the decades-old bilateral relationship. During the visit, Hu proposed the four principles to guide China–North Korea relations in the new era; namely, to continue and deepen high-level exchanges, explore and expand new areas of exchange and enrich the substance of cooperation, promote economic cooperation and seek mutual development, and engage in more active consultation on issues of mutual interests. The visit followed an earlier visit by politburo member and vice premier Wu Yi, who observed the 60th anniversary celebration of the Workers' Party of North Korea and the ceremonial opening of the China-assisted US$25 million Taean Friendship Glass Factory.[18]

In the last few years of Kim Jong-Il's rule, and especially since his reported stroke in 2008, more frequent high-level exchanges between Beijing and Pyongyang were conducted, including the final four of Kim's visits to China in an effort to pave the way for the succession of Kim Jong-Un and to seek more Chinese economic assistance. The Chinese leadership apparently conceded to the succession arrangement for no other reason than to ensure regime stability after Kim Jong-Il and perhaps increase China's influence in the North, given Kim Jong-Un's relative inexperience.[19] Beijing, meanwhile, recognising that there was little prospect of resolving the nuclear issue, decided to place the focus on peninsular stability and power transition in the North. While perturbed and at times angered by North Korean intransigence that undermines China's own interests in the region, Beijing had to carefully assess the broader geostrategic implications of various policy options (and indeed allowed and encouraged internal debates). In the end, it concluded that keeping the North Korean regime, even at the cost of a deteriorating relationship with South Korea and a closer US–South Korea alliance, would work to its fundamental benefits. One important consideration is that this is the only way that Beijing can keep maximum influence—if there is any to be had—over Pyongyang. This explains not only continued and even increased Chinese food and energy aid to North Korea but also the apparent refrain of reacting to or publicly criticising Pyongyang's provocations.[20]

In October 2009, to mark the 60th anniversary of diplomatic relations between China and North Korea, Chinese Premier Wen Jiabao made a 'goodwill visit' to Pyongyang. Wen met Kim Jong-Il and promised significant economic assistance to the North, including the construction of a new bridge over the Yalu River at a cost of US$150 million entirely funded by the Chinese side, and other economic packages reportedly worth US$50 million.[21] The years 2009 and 2010 also saw high-level military exchanges between the two countries. Chinese Minister for National Defense Liang Guanglie visited Pyongyang in November 2009; North Korean General Kim Jong-Gak visited Beijing the same month. In October 2010 the vice chairman of China's Central Military Commission, General Guo Boxiong, led a delegation to North Korea to mark the 60th anniversary of China's entering into the Korean War, during which 180,000 Chinese People's Volunteer Army members sacrificed their lives, including Mao Zedong's own son. Chinese vice president and future leader Xi Jinping attended the function at the North Korean embassy in Beijing to mark the occasion and praised the Korean War and China's friendship with North Korea.[22]

These high-level exchange visits did not symbolise a return to the solidarity of yester-year. If anything, Pyongyang remained steadfast in guarding its autonomy. In fact, Beijing's limited influence can be demonstrated by the numerous instances where North Korea simply ignored the wishes of its principal patron. For instance Hu Jintao, in his May 2010 meeting with Kim Jong-Il, proposed heightened contact between the two countries, specifically: 'reinforcing "strategic coordination"; deepening collaboration on economic and trade; increasing personnel exchanges; and strengthening "coordination in international and regional affairs".' This is a clear signal that Pyongyang should consult Beijing before it takes any provocative action that affects Chinese interests. However, Pyongyang's unequivocal response is to continue with its own ways, causing significant frustration in Beijing.[23] Indeed, as observed by a Chinese analyst, 'in its contemporary relationship with North Korea, China has often acted like a kidnapped country, kidnapped by that much weaker neighbour, depending on China's assistance.' Prior to North Korea's third nuclear test in February 2013, and the multiple satellite launches in 2012, Beijing sought to pressure Pyongyang from undertaking such provocative moves. China's diplomatic efforts failed to stop North Korea from conducting these tests. After China joined other members of the UNSC to draft and adopt sanctions, North Korea apparently retaliated by detaining Chinese fishermen. And China–North Korean high-level exchanges have slowed down significantly since Kim Jong-Un took power in December 2011. China's open criticism of North Korean missile and nuclear provocation has further strained bilateral relations. It was not until the summer of 2012 that Jang Sung-Taek made a visit to China to discuss joint economic zones with Chinese leaders. However, his request for US$1 billion in economic assistance was reportedly refused by Beijing.[24] With the execution of Jang in 2013, any prospect of Kim visiting China became ever more remote.

Indeed, North Korea under Kim Jong-Un is even more wary of China, as its economic dependence deepens given continued international sanctions and drastically reduced inter-Korea trade. While Pyongyang reluctantly accepts—and indeed has to seek—Chinese assistance for food and energy supplies, it is adamant that its political independence remains intact. The dramatic and highly public Jang Sung-Taek affair reveals at once Kim Jong-Un's insecurity and ruthless determination to stay in power, whatever it takes. Jang, Kim's uncle by marriage to his aunt, presumably a close confidant of Kim Jong-Un and reportedly the second most powerful figure in the hermit kingdom, was suddenly charged with multiple crimes, including conspiring against Kim, was stripped of all his positions and summarily executed. Jang was believed to have been one of the few trusted contacts between Beijing and Pyongyang and his fall from grace both reveals the dangerous liaison that China reluctantly maintains with its wayward client state and highlights its diminishing influence over the latter.[25] This phenomenon must be a conundrum of some sort and challenges the conventional wisdom most watchers of China–North Korea relations hold. On the one hand, China today has become North Korea's key supplier of food and energy, and its largest trading partner. On the other hand, Beijing itself claims—and it increasingly appears to be the case—that it only has limited influence over what Pyongyang does, and indeed, the North Korea's occasional wayward behaviour has actually embarrassed and proved deeply frustrating to China. Indeed, despite its unique position vis-à-vis North Korea, China remains either unwilling or unable to use whatever influence it has to make progress on issues dear to its image as a rising global power and critical to its security interests: North Korea's nuclear and missile programmes; its constant and unpredictable provocations toward its neighbours, especially South Korea, which result in unending crisis one after another; and its refusal to undertake meaningful reforms.[26]

Compared to Kim Jong-Il, who at least took China seriously despite his resistance to Chinese pleas for introducing economic reform, Kim Jong-Un has deliberately demonstrated his displeasure towards Beijing. According to Li Zhaoxing, a former Chinese foreign minister, Kim Jong-Il once rushed back from his inspection tours to Pyongyang to meet Li, as this was Li's first visit to North Korea as foreign minister.[27] In contrast, Kim Jong-Un has met few senior Chinese leaders since assuming power in late 2011. The new Chinese ambassador to North Korea, Li Jinjun, who was appointed in March 2015, has yet to be received by Kim.[28] Chinese President Xi

Jinping has met his South Korean counterpart President Park Geun-Hye at least seven times, but he has yet to meet Kim Jong-Un.[29] At the recent Chinese Victory Day parade, marking the 70th anniversary of the end of World War II in Asia, Kim Jong-Un reportedly declined Beijing's invitation to attend and sent the secretary of the Workers' Party of North Korea, Choe Ryong Hae, instead. Nonetheless, by sending Choe, who is close to Kim, it could be interpreted as a sign that Kim was seeking to mend relations with Beijing. Similarly, Kim also praised the sacrifices of the Chinese People's Volunteer Army during the Korean War. However, in the end, Choe apparently was not given any prominent treatment by the Chinese hosts.[30] In response, a recent greeting sent by Xi to Kim to mark the 67th anniversary of the founding of the DPRK was placed on page two of the *Rodong Sinmun*, while messages from Russia and Cuba were put on the front page of the paper.[31] The CCP PSC member Liu Yunshan's visit to North Korea in October 2015 led to speculations that China–North Korea relations were back on track, as Liu reportedly delivered a letter from Xi to Kim. However, any such hope was quickly dashed with the abrupt departure and cancellation of the North Korean Moranbong Band concert in Beijing in December 2015.[32] North Korea's fourth nuclear test in early January 2016 means that a meeting between Xi and Kim would at best be remote if not out of the question altogether.

Propping up North Korea for the sake of stability
Second, *juche* aside, North Korea has never been able to achieve the level of economic self-sufficiency and autonomy it desires; its failing economic system and reluctance to undertake meaningful economic reform, combined with natural disasters in the mid- to late-1990s resulted in disastrous famines. Beijing's advice to Pyongyang to restructure its economy away from a disproportionate concentration on defence and heavy industries to consumer goods had not been taken by North Korea's leadership under Kim Jong-Il, at least certainly not in a serious manner.[33] While Pyongyang allowed limited experiments in selected areas, poor infrastructure in both hardware and software and uncertain investment environments have prevented these experiments from making any headway or achieving results. Since the 1990s, Pyongyang has either announced plans or actually attempted to develop a number of economic zones: the Kaesong Special Industrial Zone; Sinuiju Special Economic Zone; Rajin–Sonbong International Trade Zone; and Mount Kumgang Special Tourism Zone. This was largely due to the Kim Jong-Il regime's concerns over potential threats to its legitimacy as a consequence of opening up, which could allow contact between North Koreans and the outside world. In other words, the Kim Jong-Il regime remained highly suspicious of the potential capitalist (and even socialist with Chinese characteristics) influence that could come with a market economy and foreign investment.[34]

Over time, China has effectively shouldered a large portion of economic aid to North Korea in terms of food and energy supplies, in addition to exports of critical materials at below market prices, just to keep it afloat and prevent a massive exodus of economic refugees from roaming into China. In the 1990s, in the wake of the loss of Soviet subsidies and the North Korean economic downturn, China provided around 1 million tons of petroleum and 1.5 million tons of coal, making up almost 90% of North Korea's energy imports. As famine struck the North, China also increased the quantity of food aid as other donors reduced theirs. Beijing pledged to provide North Korea with an annual 500,000 tons of emergency food aid up to 2000. The urgency with which Beijing dispatched energy and food aids to North Korea was influenced by its concern over the regime's stability and the possibility of massive refugee inflows into China should the economic situation further deteriorate. In other words, strategic consideration played a critical part in determining Chinese economic assistance and self-interest.[35] A US Congressional Research Service (CRS) report suggests that during the late 1990s, China's food assistance to North Korea could run as high as to 1 million tons per year. This had dropped to around 130–140,000 tons a year for 2003 and 2004. Chinese fuel supplies averaged over US$100 million per year between 1995 and 2004 and doubled in the two years after the Korean Peninsula Energy Development Organisation (KEDO) executive board halted deliveries of heavy fuel oil to North Korea in November 2002 upon the revelation of its uranium enrichment programs. It has been reported that in February 2010 China pledged US$10 billion investment in North Korea's State Development Bank. China has reportedly allocated between 25–33% of its total annual foreign assistance budgets to North Korea in recent years. From the mid-1990s to 2001, Chinese financial assistance to North Korea was estimated at US$210 million, about 10% of the total provided by the international community during the same period. It provided between 70–90% of North Korea's energy supplies, with Chinese fuel supplies estimated at over US$100 million a year.[36]

China's energy supplies have been critical to addressing North Korea's severe shortfalls and to the process of helping the country weather otherwise grave economic situations. Beijing's considerations are multiple. Preventing regime collapse, building up influence, and developing long-term economic strategies, especially for China's own energy security interests, are driving Chinese decision-making to a significant extent. At the same time, the premium is placed on long-term, strategic considerations rather than short-term urges. China has gradually shifted from offering energy supplies in the form of grand aid to at friendship prices for commercial transactions or in exchange for resources in North Korea. Indeed, a significant portion (70%) of Chinese investments in the past decade has been in the mineral and resource sectors. For instance, energy exports more than tripled between 2002 and 2007, from US$118 million to US$402 million, with increasing prices over this period. During Vice Premier Wu Yi's visit to North Korea in October 2005, the Wukang Group, China's resource trading conglomerate, bought the rights to develop the Yongdeung mine, North Korea's largest coal mine.[37]

It has been reported that during Hu Jintao's visit to North Korea in October

2005, China promised more economic assistance by signing an economic and technological cooperation agreement worth US$2 billion. This is part of the overall Chinese strategy to help North Korea revive its economy and to prod Pyongyang to remain and make progress in the six-party talks.[38] In recent years, China has sought to move the bilateral economic relationship from one of largely financial assistance to economic cooperation with mutual benefits. Over 100 Chinese companies are investing in North Korea, with activities concentrated in mining and resource-related manufacturing, to take advantage of the complementary nature of the two economies. Three areas have received particular attention: mining, the iron and the steal industry, and port development. China's growing economic activities in North Korea have led to speculation that China is now effectively turning North Korea into a resource supplier. According to Japanese media, Chinese companies have secured rights to North Korean mines containing large deposits of iron ore and copper in exchange for Chinese supplies of electricity, machinery, consumer goods and technology. Chinese businesses have also taken over a number of department stores in Pyongyang.[39]

North Korea has also increased its migrant labour in China as a source of foreign currency; workers in Chinese border cities account for the bulk of North Korean travellers. Recent reports suggest that about 40,000 North Korean workers are working in Chinese factories in its three northeastern provinces, delivering between US$140–170 million per year to North Korea. These numbers are not officially counted and could be even higher, estimated at 100,000 North Korean workers and with an annual revenue of US$1 billion.[40]

China's economic ties with North Korea have been critical for the survival and stability of the Kim Jong-Un regime, which Beijing considers to be in its national interests. China–North Korea trade reached US$6.97 billion in 2014, accounting for 90% of North Korea's global trade. China also provides over 70% of North Korea's crude oil, 80% of its consumer goods, and about 45% of its food. Chinese investments in the impoverished country represent 95% of foreign direct investment in North Korea. Chinese customs data suggests that between 2012 and 2014, North Korea imported about US$2.09 billion worth of luxury goods, items supposedly banned by UNSC sanctions. For instance, the much-publicised skiing resort that Kim Jong-Un graced a few years ago bought the Austrian-origin secondhand equipment through a Chinese company.[41]

However, notwithstanding the fact that China has become North Korea's lifeline, political strains between the two countries clearly show, as the two sides have yet to open the US$359 million Dandong–Sinuiju bridge due to a delay on North Korea's side as it continues to pursue nuclear weapons program.[42] For its part, North Korea has expanded joint fishing areas and allowed Chinese fishermen to fish near the disputed Northern Limit Line (NLL) in exchange for cash. As a result, South Korea has seen growing intrusions by Chinese fishermen south of NLL.[43] However, North Korea must have realised that to fundamentally change its economic fortune for the better, serious reforms rather than patchy tinkering of the system must be undertaken, and there have been reports that central controls have been relaxed. North Korea is also seeking greater cooperation with other countries. But whether or not the current round of reforms under Kim Jong-Un can be sustained and yield any serious results, remains to be seen.[44]

Continuity More than Change: Staying the Course

Despite these dramatic developments and major challenges it has encountered over since the early 1990s, Beijing has more or less stayed the course on the core policy issues fundamental to Chinese security interests, even as the tactics and approaches have undergone major changes. There is continuity in Chinese policies towards the Korean Peninsula in general and, to North Korea in particular.[45] First, peace and stability on the peninsula and, of necessity, regime survival in North Korea remain the most important guiding principle underpinning Chinese policy. While Beijing does not approve of Pyongyang's brinkmanship, it understands its rationale and sees no good option that could reign in its client without affecting its own interests. Along this line, Beijing has patiently sought to maintain a stable relationship with Pyongyang, despite the deep resentment from North Korea and on occasion unconcealed criticisms of Chinese economic reform programmes and its growing ties with South Korea. Indeed, while meetings between the top leaders of the two countries were effectively suspended during most of the 1990s, high-level official contacts continued and the military-to-military exchanges also seemed to have proceeded without significant downturn, even though such visits may have become largely ceremonial rather than substantive. However, ties between the older-generation Chinese and DPRK military personnel who had fought side by side during the Korean War remained undiminished.[46] This was reinforced in 2010 when Beijing and Pyongyang marked the 60th anniversary of China entering into the Korean War. There were multiple exchange visits and ceremonies by high-ranking civilian and military delegations from both countries.[47]

China has resisted attempts to undermine the North Korean regime. While maintaining a nuclear-free Korean Peninsula has always been and remains a goal, Beijing is opposed to use of force and regime change. This is as much out of concern over the consequences for China's security interests as it is for regional peace and stability. Already paranoid and feeling extremely isolated, North Korea could react strongly and even irrationally if pushed to the corner. During the 1993–94 crisis and early stage of the 2003 nuclear crisis, China had indicated its position on UNSC sanctions, opting for patient diplomacy instead. According to a Chinese report, China even refused to attend a UNSC meeting on the North Korean nuclear issue.[48] Beijing resisted repeated entreaties by the US to apply the energy leverage against North Korea. China's refusal to use its power—ranging from food aid to energy supplies—largely stems from its principled stand on the sanction issue but is also a reflection of its delicate balancing act, encouraging North Korea to come to its senses without in the process hastening its decline and collapse or otherwise provoking it to even more irrational actions. An additional factor was Beijing's concern over the potential negative consequence of withdrawing support from North Korea.[49]

Indeed, China's continued interests in peninsular stability have been driven by its long-standing appreciation of the importance of North Korea as a strategic buffer. Historically, the peninsula provided both an avenue for China to exercise its influence in northeast Asia and a passageway through which foreign powers, Japan in particular, launched invasion. Beijing is therefore highly sensitive to any power establishing dominance on the peninsula. This line of thinking explains China's entry into the Korean War and its continued involvement in the peninsular affairs.[50] Some Chinese analysts even consider the Korean Peninsula as a major asset in countering US hegemonic ambitions in northeast Asia and call for the formation of a quasi-military alignment between China, North Korea and Russia.[51] However, North Korea's strategic importance to China also provides Pyongyang with a trump card in its dealings with Beijing—China is adverse to seeing North Korea's deteriorating situation, since this would in turn affect Chinese interests, hence giving it a source of asymmetrical power.[52]

Beijing's approach to North Korea, meanwhile, began to shift towards greater economic interactions and stable diplomatic ties. Since 2009 Chinese investments in, and trade with, North Korea have steadily increased, with China now accounting for over two-thirds of all North Korea's foreign trade. In addition, the two countries have entered into agreements to develop joint special economic zones in North Korea, with major Chinese investment commitments. Two-thirds of North Korea's joint ventures with foreign partners are Chinese.[53] Likewise, diplomatic exchanges through high-ranking visits have continued despite North Korean missile and nuclear tests over the past few years, although top Chinese leaders and Kim Jong-Un have yet to exchange visits. That said, the first foreign visitor that Kim Jong-Un received since the passing of Kim Jong-Il was Wang Jiarui, the then director of the CCP's International Liaison Department. CCP PSC member and National People's Congress Vice Chairman Li Jianguo visited North Korea in 2012. Kim Jong-Un's envoy, Vice Marshal Choe Ryong-Hae, visited China and met with President Xi Jinping in May 2013 while Li Yuanchao, PRC Vice President and also a politburo member, was among the few foreign dignitaries present at the ceremonies in Pyongyang marking the 60th anniversary of the end of the Korean War in July 2013.[54]

This approach, which emphasises encouraging Pyongyang to undertake economic reform, including establishing special economic and development zones close to the Chinese border and maintaining contacts with the regime even when relations may be strained, clearly reflects Beijing's strategic thinking about this rather delicate issue. In other words, China considers the North Korean nuclear issue within the broader context of regional security, its relationships with the key players and how the escalation and containment of the problem affect and serve its national interest.[55] This places Beijing in a losing situation. As Scott Snyder has suggested, as China works closer with the US in exerting pressure on Pyongyang, it could actually lose influence over its unappreciative client. On the other hand, when it resists Washington's pressures for stronger measures such as reducing or cutting off aid, then frictions ensue in China–US relations.[56] And despite increased assistance, there is no evidence that Beijing's leverage over Pyongyang's nuclear or missile decisions has grown. Admittedly, North Korea's extreme behaviours frustrate Beijing. At the same time, isolation of North Korea or any harsh actions that threaten the regime's survival could be highly risky as far as broader Chinese interests are concerned. These considerations at once drive and impose limits on China's North Korea policy.[57]

Indeed, as Victor Cha observes,

> 'The problem today is that China is both omnipotent and impotent in North Korea. It has great material influence as the North's only patron. Yet, as the sole patron, if Beijing shut down its assistance to punish Pyongyang for its bad behavior even temporarily, it could precipitate an unraveling of the regime, which would be even more threatening to China.'[58]

From Pyongyang's perspective, while it depends on China's support, especially its economic assistance in food and energy supplies, it nonetheless harbours deep distrust towards its patron and shuns suggestions that it adopt Chinese-style economic reforms for fear of losing political control.[59] What the outside may consider to be a viable lever—the cutoff of economic aid—could well threaten Beijing's core security interest: the preservation of the North Korean regime. Jonathan Pollack argues that Pyongyang 'also believes that China's fear of the North's potential responses to heightened pressure inhibits Beijing from taking major measures against the DPRK, lest such steps trigger a far larger regional crisis.'[60] In fact, not only does North Korea ignore Chinese warnings, it sometimes deliberately and publicly humiliates Beijing by taking actions in exactly the opposite way. For instance, prior to its late 2012 ballistic missile test, a high-ranking Chinese official was dispatched to Pyongyang seeking to dissuade North Korea from undertaking the test; 12 days later it did exactly that. And then, in early 2013, the DPRK conducted its third nuclear test, further alienating the Chinese.[61] What is more, North Korea even issued a thinly veiled rebuke against China, angrily charging that 'some spineless countries are blindly following the stinking bottom of the US . . .' after Beijing joined the other countries in condemning North Korean missile tests and halted oil exports in early 2014.[62]

Another change in China's policy towards North Korea is in its efforts to encourage and push for limited economic reform, as mentioned above. This would help alleviate the hardships endured by the North Korean people, which are thus potential triggers for social and political instability; change international perceptions of the North Korean regime, making the country attractive to foreign investment; reduce China's burden of economic and financial assistance; and move China–North Korea economic relations from ones based on Chinese aid grants to new formats of investment and developments of mutual benefits. One of the initial steps to be taken would be to change perceptions of the North Korean leadership; Pyongyang remains highly suspicious and even paranoid of the potentially erosive effects of reform on regime survival. To induce such changes, in 1993 China moved from the barter trade system to trade based on foreign exchange accounts. With the almost complete disappearance of former Soviet aid, North Korea was given the choice of change or continued decline and stagnation in its economy. The message seemed to have slowly sunk in on the North Korean leaders. While Pyongyang was less receptive in the 1980s to the Chinese-style economic reform, Kim Jong-Il appeared to have taken Chinese advice more seriously, as indicated by his growing devotion to observing economic developments in China during his trips in 2009–2011. The initial reform programmes launched in the summer of 2002 have been attributed to Pyongyang's decisions in the wake of Kim's visit early in the year. Since then, a number of special economic or industrial development zones have been established. Price and income adjustments were adopted, and modest private retail activities and free markets were allowed to appear. Kim's January 2006 visit—the longest by far—to China was heavily concentrated on the Chinese economy, and included an extended tour of Shenzhen, China's first special economic zone, launched in the early 1980s.[63] Subsequent visits also involved showcasing successful Chinese enterprises and stock exchange floors. However, there is no indication that Kim was influenced by his Chinese patrons; if anything, the limited reform measures introduced in North Korea have been two steps forwards and perhaps two steps backwards. Instead of moving forwards with reforms and therefore providing any benefits for its people, Pyongyang remains resistant to any liberalisation for fear of losing control. The regime has continued to depend on highly authoritarian and illicit methods to keep control and survive. All told, Chinese efforts to induce North Korea to embark on a path of reform have so far failed.[64]

Yet another change in Beijing's North Korea policy is growing emphasis placed on bilateral economic ties, encouraged by the governments at both central and local levels, but largely undertaken by enterprises.[65] This policy shift has been driven mostly by the need to provide strategic stability to Pyongyang during an uncertain transition period. In the midst of nuclear crisis, North Korean leadership succession, which ensures stability, has become a key consideration of Beijing's policy, with promoting closer economic ties a critical component of a passive policy.[66] Despite UNSC sanctions, China–North Korea trade has continued to register growth, with US$5.9 billion in 2012, US$6.54 billion in 2013 and US$6.97 billion in 2014.[67] High-profile investment projects include an industrial park on Hwanggumpyong, an island on the Yalu River that was opened in mid-2011, where China reportedly signed a 50-year lease for joint development. The island could provide China with access to the port of Rajin, part of the Rajin–Sonbong International Trade Zone, established with Chinese assistance.[68] A predominant number of the 138 joint ventures established between 1997 and 2010 are in the extractive industries, about

41%, followed by light industry in 38%. Most are privately owned and many are losing money.[69]

Pyongyang is clearly not comfortable with its growing economic dependence on China. In 2013 90% of its exports were bound to China. China–North Korea bilateral trade remains by far and ahead of any of North Korea's other bilateral trade ties. In recent years, it has sought to expand economic ties with other countries, including Russia, which in 2012 decided to forgive 90% of North Korea's bilateral debts (about US$10 billion). In 2014 the two countries set up a joint venture to refurbish North Korea's 3500 km railway line between Jaedong and the port city of Nampo.[70]

*

North Korea's latest nuclear and missile tests have drawn immediate and strong international condemnation, and have raised serious questions about China's approach to the North Korea problem. The North Korean provocations have also cast a spotlight on China and the US, the two most consequential powers that share common interests in de-nuclearisation of the peninsular but often disagree on the best means to achieve that end. Indeed, more than a month after North Korea's 6 January 2016 nuclear test, no sanctions had been adopted, due largely to the difference of opinion between China and the US over the severity, scope and very purpose of punitive measures.[71]

Recently, Secretary of State John Kerry has publicly suggested that China's policy on North Korea has failed, triggering quick rebuke from Beijing. The Obama administration in particular raises questions about the efficacy of Chinese preferences and approaches: denuclearisation through diplomacy, specifically, to get North Korea to return to the six-party talks; resistance to wide-ranging sanctions that go beyond targeting the nuclear and missile programs; and an emphasis on peninsular stability. Washington insists that Beijing's approaches have been ineffectual, give North Korea too much latitude and too many loopholes to continue its nuclear and missile activities, and therefore need to change. These could include cutting off energy supplies to North Korea, restricting or even prohibiting North Korean cargo ships or planes from access to Chinese ports and airports.[72]

The Chinese side, on the other hand, has accused the US of failing to contribute to peninsular denuclearisation with the irresponsible policy of 'strategic patience', which in effect allows North Korea to continues with its nuclear and missile developments unhindered. In addition, the continued US military presence in South Korea, a massive show of force through large-scale military exercises, and refusal to engage with North Korea only heightens the latter's sense of insecurity. Furthermore, Beijing is suspicious that the Obama administration's North Korea policy serves its overall strategy of rebalancing Asia, since North Korean provocations provide the very rationale to strengthen its alliances in the region.[73]

While the US and China share common interests in North Korean denuclearisation and have indeed coordinated over the years, their assessments of the situation, priorities and expectations are quite different and these have prevented the two powers from developing and executing strategies with the same pace and focus. For Washington, the fact that North Korea is increasingly dependent on China for its survival should give Beijing leverage to pressure Pyongyang to give up its nuclear weapons programme. For Beijing, on the other hand, it considers the tension between North Korea and the US a major cause of the North's insecurity.[74]

North Korean provocations are seriously undermining Chinese national interests. They insult China's status as a great power just as they raise questions about China's image as a responsible power. South Korea is reassessing its approach to inter-Korea relations based on *trustpolitik* and its delicate balancing act in maintaining close ties with both the US, its security ally, and China, its key trading partner. South Korean President Park Geun-Hye has so far struck a decidedly China-friendly policy in the hope that Beijing would exercise its influence over North Korea. South Korea not only delayed discussion on the US-proposed deployment of a Terminal High Altitude Area Defense (THAAD) missile defence system, but also joined the China-led Asian Infrastructure Investment Bank (AIIB) despite pressure from the US not to. Park even went to Beijing to attend the military parade that marked the 70th anniversary of the end of World War II, much to Washington's irritation.[75]

This is, however, going to change. Facing North Korean nuclear and missile threats, South Korea is increasingly more receptive to the THAAD proposal and may eventually accept deployment on its soil despite Chinese opposition. Park has also vowed to inflict 'bone-numbing' sanctions on North Korea and, first things first, with the suspension of the Kaesong Industrial Region. The US and South Korean troops have in recent years been staging large joint military exercises and US F-22 stealth fighter jets will be stored in military bases around South Korea. Besides, Seoul is already mending ties with Tokyo following the agreement on the comfort women issue and the North Korean threat could draw the two US allies closer. None of these developments bode well for China. A strengthened US–Japan–South Korea alliance, along with the Obama administration's policy of rebalancing Asia, and Washington's active engagement with the ASEAN states, could reshape Asia's geostrategic landscape as favourable for sustaining US dominance. THAAD, if deployed, could pose a serious threat to China's second-strike capabilities, as its radar system could track Chinese strategic missiles. The new US unilateral sanction measures imposed recently not only target North Korea but also penalise Chinese entities doing business in and with North Korea.[76]

Clearly, as far as China's North Korea policy goes, business as usual is not the way to go, but finding the right balance between expressing one's frustration or even anger, and carefully evaluating and situating the North Koran issue in the totality of Chinese interests in the peninsular and regional contexts, appears to remain the guiding principle for addressing the current crisis. But the fact that Beijing finally agreed to, and was a key drafter of, the UNSC resolution 2270 endorsing much tougher sanctions, is indicative of China's frustration with DPRK.[77] Granted, China is unlikely to cut off everything to inflict real pains on Pyongyang, for fear that may lead to instability, something China has been trying to avoid for years. However, there are steps China can appear to be taking, including tightening up existing sanctions, supporting new sanctions, restricting trade and reducing economic aid to North Korea, such as in oil supplies. Indeed, Kim Jong-Un should no longer be allowed to bite the hand that feeds him.[78]

But at the end of the day, China views the North Korean situation not just as an issue of nuclear proliferation, but as something directly related to peninsula stability, the northeast Asian balance of power, the broader ramifications on US–China relations and China's role in the region, including its ties with other major powers.[79] Given the emerging China–US competition and rivalry, punishing North Korea beyond a certain extent would not necessarily benefit China, if the end game is the collapse of the North Korean regime and a unified Korea that remains allied with the US. To a significant extent, China has the least room to manoeuvre without facing some unpleasant consequences, while the US holds the key to halting, and perhaps eventually rolling back, North Korea's nuclear and missile programmes.

Conclusion

To summarise, China–North Korea relations have undergone changes over the years. Official positions aside, there are more lively—albeit still less open—discussions and debates on the issues of North Korea, ranging from China's role to the value of North Korea in China's core interests. If anything, North Korea has become one of the divisive issues facing the Chinese leadership. Chinese North Korean analysts are less optimistic about Pyongyang giving up its nuclear weapons, believe that US–North Korea distrust is a major obstacle in solving the nuclear impasse, and do not consider it beneficial for Beijing to exert pressure on North Korea. Beijing's policy since 2009 clearly indicates that China now places emphasis on regime stability more than anything else. If this goal requires that China comes to North Korea's defence, provide economic aid and even offer political support, then Beijing will do it.[80] Indeed, despite the growing frustration (and venting of it by analysts) and sheer anger over the North Korean detention of Chinese fishermen in May 2012 for ransom, not to mention the missile and nuclear tests and other provocations since Kim Jong-Un came to power four years ago, the strategic considerations convince Beijing that keeping the regime stable remains critical to China, even after North Korea's latest provocations. However, Pyongyang has to get the message that the disrespect of and even hurting of Chinese interests will not be tolerated.[81]

Despite all Beijing's frustrations, including the unpredictability of Kim Jong-Un, China continues to place stability first. Some analysts suggest that apart from both being communist regimes and North Korea providing a buffer against the US, China also derives economic benefits from cooperating with Pyongyang. But fundamentally, Beijing's concern over US intentions continues to inform a policy of caution and calculation, lest North Korea's collapse entraps it in conflicts with the US. At the same time, Beijing also needs to reassure Pyongyang that it is not abandoning it, so that defection could not take place.[82] Even though North Korea's dependence on China, from energy to food, to economic assistance, has deepened in the past few years, Beijing has not been able—nor is it willing—to convert its economic leverage into political influence over Pyongyang. If anything, the fear of regime collapse and growing strategic rivalry with the US has convinced the Chinese leadership that North Korean regime survival and stability has become critical. While this explains why China has in recent years become tougher and more open in criticising North Korean behaviour and has joined the international community in imposing sanctions on Pyongyang, China has not fundamentally changed its policy towards North Korea to the extent it decides to desert its wayward client.[83]

Finally, Beijing has to worry about the consequences of regime instability or worse, collapse—massive refugee flows, major disruption in regional economic development, not to mention the custody of North Korea's nuclear weapons and materials. Beijing opposes the use or threat of military force in solving the nuclear issue and only supports limited sanctions, while Washington has never ruled out the option of regime change and prefers tougher sanctions. China maintains that only by addressing North Korea's security concerns will Pyongyang seriously consider giving up its nuclear option.

Notes

1. John Delury and Chung-In Moon, 'Strong, Prosperous, or Great? North Korean Security and Foreign Policy', in Saadia M. Pekkanen, John Ravenhill and Rosemary Foot, eds., *The Oxford Handbook of the International Relations of Asia* (Oxford: Oxford University Press, 2014), pp. 427–445.
2. On the Korean War and China's involvement, see Sergei Goncharov, John W. Lewis and Xue Litai, *Uncertain Partners: Stalin, Mao, and the Korean War* (Stanford: Stanford University Press, 1993); and Chen Jian, *China's Road to the Korean War* (New York: Columbia University Press, 1994).
3. Chae-Jin Lee, *China and Korea: Dynamic Relations* (Stanford: Hoover Institute, 1996).
4. Chen Fengjun and Wang Chuanjian, *Yatai daguo yu chaoxian bandao* ('Asian-Pacific Major Powers and the Korean Peninsula') (Beijing: Beijing University Press, 2002), chapter 5; Chin O. Chung, *Pyongyang between Peking and Moscow: North Korea's Involvement in the Sino–Soviet Dispute, 1958–1975* (Tuscaloosa, AL: University of Alabama Press, 1978); Hong Yung Lee, 'China and the Two Koreas: New Emerging Triangle,' in Young Whan Kihl, ed., *Korea and the World: Beyong the Cold War* (Boulder, CO: Westview Press, 1984), p. 99.
5. Shen Zhihua, 'Sino-North Korean Conflict and Its Resolution during the Korean War', translated by Dong Gil Kim and Jeffrey Becker, *Cold War International History Project Bulletin* 14/15 (2004), pp. 9–24; Nobuo Shimotomai, 'Pyeongyang in 1956', *Cold War International History Project Bulletin* 16 (2008), pp. 455–461; Jae Kyu Park, 'North Korea's Political and Economic Relations with China and the Soviet Union: From 1954 to 1980', *Comparative Strategy* 4:3 (1984), pp. 273–305.
6. Andrei Lankov, *The Real North Korea: Life and Politics in the Failed Stalinist Utopia* (Oxford: Oxford University Press, 2014), pp. 15–20.
7. Lee, *China and Korea*, pp. 65–70.
8. Qian Qichen, *Waijiao shiji* ('Ten Stories of a Diplomat') (Beijing: Shijie zhishi chubanshe,

2003); C.S. Eliot Kang, 'North Korea's International Relations: The Successful Failure?' in Samuel S. Kim, ed., *The International Relations of Northeast Asia* (Lanham: Rowman and Littlefield, 2004), pp. 281–300.
9   On Chinese policy towards the Korean Peninsula since reform, see Samuel S. Kim, 'The Making of China's Korea Policy in the Era of Reform', in David M. Lampton, ed., *The Making of Chinese Foreign and Security Policy in the Era of Reform* (Stanford: Stanford University Press, 2001), pp. 371–408.
10 Joel S. Wit, Daniel B. Poneman, and Robert L. Gallucci, *Going Critical: The First North Korean Nuclear Crisis* (Washington, DC: The Brookings Institution, 2005).
11 Andrew Scobell, *China and North Korea: From Comrades-in-Arms to Allies at Arm's Length* (Carlisle, PA: Strategic Studies Institute, US Army War College, March 2004); Sukhee Han, 'Alliance Fatigue amid Asymmetrical Interdependence: Sino–North Korean Relations in Flux', *Korean Journal of Defense Analysis* 16:1 (Spring 2004), pp. 155–179; You Ji, 'China and North Korea: A Fragile Relationship of Strategic Convenience', *Journal of Contemporary China* 10:28 (2001), pp. 387–398.
12 For a comprehensive treatise of the evolution of China's Korea policy and PRC–DPRK relations over the past five decades, see Chae-Jin Lee, *China and Korea: Dynamic Relations* (Stanford: The Hoover Institute, 1996); for developments since the end of the Cold War, see Samuel S. Kim, 'The Making of China's Korea Policy in the Era of Reform', in David M. Lampton, ed., *The Making of Chinese Foreign and Security Policy in the Era of Reform* (Stanford: Stanford University Press, 2001), pp. 371–408; Yongho Kim, 'Forty Years of the Sino–North Korean Alliance: Beijing's Declining Credibility and Pyongyang's Bandwagoning with Washington', *Issues and Studies* 37:2 (March/April 2001), pp. 147–176; International Crisis Group, *China and North Korea: Comrades Forever?* Asia Report 112, February 2006. http://www.crisisgroup.org/home/index.cfm?l=1&id=3920.
13 Jin Moo Kim, 'North Korea's Reliance on China and China's Influence on North Korea', *The Korean Journal of Defense Analysis* 23:2 (June 2011), p. 259.
14 PRC Ministry of Foreign Affairs Fact Sheet on China–DPRK Bilateral Relations (Chinese version), last updated July 2015, at: http://www.fmprc.gov.cn/mfa_chn/gjhdq_603914/gj_603916/yz_603918/1206_604114/sbgx_604118/
15 Chinese Ministry of Foreign Affairs Fact Sheet on China–ROK Relations (Chinese version), updated July 2015, at: http://www.fmprc.gov.cn/mfa_chn/gjhdq_603914/gj_603916/yz_603918/1206_604234/sbgx_604238/; Samuel S. Kim and Tai Hwan Lee, 'Chinese–North Korean Relations: Managing Asymmetrical Interdependence', in Samuel S. Kim and Tai Hwan Lee, eds., *North Korea and Northeast Asia* (Lanham and London: Rowman and Littlefield Publishers, Inc., 2002), pp. 109–137.
16 *Shijie zhishi* (*World Affairs*) 10 (2004), pp. 30–31.
17 PRC Embassy to the US, 'Chinese Top Legislator Gives Four-Point Proposal on Sino–DPRK Relations', 18 October 2004. DPRK Briefing Book. Nautilus Institute. http://www.nautilus.org/DPRKBriefingBook/china/PRC_RM1.html.
18 'Liaowang Article Examines Reasons Behind Hu Jintao's Visit to DPRK', 31 October 2005, p. 44, in FBIS-CPP20051102510011.
19 Maurice Johnstone, 'Absolute Beginner: North Korea after Kim Jong-Il', *Jane's Intelligence Review* 24:2 (February 2012), pp. 8–13.
20 Dick K. Nanto and Mark E. Manyin, eds., *China–North Korea Relations* (Washington, DC, Congressional Research Service, December 28, 2010).
21 'China Brings Lavish Gifts to North Korea', *The Chosun Ilbo*, 7 October 2009.
22 Nanto and Manyin, *China–North Korea Relations*, pp. 12–13; Editorial, 'Countering Hegemonism: the Common Values of China and the DPRK', *China Review News*, 26 October, 2010; 'Xi Jinping: the Anti-US and Assisting Korea War Is Just Fight against Aggression,'

China Review News, October 25, 2010.
23 Xinhua, 7 May 2010, quoted in Jonathan Pollack, *No Exit: North Korea, Nuclear Weapons and International Security*, (London: Routledge, 2011), p. 175.
24 Bonnie S. Glaser and Brittany Billingsley, 'China–North Korean Ties in the Wake of the Death of Kim Jong Il', *Korea Review* 2:2 (November 2012), pp. 105–135.
25 Chang-hyun Jung, 'The Execution of Jang Song Thaek: Consolidating Power Pyongyang-Style', *Global Asia* 9:1 (Spring 2014), pp. 14–21.
26 Carla Freeman, ed., *China and North Korea: Strategic and Policy Perspectives from a Changing China* (New York: Palgrave Macmillan, 2015); Leif-Eric Easley and In Young Park, 'China's Norms in Its Near Abroad: Understanding Beijing's North Korea Policy', *Journal of Contemporary China* (2016). http://dx.doi.org/10.10670564.2016.1160497
27 Li Zhaoxing, *Shuo Bu Jin De Wai Jiao* (*My Diplomatic Memoir*) (Beijing: China CITIC Press, 2014), pp. 103–104.
28 Scott Snyder and See-Won Byun, 'Prospect for a Strategic Partnership?' *Comparative Connections* (September 2015).
29 Michael Ilger and Caitlin Campbell, 'Diminishing China–North Korea Exchanges: An Assessment', staff research report, US–China Economic and Security Review Commission, 23 March 2015.
30 Jess McHugh, 'North Korea China Military Parade Snub: Kim Jong Un Refuses Chinese Invitation as Border Tensions with South Heighten', *International Business Times*, 11 September 2015; Hwan Yong Kim, 'Kim Jong Un Hails Chinese Role in Korean War', *Voice of America*, 28 July 2015; Adam Cathcart, 'Assessing North Korea's "Ground Game" with China', *The Diplomat*, 27 August 2015; Chad O'Carroll, 'N Korean Delegation Get Little Attention at China's Victory Day Celebration', *North Korea News*, 3 September 2015.
31 'North Korea Snubs Greetings from China', *The Chosun Ilbo*, 10 September 2015.
32 Cary Huang, 'China's Propaganda Blitz Hints at Beijing's Closer Ties with North Korean "Blood Brother"', *South China Morning Post*, 18 October 2015; 'North Korean Bank Abruptly Leaves China, Its Concert Canceled', *New York Times*, 14 December 2015.
33 You Ji, 'China and North Korea: A Fragile Relationship of Strategic Convenience', *Journal of Contemporary China* 10:28 (2001), pp. 390–392.
34 Tat Yan Kong, 'The Political Obstacles to Economic Reform in North Korea: the Ultra Cautious Strategy in Comparative Perspective', forthcoming, *The Pacific Review*, http://dx.doi.org/10.1080/09512748.2013.846933; Even DPRK diplomats posted in China long enough would be subjected to 'debriefing' and/or 'brainwashing' lest they were contaminated by material pursuits. Interview with Chinese analyst, Beijing, December 2005.
35 Taekyoon Kim, 'Strategizing Aid: US–China Food Aid Relations to North Korea in the 1990s', *International Relations of the Asia-Pacific* 12:1 (January 2012), pp. 41–70.
36 Mark E. Manyin, *Foreign Assistance to North Korea*, (Washington, DC, Congressional Research Service, updated 26 May 2005); International China Group, *China and North Korea*, p. 3; Cheng Xian, 'North Korea's Economic Difficulties', p. 25; Andrei Lankov, 'China Raises its Stake in North Korea' *Nautilus Institute Policy Forum Online* 06–02A, 6 January 2006. http://www.nautilus.org/fora/security/0602Lankov.html; 'South Korean Media Report that DPRK Will Receive $10 Billion Investment from China', *Global Times*, 15 February 2010.
37 Julia Joo-A Lee, 'To Fuel or Not to Fuel: China's Energy Assistance to North Korea', *Asian Security* 5:1 (2009), pp. 45–72.
38 'Kyodo: PRC Aid Pledge to DPRK for Sake of Regional Stability, Tension Reduction', 29 October 2005, in FBIS-JPP20051031026002; International Crisis Group, *China and North Korea*, p. 4.
39 International Crisis Group, *China and North Korea*, p. 4; 'Japanese Journalist Says China Turning North Korea into "Second Tibet"', 14 December 2005. FBIS-JPP20051130016006

40 Ko Soo-Suk and Kang Jin-Kyu, 'China Seeks More Workers from North', *Korea JoongAng Daily*, 27 January 2016.
41 Bonnie S. Glaser, 'The US Response to North Korea's Nuclear Provocations', statement before the House Foreign Affairs Committee Subcommittee on Asia and the Pacific, 13 January 2016; Jane Perlez and Yufan Huang, 'To Build a Ski Resort Under UN Sanctions, North Korea Turned to China', *New York Times*, 5 February 2016.
42 Adam Cathcart, 'Boondoggle on the Yalu: China's Useless New Bridge to North Korea', Sinonk.com, 3 November 2014; Scott Snyder and See-won Byun, 'Beijing Ties Uneven with Seoul, Stalled with Pyongyang', *Comparative Connections* (January 2015).
43 Jeong Yong-Soo, 'North Rents Out Waters Near NLL', *Korea JoongAng Daily*, 30 May 2014.
44 Glyn Ford, 'Forks in the Road to Reform: Socio-Economic Changes Under Kim Jong Un', *Global Asia* 9:1 (Spring 2014), pp. 44–50.
45 Guo Rui and Wang Xiaoke, 'Quantificational Measurement of China–North Korea Relations after the End of the Cold War: Changes, Characteristics, and Elicitation', *Korean Journal of Defense Analysis* 25:1 (March 2013), pp. 129–146.
46 Taeho Kim, 'Strategic Relations between Beijing and Pyongyang: Growing Strains amid Lingering Ties', in James R. Lilley and David Shambaugh, eds., *China's Military Faces the Future* (Armonk, New York: M.E. Sharpe and Washington, DC: The American Enterprise Institute, 1999), pp. 321.
47 Snyder and Byun, 'DPRK Provocations Test China's Regional Role', *Comparative Connections* (January 2011).
48 Hu Kui, 'Tegao: zhongguo yong 'jingqiaoqiao fangshi' bokai chaohe 'wuyun' ('Special Report: China "Quietly" Clears Away the "North Korean Nuclear Cloud"'), *Xinlangwang*, 7 May 2003. http://news.sina.com.cn/c/2003-05-07/10271034102.shtml
49 Richard McGregor and Anna Fifield, 'China Applies Gentlest of Flicks to Pyongyang's Reins', *Financial Times*, 24 February 2005, p. 7.
50 Zhang Xiaoming, 'The Korean Peninsula and China's National Security: Past, Present and Future', *Asian Perspective* 22:3 (1998), pp. 259–272; Joseph Yu-Shek Cheng, 'China and the Korean Situation: The Challenge of Pyongyang's Brinkmanship', *East Asia* (Winter 2003), pp. 52–76.
51 Chen Fengjun and Wang Chuanjian, *Yatai daguo yu chaoxian bandao* (*Asian-Pacific Major Powers and the Korean Peninsula*) (Beijing: Beijing University Press, 2002), p. 7.
52 Samuel S. Kim and Tai Hwan Lee, 'Chinese–North Korean Relations: Managing Asymmetrical Interdependence', in Samuel S. Kim and Tai Hwan Lee, eds., *North Korea and Northeast Asia* (Lanham: Rowman and Littlefield Publishers, Inc., 2002), pp. 111–112.
53 Alexander Martin, 'North Korea Doubles Down on China Ties', *Wall Street Journal*, 30 April 2013.
54 Teddy Ng, 'Vice-President's North Korea Trip Shows Pyongyang Still Key Partner', *South China Morning Post*, 27 July 2013.
55 Zhang Huizhi and Wang Xiaoke, 'Zhongmei duichao zhengce jingzheng yu hezuo de taishi fenxi' ('SWOT Analysis on Competition and Cooperation of China and the US Policies toward DPRK'), *Dongbeiya Luntan* (*Northeast Asia Forum*) 5 (2012), pp. 31–39.
56 Scott Snyder, 'Prospects for Sino-American Policy Coordination toward North Korea', *International Journal of Korean Unification Studies* 21:1 (2012), pp. 21–44.
57 Jonathan Pollack, *No Exit*, pp. 199–204.
58 Victor Cha, *The Impossible State: North Korea, Past and Future* (New York: CCCO/HarperCollins Publishers, 2012), p. 344.
59 Kim, 'North Korea's Reliance on China'.
60 Pollack, *No Exit*, p. 207.
61 Jane Perlez, 'North Korean Leader, Young and Defiant, Strains Ties with Chinese', *New York Times*, 13 April 2013.

62 'North Korea Slams "Spineless" China', *The Chosun Ilbo*, 23 July 2014.
63 See, for example, Ji Xinlong, 'Chaoxian jingji qubian' 'North Korean Economy Looking for Change'; Gao Haorong, 'Chongfan pingrang' 'Return to Pyongyang', and Wang Mian, 'Kaicheng: xiangshijie zhanshi meili de chuangkuo', series reports on North Korea's economic reforms published in the online *International Herald Leadership*, of the China Xinhua News Agency, 26 January 2006; 'DPRK Notes Leader's PRC "Historic" Visit as "Further" Developing DPRK-PRC Friendship', 21 January 2006. FBIS-KPP20060121031003.
64 Victor D. Cha, testimony before the US–China Economic and Security Review Commission, Washington, DC, 13 April 2011; Daniel Byman and Jennifer Lind, 'Pyongyang's Survival Strategy: Tools of Authoritarian Control in North Korea', *International Security* 35:1 (Summer 2010), pp. 44–74; Bonnie S. Glaser, Scott Snyder and John Park, 'Keeping an Eye on an Unruly Neighbour: Chinese Views of Economic Reform and Stability in North Korea', (Washington, DC: US Institute of Peace, 2008); Sheena Chestnut, 'Illicit Activity and Proliferation: North Korean Smuggling Networks', *International Security* 32:1 (Summer 2007), pp. 80–111.
65 James Reilly, 'China's Economic Engagement in North Korea', *The China Quarterly* 220 (2014), pp. 915–935.
66 Mathieu Duchâtel and Phillip Schell, *China's Policy on North Korea: Economic Engagement and Nuclear Disarmament*. Policy Paper 40 (Stockholm: Stockholm International Peace Research Institute, December 2013).
67 North Korea Economic Watch, 'North Korea–China trade up 4.4% in Jan–Sept despite sanctions', GlobalPost, 11 November 2013; Glaser, 'US Response', *op cit*.
68 Barbara Demick, 'China Launches Economic Projects in North Korea', *Los Angeles Times*, 10 June 2011.
69 Drew Thompson, *Silent Partners: Chinese Joint Ventures in North Korea* (Washington, DC: SAIS, February 2011).
70 Nadège Rolland, 'North Korea's New Diplomacy', The National Bureau of Asian Research, 30 April 2015.
71 Felicia Schwartz, 'US, China Divided Over Response to North Korea's Nuclear Program', *Wall Street Journal*, 27 January 2016.
72 Laura Koran and Elise Labott, 'John Kerry: China's Approach to North Korea Hasn't Worked', CNN Politics, 8 January 2016.
73 Gao Haorong, 'US Holds the Key to N Korea Nuclear Stalemate', *International Herald Leader*, 27 January 2016.
74 Scott Snyder, 'Where China and the US Disagree on North Korea', *The Diplomat*, 9 January 2016.
75 Yuan Jingdong, 'The China Factor in South Korea's Foreign Relations', *East Asian Policy* 8:1 (Jan/Mar 2016), pp. 157–169.
76 Shannon Tiezzi, 'China Warns THAAD Deployment Could Destroy South Korea Ties "in an Instant"', *The Diplomat*, 26 February 2016; Anna Fifield, 'After Nuclear Test, Park Has Epiphanies on North Korea—and China', *Washington Post*, 20 February 2016.
77 Jonathan D. Pollack, 'China and North Korea: The Long Goodbye?' The Brookings Institution, 28 March 2016.
78 Eleanor Albert and Beina Xu, 'The China–North Korea Relationship', Council on Foreign Relations, updated 8 February 2016; Jonathan D. Pollack, 'Learning Its Lesson? What the Iran Deal Should Teach China about Sanctioning North Korea', The Brookings Institution, 11 February 2016.
79 Ha-Young Choi, 'China Values North Korea Ties Despite Sanctions: Editorial', *North Korea News*, 22 April 2016.
80 Shi Yinhong, 'New Games in Tightly Fixed Structures: North Korea's Volatile Desperation

and China's Cornered Strategy', *The Korean Journal of Defense Analysis* 23:3 (September 2011), pp. 353–368, quote on p. 360.
81 'After North Korea's Latest Nuclear Test, China Must Lead Global Efforts to Rein in Insecure Regime', *South China Morning Post*, 7 January 2016; 'North Korea Rocket Launch Testing China's Patience', *The Australian*, 5 February 2016; Colum Lynch, 'How Far Will Beijing Go to Curtail North Korea's Atomic Provocations?' Foreign Policy, 6 January 2016.
82 Han S. Park, 'North Korea as a US–China Flashpoint?' *Korea Review* 2:2 (November 2012), pp. 11–28; Nam Jong-Ho, Choo Jae-Woo, and Lee Jang-Won, 'China's Dilemma on the Korean Peninsula: Not an Alliance but a Security Dilemma', *Korean Journal of Defense Analysis* 25:3 (September 2013), pp. 385–398.
83 Andrei Lankov, 'How China's View of North Korea Is Changing', *North Korea News*, 24 July 2014; Andrew Scobell and Mark Cozad, 'China's North Korea Policy: Rethink or Recharge?' *Parameters* 44:1 (Spring 2014), pp. 51–63.

Rethinking Great-Power Rivalry: US, China and the Challenge of Nuclear Proliferation in North Korea and Iran

Robert G. Patman and Laura Southgate

Robert G. Patman is the head of the Department of Politics at the University of Otago, New Zealand, where Laura Southgate is a PhD student

Abstract

In an early attempt to move US–China relations away from a zero-sum conception of great power relations, President Obama said he wanted China to assume responsibilities commensurate with its rising power status. One of these responsibilities has been the challenge of halting or curtailing the Iranian and North Korean nuclear weapons programmes. In President Obama's view, China's role in addressing this nuclear proliferation challenge is vital. Engagement with China has therefore been a key component of the administration's nonproliferation strategy. As this paper will show, this approach has elicited mixed results. Nevertheless, attempts to cooperate on issues of mutual interest do indicate one important point—that future US–China rivalry is by no means inevitable.

From the outset, the Obama administration emphasised the importance of developing a diplomatic partnership with China in a globalising world. To achieve this goal, President Obama said the US would have to develop a closer dialogue with Beijing on a range of international issues and, for its part, a rapidly rising China should be prepared take on a more active global role. In particular, the Obama leadership believed that US–China engagement was essential for addressing the challenge of nuclear proliferation in countries like Iran and North Korea. In this chapter, we consider Paul Kennedy's historical model of great-power rivalry, Obama's stance towards China, Obama's approach to national security and nuclear nonproliferation, and US efforts to engage with China in curbing the development of nuclear weapons in North Korea and Iran. The central argument that emerges is that US–China cooperation in the area of nuclear nonproliferation has not yet lived up to expectations in the case of North Korea, but with respect to Iran such cooperation played a crucial role in producing the landmark nuclear arms agreement of July 2015.

Historical Lessons of Great-Power Rivalry

Great-power politics has traditionally been viewed in terms of an unmitigated struggle for power among nation-states. In particular, scholars like Paul Kennedy attribute the almost constant and cyclical great power conflicts to the supreme value that states attach to superior relative power.

In his 1987 book *The Rise and Fall of the Great Powers: Economic Change and Military Conflict from 1500 to 2000*, Paul Kennedy examines the politics and economics of the great powers over five centuries, and the reason for their decline. The book then predicts the fortunes of five great powers—China, Japan, the European Community (EC), the Soviet Union and the United States—in the period through to the end of the 20th century.

In essence, Kennedy accepts the realist premise that states are key actors in the international arena, but argues that the strength of a great power can only be measured in relative terms. He provides a clear and persuasively argued thesis. According to Kennedy, the ascendency of a great power over the long-term or in specific conflicts is strongly correlated to available material resources and economic performance. That is, the international standing of a great power depends on a delicate balance between its military expenditure and economic capability. Kennedy posits that military overstretch and a relative decline are the constant twin threats facing powers whose ambitions and military commitments exceed the capacity of their economic resource base.[1]

A key thrust of Kennedy's theory is distilled in the following passage:

> The triumph of any one Great Power in this period, or the collapse of another, has usually been the consequence of lengthy fighting by its armed forces; but it has also been the consequences of the more or less efficient utilization of the state's productive economic resources in wartime, and, further in the background, of the way in which that state's economy had been rising or falling, *relative* to the other leading nations, in the decades preceding the actual conflict. For that reason, how a Great Power's position steadily alters in peacetime is as important to this study as how it fights in wartime.[2]

It should be added that the interaction or balance between the military requirements and economic capacity of a great power is a dynamic one:

> The relative strengths of the leading nations in world affairs never remain constant, principally because of the uneven rate of growth among different societies and of the technological and organizational breakthroughs which bring a greater advantage to one society than to another[3]

Historically, therefore, no great power had managed to exercise its dominance permanently and Kennedy maintained there was no reason to believe that this pattern would change in the future. There would always be winners and losers when it came to great-power relations.

Using this framework, Kennedy compared the great powers of the 20th century and predicted the decline of the Soviet Union, the rise of China and Japan, mixed fortunes for the EC and the eventual decline of the United States. Kennedy's assessment of the US was based on three elements. First, the US economy was said to be declining in relation to the world's other major economies. Second, because a healthy economic base was a precondition for military strength, the US would experience a loss of military and, consequently, political power. Third, Kennedy believed that the root cause of America's economic problems was a consistent pattern of over-expenditure in its military sector. Thus, Kennedy's advice to US decision-makers was to recognise that the broad trends of decline were underway and adopt a mix of policies to help minimise the impact of this decline in the international arena. He asserted that the world was moving from a bipolar to a multipolar international system, where US power would be subject to growing challenges.[4] But provided all the great powers acted with some degree of self-restraint, the international system would remain relatively secure. For Kennedy, world politics in the 21st century was still largely determined by the competitive activities of the great powers.[5]

The Obama Administration and National Security

The advent of the Obama administration in 2009 appeared to signal a clear departure from the unilateralism of the Bush years and a revival of the 'assertive multilateralism' that had briefly characterised the US leadership approach before the Somalia debacle of 1993. Barack Obama had campaigned against George W. Bush's ideas and approach to foreign policy, and his election victory in November 2008 seemed to mark a new respect for the international impact of globalisation. According to Obama, the 'simple truth' of the 21st century is that 'the boundaries between people are overwhelmed by our connections'.[6] The Obama administration said that the US faced an 'extraordinary array of global challenges' in the post-Bush era. These challenges included 'poorly guarded nuclear weapons and material, a global financial meltdown, conflicts in Afghanistan and Iraq, Iran and North Korea building their nuclear weapons capabilities . . . pandemics and a climate that is warming by the day.'[7] Further, these 'are transnational security threats that cross national boundaries as freely as a storm. By definition, they cannot be tackled by any one country alone'[8]. To renew US leadership in the world, President Obama pledged 'to rebuild the alliances, partnerships and institutions necessary to confront common threats and enhance common security ... America cannot meet the threats of this century alone, and the world cannot meet them without America'.[9] In a July 2008 speech in Germany, Obama stated that 'partnership and cooperation among nations is not a choice; it is the one way, the only way, to protect our common security and advance our common humanity ... '[10]

Early in the Obama administration, the president had committed himself to reducing the role of nuclear weapons in the international system. According to Foot and Walter, under the Obama administration, the 'pendulum ha[d] swung back to a rhetorical emphasis on treaty-based agreements and multilateral action, marked in 2010 by a vigorous effort to achieve a final document based on a consensus at the NPT [Nuclear Non-Proliferation Treaty] Review Conference that year'.[11] The Obama administration placed great emphasis on nuclear nonproliferation in the 2010 US National Security Strategy, where it was argued that 'international peace and security is threatened by proliferation that could lead to a nuclear exchange. Indeed, since the end of the Cold War, the risk of a nuclear attack has increased ... that is why reversing the spread of nuclear weapons is a top priority'.[12] Obama took the 'symbolic step' of chairing the United Nations Security Council (UNSC) summit on nuclear nonproliferation and nuclear disarmament in 2009, the first time that a UNSC summit was chaired by a US president.[13] Then, in a major speech in Prague in April 2009, Obama stated that

> some argue that the spread of these weapons cannot be stopped, cannot be checked—that we are destined to live in a world where more nations and more people possess the ultimate tools of destruction. Such fatalism is a deadly adversary ... the United States has a moral responsibility to act. We cannot succeed in this endeavour alone, but we can lead it, we can start it. So today, I state clearly and with conviction America's commitment to seek the peace and security of a world without nuclear weapons.[14]

President Obama pledged to take steps in this direction by ratifying the Comprehensive Nuclear-Test-Ban Treaty and signing a new Strategic Arms Reduction Treaty (START) with Russia. The START treaty would limit strategic nuclear warheads deployed by each country to 1550 within seven years.[15]

By all indications, the Obama team had substantially redefined US national security interests. In US Ambassador to the UN Susan Rice's words, 'If ever there were a time for effective multilateral cooperation in pursuit of US interests and a shared future of greater peace and prosperity, it is now'.[16] This revised conception of national security recast the notion of US global primacy. To be sure, the Obama administration was saying that current global security challenges could not be met without US leadership. But while US leadership, in the words of Susan Rice, 'is necessary, it's rarely sufficient'.[17] This new stance certainly shaped the Obama administration's approach towards China.

Obama's China Policy

President Obama said that the relationship between the US and China would largely shape the history of the 21st century. It was President Obama's view that the US 'should treat China as an emergent global power and that China must assume responsibilities commensurate with its increased economic weight'.[18] During his first visit to China after winning the presidency, Obama outlined his vision of greater engagement between the US and China. He said that the US does 'not seek to contain China's rise. On the contrary, we welcome China as a strong and prosperous and successful member of the community of nations'.[19] But President Obama seemed to imply that China must be prepared to take on more global responsibilities as its economic and military power increases. He emphasised that Washington and Beijing needed to forge closer ties to address a host of international challenges, whether they be lifting the global economy out of a deep recession, combating climate change or countering nuclear proliferation. Building on a 2006 initiative, Obama and Chinese Premier Hu Jintao established the US–China Strategic and Economic as an annual platform for bilateral high-level discussions to institutionalise, in then Secretary of State Hillary Clinton's words, 'a new pattern of cooperation between our governments and a forum for discussion.'[20] All this suggests that the Obama administration has refashioned the idea of US global primacy, so favoured by Bush, to accommodate China as a possible partner in leadership.

The Obama administration set out its proposed China policy in its first National Security Strategy, issued in May 2010. That text stated that

> we will continue to pursue a positive, constructive and comprehensive relationship with China. We welcome a China that takes on a responsible leadership role in working with the United States and the international community ... we will monitor China's military modernization program and prepare accordingly to ensure that US interests and allies, regionally and globally, are not negatively affected ... we will encourage China to make choices that contribute to peace, security, and prosperity as its influence rises.[21]

The 2010 report acknowledged that the US and China 'will not agree on every issue ... but disagreements should not prevent cooperation on issues of mutual interest, because a pragmatic and effective relationship between the United States and China is essential to address the major challenges of the 21st century.'[22]

The Challenge of Nuclear Nonproliferation

According to Jeffrey Bader, Obama's senior director for East Asian affairs on the National Security Council, President Obama had a number of global foreign policy priorities, one of which was to halt or curtail Iranian and North Korean nuclear proliferation.[23] According to Bader, 'in Obama's view, China's role in all these issues was important, and in some instances critical.'[24] China also had significant relationships with both North Korea and Iran. It was hoped that China might be able to leverage North Korea regarding its nuclear weapons program. China was also 'Iran's largest trading partner and a major investor in Iran's energy sector, and therefore a player in Tehran's decisions on its future nuclear weapons program'.[25]

China has maintained a long-standing position of complete nuclear disarmament ever since it conducted its first nuclear test in October 1964. According to Hui Zhang, China's position has not changed.[26] Beijing 'believes that one key step toward a nuclear-free world is to reduce the role of nuclear weapons. To constrain their role, China has maintained a purely self-defensive nuclear strategy with a no-first-use doctrine and the pursuit of a reliable minimum deterrence nuclear force'.[27] Following Obama's speech in Prague in August 2009, Beijing officially stated: 'China is ready to work with other countries and make unremitting efforts to further promote the nuclear disarmament process and realize the goal of a nuclear-weapons-free world at an early date'.[28] At the same time however, 'many Chinese are concerned that the United States is still increasing its nuclear deterrent and continues its strategic modernization programs ... some Chinese officials and analysts suspect the intentions behind this new move toward a nuclear-free world. They argue it could aim to constrain China's nuclear modernization process'.[29] Nevertheless, on September 24, 2009, the Obama administration won the support of China at the United Nations Security Council for the objective of a world free of nuclear weapons.[30]

In 2010, Obama prioritised engagement with China as a key component of the administration's non-proliferation strategy.[31] This approach is still evident in the administration's revised National Security Strategy, released on 6 February 2015, which declared that, 'the United States welcomes the rise of a stable, peaceful, and prosperous China [and seeks] a constructive relationship with China that delivers benefits for our two peoples and promotes security and prosperity in Asia and around the world.' The text sees potential collaboration 'on shared regional and global challenges such as climate change, public health, economic growth, and [Korea's] denuclearization.'[32]

Countering Nuclear Proliferation: North Korea

From the beginning of President Obama's first term, North Korea has shown only a limited interest in international engagement.[33] In the wake of North Korea's May 2009 nuclear test, Beijing went along with tougher sanctions, 'but none that would really threaten regime stability in North Korea'.[34] China largely implemented new trade sanctions and a reduction in energy supplies. Whilst China and Washington 'share the desire for stable states on the PRC's borders', the two states struggle to 'agree on the concrete measures needed to achieve these objectives'.[35]

Tension on the Korean peninsula spiked to some of its highest levels since the 1950–53 Korean War after the sinking of a South Korean ship in 2010 which killed 46 sailors, and involved an exchange of artillery fire between the two sides, nuclear sabre-rattling from the North Korean government, and threats of war from both North and South Korea.³⁶ The escalation of the confrontation on the Korean peninsula seemed to divide China and the US. According to Plant and Rhode, the crisis in 2010 highlighted the conflicted motivations of China's policy towards North Korea. While Beijing opposes nuclear proliferation in North Korea and resents the disruption the regime in Pyongyang brings to regional peace and stability, 'these disadvantages are outweighed by the risk of regime collapse in North Korea, which would entail a large number of refugees entering northern China, and the likelihood of a reunified Korean peninsula under Seoul's control and allied with the United States'.³⁷ As a consequence, China was reluctant to be identified too closely with the Obama administration's stance during the flare up of 2010, and that was a source of frustration for an administration looking for more active PRC cooperation.³⁸

In light of the seeming contradiction between Chinese stated aims and Chinese actions with respect to areas of cooperation with the United States, the Obama administration since 2011 has increasingly pursued a two-track policy in Asia.³⁹ That is to say, the Obama administration has advanced 'bilateral relations and high-level contacts with China whenever possible', whilst strengthening alliances with other Asian countries, 'that are themselves viewing China's power ascendance with growing concern'.⁴⁰ According to Singh, 'there continues to exist a fundamental vacuum at the center of the United States' relations with China: an absence of strategic trust'.⁴¹ While the Obama administration has encouraged China to assume greater responsibilities commensurate with its position in the international system, some commentators have noted that the Obama administration has moved over time towards a stronger focus on hedging against China's power, even as it has continued to advocate Beijing's fuller inclusion in the regional order.⁴²

However, these developments have not prevented Obama and Xi from engaging in bilateral discussions relating to North Korean proliferation of nuclear weapons. In a meeting between Obama and Xi in 2013, there was an extended discussion of how to rein in North Korea. According to National Security Advisor Tom Donilon, Obama and Xi 'had a lengthy discussion about North Korea' during dinner on 7 June.⁴³ China, he added, has taken a number of steps to send a clear message to North Korea, including through enhanced enforcement of sanctions and public statements by the senior leadership in China.⁴⁴ Obama and Xi 'agreed that North Korea has to denuclearize; that neither country will accept North Korea as a nuclear-armed state; and that we would work together to deepen US–China cooperation and dialogue to achieve denuclearization.'⁴⁵

Obama also emphasised to President Xi 'that the United States will take any steps that we need to take to defend ourselves and our allies from the threat that North Korea presents.'⁴⁶ The two sides 'stressed the importance of continuing to apply pressure both to halt North Korea's ability to proliferate and to make clear that its continued pursuit of nuclear weapons is incompatible with its economic development goals.'⁴⁷ According to Donilon, 'the discussions on this issue, I believe, will allow us to continue to move ahead and work in a careful way in terms of our cooperation to work together to achieve our ends.' The bottom line 'is I think we had quite a bit of alignment on the Korean issue—North Korean issue, and absolute agreement that we would continue to work together on concrete steps in order to achieve the joint goals that the United States and China have with respect to the North Korean nuclear program.'[48]

In September 2013 at the G20 summit in Russia, Obama met with Xi to discuss nuclear proliferation in North Korea. Whilst it was confirmed that there was 'no breakthrough' on pressuring North Korea to halt its nuclear programme, the Obama administration was reportedly 'encouraged by China's cooperation on the subject'.[49] According to Ben Rhodes, the White House deputy National Security Council adviser, 'China has been a cooperative partner in underscoring the importance of denuclearisation on the Korean Peninsula'.[50] Similarly, in a joint press conference in November 2014, Obama stated that 'President Xi and I reaffirmed our commitment to the complete denuclearization of the Korean Peninsula, and we agree that North Korea will not succeed in pursuing nuclear weapons and economic development, that it can't have both'.[51]

According to some scholars, the North Korea nuclear case 'exemplifies how China limits its responsibilities on global issues (nonproliferation) in order to satisfy its immediate national concerns (maintaining North Korea's viability as a buffer state)'.[52] Notwithstanding this, hope remains in the US that China may still help with the US' North Korean denuclearisation policy. In November 2014, John Kerry said he hoped China 'will ultimately bring North Korea to the realization that its current approach is leading a dead end, and the only path that will bring it security and prosperity is to make real progress towards denuclearizing the Korean Peninsula.'[53] This came after similar remarks in October, when Kerry stated that 'the Chinese are being helpful' with regard to North Korea. After he 'went to visit last spring', Kerry said that US and Chinese officials 'engaged in a discussion where they agreed to step up their efforts with the North, and they have.' In the past year, Kerry noted, 'they've taken measures way beyond where they were . . . They've actually reduced the amount of jet fuel going into the country. They've put limitations on trade going into the country.'[54] Clearly, despite US frustrations regarding China's North Korea policy, optimism remains that China can eventually have a positive impact on halting proliferation.

This optimism has grown in 2015, with some pointing to a deteriorating relationship between China and North Korea and what appears to be a rapidly developing relationship between China and South Korea. China's nuclear experts have recently increased their estimates of North Korea's nuclear production.[55] It has been argued that this reflects China's growing concerns over North Korea's nuclear capabilities.[56] These growing concerns have coincided with what appears to be an increased emphasis on Beijing's relationship with Seoul. President Xi has met with the South Korean President Park Geun-Hye three times in the past three years.

The most recent of these was at Beijing's Victory Day parade on 3 September 2015. For some, this participation by a South Korean leader reflects an important shift in East Asian relations.[57] In addition to growing economic interests between China and South Korea, Seoul might well see enhanced relations with China as a means to counter the growing threat presented by North Korea.[58] Similarly, enhanced relations might well reflect China's growing desire to distance itself from the regime in North Korea. However, this perception has been challenged. As one scholar has cautioned, economic relations between China and North Korea have remained largely unaffected by the apparent tensions over nuclear proliferation.[59] Indeed, bilateral trade between the two has risen from US$1.7 billion in 2006 to US$6.54 billion in 2013.[60] This suggests something of a disconnect between China's rhetoric regarding nuclear proliferation in North Korea and its actions. Clearly, more needs to be done resolve this issue.

Countering Nuclear Proliferation: Iran

In addition to North Korea, the Obama administration also focused on the role China could play in halting nuclear proliferation in Iran. In 2009 Obama stated that his 'administration would engage Iran with respect and support its right to peaceful nuclear energy', but it was up to Iran to allow for 'rigorous inspections' and prove its peaceful intent, or it would face 'increased isolation' and 'international pressure'.[61] Obama emphasised the importance of relations with China to his agenda of halting nuclear proliferation in Iran. Obama was able to persuade then President Hu

> that Iran's nuclear program was a 'core interest' of the United States and that if China expected the United States to take its core interests into account Beijing needed to reciprocate on this issue.[62]

The argument that ultimately persuaded China to engage with the US on Iranian proliferation

> was that a failure to curb the program could result in an Israeli military strike or a nuclear arms race in the Middle East. Either way, the stability so essential to the extraction and shipment of oil supplies from the Gulf to China would be placed in severe jeopardy.[63]

However, Teheran did not respond positively to early overtures from the new Obama administration and, as a consequence, the Obama administration adopted a 'dual-track strategy' with Iran. That approach has rested on engagement 'without illusion'[64] and economic pressure to persuade the Iranian government to enter into negotiations on nuclear proliferation.[65] On 10 June 2010, China voted for UNSC resolution 1929 to impose sanctions against Iran, and China called on all states to implement the resolution fully and effectively.[66] However, this had not been an easy process. According to then Secretary of State Hillary Clinton, China

> do[es] not see Iran, particularly, as a threat to them. So they—after much diplomatic effort and arm-twisting, went along with the Iran Sanctions Act in the Security Council. But it's a constant, committed, determined effort for us to keep them abiding by the sanctions they agreed to.[67]

Chinese hesitancy regarding Iranian sanctions was also apparent following the release of the US–China joint statement at the Nuclear Security Summit in 2010, at which time 'many within the Obama administration held the view that a PRC endorsement of sanctions was often compromised through the continued trade of nuclear related items from China to Iran'.[68] During a visit to Beijing in September 2010, Robert Einhorn, the US State Department's special adviser for nonproliferation and arms control, expressed the US concern that certain Chinese companies were violating UN sanctions against Iran, perhaps without the knowledge of the Chinese government.[69]

Nevertheless, the Obama administration and EU officials have argued that they believe the sanctions have hindered Iran's efforts to acquire carbon fibre and maraging steel, an alloy that can be used to make centrifuges that enrich uranium to fuel a nuclear bomb. The fact that Hassan Rouhani defeated Mahmoud Ahmadinejad in the Iranian presidential elections of August 2013 may be seen as some form of vindication for the twin-track approach of the Obama administration towards Iran since 2010.

In November 2013, Beijing apparently played the role of broker in an 'historic deal' that Iran struck with six world powers, aimed at curbing Tehran's nuclear programme in exchange for initial sanctions relief.[70] It was reported that 'China pulled off a delicate balancing act in the negotiations between Iran, seen by Beijing as a long-term partner, and the US'. Hua Liming, the former Chinese ambassador to Iran, told state media that China acted as a helping broker: 'When the two parties came across irresolvable problems, they would come to China, which would "lubricate" the negotiation and put things back on track.'[71] Hua stated that Beijing welcomed the breakthrough deal with Iran, saying it would 'help safeguard peace and stability in the Middle East'.[72] Foreign Minister Wang Yi said in Geneva 'this agreement will help to uphold the international nuclear non-proliferation system [and] safeguard peace and stability in the Middle East.' Xiao Xian, an expert in international politics at Yunnan University, told reporters that regional stability was in China's long-term interest because it would enjoy more secure natural resources from Iran.[73]

However, Chinese cooperation in this regard has not always been so helpful, and its motives not always so clear. This continued to frustrate some in Washington. In November 2014, Foreign Minister Wang Yi travelled to Vienna for P5+1 talks with Iran that aimed to solve the long-standing issue of Iran's nuclear programme.

According to one commentator, Wang 'made it clear that China sees itself as a neutral arbitrator in the talks (unlike the US)'.[74] *Xinhua*, paraphrasing Wang, stated that China, 'as a responsible negotiating party', seeks 'a comprehensive agreement over the matter, which meets the common interests of the international community, including Iran'.[75] According to the reporter Shannon Tiezzi, Hua

> tacitly acknowledged that China is not quite playing the role that the Western powers, particularly the US would like to see . . . China has been moving closer to Tehran, seizing the chance to develop a sound relationship with a Middle Eastern power player while international conditions allow.[76]

Tiezzi highlights how Chinese oil imports from Iran increased to 630,000 barrels per day in the first six months of 2014, up 48% from the same period in 2013.[77] Total trade between China and Iran was worth nearly US$40 billion in 2013, with Chinese exports largely consisting of electronics, textiles, steel and industrial chemical, and with Iranian imports consisting of crude oil, ores and other raw materials.[78] And China has not only benefited from increased economic ties. China and Iran have also benefited from enhanced military cooperation. As Tiezzi notes, as Iran grows closer to China, 'there's less incentive for Iran to make sacrifices in order to secure more normal relations with the West. Even economic sanctions will have less bite as China continues to deepen its own economic engagement with Tehran.'[79] While this served to frustrate Obama's policy for cooperation on Iran's nuclear nonproliferation, it did not ultimately prevent a nuclear deal from being reached. On 14 July 2015, the P5+1 group, which included China, signed a Joint Comprehensive Plan of Action with Iran. This agreement sets limits on Iran's nuclear programme by eliminating pathways to a nuclear weapon in exchange for the gradual removal of international economic sanctions against Teheran.

According to Chinese Foreign Minister Wang Yi, China played 'a uniquely constructive role' in the signing of this agreement.[80] Wang informed the media that the deal turned 'a new page of Iran's relationship with other parties'.[81] He also stated that the 'comprehensive accord carries significance far beyond the Iranian nuclear issue itself', with particular reference to the denuclearisation of the Korean peninsula.[82] According to Wang, China's uniquely constructive role won praise from all the parties.[83] In particular, Wang is quoted as saying that:

> China has put forward the idea of the modification of the Arak heavy water reactor . . . This is the unique role China has played in resolving the Iranian nuclear issue . . . China would promote this process as initiator while enhancing communication with Iran.[84]

The assistance China offered the US with regards to the Iran nuclear deal clearly demonstrates that it is possible for these two powers to cooperate over areas of mutual interest. However, it is also clear that Sino–US methods to achieve this result differed. Having achieved a landmark agreement to curb Iran's nuclear development, it now remains to be seen whether a similar agreement can be reached with regards to North Korea.

Some Reflections on US–China Nuclear Nonproliferation Efforts in North Korea and Iran

The Obama administration clearly sees China as an important partner in curbing nuclear proliferation in both North Korea and Iran. After failing to establish to a productive bilateral dialogue with either of these countries, the Obama administration has tried to intensify multilateral negotiation efforts, involving China, to curb the nuclear ambitions of these two countries. In North Korea, these efforts have yet to yield any concrete results. In Iran, this approach has generated an historic nuclear deal after a change of government in Tehran in 2013.

The Iran nuclear agreement is important first and foremost for the tight limits it places on Iran's nuclear programmes—the major goal of the negotiations. The current deal was achieved by long and patient negotiations and is strongly supported by key US allies as well as China and Russia.[85] But the accord also has the potential to widen the diplomatic dialogue between the US and Iran, and facilitate discussions on a range of pressing regional issues such as the Syrian civil war.

It is tempting to interpret the Obama administration's more inclusive approach towards China as simply a reflection of the changing distribution of political, economic and military power between the two most prominent actors in the international system. According to this perspective, the Obama administration's willingness to work closely with China on global problems is directly linked to the fact that America, like other great powers before it, has entered a period of long-term decline and is now in the process of being gradually challenged by China as the world's number one power. In short, the more accommodating rhetoric of the Obama government towards China is essentially a function of declining US power. It is true, for example, that a report by a US government agency predicts with 'relative certainty' the emergence of a global multipolar system within the next 15 to 20 years, and that 'few countries are poised to have more impact on the world . . . than China.'[86]

But the Obama administration does not accept that the US political and economic system is in long-term decline. The US economy is now performing better than at any time since the late 1990s and there are recent signs of a slight slowdown in China's economic momentum. In fact, the Obama leadership is very confident about the vitality and sustainability of the US political system. In Obama's words, 'history offers a clear verdict. Governments that respect the will of their own people, that govern by consent and not coercion, are more prosperous, they are more stable, and more successful than governments that do not.'[87] Arguably, the Obama administration's more inclusive approach towards China has been based on calculations of China's expected actions and intentions. Obama is aware that China does not entirely trust the US. However, the administration has worked on the assumption that China will ultimately see little harm in cooperating with the US over areas it believes to be in its own interests. Obama has therefore been careful to engage China on these grounds.

The Obama leadership seems to be convinced that globalisation has fundamentally reshaped the context of global politics to the point where the idea of great power dominance in a deeply interconnected world has become deeply problematic. Most of the major economic, security and environmental challenges facing nation-states can now be resolved only on an international basis. Thus, Obama's approach to China is largely based on the conviction that unilateral options are less realistic or effective in today's world and that a democratic political system has little to fear from expanded cooperation and competition with a rising authoritarian superpower like China, although the reverse, of course, may not be true. In the period since Paul Kennedy published his seminal study *The Rise and Fall of the Great Powers: Economic Change and Military Conflict from 1500 to 2000*, the exponential increase in globalisation and interconnectivity has fundamentally reshaped the international system for all states, including great powers.

Notes

1. Paul Kennedy, *The Rise and Fall of the Great Powers: Economic Change and Military Conflict from 1500 to 2000* (London: Fonterra Press, 1987), pp. 438–39
2. Ibid., pp. xv
3. Ibid
4. Ibid., p. 691
5. Paul Kennedy, 'The Great Powers, Then and Now' *New York Times*, 13 August 2013, http://www.nytimes.com/2013/08/14/opinion/global/the-great-powers-then-and-now.html?_r=0&pagewanted=all
6. Barack Obama, 'Remarks by the President to the Ghanaian Parliament', Accra, 11 July 2009, http://www.america.gov/st/texttrans-english/2009/July/20090711110050abretnuh0.1079783.html. Accessed 2 December 2010.
7. Ibid.
8. Susan Rice, US Ambassador to the UN, 'United Nations is Vital to US Efforts to Craft Better, Safer World', New York University for Global Affairs, 12 August 2009, http://www.america.gov/st/texttrans-english/2009/August/20090813164826eaifas0.287945.html&distid=ucs. Accessed 5 March 2011.
9. Barack Obama, 'Renewing American Leadership', *Foreign Affairs* 4, pp. 2–16
10. President Obama's Speech, Berlin, Germany, 24 July 2008, http://www.nytimes.com/2008/07/24/us/politics/24text-obama.html?pagewanted=all&_r=0
11. Rosemary Foot and Andrew Walter, *China, The United States, and Global Order* (Cambridge: Cambridge University Press, 2011), p. 151
12. United States National Security Strategy, May 2010, Washington, p. 23. http://www.realinstitutoelcano.org/wpswcmconnect/81f9660042c36def87e4bf24ab1546e8/2010_national_security_strategy.pdf?MOD=AJPERES&CACHEID=81f9660042c36def87e4bf24ab1546e8
13. Foot and Walter, *China, the United States, and Global Order*, p. 151
14. Remarks by President Obama, Hradcany Square, Prague, Czech Republic, 5 April 2009. https://www.whitehouse.gov/the_press_office/Remarks-By-President-Barack-Obama-In-

Prague-As-Delivered/
15 *The Guardian*, 22 December 2010.
16 Susan Rice, US Ambassador to the UN, 'United Nations is Vital to US Efforts to Craft a Better, Safer World', New York University for Global Affairs, 12 August 2009, http://www.america.gov/st/texttrans-english/2009/August/20090813164826eaifas0.287945.html&distid=ucs. Accessed 5 March 2011.
17 Ibid.
18 Kenneth Lieberthal and Jonathan Pollack, 'Establishing Credibility and Trust: The Next President Must Manage America's Most Important Relationship,' *The Brookings Institute*, http://www.brookings.edu/research/papers/2012/03/16-china-lieberthal-pollack. Accessed 16 March 2012.
19 Barack Obama, 'Obama Answers Questions From Fudan University Students and the Internet', *America.gov*, 16 November 2009, http://www.america.gov/st/texttrans-english/2009/November/20091116095135eaifas0.900326.html.
20 US Department of State, 'Closing Remarks for US–China Strategic and Economic Dialogue', *America.gov*, 28 July 2009, http://www.america.gov/st/texttrans-english/2009/July/20090729100351emffen0.1570993.html. Accessed 5 March 2011.
21 Richard Weitz, 'Obama administration Reaffirms China Policy in Key Documents', *China–US Focus*, 16 February 2015. http://www.chinausfocus.com/foreign-policy/obama-administration-reaffirms-china-policy-in-key-documents/.
22 Ibid.
23 Jeffrey A. Bader, *Obama and China's Rise* (Washington, DC: Brookings Institute, 2012), p. 21
24 Ibid.
25 Ibid.
26 Hui Zhang, 'China's Perspective on a Nuclear-Free World,' *The Washington Quarterly* 33:2 (2010), p. 139
27 Ibid., p. 140.
28 Ibid., p. 142–3.
29 Ibid., p. 144
30 United Nations Security Council SC/9746, resolution 1887 at the 6191st meeting
31 United States National Security Strategy, May 2010, Washington, p. 43.
32 Weitz, 'Obama administration Reaffirms China Policy in Key Documents'.
33 Stephen Haggard and Marcus Noland, 'Sanctioning North Korea: The Political Economy of Denuclearisation and Proliferation', *Asian Survey* 50 (3 May/June 2010), pp. 539–568.
34 David Lampton, 'The United States and China in the Age of Obama: looking each other straight in the eyes', *Journal of Contemporary Asia* 18:62 (2009), p. 724
35 Ibid., p. 725
36 *The Guardian*, 20 May 2010
37 Thomas Plant and Ben Rhode, 'China, North Korea and the Spread of Nuclear Weapons,' *Survival: Global Politics and Strategy*, 55:2 (2013), pp. 61–80
38 Ibid.
39 Lieberthal and Pollack, 'Establishing Credibility and Trust.' 16 March 2012.
40 Ibid.
41 Robert Singh, *Barack Obama's Post-American Foreign Policy* (London: Bloomsbury, 2012), p. 141
42 Lieberthal and Pollack, 'Establishing Credibility and Trust', 16 March 2012.
43 'Obama, Xi Agree North Korea Must Denuclearize', *US Department of Defense*, Washington, 9 June 2013
44 Ibid.
45 Ibid.
46 Ibid.

47 Ibid.
48 Ibid.
49 Dave Boyer, 'Obama, Chinese president huddle on North Korea's nuclear issue at G20', *The Washington Times*, 6 September 2013.
50 Ibid.
51 Remarks by President Obama and President Xi Jinping in Joint Press conference, Great Hall of the People, Beijing, China, 12 November 2014. https://www.whitehouse.gov/the-press-office/2014/11/12/remarks-president-obama-and-president-xi-jinping-joint-press-conference
52 Martin Indyk, Kenneth Lieberthal and Michael O'Hanlon, *Bending History: Barack Obama's Foreign Policy* (Washington, DC: Brookings Institution Press, 2012), p. 38
53 JC Finley, 'US Outreach to China aims to deter North Korea Nuclear Proliferation', *UPI News*, 4 November 2014. http://www.upi.com/Top_News/World-News/2014/11/04/US-outreach-to-China-aims-to-deter-North-Korea-nuclear-proliferation/1241415140265/
54 Ibid.
55 Jeremy Page, 'China Warns North Korean Nuclear Threat is Rising,' *Wall Street Journal*, 22 April 2015. http://www.wsj.com/articles/china-warns-north-korean-nuclear-threat-is-rising-1429745706
56 Ibid.
57 Sandip Kumar Mishar, 'China–South Korea Ties: Implications for the US Pivot to Asia', *Institute of Peace and Conflict Studies*, 8 September 2015, http://www.ipcs.org/article/east-asia/china-south-korea-ties-implications-for-the-us-pivot-to-4909.html
58 Ibid.
59 Kevin Gray, 'China isn't about to abandon North Korea,' *East Asia Forum*, 29 September 2015. http://www.eastasiaforum.org/2015/09/29/china-isnt-about-to-abandon-north-korea/
60 Ibid.
61 Jill Marie Lewis and Laicie Olson, 'Iran Policy on the Way to Zero', in Catherine McArdle Kelleher and Judith Reppy, eds., *Getting to Zero: The Path to Nuclear Disarmament* (Stanford: Stanford University Press, 2011), p. 213
62 Indyk, Lieberthal and O'Hanlon, *Bending History*, p. 196
63 Ibid.
64 White House *National Security Strategy*, May 2010, pp. 26
65 Ray Takeyh and Suzanne Maloney, 'The self-limiting success of Iran sanctions', *International Affairs* 87:6, pp. 1304–05, 2011; Suzanne Maloney, 'Obama's Counterproductive New Iran Sanctions', *Foreign Affairs* 5 (2012).
66 Aiden Warren, *The Obama Administration's Nuclear Weapon Strategy* (New York: Routledge, 2014), p. 196
67 Ibid.
68 Ibid.
69 *Washington Post*, 30 September 2010; John Garve 'Is China Playing a Dual Game in Iran?', *The Washington Quarterly* 34:1, (2011), pp. 75–88. Please see also: 'The Iran Nuclear Issue: The View from Beijing', *International Crisis Group Asia Briefing* 100 (17 February 2010); John Pomfret, 'Chinese firms bypass sanctions on Iran, US says,' *Washington Post*, 18 October 2010 and Erica Downs and Suzanne Maloney 'Getting China to Sanction Iran', *Foreign Affairs* 90:1 (2011), pp. 15–22.
70 Adrian Wan, 'China plays key broker role in Iran nuclear deal', *South China Morning Post*, 25 November 2013. http://www.scmp.com/news/china/article/1364808/china-plays-key-role-broker-iran-nuclear-deal
71 Ibid.
72 Ibid.
73 Ibid.
74 Shannon Tiezzi, 'How China Complicates the Iranian Nuclear Talks', *The Diplomat*, 25

November 2014. http://thediplomat.com/2014/11/how-china-complicates-the-iranian-nuclear-talks/
75 Ibid.
76 Ibid.
77 Ibid.
78 Ibid.
79 Ibid.
80 Chen Weihua, 'China "constructive" on Iran deal: foreign minister', *China Daily*, 15 July 2015. http://usa.chinadaily.com.cn/world/2015-07/15/content_21285326.htm
81 Ibid.
82 Ibid.
83 Ibid.
84 Frank Ching, 'China's role in the Iran nuclear deal,' *EJInsight*, 21 July 2015. http://www.ejinsight.com/20150721-china-role-iran-nuclear-deal/
85 Sandy Berger, 'The Fantasy of a Better Iran Deal,' *Politico Magazine*, 5 April 2015. http://www.politico.com/magazine/story/2015/04/the-fantasy-of-a-better-iran-deal-116676
86 Kishore Mahbubani, *The New Asian Hemisphere: The Irresistible Shift of Global Power to the East* (New York: Public Affairs, 2008).
87 The White House, *Remarks by the President to the Ghanaian Parlament,* 11 July 2009, http://www.whitehouse.gov/the-press-office/remarks-president-ghanaian-parliament. Accessed 5 March 2011.

4. PERSPECTIVES OF ASIAN COUNTRIES (2)

Not Too Hot, Not Too Cold: A Vietnamese Perspective on China–US Relations

Carlyle A. Thayer

Emeritus professor, the University of New South Wales (UNSW), at the Australian Defence Force Academy (ADFA), Canberra, Australia

Abstract

Vietnam pursues a declaratory foreign policy of multilateralisation and diversification of international relations. Vietnam places a major—but not exclusive—emphasis on relations with the major powers: Since 2003, Vietnam has pursued a policy of cooperation and struggle (doi tac va doi tuong) in its relations with China and the US. With respect to China–US relations, Vietnam follows the 'Goldilocks formula'. Vietnam does not want China–US relations to become 'too hot' because it fears the states will collude against Vietnam's interests. Vietnam also does not want China–US relations to become 'too cold' because of the negative impact this would have on Vietnam. Vietnam prefers that China–US relations are 'just right' so it can leverage off the dynamic tensions in China–US bilateral relations. This paper analyses Vietnamese perceptions of China–US relations since the June 2013 informal summit between presidents Barack Obama and Xi Jinping at Sunnylands.

Introduction

Vietnam pursues a declaratory foreign policy of 'independence, self-reliance, multilateralisation and diversification of international relations, [and] proactive international integration and cooperation'.[1] Within this foreign policy framework Vietnam places a major—but not exclusive—emphasis on relations with the major powers: China (a comprehensive strategic cooperative partner), Russia (a comprehensive strategic partner), Japan (an extensive strategic partner), India (a strategic partner) and the US (a comprehensive partner). Vietnam seeks to maintain equilibrium in its relations with the five major powers. Vietnam places priority on its relations with China due to shared boundaries, historical interaction, revolutionary struggle and socialist ideology. But Vietnam resists China's centripetal pull. Vietnam shows deference to China but insists that its autonomy be respected.[2]

Vietnam pursues a robust mixed strategy of comprehensive engagement with China and hedging, or indirect balancing, in its relations with the US.[3] Since 2003, Vietnam has pursued a policy of cooperation and struggle (*doi tac va doi tuong*) in its relations with China and the US.[4] Vietnam seeks to promote cooperation across the full spectrum of bilateral relations with both major powers but faces 'struggles' (ranging from resistance to defiance) when its national interests are threatened. For example, Vietnam 'struggles' against Chinese assertiveness in the South China Sea, and Vietnam 'struggles' against US political pressures on human rights. Vietnam seeks to maintain a delicate balance between 'cooperation and struggle' in order to prevent any single issue from spilling over and negatively impacting bilateral relations in general.

Vietnam underpins its strategy of 'cooperation and struggle' with a determined self-help effort to modernise its armed forces.[5] In recent years Vietnam has acquired top of the line Sukoi Su-30 jet aircraft, stealth frigates, fast-attack missile boats, and coastal and air defence missiles from Russia. Since December 2013, it has taken delivery of four of six Kilo-class conventional submarines ordered from Russia. The fifth submarine is currently undergoing sea trials in the Baltic, while the sixth submarine was launched in late September.[6]

With respect to China–US relations, Vietnam prefers the 'Goldilocks model'. Vietnam does not want China–US relations to become 'too hot' because it fears the states will collude against Vietnam's interests. Vietnam also does not want China–US relations to become 'too cold' because of the negative impact this would have on Vietnam. Vietnam prefers that China–US relations are 'just right' so it can leverage off the dynamic tensions in China–US bilateral relations.[7]

This paper is divided into four parts. Part one provides background on Vietnam's foreign policy framework following Vietnam's normalisation of diplomatic relations with China and the US in 1991 and 1995, respectively. Part two provides an overview of the implementation of Vietnam's foreign policy of 'multilateralising and diversifying' its relations,[8] with the major powers with a specific focus on strategic partnerships. Part three discusses Vietnam's relations with China and the US after the informal summit between presidents Barack Obama and Xi Jinping in Sunnylands in June 2013. Part four provides a summary and conclusion.

I. The Framework of Vietnam's Relations with China and the US, 1991–1995

A comprehensive political settlement reached in Paris in October 1991 ended conflict in Cambodia and dramatically altered Vietnam's strategic landscape. Vietnam was now positioned to resolve the strain in its bilateral relations with China and to advance the process of normalisation of diplomatic relations with the US. In short, the post-Cambodian conflict era presented Vietnam with new opportunities as well as new challenges.

The first signs of Vietnam's strategic policy readjustment emerged at the seventh national congress of the Vietnam Communist Party (VCP), which met from 24–27 June 1991, three months before the Paris peace conference on Cambodia. The congress adopted a new orientation in foreign policy. Vietnam would now 'diversify and multilateralise economic relations with all countries and economic organisations . . .'.[9] In short, 'Vietnam wants to become the friend of all countries in the world community, and struggle for peace, independence and development.' According to the political report, 'We stand for equal and mutually beneficial co-operation with all countries regardless of different socio-political systems and on the basis of the principle of peaceful coexistence'.[10]

The political report, however, gave priority to relations with the Soviet Union, Laos, Cambodia, China, Cuba, other 'communist and workers' parties', the 'forces struggling for peace, national independence, democracy and social progress', India, and the Non-Aligned Movement. It was only at the end of this list that Vietnam's 'new friends' were mentioned:

> To develop relations of friendship with other countries in South-East Asia and the Asia-Pacific region, and to strive for a South-East Asia of peace, friendship and co-operation. To expand equal and mutually beneficial co-operation with northern and Western European countries, Japan and other developed countries. *To promote the process of normalisation of relations with the US* [emphasis added].[11]

Vietnam reaped substantial foreign policy dividends following the Cambodian peace agreement. For example, both Japan and the European Union ended restrictions on development assistance, trade and investment in Vietnam. Vietnam also succeeded in diversifying its foreign relations by moving from dependency on the Soviet Union, now in a period of disintegration, to a more diverse and balanced set of external relations. During this period Vietnam normalised its relations with all members of ASEAN and in November 1991 Vietnam and China also normalised their relations.[12] In 1989 Vietnam had diplomatic relations with only 23 states; by 1995 this number had expanded to 163.

Not all was smooth sailing in Sino–Vietnamese normalisation, however. In February 1992 China's National People's Congress passed the Law of the People's Republic of China Concerning the Territorial Sea and the Contiguous Zone, which claimed all islands in the South China Sea, including the Paracel and Spratly archipelagoes. China's law then put it on a collision course with Vietnam regarding sovereignty claims in the South China Sea. This took the form of a series of maritime incidents in the 1990s, precipitated by China's efforts to explore for oil in waters falling within Vietnam's exclusive economic zone (EEZ).[13]

In January 1994 the VCP convened its first mid-term party conference. The political report reaffirmed Vietnam's commitment to the broad outlines of economic and political renovation that emerged since the seventh congress. The political report listed eight essential tasks to be carried out, including the expansion of Vietnam's external relations.[14] The major policy theme to emerge from the mid-term conference was that priority be given to the industrialisation and modernisation of Vietnam and the mobilisation of domestic and foreign capital.[15]

In the period between the 1994 mid-term conference and the convening of the eighth national congress in mid-1996, Vietnam continued to pursue an open-door foreign policy designed 'to make friends with all countries'.[16] These efforts paid handsome dividends. In 1993–94, the US ended its long-standing objections to the provision of developmental assistance to Vietnam by the World Bank and International Monetary Fund, and gradually lifted restrictions on trade and investment with Vietnam. Vietnam thus became eligible for a variety of aid, credits and commercial loans to finance its development plans.

In July 1995 Vietnam made a major breakthrough on the foreign policy front. Vietnam normalised relations with the US, became ASEAN's seventh member, and signed a framework cooperation agreement with the European Union. For the first time, Vietnam had diplomatic relations with all five permanent members of the United Nations Security Council and, equally as important, with the world's three major economic centres—Europe, North America and East Asia.

2. Vietnam's Strategic Partnerships with the Major Powers, 1996–2013

The next turning point in Vietnam's foreign policy came at the eighth national congress, held from 28 June–1 July 1996.[17] The foreign policy section of the political report juxtaposed the potential for conflict arising from competition in the areas of economics, science and technology, with the potential for cooperation arising from peaceful coexistence between 'socialist countries, communist and workers parties and revolutionary and progressive forces' and 'nations under different political regimes'.[18]

Vietnam sought to promote cooperation with the major powers through agreements on strategic partnership. In March 2001, the Russian Federation, a 'traditional friendly state', became Vietnam's first strategic partner during the course of the visit by President Vladimir Putin to Hanoi.[19] This agreement set out broad-ranging cooperation in eight major areas. Russian arms sales to Vietnam soon became the largest and most significant component of the strategic partnership.[20] Russia became Vietnam's largest provider of military equipment and technology.[21]

After the VCP's eighth national congress in 1996 Vietnam and the US began difficult negotiations on the terms of a bilateral trade agreement (BTA). This BTA was a highly contentious issue among the party elite. It was only in mid-2000 that the party Central Committee's tenth plenum gave its approval to concluding negotiations with the US.

The ninth VCP national congress, held from 19–23 April 2001, set the goals of overcoming underdevelopment by the year 2010 and accelerating industrialisation and modernisation in order to become a modern industrialised state by 2020. According to Vu Khoan, the ninth congress resolution identified two main measures to attain this goal,

> first, perfect the regime of a market economy with socialist characteristics, and second, integrate deeper and more fully into the various global economic regimes. Integration into the global economy will tie our economy into the regional and global economies on the basis of common rules of the game.[22]

As a result, in 2001 the US granted Vietnam temporary normal trade relations status on a year-by-year basis.

The ninth congress also reaffirmed that 'Vietnam wants to be a friend and a reliable partner to all nations' by diversifying and multilateralising its international relations.[23] Priority was placed on developing relations with 'socialist, neighbouring and traditional friendly states'.[24]

In mid-2003, the VCP Central Committee's eighth plenum provided an important interpretation of two ideological concepts—'partners of cooperation' (*doi tac*) and 'objects of struggle' (*doi tuong*) in foreign relations. According to the eighth plenum's resolution, 'any force that plans and acts against the objectives we hold in the course of national construction and defense is the object of struggle.' And, 'anyone who respects our independence and sovereignty, establishes and expands friendly, equal, and mutually beneficial relations with Vietnam is our partner.'[25]

The eighth plenum resolution argued for a more nuanced dialectical application of these concepts:

> with the objects of struggle, we can find areas for cooperation; with the partners, there exist interests that are contradictory and different from those of ours. We should be aware of these, thus overcoming the two tendencies, namely lacking vigilance and showing rigidity in our perception, design, and implementation of specific policies.[26]

The eighth plenum resolution thus provided the policy rationale for Vietnam to step up cooperative activities with the US.[27] After the plenum Vietnam advised the US that it would accept a long-standing invitation for its Minister of Defence to visit Washington. Vietnam also approved the first port call by a US Navy warship since the Vietnam War.

The VCP convened its tenth national congress from 18–25 April 2006. According to the political report, Vietnam 'must strive to unswervingly carry out a foreign policy of . . . multilateral and diversified relationships while staying proactive in integrating into the world economic community and expanding international cooperation in other fields.'[28] In December 2006 Vietnam was granted permanent normal trade relations status by the US.

After the tenth congress, Vietnam stepped up efforts to consolidate its relations with the major powers as well as East Asian, European and ASEAN states through strategic partnership agreements.

In October 2006 the prime ministers of Vietnam and Japan issued a joint statement entitled 'Toward a Strategic Partnership for Peace and Prosperity in Asia'.[29] In November 2007 Vietnam and Japan issued a joint statement that included a 44-point agenda towards a strategic partnership. Point four of the agenda addressed defence cooperation including exchanges of military delegations, high-level defence officials' visits, and goodwill ship port calls by the Japan Maritime Self-Defense Force.

In July 2007 India and Vietnam adopted a 33-point joint declaration on strategic partnership.[30] It set out six areas for political, defence and security cooperation: (1) strategic dialogue at a vice ministerial level; (2) defence supplies, joint projects, training cooperation and intelligence exchanges; (3) exchange visits between their defence and security establishments; (4) capacity building, technical assistance and information sharing with particular attention to security of sea lanes, anti-piracy, prevention of pollution, and search and rescue; (5) counter-terrorism and cybersecurity; and (6) non-traditional security. Since 2007 defence cooperation has included high-level visits, an annual defence strategy dialogue and naval port visits.

In June 2008, following a summit of party leaders in Beijing, China–Vietnam bilateral relations were officially raised to that of strategic partners.[31] A year later this was upgraded to a strategic cooperative partnership (later redesignated comprehensive strategic cooperative partnership). As strategic partners, China and Vietnam developed a dense network of party, state, defence and multilateral mechanisms to manage their bilateral relations, including a joint steering committee at deputy prime minister level. China and Vietnam carried out defence cooperation in three areas: exchange of high-level visits, strategic defence and security dialogues, and joint naval patrols and port visits.

Tension between Vietnam and China over their territorial dispute in the South China Sea began to simmer from late 2007 and became more intense after May 2009. These tensions led to an increasing convergence of security concerns between Vietnam and the US. In 2010 Vietnam agreed to hold its first Defense Policy Dialogue with the US and quietly encouraged the US to contribute to maritime security by balancing Chinese military power.

The VCP held its 11th national congress from 12–19 Janaury 2011. The final resolution of the congress set the following foreign policty goals for the 2011–15 period: 'enhance external activities; firmly defend national independence, sovereignty and territorial integrity; thus creating a foundation for the nation to become a modern-oriented industrialised country by 2020.'[32] With specific reference to the main tasks ahead, the final resolution of the congress emphasised:

Intensifying the national defence and security strength and power; maintaining socio-political stability, independence, sovereignty, unity, territorial integrity, social order and security; preventing and foiling all schemes and plots of hostile forces; comprehensively and effectively carrying out external activities and *proactively taking part in international integration* [emphasis added].[33]

Following the 11th national congress, Vietnam moved to advance its defence relations with the US but in a low-key manner so as not to provoke China. At the second Defense Policy Dialogue, held in Washington in September 2011, the two sides signed their first formal memorandum of understanding (MOU) on defence cooperation.[34] This was a modest agreement that codified activities that were already being undertaken: regular high-level defence dialogue, maritime security, search and rescue, studying and exchanging experiences on UN peacekeeping, and humanitarian assistance and disaster relief (HADR). In some respects the MOU was a transparency measure directed at China.

In June 2012 Vietnam hosted a visit from US Secretary of Defense Leon Panetta under the 2003 agreement to exchange alternate visits by defence ministers every three years. Panetta visited the former US naval base at Cam Ranh Bay prior to his meeting with Minister of Defence General Phung Quang Thanh. Although Panetta's visit to Cam Ranh was rich in symbolism, Vietnam undercut any speculation that the US Navy would be permitted to return by reiterating its long-standing policy of 'three no's'—no foreign bases on Vietnamese territory, no military alliances and no use of a third country to oppose another country.[35]

Talks between Panetta and Thanh went over old ground as they reviewed progress under their MOU. Thanh proposed future cooperation in non-sensitive areas only—HADR and search and rescue. He also elicited further US financial support to address legacies from the Vietnam War (unexploded ordnance and Agent Orange); and he called for the lifting of the US ban on arms sales.[36]

Vietnam and the US held their fifth Political, Security and Economic Dialogue in Hanoi in June 2012. The following month Secretary of State Hillary Clinton held discussions with her counterpart in Hanoi. Vietnam's Deputy Minister of Defence General Nguyen Chi Vinh travelled to Washington to discuss war legacy issues. In October, as the *USS George Washington* transited the South China Sea, Vietnamese officials were flown out to observe operations. Vietnam thus signalled that it supported a US naval presence in the South China Sea. In April 2013 US Coast Guard Rear Admiral William Lee pledged support for Vietnam's fisheries protection force.

Between 2009 and 2013 Vietnam reached strategic partnership agreements with South Korea and Spain (both in 2009), United Kingdom (2010), Germany (2011), and Italy, France, Thailand, Indonesia and Singapore (all in 2013). Vietnam and the Philippines reached a strategic partnership agreement in November 2015.[37] In same period Vietnam and Australia reached agreement on a comprehensive partnership (2009), while Vietnam and Russia raised their strategic partnership to a comprehensive strategic partnership (July 2012).

3. Vietnam's Relations with China and the US, 2013–15

The proceeding two parts of this chapter outlined the multilateral context of Vietnam's relations with the major powers. During 2013–15 Vietnam and Japan raised their bilateral relations to an extensive strategic partnership (March 2014), and Vietnam and Australia agreed to enhance their strategic partnership (March 2015). This part focuses on Vietnam's relations with the US and China in the period after the Sunnylands summit between presidents Obama and Xi in June 2013, up to the recent US–China Summit in Washington in September 2015.

Vietnam–China relations prior to the Haiyang Shiyou 981 crisis

In 2013 Vietnam–China bilateral relations went on an upward trajectory. As noted above, Vietnam and China developed a dense network of party, state, and defence mechanisms to manage their bilateral relations under the umbrella of the joint steering committee at deputy prime minister level. Both deputy prime ministers were also politburo members of their respective ruling parties. In May 2013 China and Vietnam held the sixth session of their joint steering committee for bilateral cooperation in Beijing.

Vietnam and China both identified their South China Sea dispute as the major irritant in their relations and sought to contain it from spilling over and affecting their overall bilateral relations. Vietnam and China continued to manage their territorial dispute in the South China Sea under an agreement to guide the settlement of maritime issues adopted in October 2011. There was a marked drop in the number of incidents involving fishermen. During the year political relations went on an upward trajectory.

In significant respects Vietnam's defence relations with China paralleled those with the US. In January Vietnam hosted a goodwill port visit to Ho Chi Minh City by three People's Liberation Army Navy (PLAN) ships. The two defence ministers met in May on the sidelines of the seventh ASEAN Defence Ministers Meeting (ADMM) in Brunei. Vietnam and China held their Fourth Strategic Defence Dialogue in Beijing in June and agreed to establish a naval hotline between their two defence ministries. That same month China and Vietnam conducted their 15th joint naval patrol in the Gulf of Tonkin and held a search and rescue training exercise. Later, two Vietnamese naval ships paid a goodwill port visit to the headquarters of China's South Sea Fleet at Zhanjiang city.

President Truong Tan Sang made an official state visit to China in June 2013 for discussions with President Xi Jinping. The two leaders agreed to double the size of their joint development area in the Gulf of Tonkin, extend cooperation between their national oil companies until 2016 and set up a fishery incident hotline. In late July, the two communist parties held their ninth theoretical seminar in China.

China's Foreign Minister Wang Yi paid an official visit to Hanoi in August.

The high point in bilateral relations occurred in October 2013 when Premier Li Keqiang made an official visit to Vietnam at the invitation of Prime Minister Nguyen Tan Dung to advance their comprehensive strategic partnership.[38] According to the joint statement issued by Dung and Li on 15 October, the two leaders agreed to set up three joint working groups with responsibilities in three areas.

The first area was onshore cooperation and included economic issues, transport and communication connectivity, and management of the China–Vietnam land border. Two-way trade was valued at US$41.2 billion in 2012 with China enjoying a surplus of US$16.4 billion. Prime Minister Dung pressed Premier Li for a more balanced trade by easing the conditions under which Vietnamese companies could trade in China. According to the joint statement issued after their discussions:

> The Chinese side encourages Chinese businesses to expand imports of Viet Nam's competitive goods and supports Chinese firms investing in Viet Nam while being ready to create more favorable conditions for Vietnamese businesses to expand their markets in China.[39]

The two leaders set the goal of raising two-way trade to US$60 billion by 2015, if not earlier. They also discussed how to improve transport and communications connectivity. They agreed on a list of key cooperation projects and the establishment of a working group on infrastructure cooperation to plan and implement these plans. Prime Minister Dung and Premier Li endorsed the continuing role of joint land border committees and their annual work plans.

As for the second area of cooperation, the two leaders agreed to establish a joint working group on monetary cooperation. However, they only made general commitments to boosting financial transactions. The leaders encouraged their financial organisations to provide services to promote bilateral trade and investment. They also called for more research into using domestic currencies for payment.

The third area concerned cooperation on maritime issues. Dung and Li agreed to 'stringently implement' the 2011 agreement on guiding the settlement of maritime issues and to pursue maritime cooperation following the principles of 'easy-first, difficult-later' and 'step by step'.[40] They reaffirmed the role of the existing government-level mechanism on boundary and territory negotiations and agreed to pursue 'mutually acceptable fundamental solutions that do not affect each side's stance and policy, which will include studies and discussions pertaining to cooperation for mutual development.' They therefore agreed to instruct the working group on the waters off the mouth of the Gulf of Tonkin and the expert-level working group on cooperation on less sensitive issues at sea to step up their consultations and negotiations. They also agreed to establish a joint working group on cooperation for mutual development at sea under the existing government-level mechanism on boundary and territory negotiations.

With respect to their territorial disputes in the South China Sea, the two leaders reaffirmed their past agreement to implement the 2002 Declaration on the Conduct of Parties in the South China Sea, and 'based on mutual consensus, both sides will do more for the adoption of a Code of Conduct'. The two leaders also agreed 'to exercise tight control of maritime disputes and not to make any move that can further complicate or expand disputes'.[41] In this regard both sides vowed to make use of hotlines established between their ministries of foreign affairs and ministries of agriculture.

At the conclusion of their talks Prime Minister Dung and Premier Li witnessed the signing of several agreements, including:
- an agreement on the reciprocal opening of trade promotion agencies
- an agreement on the establishment of a Confucius Institute at Hanoi University
- an agreement on the construction of the Ta Lung-Shui Kou island bridge two (plus an attached protocol)
- an MOU on building a cross-border economic cooperation zone
- an MOU on establishing a joint working group to support projects supported by Chinese businesses in Vietnam

Vietnam and the US: joint statement on comprehensive partnership

In July 2010 Secretary of State Hillary Clinton visited Hanoi and reportedly proposed that bilateral relations be raised to a strategic partnership. Negotiations on a formal strategic partnership soon became bogged down by human rights and other issues.

In parallel with the improvement in Vietnam–China relations, Vietnam also moved to step up its relations with the US. A major breakthrough was announced during the official state visit of President Truong Tan Sang to Washington in July 2013. President Sang met President Obama in the Oval Office at The White House. The two presidents agreed to codify their bilateral relations by issuing a joint statement on Comprehensive Partnership.[42]

The joint statement included nine major points that basically reiterated existing areas of and mechanisms for cooperation. These included: the Trade and Investment Framework Agreement Council; the Joint Committee for Scientific and Technological Cooperation; the Defense Policy Dialogue; and the Political, Security and Defense Dialogue. The Comprehensive Partnership created a new political and diplomatic dialogue mechanism between the US Secretary of State and Vietnam's Minister of Foreign Affairs.

The Joint Statement on Comprehensive Partnership made no mention of a Plan of Action that accompanied many of Vietnam's other strategic partnership agreements. Instead, the joint statement noted that the two governments would create new mechanisms for each of the nine areas of cooperation: political and diplomatic relations, trade and economic ties, science and technology, education and training, environment and health, war legacy issues, defence and security, protection and promotion of human rights, and culture, sports and tourism. Specifically, the Joint Statement on Comprehensive Partnership committed both sides to advancing bilateral cooperation on trade and economic issues, including the conclusion of negotiations on the Trans-Pacific Partnership agreement, and to institutionalising a regular dialogue at ministerial level between the two countries.

Maritime security issues featured prominently in Vietnam–US relations after President Sang's state visit.[43] In August 2013 US Secretary of Defense Chuck Hagel met Vietnam's Minister of Defence General Thanh on the sidelines of the ADMM+ meeting in Brunei and accepted an invitation to visit Vietnam. Secretary of State John Kerry visited Hanoi in October 2013. Vietnam and the US reached agreements on cooperation between their coastguards. In December 2013 Kerry announced that the US would provide Vietnam with US$18 million to assist Vietnam in enhancing the capacity of its coastguard to conduct search and rescue by providing five patrol boats.[44]

Vietnam and China: Haiyang Shiyou 981 crisis (May–July 2014)

The upward trajectory of Vietnam–China relations was abruptly reversed when a major maritime confrontation erupted when China deployed a mega oil exploration platform, Haiyang Shiyou 981 (HYSY 981), in Vietnam's EEZ from 2 May–16 July 2014. A mixed armada of 80 vessels accompanied the HYSY 981. During the six-week standoff Chinese ships regularly rammed Vietnam's Coast Guard and Fisheries Surveillance Force vessels and used high-pressure water cannons to prevent them from interfering with the operations of HYSY 981.

China's actions provoked peaceful anti-China demonstrations in Hanoi and Ho Chi Minh City and violent attacks by Vietnamese workers on four hundred Chinese (and other foreign-owned) enterprises in three industrial estates. China evacuated several thousands of its workers, demanded compensation and imposed economic sanctions. Chinese tourism to Vietnam plummeted.

Throughout May Vietnam made more than 30 attempts to make contact with counterparts in China, either through hotlines or direct contact by the agencies concerned, to resolve the crisis. Vietnamese officials claim they were rebuffed on each occasion and China failed to respond to communications made through established hotlines.

Vietnam's leadership appeared divided on how to respond to Chinese actions. Prime Minister Dung publicly advocated taking international legal action against China. Other senior leaders were more circumspect. The Defence Minister downplayed the crisis, comparing it to an internal family spat. The VCP Central Committee convened its ninth plenum from 8–14 May 2014. By all accounts this was a heated session with some members calling for an end to Vietnam's policy of 'three no's'. Vietnam adopted a more restrained view in public. The Vietnamese media only reported that the Central Committee resolved to closely monitor the maritime standoff and called for a peaceful resolution of the dispute.

On 18 June 2014, China's dispatched State Councillor Yang Jiechi to Hanoi for testy consultations with Deputy Prime Minister and Foreign Minister Pham Binh Minh at a 'leaders meeting' of the Joint Steering Committee on Bilateral Cooperation. The term 'leaders meeting' was a diplomatic sleight of hand to enable both sides to meet without losing face.[45] The meeting between Yang and Minh focused entirely on the HYSY 981 crisis and was marked by mutual recriminations. The confrontation at sea continued.

In early July, the VCP politburo reportedly voted overwhelmingly to hold a meeting of the Central Committee in August to endorse international legal action against China; but before it could do so China brought an abrupt end to the crisis by withdrawing the HYSY 981. Nonetheless, on 28 July, 61 leading Vietnamese personalities signed an open letter criticising the government for its handling of relations with Beijing and called for legal action. The open letter also called for Vietnam to 'exit China's orbit' (*thoat Trung*).

Just as suddenly as it had erupted, the HYSY 981 crisis ended. China accepted an offer by Vietnam's party leader to send an envoy to Beijing. In August 2014 Xi Jinping and other high-level Chinese leaders met with Special Envoy Le Hong Anh, a member of the politburo, head of the VCP Secretariat and former Minister of Public Security. Anh negotiated follow-on visits by Vietnamese leaders and presented an invitation from the VCP Secretary General Nguyen Phu Trong for President Xi to visit Vietnam.[46]

The following month a high-powered Vietnamese military delegation, led by minister of defence and member of the politburo General Thanh, visited Beijing.[47] Shortly after Councillor Yang returned to Vietnam to co-chair the seventh Joint Steering Committee on Bilateral Cooperation, where both sides agreed to reset their relations.[48] Nevertheless, in December 2014 Vietnam filed a statement of interest with the Permanent Court of Arbitration in the Hague, requesting that Vietnam's interests be taken into account during deliberations by the arbitral tribunal on the case brought by the Philippines against China.[49]

In a sign of Vietnam's deference to China, on 7 April 2015 Secretary-General Trong journeyed to Beijing to meet with President Xi Jinping and other high-level Chinese leaders. After the Trong–Xi meeting, a joint communiqué stated that the leaders 'reached broad common perceptions on intensifying ties between the two Parties and countries in the new context'. The joint communiqué stated:

> They [China and Vietnam] need to consistently respect each other, hold sincere consultations and manage differences; As political trust is a foundation for the healthy and stable development of bilateral ties, both sides need to increase visits and exchanges, from the strategic heights, carrying the bilateral ties forward; win–win cooperation between Vietnam and China brings practical benefits to people in both countries and contributing to peace, development and prosperity in the region, which should be enhanced and deepened across sectors.[50]

On the vexed issue of the South China Sea dispute, the two leaders reset the clock back to October 2013 and understandings reached during the visit of Premier Li to Hanoi. Xi and Trong agreed to comply with and seriously implement the agreement on guiding the settlement of maritime issues through the already established government-level negotiation mechanism on Vietnam–China boundary and territorial issues. The leaders further agreed to 'manage disputes at sea' and 'fully and effectively' implement the 2002 Declaration on Conduct of Parties in the South China Sea and to reach agreement on a code of conduct in the South China Sea.

Trong's visit did not mark any breakthrough with respect to the South China Sea dispute. Both sides merely repeated formulations used in the past. The HYSY 981 crisis led to a loss of strategic trust by Vietnam in its relations with China. Vietnam sought to leverage its relations with the US in order to add ballast to its relations with Beijing.

Vietnam and the US

Maritime security issues featured prominently in Vietnam–US relations as a result of tensions arising from China's deployment of the HYSY 981 oil platform in Vietnamese EEZ. In May, during the HYSY 981 crisis, Secretary of State Kerry invited Vietnam's Foreign Minister Pham Binh Minh to visit Washington. Minh's trip was postponed due to Vietnamese sensitivities that it might undermine the forthcoming visit by State Councillor Yang in June. Instead, Vietnam dispatched VCP politburo member Pham Quang Nghi to Washington in July, where he held discussions with a number of Obama administration officials.

Foreign Minister Minh's rescheduled visit took place in October. Minh conferred with Kerry, who took this opportunity to announce publicly that the US had lifted the restriction on the sale of lethal weapons to Vietnam on a case-by-case basis to assist in maritime domain awareness and maritime security capabilities.[51] In March 2015 minister for public security and politburo member Tran Dai Quang met with a range of senior officials in the Obama administration.

In June US Secretary of Defense Ashton Carter visited Hanoi. After discussions with his counterpart General Thanh, the two ministers issued a joint vision statement that set out 12 areas of future defence cooperation. The fourth area included, 'expand defense trade between our countries, potentially influencing cooperation in the production of new technologies and equipment, where possible under current law and policy restrictions.

A major turning point in Vietnam–US relations was reached with the first visit of the leader of the VCP to the US from 6–10 July 2015.[52] During the course of Secretary General Trong's five-day visit, he met with President Barack Obama, Vice President Joe Biden, National Security Advisor Susan Rice, Secretary of State John Kerry, Secretary of the Treasury Jack Lew, US Trade Representative Michael Froman, and Senators John McCain and Patrick Leahy.[53]

The centrepiece of Trong's visit was his face-to-face meeting with President

Obama at the White House. At the conclusion of their talks the two leaders issued a joint vision statement that highlighted a convergence of views on six major issues.[54]

First, Obama and Trong agreed to pursue 'a deepened, sustained, and substantive relationship on the basis of respect for each other's political systems, independence, sovereignty and territorial integrity'.[55] In other words, this statement accorded *de facto* recognition to the role of the VCP in Vietnam's one-party state and the importance of the party secretary-general in Vietnam's political system, and a set a precedent for future visits from Vietnam's party leader.

The statement to respect each other's political systems is important because ideological conservatives in Vietnam voice suspicions that the US wants to overturn Vietnam's socialist regime through 'peaceful evolution'. The fact that Trong was received in the Oval Office and President Obama committed the US to respect Vietnam's political system undermined a key tenet of their worldview.

Second, both leaders pledged to advance their agreement on comprehensive partnership by stepping up high-level visits and creating mechanisms to implement cooperation in the nine major areas outlined in the 2013 agreement.[56] Obama and Trong also agreed to complete negotiations on the Trans-Pacific Partnership and Vietnam agreed to carry out reforms necessary to reach a high-standard agreement.[57]

Third, Obama and Trong pledged that the US and Vietnam would work more closely together to contribute to peace, stability, cooperation and prosperity in the Asia-Pacific, both bilaterally and through regional multilateral organisations such as Asia-Pacific Economic Cooperation, and ASEAN-related institutions, such as the ADMM+ and the East Asia Summit.

Sixth, both leaders directly addressed difficulties and challenges in their bilateral relations, including human rights and market economy status, and pledged to conduct positive, frank and constructive political dialogues to reduce these differences and build trust.

Their joint vision statement repeated the standard formulations that maritime disputes should be settled on the basis of international law and by peaceful means. Nevertheless, the leaders prefaced their remarks by noting:

> Both countries are concerned about recent developments in the South China Sea that have increased tensions, eroded trust, and threatened to undermine peace, security and stability. They recognise the imperative of upholding the internationally recognised freedoms of navigation and overflight; unimpeded lawful commerce, maritime security and safety; refraining from actions that raise tensions; ensuring that all actions and activities taken comply with international law and rejecting coercion, intimidation, and the use or threat of force.

In other words, there is considerable convergence of strategic interests regarding the South China Sea and both leaders easily accommodated the key concerns of their counterpart.

Fifth, Obama and Trong agreed to step up defence and security cooperation in maritime security, maritime domain awareness, defence trade and information sharing, and defence technology exchange. These commitments open new areas for cooperation. However, continuing restrictions under the International Trafficking in Arms Regulations remains a bone of contention,

Sixth, both leaders directly addressed difficulties and challenges in their bilateral relations, including human rights and market economy status, and pledged to conduct positive, frank and constructive political dialogues to reduce these differences and build trust.

Secretary Kerry journeyed to Vietnam in August to mark the 20th anniversary of diplomatic relations. In a public talk in Hanoi entitled 'US–Vietnam: Looking to the Future', Kerry addressed the broad range of issues that comprised the comprehensive partnership with Vietnam including dioxin (Agent Orange) contamination, human rights and the South China Sea.

The following month, Vietnam's Deputy Minister of Defence Senior Lieutenant General Vinh visited the US from 29 September–2 October to attend the sixth Defense Policy Dialogue in Washington. The two sides discussed the ongoing search for the remains of US soldiers and airmen missing in action in the Vietnam War, disposal of unexploded wartime ordnance, dioxin decontamination, peacekeeping, maritime security, search and rescue, and humanitarian assistance and disaster relief. Looking towards the future, the two sides agreed to explore cooperation in defence industry and how to enhance the ADMM+ process through practical activities.[58]

Vietnam and China

In 2015 Vietnam intensified its preparations to hold the 12th National Party Congress in January 2016.[59] On September 15, two key draft policy documents, the political report and the socio-economic plan for 2016–2020, were released for public discussion and comment. Provincial party and central bloc congresses were held to select delegates to the national congress.

Two major issues loomed large—leadership succession and Vietnam's relations with China and the US. These two issues became intertwined in intense political in-fighting in advance of the 12th plenary session of the party Central Committee held on 5 October.

The Chinese Embassy in Hanoi held an early reception on 29 September to celebrate China's national day, 2 October. Vietnam was represented by its Minister for Planning and Investment, Bui Quang Vinh. Vinh is not a member of the politburo and retired after the 2016 National Party Congress. There was intense speculation in Hanoi about why Vietnam was not represented by a more senior official from the government.

On 30 September, the day after the reception, Vietnamese media reported that Ha Huy Hoang, a former employee of the Ministry of Foreign Affairs and a former journalist with *Vietnam and the World Weekly,* had been tried and convicted for spying for China. Hoang was sentenced to six years in jail.[60] Media reporting in Vietnam on espionage cases involving Vietnamese citizens is exceedingly rare. Hoang's conviction led to speculation on the timing of the trial and who authorised media reporting. Speculation only intensified when *Tuoi Tre*, *VnExpress* and other media outlets took down their reports from their websites on the afternoon of publication. Speculation then turned to who ordered that these reports be rescinded and why.

As Vietnam completed its preparations for the 12th National Party Congress it was clear that consensus on how Vietnam should manage its relations with China and the US had not been reached. For example, the anodyne draft political report released in mid-September gave no hint of future policy directions on this vexed question. China's construction of artificial islands in the South China Sea, complete with infrastructure to support a Chinese naval and military air presence, became a major driver behind those pushing for a deeper relationship with the US.

The publicity given to the espionage trial, and the decision to rescind news reporting, was a significant sign that how Vietnam manages its relations with China and the US had not been resolved. It was evident that some elements of Vietnam's political elite approved media reporting of the espionage trial. This development followed on the heels of reports that China has been given permission to open a consulate general in Da Nang.

Those who oppose getting too close to the US highlighted the 'threat of peaceful evolution' as a national security threat.[61] They pointed to US pressure on human rights and religious freedom as part of this threat. The allegations of Chinese espionage fueled allied concerns that China continues to interfere in Vietnam's internal affairs and was attempting to influence the outcome of the National Party Congress. Hanoi-based observers privately reported that China informed selected Vietnamese leaders that it opposed the elevation of Foreign Minister Pham Binh Minh, who was viewed as pro-American.[62]

Vietnamese sources also reported that China let it be known privately that President Xi might call off his expected visit to Vietnam if Hanoi did not mute its criticism of China's construction of artificial islands in the South China Sea. Xi visited Vietnam in November with little advance warning. Vietnam, in fact, had to juggle Xi's visit with the long-scheduled visit of the president of Italy.

Those who want closer ties with the US also stress the economic advantages of membership in the Trans-Pacific Partnership. This group is now countering the argument of the 'threat of peaceful evolution' by pointing to Chinese espionage as a major threat to national security. In other words, the threat of peaceful evolution from the US is now being counterpoised with the threat of Chinese subversion.

There are other straws in the wind of a possible change in Vietnam–US relations. Despite private Chinese warnings to Vietnam to mute public statements on the South China Sea, President Sang recently stated in a media interview that China's construction of artificial islands was illegal under international law and endangered maritime security.⁶³ Sang's interview was given in New York while he was attending the annual meeting of the UN General Assembly. Sang's remarks were directed at both international and domestic audiences and may be viewed as preparing the grounds for deepening relations with the US.

Vietnamese leaders who advocate deepening ties with the US need some indication that Vietnam's actions will be reciprocated to win over their domestic critics. That is why Sang called for an end of all US restrictions on the sale of lethal weapons to Vietnam in his New York interview. Sang also repeated affirmations he made in Washington two years ago that Vietnam would engage the US on human rights. This is a precondition the US has set for advancement of defence ties and the lifting of all restrictions on the sale of lethal weaponry to Vietnam.

Obama–Xi Summit

President Barack Obama and President Xi Jinping held their first formal summit in Washington on 25 September 2015. Vietnamese officials were satisfied with the outcome because their worst fears, US–China great power collusion particularly over the South China Sea, were not realised.⁶⁴ In other words, Vietnam's preferences had been met. US–China relations were neither 'too hot' nor 'too cold'. Continued cooperation and rivalry between Washington and Beijing was 'just right' for Vietnam.

4. Conclusion

This chapter presented an overview of Vietnam's strategic framework for ordering its relations with the major powers. The main argument of this chapter is that Vietnam doggedly pursues a policy of 'multilateralisation and diversification' in its relations with the major power. This context is essential for understanding Vietnam's relations with China and the US.

Part one focused on the opportunities and challenges that opened for Vietnam following the end of the conflict in Cambodia. Four months before a comprehensive settlement was reached, Vietnam positioned itself for the post-Cambodia period with a the objective of diversifying and mutlilateralising 'economic relations with all countries . . .' Although Vietnam gave priority to enhancing its relations with traditional friendly states, such as the Soviet Union and China, it also opened the door to developing relations with 'new friends' such as Japan and normalising its relations with the US.

Within four years of the seventh National Party Congress that promoted multilateralisation and diversification of relations, Vietnam achieved notable success. It normalised diplomatic relations with China and the US in 1991 and 1995 respectively. Vietnam also became the seventh member of the ASEAN states. Normalisation of diplomatic relations, however, presented challenges as well. In the early 1990s the South China Sea emerged as a growing irritant in Hanoi's relations with Beijing. The normalisation of diplomatic relations with the US was the first step in a long process of developing economic relations.

Part two provided an overview of the framework of Vietnamese foreign policy over a 17-year period, with an emphasis on strategic policy set by five-yearly National Party Congresses—the eighth (1996), ninth (2001), tenth (2006) and eleventh (2001). An overview of this period confirms that domestic economic development and integration with the global economy were Vietnam's top priorities. Vietnam sought to become a modern and industrial country by 2020. In 2011 the 11th National Party Congress set proactive international integration as a major goal. These objectives could only be obtained by consolidating Vietnam's diversified external relations while at the same time maintaining equilibrium in Vietnam's relations with the major powers.

In the period under review (1996–2015) Vietnam developed strategic partnerships with the Russian Federation (2001), Japan (2006), India (2007), China (2008), Spain and South Korea (2009), United Kingdom and Germany (2010), and Italy, France, Thailand, Indonesia and Singapore (2013), the Philippines (2015), and reached comprehensive partnership agreements with Australia (2009) and the US (2013). Vietnam also upgraded its strategic partnerships with China (2009) and Russia (2012).

Beginning in 2007, territorial disputes in the South China Sea increasingly began to bedevil Vietnam–China relations. This led to a growing convergence of security interests between Vietnam and the US. At the same time, however, China's rise and engagement with the US posed the risk that the two major powers might collude at the expense of Vietnam's interests in the South China Sea.

Part three shifted focus to Vietnam's relations with China and the US after the informal summit between presidents Obama and Xi in Sunnylands. It was during this honeymoon period that a senior Vietnamese diplomat confided to the author that Vietnam preferred the 'Goldilocks model' in relations between Beijing and Washington. That is, Vietnam hoped that their bilateral relations were not 'too hot' or 'too cold', but 'just right' so Vietnam could leverage the dynamic tensions between Washington and Beijing.

Vietnam's relations with China and the US deepened and became more institutionalised across a number of sectors including defence and security in 2013. A high point was reached in Vietnam's relations with both the US and China with the visits of President Truong Tan Sang's to Washington in July and Premier Li Keqiang to Hanoi in October. President Sang's visit to Washington resulted in a landmark comprehensive partnership agreement, while Premier Li's visit to Hanoi resulted in agreement to deepen bilateral relations in three priority areas (on-shore, monetary and maritime) and to compartmentalise the South China Sea dispute to prevent it spilling over and affecting bilateral relations.

China's decision to deploy the HYSY 981 mega-oil drilling platform in Vietnamese waters in May 2014 proved catalytic. Strategic trust between Hanoi and Beijing was the first casualty. As a result of the six-week confrontation at sea all the goodwill flowing from Premier Li's visit dissipated. An intense debate erupted in the highest levels of the Vietnam Communist Party over whether to 'exit China's orbit' by seeking closer relations with the US.

Vietnam now sought to restore equilibrium in its relations China and the US. A special envoy of the party secretary-general was dispatched to Beijing, followed by a high-powered military delegation. In April 2015, party Secretary-General Nguyen Phu Trong held a high-level summit with Xi Jinping. Trong's visit reset economic relations but did not achieve a breakthrough on the South China Sea dispute.

At the same time as Vietnam sought to restore normalcy in its relations with China, it also sought to deepen its ties with the US. The HYSY 981 sharpened the strategic convergence between Vietnam and the US on the South China Sea. Two politburo members were dispatched to Washington in addition to Vietnam's Foreign Minister. The US lifted its restriction on the sale of lethal weapons to Vietnam on a case-by-case basis and limited sales to maritime security. Defence ministers from Vietnam and the US adopted a joint vision statement in June 2015 that included a new provision on defence trade and technology.

The high-point in Vietnam–US relations was reached in July 2015, with the first visit of the VCP secretary general to Washington and his meeting with President Obama at the White House. Of the six major outcomes of Trong's visit, none was more important than US recognition of the legitimacy of Vietnam's one-party system and the role of the party Secretary-General in that system. This outcome was a powerful antidote to those who opposed deepening ties with the US on the grounds that the US was seeking to overthrow Vietnam's socialist system through 'peaceful evolution'.

The question of how Vietnam will manage its relations with China and the US gained new urgency in late 2015, with China's continued construction of infrastructure on its artificial islands. Leadership changes at Vietnam's 12th National Party Congress witnessed the elevation of Foreign Minister Pham Binh Minh to the politburo and the retention of party Secretary-General Trong for a third term in office. In the lead-up to the national party congress, officials identified Vietnam's relative quiescence in responding to Chinese assertiveness in the South China Seas as a shortcoming. This was soon rectified. In April 2016 Vietnam arrested a Chinese trawler and protested the relocation of the HYSY 981 in contested waters in the Gulf of Tonkin, a sign of stiffening in Vietnam's position. Vietnam received President Barack Obama in May 2016 after the postponement of his visit in 2015. The future trajectory of bilateral relations, however, will be dependent on the outcome of the US presidential election in November 2016.

Notes

1   'Enhancing the Party's Leadership and Combat Capability, Bringing into Full Play the Entire Nation's Strength, Comprehensively Boosting the Renewal Process, and Quickly Delivering the Country from Its Underdeveloped Status, Political Report of the Communist Party of Viet Nam's 9th Central Committee to the 10th National Party Congress', *85 Years of The Communist Party of Viet Nam (1930–2015): A Selection of Documents from Eleven Party Congresses* (Hanoi: The Gioi Publishers, 2015).

2   Brantly Womack, *China and Vietnam: The Politics of Asymmetry* (New York: Cambridge University Press, 2006).
3   Carlyle A. Thayer, 'New Strategic Uncertainty and Security Order in Southeast Asia', in Elena Attanassova-Cornelis and Frans-Paul van der Putten, eds., *Changing Security Dynamics in East Asia: A Post US–Regional Order in the Making? Critical Studies of the Asia-Pacific.* (London: Palgrave Macmillan, 2014), pp. 127–146.
4   Carlyle A. Thayer, 'The Rise of China and India: Challenging or Reinforcing Southeast Asia's Autonomy?', in Ashley J. Tellis, Travis Tanner and Jessica Keough, eds., *Strategic Asia 2011– 12: Asia Responds to its Rising Powers, China and India.* (Seattle: National Bureau of Asian Research, 2011), pp. 336–37; Carlyle A. Thayer, 'The Tyranny of Geography: Vietnamese Strategies to Constrain China in the South China Sea', *Contemporary Southeast Asia*, 33:3 (2011), p. 351.
5   Carlyle A. Thayer, 'With Russia's Help, Vietnam Adopts A2/AD Strategy', *The Diplomat*, 8 October 2013. http://thediplomat.com/flashpoints-blog/2013/10/08/with-russias-help-vietnam-adopts-a2ad-strategy/; Carlyle A. Thayer, 'The Bear is Back: Russia Returns to Vietnam', *The Diplomat*, 26 November 2013. http://thediplomat.com/2013/11/the-bear-is-back-russia-returns-to-vietnam/; Carlyle A. Thayer, 'The Philippines, Malaysia and Vietnam Race to South China Sea Defense Modernisation', *The Diplomat*, 23 January 2015. http://thediplomat.com/2015/01/the-philippines-malaysia-and-vietnam-race-to-south-china-sea-defense-modernisation/; Carlyle A. Thayer, 'Vietnam's Advanced Kilo-class Submarines and South China Sea', Chennai Centre for China Studies, C3S Paper 0166/2015, 25 August 2015. http://www.c3sindia.org/china/5212
6   Anh Son, 'Russian shipyard launches last "Black Hole" sub built for Vietnam Navy', *Thanh Nien News*, 28 September 2015.
7   The title of this paper draws on a conversation with a senior Vietnamese diplomat who invoked the children's story 'Goldilocks and the Three Bears' as a simile for how Vietnam would like China–US to develop. For the Goldilocks story see: http://learnenglishkids.britishcouncil.org/sites/kids/files/attachment/stories-goldilocks-and-the-three-bears-transcript.pdf.
8   7th National Congress Documents (Hanoi: Vietnam Foreign Languages Publishing House, 1991), p. 134.
9   Communist Party of Viet Nam, 7th National Congress Documents (Hanoi: Vietnam Foreign Languages Publishing House, 1991); Vu Khoan, 'Mot so van de quoc te cua dai hoi VII quan,' in Bo Ngoai Giao, Hoi nhap quoc te va giu vung ban sac (Hanoi: Nha xuat ban chinh tri quoc te, 1995) pp. 71–76; Carlyle A. Thayer, 'Indochina', in Ramesh Thakur and Carlyle A. Thayer, eds., *Reshaping Regional Relations: Asia-Pacific and the Former Soviet Union* (Boulder, San Francisco and Oxford: Westview Press, 1993), p. 221.
10 Communist Party of Viet Nam, 7th National Congress Documents, (Hanoi: Vietnam Foreign Languages Publishing House, 1991), p. 134.
11 Ibid, p. 135.
12 Carlyle A. Thayer, *Asia–Australia Briefing Papers* (Sydney: The Asia–Australia Institute, The University of New South Wales, 1992), pp. 55–62; Carlyle A. Thayer, 'Internal Southeast Asian Dynamics: Vietnam's Membership in ASEAN', in Hadi Soesastro and Anthony Bergin, eds., *The Role of Security and Economic Cooperation Structures in the Asia Pacific Region: Indonesian and Australian Views*, (Jakarta: Centre for Strategic and International Studies, 1996), pp. 78–88.
13 Ibid.
14 'CPV Central Committee Political Report', *Nhan Dan*, 21 January 21 1994, translated and reprinted in 'United States Foreign Broadcast Information Service Daily Report', EAS-94-031, 15 February 1994, p. 64.
15 After the conference the official Vietnamese media highlighted what it termed the challenges

of 'four dangers' facing Vietnam: the danger of being left behind (tut hau) economically by regional countries; the danger of peaceful evolution against socialism; the danger of corruption; and the danger of the breakdown of social order and security. See: *Voice of Vietnam*, 22 January 1994.

16   Vo Van Kiet, 'Thu cua Ong Vo Van Kiet Gui Bo Chinh Tri Dang Cong San Viet Nam' ('Letter from Mr Vo Van Kiet to the Political Bureau of the Communist Party of Vietnam'), 1995.

17   For the first time delegates from Southeast Asia were included (representing the non-communist ruling parties in Cambodia, Malaysia and Singapore).

18   Dang Cong San Viet Nam, 7th National Congress of Representatives. Draft Statutes (amended and revised) Hanoi, 1996.

19   Carlyle A. Thayer, 'Vietnam On the Road to Global Integration: Forging Strategic Partnerships Through International Security Cooperation', in *Vietnam on the Road to Integration and Sustainable Development The Fourth International Conference on Vietnamese Studies* (Hanoi: Vietnam Academy of Social Sciences and Vietnam National University, 2012). pp. 206–214.

20   For background see Thayer, 1997.

21   Carlyle A. Thayer, 'Russia–Vietnam Relations', Global Insider, *World Politics Review* (8 June 2011), http://www.worldpoliticsreview.com/trend-lines/9099/global-insider-russia-vietnam-relations; Carlyle A. Thayer, 'The Russia-Vietnam Comprehensive Partnership', *East Asia Forum*, (October, 2012). http://www.eastasiaforum.org/2012/10/09/the-russia-vietnam-comprehensive-partnership/; Carlyle A. Thayer, 'With Russia's Help, Vietnam Adopts A2/AD Strategy', *The Diplomat*, 8 October 2013. http://thediplomat.com/flashpoints-blog/2013/10/08/with-russias-help-vietnam-adopts-a2ad-strategy/

22   Vo Khoan, 'Tich Cuc va Chu Dong Hoi Nhap Kinh Te Quoc Te', Tap Chi Cong San, 2006, p. 119; This was the first time the concept of 'market economy with socialist characteristics' was endorsed, in Le Xuan Tung, 'Nhung Dot Pha Tu Duy Ly Luan ve Kinh Te Thi Truong o Nuoc Ta', *Tap Chi Cong San* 16:715 (2004), pp. 14–21.

23   Carlyle A. Thayer, 'Vietnam in 2001: The Ninth Party Congress and After', *Asian Survey* 42:1 (2002), pp. 81–89.

24   A Vietnam Politburo Bureau resolution adopted in November 2001 sketched Vietnam's diplomatic strategy as follows: 'continue to strengthen relations with Vietnam's neighbours and countries that have been traditional friends; give importance to relations with big countries, developing countries, and the political and economic centers of the world; raise the level of solidarity with developing countries and the non-aligned movement; increase activities in international organisations; and develop relations with Communist and Workers' parties, with progressive forces, while at the same time expanding relations with ruling parties and other parties. Pay attention to 'people's diplomacy.' (Vu Duong Ninh, 2002, p. 110).

25   Vietnam Communist Party, Commission on Ideology and Cultural Affairs, 'Documents of the Eighth Central Committee of the Vietnam Communist Party' (Hanoi: The National Politics Publishing House, 2003), quoted in Nguyen Vu Tung, 'Vietnamese Foreign Policy: At a New Crossroad?', Paper Presented to Strategic and Foreign Relations, 'Vietnam Update' (Singapore: Institute of Southeast Asian Studies, 25–26 November 2004).

26   Ibid.

27   Carlyle A. Thayer, 'The Prospects for Strategic Dialogue', in Catharin E. Dalpino, ed., *Dialogue on US–Vietnam Relations: Ten Years After Normalisation* (San Francisco: The Asia Foundation, 2005), pp. 26–30.

28   Carlyle A. Thayer, 'Vietnam: The Tenth Party Congress and After', in Daljit Singh and Lorraine C. Salazar, eds., *Southeast Asian Affairs 2007* (Singapore: Institute of Southeast Asian Studies, 2007), pp. 381–397.

29 Carlyle A. Thayer, 'Vietnam On the Road to Global Integration: Forging Strategic Partnerships Through International Security Cooperation', in *Vietnam on the Road to Integration and Sustainable Development, The Fourth International Conference on Vietnamese Studies* (Hanoi: Vietnam Academy of Social Sciences and Vietnam National University, 2012), pp. 206–214.
30 Ibid.
31 Ibid.
32 'Resolution of the 11th Party National Congress', Communist Party of Vietnam Online Newspaper, 23 January 2011, http://www.cpv.org.vn/cpv/Modules/Preview/PrintPreview_En.aspx?co_id-30180.
33 Ibid.
34 Carlyle A. Thayer, 'Vietnam Gradually Warms Up to US Military', *The Diplomat*, 6 November 2013, http://thediplomat.com/2013/11/vietnam-gradually-warms-up-to-us-military/
35 Carlyle A. Thayer, 'Hanoi and the Pentagon: A Budding Courtship', US Naval Institute, 11 June 2012, http://news.usni.org/news-analysis/hanoi-and-pentagon-budding-courtship.
36 Ibid.
37 'Viet Nam, Philippines issue joint statement on strategic partnership', *Viet Nam News*, 19 November 2015, http://vietnamnews.vn/politics-laws/278770/viet-nam-philippines-issue-joint-statement-on-strategic-partnership.html.
38 Carlyle A. Thayer, 'Le Premier minister chinois Le Keqiang au Vietnam', *Étude quadrimestrielle* 1 (2013–2014), pp. 13–15. http://www.centreasia.eu/sites/default/files/publications_pdf/etude_etude_quadrimestrielle_n_1_janv2014.pdf.
39 Vietnam Government Portal, 'VN, China issue joint statement', Ministry of Foreign Affairs, 15 October 2013.
40 Thayer, 'Le Premier . . .'
41 'VN, China issue joint statement', Vietnam Government Portal, Ministry of Foreign Affairs Vietnam, 15 October 2013, http://www.mofa.gov.vn/en/nr040807104143/nr040807105001/ns131016041515.
42 Carlyle A. Thayer, 'The US–Vietnam Comprehensive Partnership: What's in a Name?', *cogitASIA*, Center for Strategic and International Studies, 30 July 2013. http://*cogitASIA*.com/the-u-s-vietnam-comprehensive-partnership-whats-in-a-name/; Carlyle A. Thayer, 'The US-Vietnam Comprehensive Partnership: What's in a Name?', *The Strategist* (Australian Strategic Policy Institute Blog), 31 July 2013. http://www.aspistrategist.org.au/the-us-vietnam-comprehensive-partnership-whats-in-a-name/.
43 Carlyle A. Thayer, 'US–Vietnam: From Comprehensive to Strategic Partners?', *cogitASIA*, 20 March 2014, http://*cogitASIA*.com/u-s-vietnam-from-comprehensive-to-strategic-partners/.
44 Carlyle A. Thayer, 'Japan and the US Renew Commitments to Maritime Security', *The Diplomat*, 28 December 2103, http://thediplomat.com/2013/12/japan-and-the-united-states-renew-commitments-to-maritime-security/
45 This was the first co-called leaders' meeting.
46 Carlyle A. Thayer, 'China and Vietnam Eschew Megaphone Diplomacy', *The Diplomat*, 2 January 2015 http://thediplomat.com/2015/01/china-and-vietnam-eschew-megaphone-diplomacy/.
47 Carlyle A. Thayer, 'China–Vietnam Defense Hotline Agreed: What Next?', *The Diplomat*, 20 October 2014. http://thediplomat.com/2014/10/china-vietnam-defense-hotline-agreed-what-next/.
48 Carlyle A. Thayer, 'How Vietnam Woos China and India Simultaneously', *The Diplomat*, 28 October 2014, http://thediplomat.com/2014/10/how-vietnam-woos-china-and-india-simultaneously/.
49 Carlyle A. Thayer, 'Vietnam Files Statement of Interest with the Permanent Court of

Arbitration', *cogitASIA*, 15 December 2014, http://*cogitASIA*.com/vietnam-files-statement-of-interest-with-the-permanent-court-of-arbitration/.

50   Vietnam News Agency, 'Viet Nam, China issue joint communiqué', Ministry of Foreign Affairs, 8 April 2015, http://www.mofa.gov.vn/en/nr040807104143/nr040807105001/ns150409005752.

51   Carlyle A. Thayer, 'The US Lifts Arms Embargo: The Ball Is in Vietnam's Court', *The Diplomat*, October 2014, http://thediplomat.com/2014/10/the-us-lifts-arms-embargo-the-ball-is-in-vietnams-court/.

52   Carlyle A. Thayer, 'Is Vietnam Pivoting Toward the US?', *The Diplomat*, 6 July 2015 http://thediplomat.com/2015/07/is-vietnam-pivoting-toward-the-united-states/.

53   Secretary-General Trong also met with American religious leaders, Vietnamese–American community representatives, American entrepreneurs, the head of the Communist Party of the US, former president Bill Clinton, a group of Harvard University professors and United Nations Secretary-General Ban Ki-Moon.

54   Carlyle A. Thayer, '8 Developments in US–Vietnam Relations Show Emerging Partnership', *The Diplomat*, 13 July 2015. http://thediplomat.com/2015/07/8-developments-in-us-vietnam-relations-show-emerging-partnership/; Carlyle A. Thayer, 'Setting the Foundation for Strategic Trust', Russian International Affairs Council, 13 July 2015. http://russiancouncil.ru/en/inner/?id_4=6325#top-content.

55   VTV4 [Vietnam Television 4], 'Vietnam–US convene 6th Defense Policy Dialogue', 5 October 2015. http://english.vtv.vn/news/vietnam-us-convene-6th-defense-policy-dialogue-20151005153703384.htm.

56   On 7 July the US and Vietnam signed four agreements, including on double taxation, cooperation in addressing emerging pandemic threats and technical assistance for aviation safety. Vietnam's Deputy Minister of National Defence Senior Lieutenant General Nguyen Chi Vinh and US Assistant Secretary of Defense for Asia-Pacific Security David Shear signed a memorandum of understanding on US assistance to Vietnam for UN peacekeeping. Vietnam is poised to raise it commitment to the UN from five military officers to deployment of a level-2 field hospital and an engineer company. In addition, PetroVietnam and Murphy Oil signed a cooperation agreement, Harvard University was given approval to establish the Fulbright University in Vietnam, and Vietnam took delivery of its first Boeing 787 Dreamliner aircraft.

57   There are several hurdles to be overcome. The US insists that Vietnam meet four principles included in the International Labor Organisation's 1998 Declaration on Fundamental Principles and Rights at Work. One of the principles is the right of workers to 'freely associate' and to bargain collectively (form their own labour union). Vietnam is pushing the US to grant it market economy status so that tariffs will be lowered on imports to the US.

58   Vietnam News Agency, 'Vietnam, US convene 6th Defense Policy Dialogue', *VietNamNet*, 2 October 2015, http://www.businessinsider.com/ap-vietnam-leader-china-island-work-violates-international-law-2015-9?IR=T.

59   Carlyle A. Thayer, 'Vietnam's China Factor', Policy Forum Canberra: The Crawford School, The Australian National University, 9 September 2015. http://www.policyforum.net/vietnams-china-factor/; Carlyle A. Thayer, 'Vietnam is Changing . . . And So Is the Balance of Power in Asia', *The Diplomat*, 2 October 2015. http://thediplomat.com/2015/10/vietnam-is-changing-and-so-is-the-balance-of-power-in-asia/.

60   'Vietnam Jails Journalist Accurse of Spying For China', *Radio Free Asia*, 30 September2015. http://www.rfa.org/english/news/vietnam/vietnam-jails-journalist-accused-of-spying-for-china-09302015130324.html.

61   See Nguyen Duc Thang, 'No ground for any claims to 'depoliticise' the armed forces', *People's Army Newspaper Online*, 13 September 2015 and 'Units active in combating 'peaceful evolution

plot', *People's Army Newspaper Online*, 2 October 2015.
62 Thayer, 'Vietnam is changing . . .'
63 John Daniszewski and Matthew Pennington, 'Vietnam Leader: China island work violates international law', *Associated Press*, 28 September 2015.
64 Differences between Obama and Xi over the South China Sea emerged at a joint press conference following their meeting; see: Jacquelyn Bengfort, 'Chinese President Reasserts Astroturf Sovereignty Claims in South Chia Sea', *Vice*, 30 September 2015 and *Reuters*, 'Obama and Xi remain at loggerheads on S China Sea', *Today Online*, 30 September 2015.

A view of the audience in the Council Chamber of the Victoria University Hunter building during the conference

The US–China–India Strategic Triangle

Manjeet S. Pardesi

Lecturer in international relations and an Asia Research Fellow at the Centre for Strategic Studies at Victoria University of Wellington, New Zealand

Abstract

India views the China–US relationship both as an opportunity and as a source of uneasiness. Anxiety about China makes India an attractive partner for the US. India believes that US capital, technology and diplomatic support are important for facilitating India's own rise. But exigencies of geography and the growing economic relationship with China mean that India does not want the China–US relationship to deteriorate to a point that would force it to make a choice between them. India also remains concerned about any China–US rapprochement that may reduce it to a secondary power in Asia. India worries about the fact that while China is a significant factor in the US–India relationship, India has not yet attained the same significance in China–US relations.

Introduction

China, the US and India—in that order—are expected to emerge as the world's three biggest economies by 2030 (when measured at market exchange rates).[1] Similarly, the US, China and India—in that order—are expected to be emerge as the world's three biggest defence spenders by 2020.[2] While much attention has been devoted to the bilateral US–China, US–India and China–India relationships, we are still in the early stages of understanding the US–China–India triangular dynamics.[3] This paper makes a limited attempt to address this gap and argues that India views the US–China relationship both as an opportunity as well as a source of uneasiness.

Anxiety about China makes India an attractive partner for the US. India believes that US capital, technology and diplomatic support are important for facilitating India's own rise. At the same time, given the exigencies of geography and India's rapidly expanding economic relationship with China, India does not want the US–China relationship to deteriorate to a point that would force New Delhi to make a choice between them. India also remains concerned about the possibility of a US–China rapprochement that may reduce it to a secondary power in Asia. India worries about the fact that while China is a significant factor in the US–India relationship, India has not yet attained the same significance in US–China relations.

This chapter offers a brief overview of the US–China–India strategic triangle that (arguably) formed for the first time immediately following India's independence and the creation of the People's Republic of China (PRC) in the late 1940s. However, even as there were specific events during which their strategic relationship displayed a triangular dynamic, no sustained US–China–India strategic triangle emerged until the end of the 20th century. The basis for a sustained triangular relationship only emerged around the beginning of the 21st century, as the US began to think of India in the context of the rise of China, while China also began to pay more attention to the US–India relationship. India's rapidly growing economy over the past two decades has been the key to America and China's changing perceptions of India. However, this triangle is in its early stages of formation. Finally, it is also argued that the US–China–India strategic relationship will interact with at least three other triangles—Russia–China–India, China–India–Pakistan, and China–Japan–India.

The Evolution of the US–China–India Triangle

Independent India's adoption of a secular-democratic path, around the time of the communist revolution in China in the late 1940s, made many Americans think of democratic India as an alternative model for the developing world in contrast to communist China. In fact, US policymakers also understood the strategic implications of augmenting democratic India's power through economic and technological assistance.[4] However, independent India's quest for strategic autonomy through a policy non-alignment and its relatively closed economic system was a disappointment for the US. Therefore, even as India tried to play the role of a diplomatic interlocutor between the US and China during the 1950–53 Korean War (given the absence of direct diplomatic links between Washington and Beijing), India won no friends as the US suspected India of having pro-China (and pro-communist) sympathies, while China believed that US power and interests were lurking behind Indian diplomacy.[5]

While the US began to lose interest in India in the 1950s, China–India tensions over Tibet provided an important covert avenue for tacit cooperation between Washington and New Delhi beginning in the late 1950s.[6] Later, at Prime Minister Jawaharlal Nehru's request, the US provided overt diplomatic and military support to India during the 1962 Sino–Indian War.⁷ This was the first time that two of these three powers openly aligned themselves against the third. However, Cold War geopolitics and the US–Pakistan relationship meant that the nascent US–India strategic partnership came to an abrupt end with the outbreak of the 1965 India–Pakistan War.⁸ In spite of this, the US played an important diplomatic role by discouraging China from opening a second front against India in 1965 in support of its Pakistani ally.⁹

The US' dramatic opening to China in 1971 under National Security Advisor Henry Kissinger and President Richard Nixon created a US–China entente directed at India (and the Soviet Union). In fact, the alignments in the US–China–India strategic triangle had changed so dramatically since 1965 that the US gave China its tacit approval to open a second front against India during the 1971 Bangladesh War.¹⁰ A China–India war was avoided in 1971 due to a combination of Chinese hesitancy and because of the 1971 Indo–Soviet Treaty of Friendship and Cooperation (as a result of which the Soviet Union threatened to open a second front against China in the event of a Chinese attack on India). However, India also perceived a security threat from the US in 1971 as a US carrier group, the *USS Enterprise* (that was believed to be nuclear-armed by strategists in New Delhi), made its appearance in the Bay of Bengal to reassure Pakistan and to send a positive signal to the US' new ally, China.¹¹

This pattern of US–China alignment against India (and the Soviet Union) remained in place for the rest of the Cold War. While US–China relations dramatically deteriorated in the aftermath of the 1989 Tiananmen Square massacre,¹² India did not join the Western- and Japanese-led condemnation of China. In fact, Sino–Indian relations had just begun to recover in the aftermath of the 1986–87 Sumdorong Chu crisis (which had almost brought China and India to blows again).¹³ Prime Minister Rajiv Gandhi paid a successful visit to China in 1988, at a time when a Chinese crackdown in Tibet was underway.¹⁴ In the meanwhile, US–China relations deteriorated further during the 1995–96 Taiwan Strait Crisis. Consequently, the US began to worry about China's growing military power, while Beijing became concerned about US gunboat diplomacy.¹⁵ It was in this context that India's May 1998 nuclear tests provided the US and China with an opportunity to cooperate and to reverse the decline in their post-Cold War relationship.

The Indian Prime Minister Atal Bihari Vajpayee had justified India's nuclear tests after citing a threat from China and because of the China–Pakistan nuclear and missile connection in a confidential letter to US President Bill Clinton. However, the Clinton administration made this letter public.¹⁶ In the meanwhile, China not only rejected India's 'China threat theory', but also decided to form a partnership with the US to condemn India's nuclear tests and to bolster China's position on nonproliferation.¹⁷ The US–China joint statement on South Asia that was released a month after India's nuclear tests noted that the US and China 'can jointly and individually contribute to the achievement of a peaceful, prosperous, and secure South Asia.'¹⁸

From New Delhi's perspective, this was the worst of all possible outcomes, since not only had India's diplomacy backfired, but the US was legitimising China's role in the security affairs of South Asia, a region that India deemed to be its own sphere of influence. The US–China joint statement also demonstrated that even as late as 1998, the US did not think of India as a balancer of China's growing power in Asia. It must be noted that throughout the period from the late 1940s until India's 1998 nuclear tests, the alignments in the US–China–India strategic triangles were event-specific, that is, it was specific events that caused the strategic alignment of the US with either India or China against the other, and that this alignment disappeared soon after the passing of that event. These strategic triangles were not a consistent feature of the strategies of any of these three powers because India was a secondary actor during the Cold War and remained at the margins of global geopolitics even in the first post-Cold War decade because of its relatively small economy.

After India's May 1998 Nuclear Tests

However, there was a dramatic US and Chinese reassessment of India's potential after India's nuclear tests given that it came just years after India had launched its economic reforms and began to gradually embrace the market after the end of the Cold War. Soon after its nuclear tests, Jaswant Singh, India's Minister for External Affairs, began bilateral talks with Strobe Talbott, the US Deputy Secretary of State, in order to explain India's strategic worldview and predicament to the US. This resulted in 14 rounds of talks between them, the first-ever set of sustained talks between India and the US on their strategic view of the world.[19]

That the US had favourably reassessed the strategic importance of India became apparent just before President George W. Bush assumed office in 2001. Writing in *Foreign Affairs* almost a year before she became President Bush's National Security Advisor, Condoleezza Rice noted that America 'should pay closer attention to India's role in the regional balance [in Asia].' She added that it was important to think of India beyond the India–Pakistan dispute over Kashmir and nuclear nonproliferation since 'India is an element in China's calculation, and it should be in America's too. India is not a great power yet, but it has the potential to emerge as one.'[20]

It soon became evident that the US was beginning to think of India as an element in the Asian (and global) balance of power as a result of New Delhi's sustained economic growth throughout the 1990s and its growing military (and nuclear) power. In 2005 a US State Department spokesperson noted that it was America's 'goal . . . to help India become a major world power in the 21st century', before adding that the US understood the 'implications, including military implications, of that statement.'[21] In the same year, the US and India also began the process of ending India's isolation from the global nuclear order by launching the process of entering into a civil nuclear agreement with India. This process, which culminated in the 2008 US–India Civil Nuclear Agreement, involved changing US domestic law. At the same time, the US also spent political capital at the international level— at the International Atomic Energy Agency (IAEA)—to make an exception for

India as New Delhi is not a signatory to the Nuclear Non-Proliferation Treaty. As a consequence, India has become a *de facto* nuclear weapons state.

Just like the US, China has also noted the strategic impact of India's rapidly expanding economy.[22] At the same time, Chinese analysts are also concerned about India's growing military power, its Look and Act East strategies, and the dramatic transformation in US–India relations in recent years.[23] However, the China–India rivalry has intensified as a consequence of India's growing power and the transformation in US–India relations, despite the growing economic links between China and India.[24] Not only has no progress been made in resolving the China–India border dispute, but we are also witnessing the emergence of a nascent rivalry between China and India in the Indian Ocean.[25] In the meanwhile, instability in Tibet and the presence of the Dalai Lama and the Tibetan government-in-exile in India (although not recognised by the government of India), continue to remain important sources of tension in the China–India relationship.[26]

Therefore, it is perhaps not surprising that India and the US are in the process of creating a strong strategic partnership. America's important role in ending India's nuclear isolation made Indian policymakers realise that support from Washington is crucial for enhancing a rising India's diplomatic profile as well as its acceptance by many important states in Asia and beyond. Furthermore, India's leadership is also cognizant of the fact that the US possesses the capital and technology to help transform the Indian economy (and military).[27] Notably, India and America now conduct more military exercises with each other than either conducts with any other country, and that these exercises include all military services as well as all significant conventional military operations.[28] In recent years, India has also emerged as the largest buyer of US military equipment.[29] Finally, in a significant move, India and the US released a joint strategic vision for Asia and the Indian Ocean in 2015, in which they specifically called for 'freedom of navigation and over flight throughout the region, especially in the South China Sea.'[30] Not surprisingly, China has warned the US and India from any cooperation aimed at containing Chinese power.[31]

Conclusion

However, it would be mistake to think that the US and India are in the process of creating an alliance to balance China's growing power in Asia for four main reasons. First, it is not clear that either the US or India want to pursue a policy of containment towards China (with or without the help of the other). Given China's integration with the global economy and the fact that China is one of the largest trading partners of both the US and India, containment is clearly not a viable policy.

Furthermore, given India's geographical contiguity with China, India would certainly not like to play the role of a frontline state in any US-led policy of the containment of China (assuming that the US would like to pursue such a policy). It should also be noted that the most likely source of military tensions between the US and China is maritime in nature and is focused on the South and East China

Seas. However, the immediate Chinese military challenge for India is continental in nature, given the China–India border dispute along the Himalayas. As such, it is not clear if the US and India can (or will) provide the other side with overt military assistance in the event of a show of force with China. Nevertheless, the US is comfortable with it growing partnership with India as a powerful India contributes to the creation of a more equitable balance of power in Asia.

Second, India is concerned that the US and China may seek rapprochement that may come at the expense of Indian interests, thus reducing India into a secondary power in Asia. While there is historical precedent for a US–China alignment aimed at India (in 1971 and after India's 1998), the two sides have also sought accommodation in recent years. For example, many US analysts (as well as President Barack Obama according to some accounts) were in favor of a US–China 'G2' to manage global problems during Obama's early presidency.[32] Similarly, President Xi Jinping's proposal of 'a new type of great-power relations'[33] between the US and China hoped to create a bipolar world order as opposed to one that was multipolar.[34] In fact, officials in New Delhi were particularly alarmed when the US–China joint statement issued in 2009 mentioned that the US and China would like to 'work together to promote peace, stability, and development' in South Asia.[35]

However, China's more assertive policies in maritime East and Southeast Asia and the US' 'rebalancing' has dashed hopes of such a G2. In fact, the Pentagon now 'sees a strategic convergence between India's "Act East" policy and the US rebalance to the Asia-Pacific region', and is 'seeking to reinforce India's maritime capabilities as a net provider of security in the Indian Ocean region and beyond.'[36] Nevertheless, India will continue to remain wary of accommodation between the US and China that relegates India to the role of secondary power in Asia.

Third, given the power disparity between China and India,[37] and India's own tradition of strategic autonomy, New Delhi would like to avoid both—antagonising China as well as getting too close to the US. Indeed, New Delhi prefers a multipolar world order, with India as one of its poles. Notably, India has been institutionally involved with groupings and organisations that do not involve the US, including those that are led by China. For example, India continues with its meetings at the trilateral level with Russia and China with the explicit aim of promoting a multipolar world order.[38] Similarly, India has joined the China-led Asian Infrastructure Investment Bank (AIIB), where it is the second-largest stakeholder, although the US has disapproved of it (and even as the US tried to unsuccessfully prevent its close allies, the UK and Australia, from becoming members). India has also become a full member of the China-led Shanghai Cooperation Organisation.[39] However, none of this is to imply that India will play second fiddle to China. Notably, India has not endorsed China's One Belt, One Road initiative.[40] New Delhi's aim in joining China-led institutional initiatives is to raise India's international profile through its decision-making role within those international organisations, and should not be read as India's endorsement of China's primacy in Asia.

Finally, it should be noted that China is already responding to the growing relationship between the US and India by supporting India's subcontinental rival, Pakistan. Notably, China responded to the US–India Civil Nuclear Agreement that was endorsed at the multilateral level by the International Atomic Energy Agency (IAEA) by entering into a civil nuclear deal with Pakistan (at the bilateral level and without seeking IAEA approval).[41] Not only is Pakistan viewed as 'China's Israel',[42] but the China–Pakistan entente has also been described as 'the *most* stable and durable element of China's foreign relations.'[43]

China has consciously exported nuclear and missile technology to Pakistan, and Pakistan has now emerged as the largest buyer of Chinese conventional weapons.[44] China has also pledged US$46 billion for the construction of the China–Pakistan Economic Corridor, which will not only serve as the economic lifeline for Pakistan but is also rife with strategic implications.[45] The proposed corridor passes through Pakistani–Kashmir, a disputed territory between India and Pakistan. At the same time, the corridor terminates at the Arabian Sea port of Gwadar in Pakistan's Balochistan region. Indian strategists worry that Gwadar may be used by the Chinese navy in the future. Not surprisingly, India has begun to 'Act East' in earnest and is in the process of forming a closer strategic partnership with Japan, China's major rival in East Asia.[46] At the same time, India will also intensify its growing partnership with the US. Given that the US, China and India are likely to have the three largest economies and militaries in world over the next decade or so, this strategic triangle is fast emerging as one of Asia's most important relationships.

Notes

1. China, the US and India—in that order—are already the world's three largest economies (when measured in terms of purchasing power parity). See *The World in 2050: Will the Shift in Global Economic Power Continue?* (PricewaterhouseCoopers, February 2015), p. 3, 40. https://www.pwc.com/gx/en/issues/the-economy/assets/world-in-2050-february-2015.pdf
2. Sounak Mitra, 'India to be the third-biggest defense spender by 2020', *Business Standard*, 19 December 2014, http://www.business-standard.com/article/economy-policy/india-to-be-third-largest-spender-on-defence-by-2020-114121900369_1.html
3. There is a voluminous literature on these bilateral relationships. On the US–China relationship, see Warren Cohen, *America's Response to China: A History of Sino–American Relations* (New York: Columbia University Press, 2010); on the US–India relationship, see Rudra Chaudhuri, *Forged in Crisis: India and the US since 1947* (New York: Oxford University Press, 2014); and on the China–India relationship, see John Garver, *Protracted Contest: Sino–Indian Rivalry in the Twentieth Century* (Seattle: University of Washington Press, 2001).
4. For such a favourable assessment of India by Chester Bowles, the US ambassador to India from 1951–1953, see Chester Bowles, *Ambassador's Report* (New York: Harper and Brothers, 1954), pp. 156–158, 170–172, 199–200 and 327–331.
5. Charles Heimsath, *India's Role in the Korean War* (PhD Dissertation, Yale University, 1956).
6. According to the available evidence, India turned a blind eye to US support for Tibetan exiles in India in the 1950s. See Kenneth Conboy and James Morrison, *The CIA's Secret War in Tibet* (Lawrence: The University Press of Kansas, 2002).
7. Bruce Riedel, *JFK's Forgotten Crisis: Tibet, the CIA, and the Sino–Indian War* (Washington,

DC: Brookings Institution, 2015).
8   Robert McMahon, *The Cold War on the Periphery: The US, India and Pakistan* (New York: Columbia University Press, 1996).
9   Paul McGarr, *The Cold War in South Asia: Britain, the US and the Indian Subcontinent, 1945–1965* (Cambridge: Cambridge University Press, 2013), pp. 301–344.
10 See chapters 10 and 11 in Gary Bass, *The Blood Telegram: Nixon, Kissinger, and a Forgotten Genocide* (New York: Alfred A. Knopf, 2013).
11 Srinath Raghavan, *1971: A Global History of the Creation of Bangladesh* (Cambridge: Harvard University Press, 2013), pp. 184–204.
12 Robert Ross, 'The Diplomacy of Tiananmen: Two-Level Bargaining and Great-Power Cooperation', *Security Studies* 10:2 (2000).
13 Robert Sutter and Richard Cronin, 'China–India Border Friction: Background Information and Possible Implications', *CRS Report for the Congress*, Congressional Research Service, 19 June 1987.
14 In fact, China declared martial law in Tibet just weeks after Gandhi's visit. See Ronald Schwartz, *Circle of Protest: Political Ritual in the Tibetan Uprising, 1987–1992* (New York: Columbia University Press, 1994).
15 Robert Ross, 'The 1995–96 Taiwan Strait Confrontation: Coercion, Credibility, and the Use of Force', *International Security* 25:2 (2000).
16 'Nuclear Anxiety: Indian's Letter to Clinton on the Nuclear Testing', *New York Times*, 13 May 1998.
17 Manjeet S. Pardesi, 'China's Nuclear Forces and Their Significance to India', *The Nonproliferation Review* 21:3–4 (2014).
18 'Text: US–China Joint Statement on South Asia', 27 June 1999, http://fas.org/news/china/1998/sasia.htm
19 On their personal view of these talks and of the US–India relationship, see Jaswant Singh, *A Call to Honour: In Service of Emergent India* (New Delhi: Rupa, 2006); and Strobe Talbott, *Engaging India: Diplomacy, Democracy, and the Bomb* (Washington, DC: Brookings Institution, 2010).
20 Condoleezza Rice, 'Campaign 2000: Promoting the National Interest', *Foreign Affairs* 79:1 (2000), p. 56.
21 Background Briefing by Administration Officials on US–South Asia Relations, US Department of State, 25 March 2005, http://2001-2009.state.gov/r/pa/prs/ps/2005/43853.htm
22 Manjeet S. Pardesi, 'Understanding (Changing) Chinese Strategic Perceptions of India', *Strategic Analysis* 34:4 (2010).
23 Lora Saalman, 'Between "China Threat Theory" and "Chindia": Chinese Responses to India's Military Modernization', *The Chinese Journal of International Politics* 4 (2011).
24 Manjeet S. Pardesi, 'India's China Policy', in Sumit Ganguly, ed., *Engaging the World: Indian Foreign Policy Since 1947* (New Delhi: Oxford University Press, 2016).
25 Francine Frankel, 'The Breakout of the China–India Strategic Rivalry in Asia and the Indian Ocean', *Journal of International Affairs* 64:2 (2011).
26 Manjeet S. Pardesi, 'Instability in Tibet and the Sino–Indian Strategic Rivalry: Do Domestic Politics Matter?', in Sumit Ganguly and William Thompson, eds., *Asian Rivalries: Conflict, Escalation, and Limitations on Two-Level Games* (Stanford: Stanford University Press, 2011).
27 Former Prime Minister Manmohan Singh listed the US along with Germany and Japan as the countries that had the capital and technology to 'transform' India. See Indrani Bagchi, 'India should bond with Japan and stop looking over its shoulder at China', *The Economic Times*, 27 May 2013.
28 'Report to the Congress on US–India Security Cooperation', US Department of Defense, November 2011, p. 3; and Richard L. Armitage, R. Nicholas Burns and Richard Fontaine,

'Natural Allies: A Blueprint for the Future of US–India Relations', Center for a New American Security, October 2010, p. 5, <www.cnas.org/files/documents/publications/CNAS_Natural%20Allies_ArmitageBurnsFontaine.pdf>. See also John Ryan, 'China and Indo–US Relations: An Emerging Triangle? An Interview with Shivshankar Menon', The National Bureau of Asian Research, June 26, 2015, <www.nbr.org/research/activity.aspx?id=582>.

29 Gill Plimmer and Victor Mallet, 'India Becomes Biggest Foreign Buyer of US Weapons', *Financial Times*, 24 February 2014.
30 US–India Joint Strategic Vision for the Asia-Pacific and Indian Ocean Region, The White House, 25 January 2015. https://www.whitehouse.gov/the-press-office/2015/01/25/us-india-joint-strategic-vision-asia-pacific-and-indian-ocean-region
31 'China Warns on South China Sea as US, India Consider Patrols', *Reuters*, 11 February 2016, http://www.reuters.com/article/us-southchinasea-china-idUSKCN0VK0WQ
32 Richard Bush III, 'The US and China: A G-2 in the Making?', *Brookings*, 11 October 2011, http://www.brookings.edu/research/articles/2011/10/11-China–US-g2-bush
33 David Lampton, 'A New Type of Major-Power Relationship: Seeking a Durable Foundation for US–China Ties', *Asia Policy* 16 (July 2013).
34 Yan Xuetong, 'Why a Bipolar World is More Likely That a Unipolar of Multipolar One', *New Perspectives Quarterly* 32:3 (2015).
35 US–China Joint Statement, The White House, 17 November 2009, https://www.whitehouse.gov/the-press-office/us-china-joint-statement
36 Asia-Pacific Maritime Security Strategy, Department of Defense, July 2015, p. 28. http://www.defense.gov/Portals/1/Documents/pubs/NDAA%20A-P_Maritime_SecuritY_Strategy-08142015-1300-FINALFORMAT.PDF
37 The Chinese economy is five times larger than the Indian economy today and is expected to still be twice as large (at market exchange rate) even as late as 2050. See footnote 1.
38 'A Role for the RIC Trilateral', *The Hindu*, 17 November 2010.
39 'India, Pakistan Become Full SCO Members', *The Hindu*, 10 July 2015.
40 Charu Sudan Kasturi, 'India Wrinkle on China Silk', *The Telegraph*, 21 July 2015.
41 Ashley Tellis, 'The China–Pakistan Nuclear Deal: Separating Fact From Fiction', *Carnegie Policy Outlook*, 16 July 2010, http://carnegieendowment.org/files/china_pak_nuke1.pdf
42 Andrew Small, *The China–Pakistan Axis: Asia's New Geopolitics* (New York: Oxford University Press, 2015).
43 Garver, *Protracted Contest*, p. 187.
44 'Pakistan Largest Importer of Chinese Arms: Study', *Dawn*, 16 March 2015, http://www.dawn.com/news/1169906
45 'Is China-Pakistan 'Silk Road' a Game-Changer?', *BBC News*, 22 April 2015, http://www.bbc.com/news/world-asia-32400091
46 Manjeet S. Pardesi, 'India's Relations with Japan and South Korea', in Ganguly, *Engaging the World*.

5. PACIFIC PERSPECTIVES

Top: The roundtable panel (from left), with Professor Bo Zhiyue, New Zealand; Professor Wang Gungwu, Singapore; Ambassador Wu Jianmin, China; Dr Charles Morrison, Hawaii, US; Professor Bob Carr, Australia; and Professor Robert Ayson, New Zealand.

Bottom: Professor Wang Gungwu (second from left), talking about perceptions and misperceptions of the China–US relationship.

China and the US: Trading Arrangements in a Post-TPP World

Crawford Falconer

The Sir Graeme Harrison Professor of Global Value Chains and Trade at Lincoln University, New Zealand

No one should relish the prospect of a world where China and the US are pursuing mutually exclusive trading arrangements, even if it is not planned that way. Forget the economics, which may even be roughly manageable for a while. It's terrible politics. And terrible politics eventually messes up the economics. The big risk is that things are left to drift.

But there is (fortunately) an enormous potential to create a mutually beneficial outcome. The bedrock for that fortunate prospect is that China is in the market for undertaking a major reform programme in the near future that will be good for China but also for its trading partners.[1]

China still has huge economic and trade reforms to make if it is going to avoid the so-called 'middle-income trap'. The Chinese leadership knows this and knows real action is needed soon. Such changes will mean opening up its inefficient services and state-owned enterprise sectors, freeing up its investment regime and liberalising its capital account. One can gamble on China doing all this on its own and all the rest of the world gets the benefits in due course.

But the evidence suggests that China has not been able to quite turn its good intentions into action.[2] Might it not be the case that, in order to get there, China will need a little help from its friends? In fact, is there not the making of a grand bargain here for China and its trading partners in the not-too-distant future?

The obvious home for such a grand bargain should be the WTO—just like it was once before under Mike Moore's leadership way back in 2002. But, alas, the WTO now is not the WTO then. And Mike Moore isn't running it now.

Don't get me wrong. Serious people should still be looking to make this work in WTO terms. It is of course the most sensible way to deal with this—and so many other things. In fact, they should have been doing so a long time ago.

But they are not. And if they are not, one has to look, however reluctantly, at a second-best alternative. It is not without its own risks, but as long as the WTO remains ineffectual, the only realistic second-best alternative is to bring China into inclusive regional arrangements here in the Asia-Pacific. A successful TPP has created the essential conditions and generated massive momentum for that to happen.

New Zealand can and should play its honest-broker role in bringing the giants together. After all, nothing less than the future of our national economic security is at issue. All the more reason for strenuous efforts to be made on all sides at reinvigorating a long tradition of transparent and inclusive bipartisanship. Without it, our hand (and our prospects) in future processes will be materially diminished.

Situation and Prospects

Since at least the third plenum, China has foreshadowed that it intends to undertake further significant economic reform. It is unquestionable that it needs to do so. China clearly knows well enough that it is in its interest. The main international institutions are not hesitant to lecture accordingly. And nearly all, if not all, of China's major economic partners share that view.[3]

Of course, many of those changes go way beyond trade-focused matters. They cover a broad range of policies needed to move from an investment and export-oriented growth model to one that is more balanced with consumption. They go well beyond that to matters such as more efficient revenue raising, development of more effective social safety net arrangements, and rebalancing the relationship between the centre and the regions. It is a huge agenda.

The real issue is whether the Chinese leadership is going to be in a position to make that transition in a way that can be managed politically. It is by no means clear whether or how that is going to be done.

Right now, some observers see drift (or worse).[4] Others see shrewd incrementalism at work.[5] As to the more trade-related side of that (undoubtedly in many respects less significant than, for example, fiscal or tax reform), there are potentially some huge changes involved in moving such a general reform agenda ahead.

Reforms, notably in the areas of foreign direct investment, services and state-owned enterprises, are essential if China is going to move up the value chain seriously. And Chinese policymakers understand this perfectly well. Doing so would also have significant opportunities for China's trading partners. Is China going to prove willing and able to make those changes autonomously?

The scope for change is considerable. By way of illustrating what is potentially at stake, one can compare China's current restrictiveness in its major services sectors with the average levels of restrictiveness in OECD members and the BRICS states.

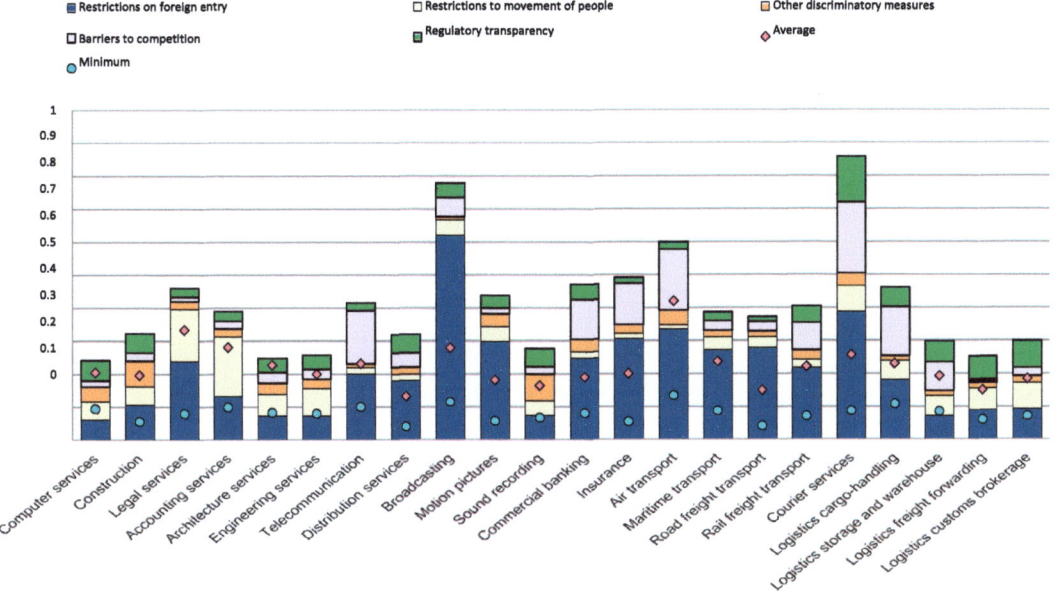

The case for doing so is, doubtless, that it would be in China's own interests. This logic applies no less to China than to any other country contemplating reform. But it is true that economies have often found it politically easier to undertake reform when they are in the company of others.

Indeed, we know that China itself has already used its relations with economic partners to reinforce a major economic change once this century. China's huge move to open up to the outside world was inextricably tied in with its accession to the WTO, finally achieved in 2002. Could China decide to do something like this again?

Of course, China does not need to do so. Indeed, most reputable economists would urge China to do itself a favour by advancing reform unilaterally without delay.

One has no quarrel with the logic. But there is the little matter of the politics.

The seeming hesitancy with which the leadership appears to be approaching its own declared trade-related reform agenda at least does more than suggest significant political difficulties with proceeding at this point.

Are China's trading partners missing a trick here?

Is it not just possible that the political forces could be more favourable realigned in circumstances where there is manifest additionality to China through others also contributing? Or, looking at it from the other end of the telescope, would it not make sense for China's trading partners to provide some positive inducements which might facilitate mutually beneficial arrangements?

The short answer appears to be, seemingly not. The default position all round seems to be let things slide. Which leaves you with three alternatives.

You can choose to believe that China will (eventually) proceed autonomously and China's trading partners will, in due course, gain benefits also without the need to act on their own part.

You can choose to believe that China is stuck but that there is nothing that anyone can do from outside that will make any difference whatsoever.

You can choose to believe that China is currently stuck, but that outside engagement might just make enough difference to move things forwards decisively to the benefit of both China and its trading partners.

This note lightly explores the third alternative. If it was to be pursued, what would be the most promising way forwards?

China and the WTO

The WTO was once decisive for China's reform, so let us start there.

The reality is that the (nigh on terminal) decline in the WTO's negotiating function would have seriously diminished the scope for any so minded within the Chinese system to argue seriously for the WTO as a principal vehicle for action.

It is worth noting, however, that China did signal that it wanted to join the WTO Trade in Services Agreement (TISA). By that time, the Doha Round was generally moribund and China had taken a position at the third plenum, which foreshadowed significant upcoming reform, particularly in the services area. The US and EU had, for their part, moved their attentions to the plurilateral route (apart from their FTA agenda), and TISA was the most economically significant sector under serious negotiation.

Certainly, on its face, it presents the form at least of a classic case of looking for a vehicle to facilitate reform with a *quid pro quo*.

The US rebuffed it.[7] The EU did not and, within the EU private sector at least, there were powerful voices urging that China be admitted to that process. The US argued that, in effect, China was not really serious. This, it may be noted, was at a time when the US was going seemingly going full steam ahead with its own bilateral investment treaty with China!

I have no way of knowing who was wrong and who was right as to what were the 'real' Chinese intentions. What does seem reasonable to conclude is that if there had been any intention on the part of China (or perhaps more particularly on some players inside the Chinese system) to move cautiously in the direction of looking to the WTO as an external vehicle to foster a process of domestic reform, they would likely have been disincentivised by that outcome.

All of which would seem to argue against either the likelihood or the desirability of China pursuing any grand bargain in the WTO. In principle, it still makes powerful sense. It would be optimal if serious minds were prepared to sit down and try to construct a serious package that could, over time, take participants through the Doha Round mandate and beyond to encompass a deal with China of the magnitude that is potentially on offer.

That would have to be the first best option. Of course, the problem is that perception of WTO viability is poor. I would be the last person to discourage, let alone dissuade, anyone from undertaking such an initiative. I can even see many powerful advantages to China for pursuing this route.

It is not so fully exposed to the US as it would be in the TPP. It would potentially be part of a deal that brought in all of its trading partners and not just the US, which would be far more in accord with its economic interests. It would suit its role vis-à-vis developing countries far more comfortably under a WTO banner.

And, as a global player itself, it would benefit hugely from a general reconsolidation of the multilateral system. It would doubtless also drive these fragmented and fragmenting arrangements more generally into a more coherent multilateral arrangement. It would be doing all players in the trading system a huge favour.

But it is also true that no other major player seems to be seriously pursuing the multilateral agenda. China would have to be prepared to assume a huge leadership role, at least for some period of time. One would not want to discourage it. It would be a huge breath of fresh air in the international system. It could even prove to be a major political coup.

But, one is entitled to ask for proof of life. The WTO ministerial conference in Nairobi was better than many had expected it to be, but it hardly amounted to a genuine resurrection. Without it, yes, it would doubtless run a risk of failure. And the harsh reality is that no politician much likes being associated with failure. That, alas, is still the WTO negotiating brand these days. Politicians always like to back a winner. And that winner right now is manifestly half a world away in the Asia-Pacific, going by the acronym the TPP.

The Post-TPP Regional Trade Agenda

By contrast, the serious action is regional these days. China, for its own part, has a series of FTAs. Its trilateral negotiation (China–Korea–Japan) had stalled for essentially political reasons with Japan, although there are indications—post TPP—that it may be revived. A less than first-rate deal has been done with Korea.[8]

More broadly, RCEP has been under way for some years, but there has been no real sense, to outside observers at least, that this is yet on the way to being a serious negotiation. Indeed, with India in the mix it is difficult to see it reaching any high quality outcome anytime soon.[9]

But China now knows that the major players—US and Japan—have done a deal and others are in the mix with the TPP. It will also guess that it is only a matter of time before Korea and others seek to join. The Philippines and Indonesia appear to be in that category already, and others will inevitably follow. It knows that the US and EU are trying to put together a deal of their own.

So, what does China do? It could try to up the pace in RCEP—that seems almost certain. The jury is still out on whether it can deliver something serious within a reasonable period of time.

It is certainly difficult to see RCEP being a vehicle capable of delivering the kind of reciprocal *quid pro quo* that would facilitate significant domestic reform. Leave aside whatever guess one may make about the intrinsic merits of such a deal. The fact is, that it does not involve such huge trading partners as the US and the EU.

It is also difficult to imagine any other novel or significant regional configuration even being initiated, let alone being carried through, to generate an outcome that would genuinely improve prospects for significant trade-related domestic reform.

It would perhaps be too much of an exaggeration to see the One Belt, One Road initiative as a reaction to TPP exclusion. There are doubtless intrinsic strategic, as well as economic, reasons why China would pursue this, irrespective of whether or not it was more directly involved, for instance, in free trade initiatives across the Pacific.

It is not really a free-trade-area type of initiative, although it doubtless has important and valuable economic and strategic linkages for China.

It is evident that the TPP has an attraction to China, and there have been senior voices expressing that sentiment publicly. In terms of pursuing its actual trading interests, it would at least involve the US, and I suspect that, even aside from whatever economic advantages that it is perceived to entail, it would have strong political attraction to China as an economic superpower-to-superpower partnership. And it is certainly difficult at this point to see any other vehicle presenting itself.

The prospect of a Free Trade Area of the Asia-Pacific (FTAAP) is a much more complicated arrangement. All the economies of the Asia-Pacific may get there at some point but hardly in a single bound. RCEP might be complementary but the momentum is unlikely to evolve into an inclusive arrangement that takes in the other side of the Pacific. All the momentum is with the TPP. You can see that with the reactions of the Philippines and Indonesia alone.

If it is going to be anything it will involve some kind of engagement with or evolution of TPP. But I do think that this is not without downside risks for China. If the whole logic of going down that road is some kind of reform-enhancing reciprocity, it does have some serious flaws from a Chinese perspective.

First, the US influence within the TPP is high. That might be politically attractive in the sense alluded to above, but it does mean, on the other hand, that the US will be able to exert enhanced leverage in a negotiating sense. Whatever it is called, it will be a negotiation where the terms of engagement have been largely set by the US. Of course, China has huge leverage of its own and where it starts is not where it will end up. But it will start off in a position that is a good distance away from being a neutral basis from day one.

Second, China will secure some commercial advantages vis-à-vis the US, but that is about it. Presumably not much, if anything, vis-à-vis Japan, on the assumption that the trilateral has already delivered that in the meantime. And nothing at all vis-à-vis all the other major players in the world economy: the EU; Brazil; India. China is a truly global trader. If the primary logic of engagement is to secure reform-enhancing reciprocity, it does have its limits.

Third, China may well perceive that this is an arrangement seen around the world, rightly or wrongly, as a US brand, and that this carries with it a political profile cost in relation to how it is seen by the rest of the world, particularly by the developing world.

All of which are reasons to point China—and everyone else—to the WTO umbrella, as alluded to above. But for as long as that remains out of reach, you are seriously in the world of the second best.

You have to make the best of what you have got. And that presents itself as doing as little harm as possible. Which, in practical terms means, at least bring the giants together rather than let them wander off down separate paths. But, even here, there is certainly no inevitability about it. Indeed, it will require considerable skill, guile, persistence and patience to make it happen.

Making signals that you are interested is one thing. But it is perfectly conceivable that China would not actively pursue a serious initiative to join the TPP. This is partly due to its negotiating tactics. The more you appear to want something, the more the price goes up.

But that's not the main reason. A nation with the weight and bearing of China is hardly going to go cap-in-hand, as it were, seeking to join a club to which it has not been seriously invited. If it was to make that effort it would only be conceivable in circumstances where a positive answer was guaranteed. Getting to that point would not be straightforward. It would require many things, not least skilful trade diplomacy.

The reality is that the TPP has been generated without involving China, and the view has been expressed up to the highest political levels that the reason that, for example, the US should prepare to agree to this, is that if it does not, 'China sets the rules'.[10]

It is going too far to say that the TPP was and is aimed at excluding China. Australia and New Zealand have been explicit in saying they reject any such view.[11] I think, more generally, that the jury is still out on that, even in Washington. But it is clear that there are a good number of political figures who hold that view. And there is no doubting that Chinese participation was never seriously contemplated as a possibility in the negotiating process to this point.

The US has, for various reasons, adopted largely combative rhetoric when it comes to China trade issues. There is plenty of stick but no discernible carrot. And China can give as good as it gets, irrespective of whatever view one holds about its exchange-rate policies.

In the meantime, China is busy doing what it can outside the TPP negotiation with RCEP, and other arrangements. It is also carefully signalling that it is potentially open to the TPP. The US is, meanwhile, carefully avoiding giving any kind of positive response whatsoever.

Of course, there is a form of competition going on here. And while, at least for the moment, matters are in a roughly manageable and nonthreatening state, it would be folly to imagine that this could not change. On the contrary, the risks of friction increase the higher the political and economic stakes are. Prudent policy would be to act precisely at a point before things look like they might actually go off the rails.

The US, for its part, will now go through a difficult implementation debate. It will have a presidential (and congressional) election cycle. It seems unlikely that anyone in the immediate foreseeable future will see any votes to be had by arguing for a free trade agreement with China, whether involving the TPP rubric or otherwise.

From the most optimistic perspective, one would be looking at a new US administration in 2017—and well into 2017—at the absolute earliest before anything like serious thought might be given to this. There are certainly plenty of voices that have seemingly entrenched opposition to engaging China. But there are other voices with a different view. It would doubtless be a difficult debate if it was ever seriously engaged with.

But it is difficult to see how objective observers could have much comfort if these two giants went their separate ways in separate trading arrangements for a prolonged period. Differences all too easily harden into disagreements over periods of time. And the risks of that are even greater if the WTO was to remain dysfunctional as well.

This is not to underestimate the actual substantive negotiating challenges, particularly for China. The TPP template will have some serious challenges for China. It is fair to say that China was not in fact in a position to live with the current elements of the TPP right now, irrespective of whether there had been a readiness to engage China from day one.

But they may not prove to be insurmountable. The whole premise is that China will be moving to a point where it is ready and willing to undertake reform. The absolute earliest that any process could commence would be 2018, and it would take years to negotiate—these things always do. Even if it was done in a lightning-fast timescale (say three years), then you have the phase in process. Five years? So before you know where you are, you are talking changes of the hardest stuff taking effect no earlier than 10 years away.

All of which would suggest there are hugely positive elements available to make this work. There must surely be a crucial role for a small trusted player such as New Zealand to help out these giants. Once upon time, we did that in the WTO. And we should not stop doing so, despite the odds. But we should also up the game in this area. There is much to lose if this fails, and quite a bit to gain if it succeeds. And it needs broad-based consensus because it will take years of effort to bring it to fruition. A light-switch effort will get us nowhere.

Notes

1. The essential document is 'Decision of the Central Committee of the Communist Party of China on some Major Issues Concerning Comprehensively Deepening Reform'. But see also 'Explanatory Notes' under President Xi's name alone, China.org, 13 November 2013, http://www.china.org.cn/china/third_plenary_session/2013-11/16/content_30620736.htm
2. 'Walled In: China's Great Dilemma', Investment Strategy Group, Goldman Sachs, January 2016.
3. IMF, PRC 2015 Article IV, Consultation Staff Report, Washington, DC, 2015
4. David Shambaugh, 'The coming Chinese crack-up', *Wall Street Journal*, 6 March 2015.
5. Daniel H. Rosen, 'Avoiding the Blind Alley', Asia Society Policy Institute report, October 2014.
6. OECD Services Trade Restrictiveness Index, www.oecd.org.
7. Schott and Miner, 'US–China Trade Relations: Projecting the Path Forward' in 'China's Economic Transformation', Peterson Institute for International Economics (PIIE) 2015 report, p. 15
8. Schott, Jung and Cimino-Isaacs, 'An Assessment of the Korea–China Free Trade Agreement', Policy Brief, PIIE, December 2015, pp. 15–24
9. 'Trading bloc to India: Cut tariffs or exit FTA talks' in *The Hindu,* 20 April 2016
10. 'With TPP, China doesn't set the rules in that region, we do,' qtd in *China Daily USA* 30 January 2016.
11. 'At least one Australian Trade Minister and I have said in public, neither Australia nor New Zealand would be part of TPP if it became a "China containment" strategy.' Tim Groser, New Zealand Minister for Trade, qtd in *Xinhua Global Times*, 30 June 2015.

Making Trans-Pacific Friends: New Zealand, China and the US

Stephen Jacobi

Executive director of the New Zealand International Business Forum, New Zealand

Abstract

New Zealand enjoys close relations with both China and the US, but has free-trade relations only with the former and not the latter. The Trans-Pacific Partnership (TPP) provides a pathway to realising the long-held vision of deeper economic relations with the US, along with ten other economies. The TPP is also seen as a pathway to a broader instrument for economic integration in the Asia-Pacific region, which will need to include China if it is to be successful. The following chapter will explain, from a business perspective, why the TPP is an important element to bridging New Zealand's important friendships on both sides of the Pacific and how this might be achieved.

In this chapter I would like to focus on three key issues:
- how business in New Zealand sees its relationships with China and the US in an economic and commercial context
- what the Trans-Pacific Partnership (TPP) has to do with all this; and
- how the TPP and, more importantly, what might flow from it, could lead to a new framework for trade and investment across the Pacific, encompassing both these key partners for New Zealand.

The NZ–China–US Relationship in a Commercial Context

Having spent the larger part of my professional life involved in trade and trade negotiations, I still find it surprising that New Zealand has, for the last seven years, enjoyed the benefits of a free-trade relationship with China while a similar set of arrangements with the US has continued to elude us. The situation is all the more surprising when you think that New Zealand shares fundamental values and principles with the US as well as a shared history as an erstwhile ally and still a 'very, very, very' good friend to use the terminology of former secretary of state Colin Powell.

As we know, the reason for this anomaly has to do mostly with factors in the political relationship between New Zealand and the US which meant we were unable, as had been the expectation at the time, to follow in the footsteps of Australia in securing an FTA in 2004.

In the period 2005–14 I personally led the work of the NZ US Council, a nonpartisan organisation funded by business and government to strengthen the relationship with the US and prepare the way for a future FTA negotiation. I am delighted that those past political difficulties have now been overcome; the political relationship is now in a better space than it has ever been and the TPP—now concluded, signed and awaiting ratification—has the potential to deliver the free-trade relationship we have sought for so long.

None of this has stopped New Zealand from actively pursuing a closer economic relationship with China—building on the famous 'four firsts' and culminating with the successful conclusion of an FTA in 2008. Much of the academic discourse around these important relationships seems to be focused on whether New Zealand might one day be forced to choose between one of these partners, but this tends to overlook that an important choice has already been made.

A generation ago New Zealand faced some difficult rebalancing of our external economy as a result of the consequences of Britain joining the European Economic Community in 1973. At that time we made the inevitable but nonetheless conscious choice to diversify our exports and seek to align ourselves economically with the Asia-Pacific region.

Today that choice sees over 70% of our exports going to that region whose economic pulse to a large extent is determined by both China and the US. In the last decade, the nature of trade has changed considerably. Models based on import and export are slowly being replaced by much more complex global value chains and networks. Trade in goods is being supplanted by trade in services and by both inward and outward investment, particularly as firms seek to be closer to their customers and to benefit from innovation on a global scale.

New Zealand is not immune to these developments. We connect to global value chains in different ways, increasingly incorporate services into our trade in goods, actively seek new foreign investment and, although in my view at too slow a pace, invest ourselves in other economies. Many of these value chains incorporate both China and the US—think for example of Pumpkin Patch designing clothes in Auckland, manufacturing them in China and selling them in New York. Or Fisher & Paykel linking innovation teams in Auckland and China, manufacturing dishwashers in Mexico and then selling them throughout the US.

Therefore, it should come as no surprise that to ask business to make some sort of choice between China and the US is a question that simply does not make sense in light of the reality of these global business networks. Rather, business in New Zealand seeks the best possible environment for doing business with *both* partners. That is unquestionably the sort of environment that high quality FTAs seek to create.

New Zealand is fortunate to have enjoyed the benefits of the NZ–China FTA for a number of years now. The FTA has given rise to an extraordinary increase in two-way trade due as much to what is called the 'dynamic gains of trade' as to the progressive elimination of tariffs and other trade barriers. Those dynamic gains of trade have to do with the increased commercial attention that an FTA tends to put on a relationship, as well as the framework that an FTA provides to improve the relationship over time. New Zealand has experienced these same dynamic gains arising from the Closer Economic Relations (CER) agreement with Australia over the last 30 years. I fully expect to see these dynamic gains arising from the TPP once it is ratified and has entered into force.

China and New Zealand are about to embark on an upgrade of the FTA in an effort to sustain the momentum of trade growth in recent years. The upgrade is of great interest to business because FTAs always need continuous improvement and because trade agreements are always lagging behind market realities. Some of the elements of the China FTA urgently require updating, such as the safeguards applied to dairy exports, which no longer reflect the growth of the market in recent years, and the rather cumbersome bureaucratic arrangements around the issuing of certificates of origin, which are out of step with the direction of trade growth.

There will likely be a range of issues on both sides that will be brought to the table to ensure the FTA remains a driving force in the economic and commercial relationship. This is all the more necessary now that our other good friend and competitor Australia has concluded a ground-breaking FTA with China—a very good one for Australia and one which will mount a challenge to New Zealand over time as Australian exporters enjoy similar and, in a few areas, better arrangements than in New Zealand.

And what of the US? As I mentioned earlier Australia has enjoyed an FTA with the US since 2004 and has used this agreement to good advantage in developing its commercial relationship, although primarily in areas that have not disadvantaged New Zealand. Meanwhile the US has clearly been disadvantaged in the New Zealand market as our arrangements with China have led to a loss of market share. While this might not cause much lost sleep in Washington, it does reflect the impact FTAs can have on trade flows.

The rise of China's economic profile in New Zealand has also led to calls for a new diversification of the economy, which would allow the risks of dependence to be spread across a range of partners. Somewhat ironically in light of history since 1973, such diversification needs to include the European Union, with which we hope soon to start a new FTA negotiation.

The fact of the matter is that *both* China and the US matter to New Zealand—as markets for goods as well as services, as import sources, as partners for investment and as sources of innovation, entrepreneurship and business ideas. It follows also that the relationship between them matters as well, particularly in the new global economic context in which we now operate.

The Significance of the TPP

This is where the TPP comes in. The organisers of the conference on 'China–US Relations in Global Perspective' must have had incredible foresight in choosing the timing of this gathering—the week following the decisive ministerial meeting in Atlanta at which the conclusion of the long-running TPP negotiations was achieved.

The time taken to conclude the TPP—not quite as bad as the WTO Doha Round—reflects the complexity of the issues under negotiation by the 12 parties which include the US and New Zealand. It's worth remembering that the TPP was essentially a New Zealand idea, born of a vision for a more seamless environment for trade and investment in the Asia-Pacific region, which was born in the early 1990s towards the end of the Uruguay Round and pursued with resolve over the last 20 years.

Decisive steps forwards were taken in the conclusion of the first TPP between New Zealand, Brunei, Chile and Singapore in 2006 and when the US joined the enlargement process in 2008. New Zealand's vision from the very beginning has always been for open regionalism—the widest possible membership of economies, the greatest possible coverage of issues and the highest quality of agreement.

In its earliest stages the TPP was open for any economy within APEC to join: at the APEC summit in Peru in 2008 this brought in Australia, Peru and Vietnam (at first in an observer capacity). Later Malaysia joined and then, very late, Mexico, Canada and Japan—by that stage the processes to join what was already an advanced negotiation had become a lot more complicated.

I repeat this history to underline an important point—the idea that the TPP has been devised to somehow contain China or that China has been prevented from joining simply does not hold water. It is completely understandable of course that the Chinese government felt unable to commit to such an ambitious negotiation at an early stage, but it has been very clear throughout the TPP process that China has followed the negotiations closely and no doubt has been kept informed by New Zealand.

At the TPP leaders' meeting held on the margins of APEC in Honolulu in 2011, it was agreed that the final agreement would be 'high quality, ambitious and comprehensive'. This wording reflected the original vision of the negotiating parties and the opportunity to create a new framework for trade and investment that would have a significant impact on sustainable growth and job creation.

Over time that vision appears to have been diluted—to the point that what came out of Atlanta, while undoubtedly a major step forwards, is something not quite as ambitious as what the architects of the TPP had in mind. Perhaps we should not be so surprised about that. The forces of protectionism and anti-competition are alive and well in many economies, including our own.

The Asia-Pacific region's economy has been subject to both rise and fall during this long period, affecting the willingness of politicians to embrace significant reform—reforms are inevitably put off in the bad times and seen as unnecessary in the good times. It must be admitted that the time taken with the TPP and the unavoidable limits on transparency in the negotiating process, have given rise to deep distrust on the part of civil society, even here in free-trade-loving New Zealand.

The final TPP is very positive indeed but still something less than what was on offer in Honolulu four years ago. It is disappointing from a New Zealand perspective that the final deal falls short of the goal of comprehensive tariff elimination—all duties on all products—even if no sector is completely off the table.

One might have thought that a deal focused firmly on the 21st century would have found a way to deal with issues from the 20th or even 19th centuries, but agricultural protectionism runs deep in the US, Japan and Canada, especially when it comes to dairy products. The TPP outcome on dairy marks the beginning of a further process to address wrong-headed protectionism, but on other agricultural products there are some very positive gains.

On another product of key interest to New Zealand—beef—the goal of complete tariff elimination in Japan continues to elude us, but there are very significant cuts to tariffs from 38.5% to 9% which should make a material difference to New Zealand exports. And in horticulture, wine, seafood, forestry and manufactured products there are also extremely useful advances which can be welcomed.

But the TPP was always meant to be about more than agriculture. In that respect what the TPP does is set up a more contemporary framework of rules for trade and investment that will lower costs, reduce the time it takes to do business, provide greater certainty and security for business and ensure that over time there is a more consistent approach to setting regulations and standards across the region.

That this has been achieved without the likelihood of significant adjustment for New Zealand in areas like medicines, investment, intellectual property or the management of state owned enterprises reflects both the skill of our negotiators and the fact that New Zealand is already at the level of world's best practice in these areas.

On medicines, the TPP preserves the operations of Pharmac, albeit with some modifications to the way Pharmac interacts with industry. On investment the TPP retains the right to regulate in areas such as public health, the environment and the Treaty of Waitangi, and provides an exemption for New Zealand's existing approach to regulating investment through the Overseas Investment Act. The TPP also limits the scope of investor state dispute settlement to measures affecting tobacco—an extraordinary facing down of the powerful tobacco lobby in the US.

On intellectual property the TPP upholds existing policy settings except in relation to the copyright term (where in New Zealand the term will rise from 50 to 70 years after death of the author or first release in the case of a recorded work) and the period of data protection for biologic drugs (where we understand the term will stay at five years as presently with some additional market protection measures).

On state-owned enterprises the TPP's disciplines are likely to be close to what we already have here and should not call into question government ownership of entities in New Zealand. The government is on record as saying that the costs and any risks arising from these changes can be managed.

The final text of the TPP treaty was released to the public in November and is still being pored over by stakeholders of all persuasions. This will hopefully enable a robust debate about the implications for New Zealand on the basis of facts, and should enable conclusions to be drawn in the context of the select committee process that will precede the ratification by the government. A release of the text will also be useful for partners like China and others not yet part of the TPP to enable them to judge their ability to join the TPP at a later date.

This was always the strategy—build on each agreement incrementally to expand the vision of freer trade and investment across the whole region: in that sense the TPP is not just about the 12 but about the whole 21 members of APEC, eventually including China.

Towards a New Framework across the Asia-Pacific

When the earliest moves to expand the TPP got underway there was a debate particularly in the US about not wanting to build a wall down the middle of the Pacific Ocean. The aim of the TPP was therefore to link both sides of the Pacific and also developed and developing economies. Thus the TPP today includes dynamic economies in both Asia and Latin America. The broader vision of which the TPP is a key part is for a future Free Trade Area of the Asia-Pacific (FTAAP).

In 1994 the APEC economies proceeded to adopt the famous Bogor goals, which committed them to achieving free trade and investment in the region by 2010 for developed economies, and 2020 for developing economies. It was envisaged that these goals would be achieved through a mix of unilateral, bilateral and multilateral efforts. However, it took another ten years before the APEC Business Advisory Council (ABAC) first started to think seriously about developing a more ambitious proposal to achieve comprehensive free trade in the region. Business leaders in ABAC were getting impatient at the time being taken to make meaningful progress towards achieving the Bogor goals.

The FTAAP concept arose due to a lack of progress in the Doha Round of WTO negotiations, which has not improved in the intervening period. By 2006 at the APEC leaders' summit in Hanoi, President Bush proposed that APEC adopt the vision of the FTAAP. After much debate the leaders decided that the FTAAP would be achieved through a range of practical and incremental steps—something that the trade negotiators in the room will be quick to assure you means no progress whatsoever.

In 2007 APEC economic leaders endorsed the report 'Strengthening Regional Economic Integration', which contained no less than 53 agreed actions aimed at strengthening work among APEC economies. These included reference to the FTAAP, but as a 'long-term' prospect.

At the 2010 APEC Japan meeting, it was agreed that the FTAAP would be achieved through a series of negotiating pathways including the TPP and the recently launched Regional Comprehensive Economic Partnership (RCEP), linking 16 Asian economies including New Zealand and Australia. The achievement of the FTAAP remained hostage to the conclusion of these negotiating pathways with all their attendant difficulties.

It was not until China's leadership of APEC in 2014 that some real momentum was injected into the FTAAP, with strong Chinese advocacy of a work programme to complete the broader vision. It was more than a little ironic that China's advocacy received a lukewarm reception from the US, whose legislative processes remained fixed on securing the TPP in the first instance.

Other economies like New Zealand were more appreciative, suggesting it was possible to chew gum and walk at the same time—meaning, continue to work to conclude TPP as a bottom-up approach while initiating work on the FTAAP from the top down. This is essentially what is happening now as APEC pursues a 'collective strategic study' to prepare the ground for FTAAP. The study is to be completed by the end of 2016—by then, hopefully, the TPP will be about to enter into force and RCEP, hopefully too, will have made significant progress.

Both agreements will contribute to achieving the FTAAP, bearing in mind of course that the 'A' in FTAAP stands for 'area' rather than 'agreement'. What that means in effect is that the FTAAP may not take the form of a conventional FTA negotiation, but may be achieved by a merging and docking of existing arrangements. In that way the FTAAP may serve to bring together the two largest economies in the region—the US and China—building also on the progress made between them in the interim such as through the bilateral investment treaty currently under negotiation.

The point is that the launching of the APEC collective strategic study process and the conclusion of the TPP in Atlanta bring the prospect of a future arrangement between the US and China that much closer. What once seemed an impossible dream now seems an achievable goal. Commitment, perseverance and a long-term vision are all indispensable elements in this journey to unite both sides of the Pacific.

Conclusion

The US baseball player and part-time philosopher Yogi Berra, who died last year, once said 'the future ain't what it used to be'. This observation is most certainly true when it comes to the future architecture for trade and investment in the Asia-Pacific region. It is also true in describing the way business is being done today through complex global value chains and networks. New Zealand has a major stake in the success of the region and in closer economic relations with the region's two major economic powers, China and the US.

What we have achieved with China through our FTA, we now—at last—have the prospect of achieving with the US through the TPP. And the TPP together with the collective strategic study underway within APEC provides a means to move forwards with the even broader vision of linking both sides of the Pacific in a new area of economic opportunity.

Making trans-Pacific friends is something that comes naturally to New Zealanders. We hope that this habit of expanding friendship across the region will become a means of achieving economic and social progress right across that great ocean which is our common home.

How Robust is New Zealand's China–US Strategy?

Robert Ayson

Professor of strategic studies at Victoria University of Wellington, New Zealand

Abstract
Denying that a choice needs to be made between China and the US, New Zealand argues it has a different type of relationship with each of the two great powers, who both understand this position. Hence if relations with China and the US are interdependent, they are not connected in zero-sum terms. This paper explores the robustness of New Zealand's informal China–US strategy against two types of change. One is the familiar scenario of a severe crisis between a stronger China and a still-strong US. But should the US unexpectedly become significantly less willing to maintain its presence in Asia, or should China experience severe economic and political challenges, what happens to regional relations and New Zealand's role in them?

What Is New Zealand's China–US Strategy?
New Zealand's China–US strategy is not laid out clearly in a single document. But it is possible to detect elements of that strategy by bringing together scraps of data and reading between the lines. In this spirit, here are ten points I believe comprise the New Zealand government's approach China–US relations.

    1. New Zealand recognises China and the US as the two most important players in the region. It also believes the bilateral relationship between the US and China is the most crucial of all relationships for Asia's future.

    2. New Zealand sees relationships with China and the US as two of its most important relationships anywhere in the world. They are bettered only by our number one partner, Australia, which itself places the US and China at the top

of its own list. (Incidentally, Australia's top four relationships probably include Indonesia and Japan, and not New Zealand.)

3. Wellington is aware that both China and the US want to intensify their own bilateral relationships with New Zealand, as they do with a range of Asia-Pacific countries. Wellington recognises this as a sign of competition for regional influence between China and the US.

4. New Zealand believes that the US and China also have some important common interests in Asia alongside their more competitive tendencies. These common interests include a mutual desire for greater prosperity (including through regional economic linkages) and the avoidance of catastrophic war. Opportunities for the two giants to focus on their common interests, such as at the recent Obama–Xi summit at Sunnylands, California, are welcomed by New Zealand.

5. New Zealand believes that the cooperative elements of China–US relations can be used to moderate some of the more competitive aspects. Working with its regional partners, New Zealand believes it can encourage the US and China to focus on what they have in common. This is one reason for New Zealand's active participation in regional multilateral forums, including the East Asia Summit, the ASEAN Defence Ministers Meeting-Plus (ADMM+) and the ASEAN Regional Forum. Likewise New Zealand has also been encouraging collaboration among the five permanent members of the UN Security Council, which include the US and China.

6. New Zealand recognises that China and the US are different actors with different strengths. Their contributions to Asia's future order will also be different. China's recent influence has been built, above all, on its economic growth, and its increasingly central role in Asia's economic integration. This is now translating into greater diplomatic and military influence for China, but there are limits to these elements. By comparison, having experienced its own gilded age over a century ago, the US is a more complete great power. The signing of the TPP advances the regional economic profile of the US. But unlike China, the US also has a unique security role in Asia thanks to its long-standing network of military and intelligence relationships.

7. New Zealand wants enhanced partnerships with both China and the US but realises these will be built differently. Not long ago China became New Zealand's leading trade partner and the two regularly point to a series of 'firsts' in the economic aspects of their relationship. Defence cooperation between New Zealand and China is increasing, and New Zealand welcomes China's participation in regional security cooperation. But China is unlikely to become an intimate security partner along the same lines as New Zealand's traditional relationships. The economic element is also important in New Zealand's relationship with the US. Having the US play a fuller role in Asia's economic integration has been judged by New Zealand to be worth the dairy sector trade-offs in the TPP. But whatever happens to that agreement in Congress, New Zealand enjoys a defence and security relationship with the US

(including on intelligence matters) unlike the relationship it can have with any other Asian-Pacific great power. I do not think it likely that a future New Zealand government will turn down the opportunity to continue these renewed links.

8. New Zealand believes that its close partnerships with China and the US are not mutually exclusive. In New Zealand's view, there is little need to think in zero-sum game terms. A warmer relationship with China need not mean a cooler one with the US, and vice versa. But New Zealand is aware that in order to keep things this way, some care is needed. It is possible to get too close to one party at the expense of friendship with the other. So far, New Zealand has stayed within the limits.

9. At least in its public comments, the New Zealand government does not buy into the argument that it needs to make a fundamental choice between China and the US. New Zealand is aware that other countries in the Asia-Pacific may may feel they are much closer to making such a massive decision. Some may already have gone past a point of little return, including one or two countries around China's periphery and some of America's leading allies. But New Zealand may have good reasons, including geographical ones, to feel less vulnerable on this score than other countries in the region. For example, our strategic debate has not witnessed the same anxiety over the choice between the two great powers as our neighbour Australia has.

10. New Zealand believes that one of the best forms of protection against such unwanted choice-making is to avoid becoming too closely and exclusively aligned to either China or the US. New Zealand's leaders give the impression that they are confident the two major powers understand these limits and that they do not push us too hard as a consequence. Some New Zealanders may even feel that if the rest of the region took a middle-ground approach, we are more likely to see a peaceful and stable regional order in which China and the US are engaged simultaneously and beneficially. We have that inclination perhaps because of a belief in the power of fairness.

How Robust is New Zealand's Strategy?

This depiction of New Zealand's China–US strategy can be challenged in some of its detail. Indeed, you may still be wondering if this strategy really does exist. But assuming I have got at least some of the central aspects right, there are also some important questions that can be raised about how well suited this approach is to New Zealand's needs in a changing region. So here is a further set of ten points:

11. New Zealand's political leaders do talk about this country's relationships with China and the US. But they seldom do so at the same time. Nor do we have much specific knowledge on how New Zealand's approach to one of these relationships affects its approach to the other. A strategy is a strategy when it acknowledges the interdependence of expectation and action between two or more purposeful actors. Our public debate is short of this kind of strategic analysis.

12. New Zealand's leaders occasionally invoke an interaction between the China- and US-factors in their thinking about the region. But these moments are fleeting

and leave a good deal to the imagination. I can recall two such examples from current New Zealand prime minister, John Key. During his first term he said that New Zealand was comfortable with the idea of there being two superpowers in the region. And just before his most recent electoral success, he said that New Zealand enjoys different relations with the US and China and that both of these countries understood this situation. Gerry Brownlee's recent speech in China was one of the first (and only) times I can recall a New Zealand cabinet minister comparing our defence relations with the two countries. 'We do not see our defence relationships with the US and China as mutually exclusive,' New Zealand's defence minister told his audience at the PLA National Defence University in Beijing. 'We believe that the US and China want the same thing for the Asia-Pacific—peace and prosperity.'[1] Whether or not we agree with these observations, at least they confirm the fourth and ninth points of my depiction of New Zealand's strategy. But they are just the starting point for the grander discussion we need in New Zealand, in which our political leaders and leading officials should be engaged.

13. We may wonder if New Zealand's position of enjoying close relations with both China and the US is much more than a happy coincidence of these two largely separate relationships. There have been some initial signs of trilateral interaction. On the military side, China and the US have participated in exercises led by New Zealand such as Exercise Tropic Twilight in the Cook Islands and the humanitarian Exercise Phoenix Spirit. But in overall terms it is important to wonder how much the New Zealand government consciously manages these two relationships as parts of an interdependent strategic approach. Strategies are deliberate. They are not accidents of history. That does not mean they have to be written down. A lot of good strategy is implicit. But because so little is written down, our reasons to ponder the ratio between management and coincidence tend to grow.

14. A wise New Zealand approach to the China–US question cannot be derived by the maximisation of both of these relationships. The equation is not China–US Strategy = US Strategy + China Strategy. While we may be able to avoid zero-sum games, we cannot pretend there are any purely cooperative ones out there. But that means we need to be a little cautious about the 'NZ Inc' strategies which the Key government has published. These include a China strategy that sets big targets for trade and investment gains. I tend to see these as plans designed to coordinate New Zealand behaviour around a common ambition. But I doubt they are strategies focusing on the management of encounters with purposeful strategic actors who may see the world quite differently. There is of course a lot of hard bargaining in trade negotiations, but the parties still see negotiation as a common endeavour. New Zealand's leaders have sometimes viewed foreign policy through a trade-promotion lens. When there is no such thing as too many FTAs in Asia, some of the other questions can be obscured.

15. The test of New Zealand's China–US strategy will not necessarily be a war between the two great powers where we face an ugly all-or-nothing choice such as

whether we side with an emerging China or the traditionally strong US. This is quite unlikely. Asia now boasts a record of several decades of major-power peace. There are points of tension and risks of escalation, but it is unwise to assume this record will come adrift any time soon. So the issue is not the terms of Asia's future war and New Zealand's position between and amongst the warring parties. The issue is more likely to be the terms of Asia's future order. But even if Asia remains technically peaceful, there will be all sorts of ways in which actors can exploit potential violence. This we already know in the East China and South China Seas. This means that there are still some important everyday choices for New Zealand to make in a peacetime Asia. These are choices about the rules which govern Asia's order. Many of these rules will be informal and implicit ones: they will be the rules of the game. And in addressing them, let us not assume for a moment that New Zealand can rest on its participation in the UN and Asia's regional organisations.

16. It may be possible to get a little carried away here, but potentially everything New Zealand says and does in relation to either China or the US, and certainly when it relates to both, is a potential signal of where we stand. This has applied to our position on the Trans-Pacific Partnership and China's investment bank. It applies to our approach to the US 'rebalance' and to China's growing military role. It applies to our positions on human rights, military intervention and cybersecurity. It applies to the cooperation we pursue with Australia, Japan, South Korea and our ASEAN partners. It applies to the large powers we choose to work with in the South Pacific region. It applies to the approach we take on maritime troubles in East Asia. It applies to what we say and don't say about sensitive issues that China deems as its core interests and about the values that matter to the US. And it certainly applies to the military capabilities we choose to develop, the exercises we engage in, our involvement in information gathering and the overseas deployments we commit to.

17. In this series of everyday tests, the New Zealand government's default position appears to be to say 'yes' often enough to both China and the US so that all are aware of our standards of fairness. I refer to a 'default position' because this is suitably vague. It may imply something that occurs automatically as we think and act on the two relationships in isolation. Or it may be our bottom line as New Zealand prudently make a series of choices designed in their combination to evoke a deliberate balance. Taking the more inspiring second option, one might see a pattern emerging. On one day, for instance, New Zealand agrees to a limited role in training Iraq's armed forces whereas on another day we agree to be part of China's One Belt, One Road initiative.

It is difficult to be sure how much conscious interaction there is between these choices, because there may be good independent reasons to do each of them. But I think we can give New Zealand some of the benefit of the doubt here. There is at least a sense of an interdependent and thus strategic approach, where we are managing and moderating one relationship partly because of what it means for the other. For example, New Zealand ministers have studiously avoided the two 'A' words (alliance and ANZUS) in talking about the burgeoning US relationship. This is not just because of what China may think, but this will be part of its consideration. And New Zealand has been getting a stronger in words spoken publicly to China about the South China Sea. Again, this is not just because of what Washington will think, but we do know the US is more content the more we move in this direction.

18. If the immediate goal is for New Zealand to enjoy a level of comfort in its international affairs, then this balanced approach may succeed in providing just that. Neither of the great powers is completely pleased with us, but they have no reason to be completely displeased either, and we all sail along accordingly. This may foster a view that New Zealand would be happy with a future Asian order where China and the US are matched evenly enough to produce a regional equilibrium. But that is actually not what quite a number of our regional partners want. Regardless of what some of them say in public, they prefer a preponderance of power for the US to a balance of power between the US and China, let alone preponderance in China's favour. And we know that US preponderance is the preference of Australia, New Zealand's leading ally and partner. Australia is not alone here.

19. The preponderance of the US is also more likely to be New Zealand's preference than our current tactics suggest. On the rules of the game that will make up Asia's evolving order, we will not have identical positions to the ones held by the US. But on many issues, our position will be significantly closer to that of the US than it will be to China's. These include our desire for a broad notion of Asian regionalism, which is more Asia-Pacific than specifically East Asian and in which the US is included. They include New Zealand's preferences regarding norms on cyberspace (including on the openness of the internet), on the application of international law to the freedom of navigation, on the relationship between citizens of countries and their governments, on the style of governments we are happy to see our South Pacific neighbours maintain and on the future of the southern oceans and Antarctica. Does this mean that US power is unproblematic for us? The answer is no. The ways in which the US projects power into Asia can cause us some difficult moments. But these are small by comparison to what would worry us should China come to dominate the region.

20. There is a final problem in that preferences are not strategy either. All the ambitions in the world count for little if they completely outstretch available means. Perhaps there is more talk of the system of rules (and the liberal values) that have worked for New Zealand when we are concerned those rules are being challenged. Likewise, the appeal of US preponderance may grow the more it is challenged. What does it mean for our strategy if the Asian order that works for us is becoming increasingly less tenable? Unlike China's leaders, who watch on from the heart of East Asia, US leaders must choose for their country to project power from some distance into the heart of the region. The US may be a resident Pacific power, but it is not an East Asian continental power that is now extending its maritime reach. The Obama administration, its successor and its successor's successor will continue

to tell New Zealand that the US remains committed to the region and sees itself in a leadership role. These will be genuine commitments and we will treat them as such. Yet all preponderances of power come to an end at some stage. If we think such a change is likely, that it is already happening, or even that it is possible, there might be good reason to butter our bread on both sides.

But of course China's trajectory is unlikely to be smooth. The socio-political, economic and environmental pressures it faces are truly immense. A China that is unable to cope with those pressures may be more troubling to New Zealand than a less-influential US. But the combination of these factors could be deeply destabilising for Asia as a whole, in which case the uncertain future roles of Japan and India become more significant. Something tells me that, in all of this, New Zealand's China–US strategy, while passable in the short-term, is going to be found wanting at some stage. Of course the same might be said for the China–US strategies of many of our regional partners. At least we will not be alone in our confusion.

Notes

1   For analysis of this speech, see the piece I have written with David Capie for *Incline*, a blog on New Zealand's place in the world, http://www.incline.org.nz/home/-cooperation-and-concern-in-new-zealands-view-of-china

Top: Professor the Hon. Bob Carr, Australia, discussing how to manage China's rise.

Bottom: Dr Charles Morrison, president of the East–West Center, Hawaii, US, talking about China's role in global affairs.

Conclusion: The Future of China–US Relations

Edited by Bo Zhiyue

Abstract

The China–US relationship is one of the most important bilateral relationships in today's world. How the relationship evolves in the future is of great interest not only for the two giants but also for the rest of the world. If the two countries could manage their relationship well, the Asia-Pacific region in particular and the entire world in general will benefit. If there is a tension between the two, countries and regions in the region will be torn apart. Maintaining a good relationship between China and the US involves many factors across many dimensions. In the following, experts share their views on the future of China–US relations.

Wang Gungwu

University professor and chairman of the East Asian Institutue at the National University of Singapore

Perceptions and Misperceptions, and the Future of China–US Relations

Conversations about China and the US are not just the crux of the matter here in this volume, but can be found everywhere I turn these days. My understanding of what goes on in these conversations is that misunderstandings and misperceptions are often found together with genuine efforts to understand the relationship between these two countries. It is important for us to know that some of these misperceptions may have consequences on the future. But how you sieve through today's dynamics of the China–US relationship to gain insights into the future, I do not know. What I am certain of in modern history is that change tends to occur at a moment's notice. With global affairs in a state of flux, it is expected that unforeseen changes will continue to happen.

For someone who has been keeping track of China's development over the last few decades, I will personally share with you that I have been surprised beyond count. Perceptions, then, are central to the creation of surprises as they influence human behaviour in ways we cannot predict. For example, incidents in the Senkaku (Daioyu) and Spratly Islands have shown us that nothing can be taken for granted. Every action remains hard to predict and bears consequences that are potentially disruptive to the global world order.

What I would like to do to elaborate the importance of perceptions in the China–US narrative is to identify two key misperceptions I see that the world and, more specifically, the US may have about China today.

The first misperception lies in the realm of economics, and over which direction is

China heading towards. It is a matter of fact that the rise of China is inevitable and will go on for quite some time. But is that a perception or a reality? Let us assume it is a reality. There can be no misperceptions over that. China's growth has been phenomenal over the past few decades, but for how much longer I do not claim to know.

The tendency to evaluate China's growth as a zero-sum game, where China's rise is accompanied by a relative decline in another country, creates a set of misperceptions that could ultimately prove to be a terrible mistake. In the world of economic development, there is a lack of zero-sum calculations. Everyone gets the opportunity to grow and be richer. However, I have always been given to understand that in politics, realities are often framed in a zero-sum game mindset. Since politics has to take the form of a zero-sum game, the perception of someone improving their position at the expense of others has become influential in our thinking, even if it is not true.

I am aware that many in China who know that China is rising would therefore assume that the US must be declining. This assumption is often taken for granted. It is not possible to ignore it, as such views are now commonplace in China. The perception of one rising and the other falling by comparison seems to me to be one of the key factors in the political game. But I would like to bring your attention to the importance of economic possibilities through trade and negotiation that might change the behavioural pattern of these two countries.

On the other hand, it is important to consider the zero-sum game from the US perspective. How many people in the US assume China is rising at their expense? I hope that is not the case, but if that is so, these kinds of mutual perceptions are bad factors in any equation. It is important that such negative perceptions of each other do not become a key determinants in future political calculations. If you think like that, it will increase the possibility of further misunderstandings based on poor miscalculations. This will set off a chain of bad decisions that arise from such misunderstandings. So that's the first misconception I am concerned about—charting China's growth as a zero-sum game.

The second misperception is a question of geographical territory and status. These are very difficult things to measure. In that sense, I always envied the economist, who works with quantifiable data. Unfortunately, hard data is hard to come by in the world of politics and perceptions. Over the last few years, the perception that China is building a navy to project her naval power into the Pacific and challenging US hegemony in the region is fast gaining credence. Personally, I do not know how many people actually believe that. I hate to think that Chinese admirals actually buy into the notion and are actively seeking such an outcome in the Pacific. Conversely, I do not want to think what would happen if the US thought that a hegemonic challenge to them was the only rational outcome of the Chinese national interest. I would remind you that such concerns represent the most unnecessary part of speculating about the future. I believe that such propositions are unrealistic for a variety of reasons—the nature of China's trade as a maritime nation and her historical attachment to the Eurasian hinterland.

Over the past few years, the Chinese have come to realise that they are more economically dependent on maritime trade, and development has come about because they opened their economy to sea trade. Although this may be speculative, we need to take into account how a maritime capitalist/market economy is vital to Chinese economic development. The Chinese are perfectly aware of this, so they are going to be more active economically to further embed themselves permanently in the global maritime trade network.

As China finds herself to be a key maritime trading nation, it does not mean that such a development should be accompanied by a naval or military challenge in the oceans. There is no need for that at all. I think the existing situation allows the Chinese economy to continue growing, and any tenuous links should not be made between military aggression and maritime trade development. That should be a key point to remember when assessing the future of the China–US relationship.

As well, with China recently cementing its status as one of the world's major powers, I believe it is continually reminded that its continent is of geostrategic importance. In my introduction, I mentioned the Old and New Worlds. I think the Chinese are perfectly aware that they belong to the Old World of Eurasia, part of the Eurasian continent. Hence, historical threats from the continent are real and will continue to be very meaningful to China. In the end, this contributes to its thinking on how it important it is to develop its Eurasian hinterland and reduce its reliance on a maritime economy centred along the Chinese coasts. As we saw from the map shown the other day, the population of China today shows a high concentration of along the coastline.

However, the significance of the interior economy cannot be understated. Around 80% of China's economy is derived from the internal markets of continental Eurasia. That dependence will not change, as it is a fact of historical geography, so to speak. Therefore, we can see that the interior is of great geostrategic importance to China. Now, let us assume that this scenario still holds good, and China is aware of it, which I think it is. I would believe the speculations on the purpose of the One Belt, One Road initiative. We are not entirely sure what China is going to do, but I think this represents the beginning of a consciousness that it cannot afford to neglect the continental side of development.

If we allow for some speculation, there are suggestions that the One Belt, One Road project is a message sent to the US, saying that China will not challenge them in the Pacific and Indian Oceans. China's real future lies in the balance between its dependence on the sea and responsibility towards the continental interior. China's interior represents China's future growth. If China and the US can divide their responsibilities as leading global nations, the US can look after the Indo-Pacific Oceans while China not only looks after the maritime neighbourhood in its vicinity, but also the continental interior as well. This continental interior is important to the maintenance of global stability, for it encompasses the Middle East, eastern and central European regions. The Eurasian continental mainland is an area where China can play a responsible and probably much more successful role than what the US has done in recent years, as evident from their mistakes in the region. The segregation of global policing in this manner might be in US interests, where responsibilities are clearly delineated, minimising the potential for quarrels. That is my optimistic speculation of the future.

Maybe the next step in this One Belt, One Road development is for Xi Jinping and his advisers to work harder and ensure that China's maritime trade and domestic economy is channelled into the development of Eurasia. It is not about the naval supremacy on the oceans, though that is now commonly accepted as part of the thinking on China–US relations. Given today's circumstances, the best possible outcome can be realised if China and the US could separate their political and military roles clearly. That is one thought.

My last thought is to simply seek your forgiveness for talking too much yesterday about whether the leaders should meet or not. When the leaders of China and the US never met, nothing went wrong. Both countries were doing very well. In fact, both were heading in opposite directions, with or without the help of any leaders' meeting. Had they met, it wouldn't have made any difference anyway. So today the question is, does it matter if the leaders meet? Maybe it does now. If it does, if meeting between leaders is now important, then something has changed in the world today. The world has become smaller and things move faster. Leaders have to meet eye to eye and actually get the opportunity to like each other or trust each other, and that becomes important. I hope not, because it becomes more troublesome when you think about who is going to meet who next time. I am quite sure about Xi Jinping for the next seven or eight years, but I am not sure who he is going to meet the next time in the US. That part does not excite me very much; I'm not very happy about that. The idea that in the future, where meetings between leaders should become the norm and whether leaders actually like or trust each other is important, creates a big question mark. So let me leave you with that intriguing possibility.

Wu Jianmin

Former member of the Foreign Policy Advisory Group of the Chinese Foreign Ministry, special research fellow of Counselors' Office of the State Council, member and vice president of the European Academy of Sciences and honorary president of the International Bureau of Exhibitions (BIE)

A Sound China–US Relationship Requires the Two Sides to Deal with Their Differences Properly

Looking down the road on the China–US relationship, I am cautiously optimistic for three reasons:

1. The fundamentals of the China–US relationship remain unchanged. They are included in the historical consensus reached by President Xi and President Obama in June 2013 in Sunnyland, California. Specifically, the fundamentals are as follows: building a new type of major-power relationship, adhering to interdependence and acknowledging the overarching importance of the two countries' common interests vis-à-vis their differences.

2. The China–US relationship is growing mature. The past 44 years since Dr Henry Kissinger's first visit to China in 1971 have seen eight US presidents: Nixon; Ford; Carter; Reagan; Bush Snr; Clinton, Bush Jnr; and the incumbent Obama. All of them have continued to maintain good bilateral relations with China, notwithstanding some temporary fluctuations. It indicates a bipartisan consensus in the US with regard to this relationship. On the Chinese side, we have had Mao Zedong; Deng Xiaoping; Jiang Zemin; Hu Jintao; and the incumbent Xi Jinping. Five generations of leaders have been committed to carrying on bilateral relations with the US. It indicates a unanimity of views in the Chinese leadership towards developing a sound relationship with the US. The continued commitment from both countries signifies a maturing relationship which is achieved through arduous efforts from both sides.

3. The history of the China–US relationship serves as a good lesson for both our two countries. China and the US were allies during World War II. We fought together against Japanese militarism. Unfortunately, after the founding of the People's Republic of China, our bilateral relationship kept moving downward. We fought each other on the battlefield in Korea and then in Vietnam. Both paid a heavy price. However in 1971, the China–US relationship began to improve and since then has grown tremendously. It has benefited both the Chinese and US peoples, and the entire international community as well. This history shows that confrontation makes us both losers, while mutual cooperation makes us winners.

It is true that there are many differences between China and the US. We have differences now. Even in 100 years, we may still have differences of this or that kind. As the saying goes, 'It takes two to tango', so a sound China–US relationship requires the two sides to deal with their differences properly. It means that we have

to do the following:
   a. We have to acknowledge that it is natural for China and the US to have differences, because we have different histories, cultures, political systems, and we are in different stages of development.
   b. We have to deal with our differences through dialogue, which is the only viable and right way. When we look at our differences, we may find some that can be resolved today, while others can be resolved tomorrow and still others the day after tomorrow or even later. For the differences that can only be resolved tomorrow or even later, we should not try to do it today. That will only prove to be futile.
   c. We should not let the differences stay in the way of mutual cooperation. If we can prevent differences from interfering in our bilateral cooperation, I am sure it will be good news not only for our two countries, but also for the whole world. A sound China–US relationship is in the interests of world peace and prosperity.

Charles Morrison

President of the East–West Center, Hawaii, US

The Relationship between the US and China from a Global Perspective

In the past, the US–China dialogue was mainly about regional issues. But recently, issues dominating the dialogue are increasingly global in nature and I think it is a direction that we will continue on as China flexes its diplomatic muscles as a global power. It is often said that India, as a neighbour and potential rival to China, has punched well below its weight. However, China is not too dissimilar to India in this regard, as it continues to find its way in today's world where modern realities of international affairs are often contrasted with its emergence from its isolationist past. China is dealing an international language that is not its own, so there are a lot of experiences to be gained from its rise as a global power.

A certain belief that I find credence in is that US interest would mean involving China as a responsible stakeholder in the international system. I think we can agree on the meaning of stakeholder. We are all stakeholders, but responsibility is a matter of semantics. This is where I think third-party countries such as New Zealand become more prominent in mediating a common ground on what responsibility is. The US views responsibility in one way, while China may base their understanding of responsibility on Chinese beliefs. Among such competing interpretations of responsibility, the real definition would be a global one where lots of voices can be heard. So I think the world of the future is one where we have to function as a human community, organising our interests along values of humanity despite our diverse origins. The basic traditions that were formative of a nation's current status in the international system are important and should not be forgotten. However, we have to try and make such diversity fit together in a 'win–win' proposition.

One of the areas we may have skipped over a little bit is the economic dimension. I think this is an important element of the future, where China may already be or will be at an inflection point in the future. Not wanting to be alarmist, but China has been following a growth model that is reaching its end, and what is happening now in fact represents a search for a new growth model. The increasing emphasis on a domestic consumer society, changes in the state-owned enterprises and attempts to deal with the middle-income trap strike me as examples of China's desire to proceed into the new stage of economic development. These changes are not easy to negotiate or circumvent, and I think we have a scenario where China needs to interact with other countries more often and more closely so we can all work through the problems together.

Let me now turn to the issue of grand bargains and regional institutionalism. I am sceptical about those who think that there can be grand bargains, or those who propose grand new regional institutions. On the former, I think it is almost politically impossible to achieve. It is common sense that third parties always feel that a grand bargain struck between two nations would inevitably disadvantage those who are not at the table. In hindsight, what may appear to be a grand bargain may not be so grand after taking into account its implications at a global level.

On regional institutions, there is the tendency to think that building regional architecture is the answer when it is really only an invitation for a discussion. I am sceptical about institutions like APEC (Asia-Pacific Economic Cooperation) as to what purpose they really fulfil. But discussions among leaders in this day and age are very important. A meeting of leaders provides a multilateral framework where people can easily and efficiently see each other. I recall that former US President Bush Snr, on his last trip around Asia, travelled 25,000 miles and only saw four leaders, while falling sick towards the end. These days, such regional forums would allow one leader to gain access to the other 20 leaders at an APEC meeting. It is a consensus-building process because it is not bilateral. This results in a common desire for wanting these meetings to go well. It drives progress because you make commitments every time you meet. There is the need to announce some form of progress or honour a commitment at every meeting. I think this is important.

On the other hand, I feel that it is strange that the North-Pacific region has no institutions like APEC. I noticed that in a larger framework, the Chinese and Japanese would sometimes compete among themselves over the other countries. Given this area has a large number of economies, it is often hard to get things done. I am not arguing that for cooperation to happen, it has to be in the form of a regional organisation. But it remains a useful framework in looking at some of their common interests and developing a consensus around that.

As Professor Wang Gungwu said earlier, perceptions among countries, how we see each other, are key to understanding each other. I think it is important for the US to not see China rising as a threat, but Asia rising as a whole. It is an opportunity to take advantage of. This is up to US leadership to try and define it that way. However, in every country and certainly for those who read *Weibo*, a lot of commentary on the US–China relationship remains uncomplimentary and not encouraging. It is not surprising for very nationalistic and short-term views to dominate the conversation in mass media. Such views need to be placed into perspective and our leaders should be doing that because that is the essence of leadership. But there remain a lot of obstacles due to the short attention span and sensationalist outlook in social media these days. It is essential that we retain some insight over the long-term nature of US–China relations, which is continually developing, brick by brick.

Let us return a while to the discussion about economic relations between the US and China. Bilateral investment treaties are mutually beneficial to both states. However, getting two-thirds of the Senate to ratify it would be very hard, especially for a Chinese bilateral investment treaty. The currency conversion issue remains a sticking point in negotiations, and it is important that both do not create a set of unrealistic expectations and dash such hopes. Therefore, perceptions need to be managed carefully as they are crucial to creating convergence in their economic interests.

Finally, I am not just cautiously optimistic, but very optimistic about the future of US–China relations. Interests are a motivating factor for greater cooperation. In many cases converging interests between both countries are reliant on the freedom of navigation. In some ways, the US and China share similar issues on global maritime security. A huge portion of global prosperity and security hinges on the US–China relationship. There are billions of people benefiting from such a relationship. If it were to turn sour, you would have lot of unhappiness in both countries and the world. Both countries would have to continue to work hard and build on existing efforts at cooperation. Of course, meetings such as the one that we are currently at are essential to helping build further progress.

Hon. Bob Carr

Director at the Australia–China Relations Institute, Australia

Chinese Nationalism and China–US Relations

In my presentation I shall simply hone in on the summation of the challenges found in former Australian Prime Minister Kevin Rudd's report, 'US–China 21: The Future of US–China Relations Under Xi Jinping'. In this report, sponsored by the Belfer Center for Science and International Affairs at Harvard's John F. Kennedy School of Government, it is not so much Chinese nationalism that will dictate US and China relations, but the lens through which each state sees one another. Each side has a very different perspective. In Rudd's view, China sees the US employing an isolationist stance in an attempt to reduce their standing in global politics, internally divide the country and sabotage their leadership. Such a view is the consensus of the Chinese leadership. On the other hand, the US sees China's foreign policy as being geared towards the removal of the US as the regional hegemon, stripped of all primacy and dominance in Asia.

These competing perceptions are very worrying. However, what Rudd has sought to do in his report is to hypothetically recommend very realistic agendas that the two countries can commit to. First, they agree to the agenda. After a consensus is reached, they should sit down and work through the issues carefully. A case in point would be the arms sales to Taiwan. We should get the two sides working on an agenda that diffuses tensions and establishes trust.

But back to reality now. The issue of sovereignty in the South China Sea is a flashpoint in US–China relations. Today, international media has reported that the US is committed to challenging Chinese claims in the South China Sea. I have noticed that such a move has deeply divided the US political and military establishment. Evidently, the White House and Pentagon are in disagreement over their approach to China's increasing sphere of influence in the South China Sea. But such disagreements have not prevented the move to approve US naval forces to challenge Chinese claims in the South China Sea, sailing inside the 12-mile territorial limit that is being claimed by China for its manmade island chain. Such a move has gone uncontradicted by US military officials and it seems to set the US on her current course in the region. In response, there are reports that Beijing is on alert, readying herself for US naval incursions near the artificial islands.

These are practical examples of misunderstandings on both sides. China's insistence on her island-building campaign in the South China Sea is premised upon an historical claim that the area was always Chinese. Therefore, it is its entitlement to make such claims around the artificial islands produced by processes of dredging. Conversely, the US view is rooted in the legalist framework of international relations where international law permits them to sail within the 12-mile limit around the artificial islands. What disturbs me the most is the US commitment to test Chinese claims in the region, as China's subsequent response will only chart a path into murkier waters.

Robert Ayson

Professor of strategic studies at Victoria University of Wellington, New Zealand

The US, China and New Zealand

China and the US have enough common interests that we should not be surprised when they show clear signs of cooperation. These shared interests extend beyond their economic interdependence from trade and investment and the benefits they both gain from Asia's prosperity. They extend as well to a shared interest in avoiding a catastrophic war between themselves. Beijing and Washington also have common interests in the avoidance of conflicts on the Korean peninsula, over significant disputes across the Taiwan Strait and over further nuclear proliferation in Asia. Neither of them wants disagreements in the South China Sea to trigger armed conflict, nor do they have an interest in Russia's macho diplomacy under Putin becoming an international standard.

Many of these common interests are likely to persist over the next 20 or 30 years. But singly or in combination, they are not enough to resolve China–US tensions. Promises of a new era in great-power relations can only be realised if both agree to look past areas in which their interests (and values) clash. That seems unlikely. Even when they have common interests, one of the great powers may be gaining more than the other: China's rise and the economic gains that have resulted for Asia are self-evidently more to Beijing's benefit than to Washington's. As the rising power, China probably gains more from Asia's peace than does the US. And on subjects such as the norms of freedom of navigation as they apply in the South China Sea, the two appear at loggerheads even if neither of them wants to resort to hostilities over the issue. Their partnership on North Korea and the Taiwan Strait is very much an incomplete one: their interests overlap to some extent but compete in other ways.

Thinking about the US and China as adversarial partners is probably a healthy way of thinking about their complex relationship. From this point it is easy to come to the view that what matters is how each side manages their relationship with the other. In particular, it might be thought that the China–US relationship, and how this is conducted in Asia, is itself the answer to whether the region's relative peace and prosperity holds up; an issue of ongoing interest for New Zealand and all of its neighbours and partners in the wider region.

To see the fate of the region resting on how Beijing approaches its relationship with Washington, and what happens in reverse, is tempting but problematic if we think the answer therefore lies in adroit diplomacy, military restraint and growing capacities for bilateral crisis management. All of these factors are very important. But the future of China–US relations may depend less on the conduct of external policy itself and much more on what is occurring within both countries (and how this then spills over in to the international arena).

The greatest uncertainty in China–US relations may well be the future course of political and social affairs in China, including the strains on the CCP as it seeks to retain its singular preeminence. No amount of repeating the mantra that one party rule is a core interest will ensure China against significant questions over legitimacy, popularity and political consent that are bound to arise within this vast and changing country, despite Xi Jinping's efforts to reinforce the party's authority. There is no obvious alternative model available, but while we can be sure that China's only options go beyond a choice between the political status quo and complete anarchy, a politically volatile China could still make for a difficult adversarial partner for the US. In the period since Mao came to power in 1949, there appears to be an historical correlation between domestic instability in China and a non-cooperative tendencies in Beijing's external policies. And because the US cannot by itself ensure Asia's peace and prosperity, the absence of an occasional partnership with China (despite its evident differences today) would be bad for the region.

Looking on at what has become a fascinating but polarising US presidential contest, China's leaders may also wonder what sort of adversarial partner they will have in Washington in future years. They may have been tempted to think that one of the worst outcomes for the expansion of Beijing's influence is an America which offers a consistent and vigilant balancing of China's rise in Asia. But if Beijing's leaders have to work with the prospect of a US that is fractured by its own domestic political turbulence and is unable to offer consistent policy abroad, the outcome could be worse. China relies more on an adversarial partnership with the US than vice versa, and the alternative is not a peaceful Asia under Beijing's sway and US weakness, but a nervous region combined with an unpredictable, but still very powerful, US.

Hopefully, for all of our sakes, the domestic politics of both great powers will be sufficiently steady and functional for none of this to eventuate. But this will probably require significant concessions by the one and only party in charge in China and the emergence of some newly fashioned bipartisan common ground in the US. And neither of these, at the time of writing, can be guaranteed.

Robert Sutter

Professor of Practice of International Affairs at the Elliott School of George Washington University

US–China Relations: 2016 and beyond

US government policy and practice towards China is in the midst of significant change. The change comes amid growing US resolve to counter initiatives of Chinese President Xi Jinping that undermine important US interests. The forecasting of rising tensions with China is accepted as the unavoidable consequence of US need to protect interests from negative Chinese practices.

President Barack Obama and his administration long saw US China policy as a mix of positive goals sought by the US along with negatives reflecting often longstanding differences with China. The US president and former Chinese president Hu Jintao (2003–13) appeared to share common ground in emphasising positive engagement and avoiding serious problems with one another. Notably, both leaders were preoccupied with domestic and foreign problems elsewhere. In contrast, President Xi has boldly taken initiatives that seek Chinese ambitions at the expense of others, notably that of the US. In particular, Xi's China:

- uses coercive means short of direct military force to advance Chinese control in the East and South China Sea at the expense of neighbours and US interests in the regional order.
- uses foreign exchange reserves and excess industrial capacity to launch self-serving international economic development programmes and institutions that undermine US leadership and/or exclude the US.
- advances China's military build-up targeted at the US in the Asia-Pacific region.
- continues cyber theft of economic assets and intellectual property, market access and currency practices, and intensified repression and political control—all with serious adverse consequences for US interests.

Though he rarely publicly discussed differences with China during his first six years in office, since 2014 President Obama became outspoken about Chinese behaviour on the above issues. President Xi publicly ignored the complaints, which were dismissed by lower-level officials. Xi emphasised a purported 'new great-power relationship', which US critics increasingly saw as Xi playing a double game at America's expense.

Since the strained US–China summit in Washington in September 2015, President Obama has less to say about China. Rather, he is taking stronger action. Salient examples include:

- much stronger pressure than seen in the past to compel China to rein in rampant cyber theft of American property.
- much stronger pressure than seen in the past to compel China to abide by international sanctions against North Korea.

- China's continued militarisation of disputed South China Sea islands followed President Xi's seemingly duplicitous promise made during the September summit not to do so. In tandem came much more active US military deployments in the disputed South China Sea, along with blunt warnings by US military leaders of China's ambitions.
- more prominent cooperation with allies Japan, the Philippines and Australia, along with India and concerned Southeast Asian powers that strengthen regional states at odds with China over the South China Sea and create webs of regional cooperation that complicate Chinese bullying.
- the abrupt decision in March 2016 halting access to US information technology that seriously impacted China's leading state-directed Chinese electronics firm ZTE. Reportedly ZTE had agreed under US pressure to halt unauthorised transfers to Iran of US-sourced technology and then created shell companies to continue the unauthorised transfers.
- the unprecedented US-led rebuke of negative Chinese human rights practices in a joint statement to the UN Human Rights Council in March 2016, which was endorsed by Japan, Australia and nine European countries.

Outlook

The US and China are big countries not easily influenced by outside pressure. President Xi Jinping's bold assertiveness has been warmly embraced by very self-righteous Chinese opinion which views Hu Jintao's previous discretion with disdain. Thus China's recent assertiveness seems likely to continue. The US, too, is known for its self-righteousness. All US presidential candidates who have spoken on China-related issues have adopted more hard-line approaches than President Obama. Thus, informed US officials seem correct when they advise that there will be greater 'friction and tension' in the period ahead.

Editor's Acknowledgements

This volume is based on an international conference on the same topic, organised by the New Zealand Contemporary China Research Centre on 8–9 October 2015 in Wellington, New Zealand.

It is our great honour that the Right Honourable John Key, Prime Minister of New Zealand, has written the preface for this volume. We are truly grateful for his reflections and insights on New Zealand's perspective on the bilateral relationship and New Zealand's good relations with both China and the United States.

On behalf of the New Zealand Contemporary China Research Centre, I would like to thank all participants in our conference on 'China–US Relations in Global Perspective'. This long list includes Professor Grant Guilford, vice-chancellor of Victoria University of Wellington, who opened the conference; two ambassadors, H.E. Mr Wang Lutong, Chinese Ambassador to New Zealand, the Cook Islands and Niue, and H.E. Mr Mark Gilbert, American Ambassador to New Zealand and Samoa, both of whom offered opening remarks; Professor Wang Gungwu, board chairman of the East Asian Institute, National University of Singapore, who gave a keynote address; and presenters, chairs and discussants. In particular, I am grateful for the additional contributions from Professor Crawford Falconer, the Sir Graeme Harrison Professorial Chair at Lincoln University; Professor Robert Sutter of George Washington University; and Dr Liu Dongmin and Dr Bei Gao of the Chinese Academy of Social Sciences. I would also like to acknowledge the assistance of Mr Chris Wilson and Dr Jim Rolfe of Victoria University of Wellington, who helped to launch the conference, and of Colin McDiarmid, university photographer, for his wonderful photos.

I would like to express our gratitude for the generous financial contributions from the following institutions and individuals: Victoria University of Wellington, the Embassy of the People's Republic of China, the Embassy of the United States of America, New Zealand Trade and Enterprise, the Ministry Foreign Affairs and Trade, Education New Zealand, the Ministry of Business, Innovation and Employment, the Ministry of Defence, the Lee Foundation (Singapore), KVB Kunlun, Treasury, and an anonymous individual.

On a personal level, I am grateful for the support I have received during my first year as director of the New Zealand Contemporary China Centre, from my advisory board as well as our associate directors from member universities. My thanks also go to Lai Ching Tan and the Victoria staff, who have provided necessary logistical support, and to my two research assistants, Yin Cheung Lam and Xiaoming Xue, who helped with transcribing remarks and merging chapters into a single volume. I would also like to acknowledge the valuable guidance provided by Fergus Barrowman and Holly Hunter at Victoria University Press for preparing the publication of this volume.

NEW ZEALAND CONTEMPORARY CHINA RESEARCH CENTRE

Director: Professor Bo Zhiyue, PhD in political science (University of Chicago)

Associate directors: Professor Paul Clark (University of Auckland); Associate Professor Coral Ingley (Auckland University of Technology); Professor Brian Mologhney (University of Otago); Professor Alex Tan (University of Canterbury); Dr Ed Weymes (University of Waikato); Sharon Lucock (Lincoln University); and Professor James Liu (Massey University)

The New Zealand Contemporary China Research Centre is a nationwide research centre on contemporary China in New Zealand, possibly one of its kind in the world. Based at Victoria University of Wellington, the Centre comprises all eight universities in New Zealand: **Victoria University of Wellington, University of Auckland, Auckland University of Technology, University of Canterbury, University of Otago, University of Waikato, Lincoln University and Massey University**.

The strategic vision of the Centre is to become a global leader in knowledge acquisition and knowledge-sharing on the political, economic and social life of contemporary China among tertiary institutions, the business sector and the policy community for the benefit of New Zealand.

The Centre has four goals. The first goal is to become a think tank on China policies for the New Zealand government. The second goal is to become a management consultant for the business community in New Zealand and elsewhere. The third goal is to become a global leader in research on contemporary China among tertiary institutions. The fourth goal is to provide the public with up-to-date information on a changing China.

The Centre holds annual international conferences on contemporary China: 'China's Development' (2009); 'China and India: the End of Development Models' (2010); 'China and Japan in Modern Economic Growth' (2011); 'Chinese Model of Modern Economic Development and Social Transformation' (2012); 'China's Global Course: the Political Economy of China Going Global' (2013); 'China at the Crossroads: What the Third Plenum means for China, New Zealand and the World' (2014); and 'China–US Relations in Global Perspective' (2015). The Centre also holds conferences in conjunction with leading universities in China and other countries, such as China and the Pacific (2015).

Index

bold signifies a photograph;
italics signifies a figure or table

A

Abe, Shinzō, 83, 84, 96, 127, 128, 146–147, 149, 158
Abramowitz, Morton, 159
Afghanistan, 66, 69, 76, 78, 84, 198
African Development Bank (AfDB), 109, 111–113, 115, 137
aging populations, 65
agriculture, 264
Ahmadinejad, Mahmoud, 205
aid comparisons, 76, 98
Air Defence Identification Zone (ADIZ), 83–84
AirSea Battle concept, 66–67
alliance structure (United States)
    and China's response, 68–69, 154, 159–163, 165–168, 187
    partners, 157–158, 272–273
    and South Korea, 162–163, 164, 174, 178, 188, 202
American Dream, 30
Antarctica, 47, 273
Anti-Ballistic Missile Treaty (1972), 66
APEC Business Advisory Council (ABAC), 265
ASEAN Infrastructure Fund, 92
Asia Pacific Economic Cooperation (APEC), 139, 263, 265–267, 282
Asia Regional Forum (ARF), 69
Asian Development Bank (ADB)
    and AIIB, 99, *100*, 103, 115–117
    cooperation and co-financing, 120, 137
    governance and role, 109–113, 128, 134
    Japan's influence on, 96, 110–111
    lending figures for, 92–93, 97–98
    loan influences, 113
Asian Infrastructure Investment Bank (AIIB)
    and China/US rivalry, 59, 71, 95–96, 102, 188, 245, 272
    cooperation and co-financing, 120, 138
    founding and capital, *94*, *100*, 116–117, 119
    governance, 117–118, 138, 145
    and infrastructure needs, 92–93
    investment model, 126–128, 131
    and isomorphism, 108–109, 122
    loan approval, 118
    and One Belt, One Road, 132
    role, 96–97, 99, *101*, 117, 128, 131, 134–136, 140
    voting and oversight, 117–118, 121
Asian–African Conference, 160
Asia-Pacific Economic Cooperation (APEC), 81, 228
Aso, Taro, 158
Association of Southeast Asian Nations (ASEAN)
    and China, *101*, 102, 148
    and international financial system, 133
    partnership role, 38, 68–69, 161–162, 217–218, 228, 269, 272
asymmetric parity, 56, 61–65, 70
Atlas estimates (World Bank), 61–62
Australia
    relations with China, 56, 245, 268–269, 270
    relations with NZ, 262, 268, 272
    relations with US, 69, 158, 162, 245, 261, 268–269, 270, 273, 288
    relations with Vietnam, 221–222, 232
    and TPP, 150, 257, 263
    wealth ranking, 65
Australia New Zealand US Alliance (ANZUS), 158, 272–273
Ayson, Robert, 250, 285

B

Bader, Jeffrey, 200
Bangladesh War, 242
bargaining leverage (of smaller states), 64

Bei Gao, 126
Beijing Olympics, 82
Berra, Yogi, 267
Bhagat, Chetan (*Half Girlfriend*), 129
Biden, Joseph, 46, 227
bilateral dialogues, 81
bilateral investment treaty (China/US), 48, 254, 266, 283
bilateral relations, strains on, 48, 56, 58, 80–81
birthrates, 64
Bo Xilai, 148
Bo Zhiyue, 80, 250
Boehner, John, 85
Bogor goals, 265
Brazil, 63–64, 65, 95, 97, 119, 257
Bretton Woods system, 91, 99
BRICS countries (Brazil, Russia, India, China, South Africa), 94–95, *101*, 111–112, 119, 134, *253*
Britain, 127, 261. *see also* United Kingdom
Britain/China trade (historic), 29
Brownlee, Gerry, 271
Brunei, 263
Bui Quang Vinh, 229
Bush, George H.W., 280, 282
Bush, George W., 81–82, 198, 200, 243, 265–266, 280

C

Cambodia, 92, 216–217, 231
Canada, 65, 116, 263, 264
capitalisation levels, 62
carbon emissions, 47, 48
Carr, Bob, **153**, **250**, **275**, 284
Carter, Ashton, 227
Carter, Jimmy, 53–54, 280
Center for a New American Security (CNAS), 159
central/regional balance (China), 252
Chan, Gerald, 91
Chen Shuibian (Taiwan), 81
Chiang Mai Initiative Multilateralisation (CMIM), *101*, 133
Chile, 263
China Development Bank, 97, 102
China Dream, 30, 31, 57, 160
China Federation for Defending the Diaoyu Islands, 149
China Investment Corporation, 97
China Overseas Port Holdings, 98
China Silk Road Fund Limited Liability Company, 97
'China-led international financial institutions' (table), *94*
China–Pakistan Economic Corridor, 98, 245
China–US Strategic and Economic Dialogue (S&ED), 81, 82
China–US Strategic Economic Dialogue (SED), 81
Chinese Academy of Social Sciences, 78
Chinese Communist Party (CCP), 31, 36, 38, 80, 147, 148, 176, 180, 184, 286
Chinese delegation (to UN General Assembly), 53
Choe Ryong Hae, 180, 184
Choo, Jaewoo, **153**, 154
Citigroup, 98
civil war (American), 32
civil war (Chinese), 36
civilisation-*wenjiao*, 27–28
Cixi, Empress Dowager, 33, 34, 37, 39
Clean Power Plan (US), 85
climate change, 43, 46–48, 65, 84, 85, 154, 198, 200, 201
Clinton, Bill, 242, 280
Clinton, Hillary, 75, 147, 161, 200, 205, 221, 224
Cold War, 38, 56–58, 66–67, 76, 82, 108–109, 115–116, 157, 160, 175, 199, 241–243
Confucian principles of governance, 29, 33
conservation, 47
containment
  of Soviet Union, 67–68
  US policy of, 156–157, 159
continental interests (China), 29–30, 38, 245–246, 278–279
Contingency Reserve Arrangement (CRA), *101*
cooperative tourism initiative, 49
coordinated development mechanism (for

MDBs), 137–139
core interests (China), 57, 82–83, 189, 204, 272
Council for Mutual Economic Assistance (COMECON), 58
counter-terrorism, 43
Cuba, 180, 217
Cuban Missile Crisis, 66
cybersecurity, 43, 48, 52, 66–67, 84, 86, 148, 272, 287

D

Dai Bingguo, 82
dairy industry, 264
Dalai Lama, 82, 244
Dandong–Sinuiju bridge, 178, 182
Democratic Party of Japan, 150
democratic peace theory, 59
Democratic People's Republic of Korea (DPRK), *see* North Korea
demographic power, 65, 70
Deng Xiaoping, 54, 280
dependency ratios, 64
Development Bank for Latin America (CAF), 118, 121
development finance system, 127, 139
development model (new), 102–103, 139–140
development policies (of MDBs), 110–111, 113, 114–115, 117, 119–120
diplomatic influence (China), 269
diplomatic ties, US–China establishment, 53–54
Doha Development Round, 133, 254–255, 263, 265
Dollar, David, 96
domestic politics (China), 148, 286
domestic protectionism, 60
Dongmin Liu, 126
Donilon, Tom, 202–203
'dynamic gains of trade,' 262

E

East Asia Summit, 69, 150, 160, 228, 269
economic asymmetry, 62
economic capability, 197–198
economic cooperation, 48, 75–81, 139, 177, 182, 224
economic espionage, 48
economic growth
  Afghanistan, 76
  China, 269, 277–278, 282
  global, 43, *103*
economic integration (Asia), 269
economic interdependence, 59–60, 157, 285
economic partnership agreements, 150
economic reforms, 59, 251–254
economy
  Asia-Pacific, 264
  China, 31, 56–57, 61–62, 77, 103, 132–133, 146–147
  global, *see* global economy
  Japan, 61–62, 146
  rankings, 65
  Soviet Union, 57
  United States, 57, 61–62, 207
  Ecuador, 97
education, 34, 49
educational exchanges, *see* student exchanges
Egypt, 92, 95
Einhorn, Robert, 205
electricity price comparisons (South Asia), 130
emissions, 84–85
energy consumption, 47
energy cooperation (China), 77
energy resources, 76, 78, 129
enmeshment, 60, 63–65
espionage allegations, 229–230
Eurasia (China links to), 278–279
Eurasian Land Bridge, 77, 78
European Bank for Reconstruction and Development (EBRD), 109, 111, 115, 117
European Community (EC), 197–198
European Economic Community (EEC), 261
European Union (EU), 217, 218, 254, 255–257, 263
Eurozone crisis, 99

exclusivity (consequences of), 64
Export Import Bank of China, 97
exports, US to China, 46

F

Falconer, Crawford, 251
financial cooperation, 78
financial diplomacy, 92, 103
Fisher & Paykel, 262
Ford, Gerald, 280
foreign direct investment (China), 103, 252
foreign policy priorities (China), 44
foreign policy/national goals relationship, 155–156
fragmentation, 132–134, *134*, 137, 255
France, 71, 221, 232
free trade agreements, *see also* Trans-Pacific Partnership (TPP)
  and Asia-Pacific, 265–266
  Australia–US, 262
  China–NZ, 261–262
  Japan–China–South Korea, 147, 150
  time scale for, 258
  and WTO, 133, 254–256
Free Trade Area of the Asia-Pacific (FTAAP), 256, 265–266
freedom of navigation, 49, 161, 228, 244, 273, 283, 285
Froman, Michael, 227
Fu Ying, 132
fuel efficiency standards, 47–48
Fukuda, Yasuo, 147
future order (Asia), 273–274

G

G7 states, 112, 113, 115, *122*
G20, *101*, 102, 137, 139, 203
Gandhi, Rajiv, 242
Gao Hucheng, 147
'GDPs of the BRICS, 2014' (table), *95*
general theory of world politics, 61
geo-neo-functionalism, 92, 103
Germany, 56, 63, 65, 71, 117, 221, 232
Gilbert, Mark, 46
ginger industry (case study), 128–131
Global Competitiveness Report, 129–130

global convergence, 64
global development financing, 91, 101
global economic governance, 139
global economy, 56, 61, 127, 132, 200, 244
global financial architecture, 91, 92, 135
global financial crisis (2008), 56, 63, 77, 98, 99, 113, 198
global GDP, 92, 93, 95, *103*
Global Infrastructure Facility (GIF), *93*, 96, 137
Global infrastructure investments (table), *93*
global manufacturing economy, 55
global oil market, 99
global political economy, 55, 70
global positions, 31–32, 37, 55, 59, 281
global security, 47, 199, 278–279, 283
global value chains (GVC), 60, 63, 128, 130–131, 252, 261–262, 267
global warming, *see* climate change
globalisation, 55, 63, 70, 71, 102, 132–134, 157, 198, 208
goals
  China, 38, 44, 58, 155, 159–162, 165–167
  differing, 155
  North Korea, 174
  United States, 155, 156–159, 165–167, 243
  Vietnam, 219
'Goldilocks model' (Vietnam), 215–216, 231–232
grain cooperation mechanism, 78
'great-power relationship', *see* 'major-country relationship'
Green Climate Fund (US), 47
growth models (China), 252
Guilford, Grant, 11
Gulf of Tonkin, 222, 223, 233
Guo Boxiong, 178
Gwadar (port), 98, 245

H

Ha Huy Hoang, 229–230
Hagel, Chuck, 83–84, 225
Haiyang Shiyou 981 crisis, 225–227, 232
Hakka rebellion, 32–33

Hatoyama, Yukio, 150
Hawaii, 36
hegemony, 55, 56, 61, 63, 71, 155, 184, 277, 284
historic relationship (China–US), 29
Hong Xiuquan, 32–33, 37
HSBC (bank), 93, 98
Hu Jintao, 81–82, 86–87, 176–178, 181–182, 200, 204, 280, 287–288
Hua Liming, 205, 206
Hui Zhang, 201
human rights, 52, 272, 288
Huntington, Samuel, 39
hydrofluorocarbons (HFCs), 47

I

India
  ambitions, 240–241, 245
  China rivalry, 241, 244, 281
  defence spending, 240
  economic relations (China), 240–241, 244, 255
  economy, 56, 65, 95, *103*, 150, 241, 243–244, 257
  global role, 63, 243–244, 274
  independence, 241
  infrastructure needs, 92
  and Korean War, 241
  military capabilities, 243–244
  and new MDBs, 117, 119
  non-alignment policy, 241
  nuclear ambitions, 242–244
  Project Mausam, 132
  relations with Japan, 245
  relations with US, 75–76, 158, 161, 241–242, 244, 288
  relations with Vietnam, 215–216, 217, 220, 232
  Sardar Sarovar dam project, 115
  and South Asia security, 242–243, 245
  strategic interests, 241, 243, 244
  trade growth, 98, 101
  trade relations with Nepal, 128–131
  triangular relationship dynamics, 240–246
  and US–China alignment, 242–243
  US–India Civil Nuclear Agreement, 243
  wars, territorial disputes, 241–244
  world rankings, 240
India–Pakistan War, 242
Indonesia, 65, 91–92, 131–132, 221, 232, 255–256, 269
Industrial and Commercial Bank of China, 98
infrastructure deficiencies, implications of, 129–131
infrastructure development, 78, 91–93, 96–97, 102–103, 110, 117, 128, 139
infrastructure diplomacy, 92, 93, 95, 96, 98, 103
infrastructure investment gap, 92–93, 116, 127, 134–136, *135*
intellectual property, 48, 59, 264–265
Inter-American Development Bank (IDB), 109, 111–113, 115
International Atomic Energy Agency (IAEA), 243–244, 245
International Development Corporation, 96
international economic position (US), *102*
International Monetary Fund (IMF), 57, 99, *101*, 103, 111–112, 132–133, 136–137, 218
internet openness, 273
investment, China in US, 46
investment cooperation strategies, 131
investment needs (for infrastructure), 93
investment regime (China), 251
invulnerability (pursuit of), 66
iPhone production, 60
Iran
  nuclear ambitions, 47, 196–198, 200–201, 204–208
  relations with China, 98, 200–201, 204–207, 288
  relations with US, 69, 76
  sanctions against, 48, 71, 204–206
Iraq, 66, 69, 71, 198, 272
Ishihara, Shintaro, 149
ISIS, 69
Islamic Development Bank, 137
isomorphism (in MDBs), 108–109, 112–115, 119, 120, 121

Israel, 204
Italy, 221, 232

J

Jacobi, Stephen, 260
Jang Sung-Taek, 179
Japan
   defeat of China (1894), 34
   economy, 56, 146, 150
   free trade agreements, 133
   future role, 274
   infrastructure aid, 96, 128
   investment in China, 147
   and multilateral institutions, *100*, *101*, 110–113, 116–117, 127
   predictions for, 197–198
   relations with Australia, 269
   relations with China, 58, 82–83, 145–151, 158–159, 184, 255, 256, 282
   relations with India, 241, 245
   relations with NZ, 272
   relations with Vietnam, 215, 217, 220, 222, 231–232
   and TPP, 263–264
   as US ally, 69, 83, 95, 127, 145–151, 157–158, 162–165, 168, 288
   and WWII, 37
Japan–China–South Korea trilateral FTA, 147, 150
Japan–US Security Treaty, *see* US-Japan Security Treaty (1952)
Jiang Zemin, 81, 82, 165, 176, 177, 280
Jin Liqun, 96, *100*, 116, 118
Jin Qi, 97
Joint Comprehensive Plan of Action (JCPOA), 71, 206

K

Kaesong Industrial Region, 188
Kamath, K.V., 94, 119
Kashmir, 243, 245
Kazakhstan, 91
Kennedy, Paul, 196–198, 208
Kenya, 92
Kerry, John, 187, 203, 225, 227, 229
Key, John, 9, 271

Kim, Jim Yong, 96, *100*
Kim Dae-Jung, 164, 176
Kim Il-Sung, 174–176
Kim Jong-Gak, 178
Kim Jong-Il, 176–180, 184, 186
Kim Jong-Un, 177, 179, 182–184, 189
Kim Yong-Nam, 176, 177
Kim Young-Sam, 176
Kissinger, Dr Henry, 52, 69, 242, 280
Korean Peninsla Energy Development Organisation, 181
Korean peninsula, 158, 162–165, 177, 183–184, 201–202, 206, 285
Korean War, 155, 159–160, 164, 174–175, 177–178, 180, 183–184, 201, 280
Kuomintang (KMT), 36

L

Laos, 92, 217
Le Hong Anh, 226
League of Nations, 37, 38
Leahy, Patrick, 227
Lee, William, 221
Lee Myung-Bak, 164, 176
Lew, Jack, 227
Li Jianguo, 184
Li Jinjun, 179
Li Kequiang, 116, 223–224, 227, 232
Li Peng, 165
Li Yuanchao, 184
Li Zhaoxing, 179
Liang Guanglie, 178
Lichtenstein, Natalie, 96
Lincoln, Abraham, 32, 34, 37, 39
Liu Baocai, 162
Liu Yunshan, 180
loan comparisons, 97–98
logistics, 78
Lou Jiwei, 132

M

Macartney, Lord, 29
macro-economic restructuring, 110
'major-country relationship,' 44, 51–52, 59, 80–83, 85–86, 148, 245, 280, 287
Malaysia, 263

Mandarin language (in US), 49, 85
Mao Zedong, 33, 53, 149, 154, 155, 159–160, 175, 178, 280, 286
Marine Protected Area (Antarctica), 47
maritime disputes, *see* territorial disputes
maritime interests (China), 38, 148, 278
Maritime Silk Road (China), 76–78, 91–92, *see also* One Belt, One Road
Marshall Plan, 67, 98
Matsumoto, Shigeharu, 145
McCain, John, 227
media, 85, 128, 132, 182, 205, 206, 225, 229–230, 283, 284
Meiji Restoration (Japan), 34
Mexico, 262, 263
Middle East, 58, 66, 67, 204, 205, 279
middle-income trap, 251, 282
military alliances, 83–84, 157, 184
military capabilities
   China, 66, 145, 161, 272, 277, 287
   India, 243–244
   New Zealand, 272
   North Korea, 174
   United States, 66, 70
   Vietnam, 216, 218, 227
military contact risks, 60–61, 147, 287–288
military cooperation, 206, 271
military expenditure, 60, 197–198
military influence (China), 269
military withdrawal
   from Afghanistan, 76, 78
   from South Korea, 162–165
Ministry of Defence (China), 83
Ministry of Finance (China), 97
Ministry of Foreign Affairs (China), 78
missionary culture (in China), 29
Mongolia, 92, 132, 158
Moore, Mike, 252
Morrison, Charles, **250**, **275**, 281
multilateral development banks (MDBs), *see also individual bank entries*
   accountability, 115, 118, 122
   anti-corruption mechanism for, 138
   co-financing, 120, 136
   coordinated development mechanism for, 137–139
   development policies, 110–111, 113–115, 117, 119–120
   formation of, 154
   function and structure, 109–111, 117–119
   governance, 109, 111–112, 117–119, 127
   isomorphism in, 108–109, 112–115, 119–122
   lending standards for, 138
   role, 136
   social, environmental safeguard policies, 114–115, 118, 120–122, 138
   US dominance of, 112–115, 120, 122
   voting systems, 111–112, 117, 119, *122*
multilateral financial involvement (China), *101*
multilateral global system, 255
Multilateral Interim Secretariat (MIS), for AIIB, 116
multilateral organisations, 66, 68, 269, 272, 282, *see also individual organisations*
multilateralism, 158–159, 161, 165–168, 198
multinational firms, 60
multi-nodal world, 55, 63–64, 65, 67, 71, *see also* multi-polar international system
multi-polar international system, 197–198, 207, 245. *see also* multi-nodal world
Myanmar pipeline, 98–99

N

Nakao, Takehiko, *100*
National People's Congress, 132, 177
National Security Strategy (NSS), 161, 199–201
nationalism, 35, 38, 148, 151, 284
natural gas pipeline, 78
navigational rights, 49, 161, 283, 285
Nehru, Jawaharlal, 241
Nepal (ginger industry case study), 128–131
Netherlands, 129
New Asian Security Concept (NASC), 154, 159

New Development Bank (NDB), 92,
    93–95, *101*, 102, 108–109, 119–120,
    122, 133–134
New Komeito Party (Japan), 147
New Silk Road initiative (United States),
    75–76, 78–79
New Zealand
  business viewpoint, 260, 262
  China strategy, 271
  China-US strategy, 268–274
  dairy and beef industries, 262, 264, 269
  exports, 261
  foreign policy, 44–45
  free trade agreements, 262–263, 267, 269
  and global value chains, 261–262, 267
  investment, 261, 264
  military response choices, 272
  Pharmac, 264
  relations with Australia, 262, 268, 272
  relations with China, 44–45, 257,
      260–263, 267–274
  relations with other countries, 272
  relations with US, 260–263, 268–274
  role in regional relations, 252, 258, 269,
      281
  security relationships, 158
  security relationss, 269–270
  state-owned enterprises, 265
  strategic analysis, lack of, 270
  and TPP, 261–267, 269, 272
Nguyen Chi Vinh, 221
Nguyen Phu Trong, 226–229, 233
Nguyen Tan Dung, 223–224, 225
Nigeria, 110
Nixon, Richard, 242, 280
Noda, Yoshihiko, 149
North Atlantic Treaty Organization
    (NATO), 67, 68, 159, 162
North Korea, *see also* Korean peninsula;
    Korean War
  China criticism of, 176, 179
  Dandong-Sinuiju bridge, 178, 182
  detention of Chinese fishermen, 179, 189
  economic assistance to, 175–181, 183,
      185–186, 189, 190
  economic zones, 180, 184, 186
  famines, 174, 176, 180, 181
  foreign currency earnings, 182
  goals, 174, 202, 203
  high level exchanges, 176–180, 183–184
  investment in, 181, 182, 184, 186–187
  migrant labour, 182
  military exchanges, 178
  mineral and resource sector, 181–182
  Northern Limit Line, 182
  nuclear ambitions, 149, 163–165, 173–
      190, 196–198, 200–201, 201–204
  provocative actions, 173–174, 178–179,
      185, 188, 189
  reforms, 184, 185–186
  regime survival, 173–174, 181, 182, 183,
      185–186, 189–190, 201–202
  relations with China, 164–165, 173–190,
      203–204, 285
  relations with South Korea, 163, 175,
      179, 188
  relations with United States, 162–163,
      173–175, 285
  security, 164, 173–174, 175–176, 190
  stance on USFK, 162–164
  State Development Bank, 181
  strategic interests, 163, 173
  trade, 179, 184, 186–187, 189, 203, 204
  UN sanctions against, 173–174, 178–
      179, 182, 183, 186, 188–189, 201,
      287
  Yongdeung mine, 181
north-south cooperation, 139
nuclear ambitions
  Iran, 196–198
  North Korea, 163–165, 173–190, 196–198,
      201–204
nuclear nonproliferation
  China's role, 163, 173–190, 196–197,
      200–208
  China–US cooperation, 43, 47, 71, 285
  and India, 242–244
  US strategy, 149, 158, 196–201, 203,
      204–208
Nuclear Posture Review (NPR), 161
Nuclear Security Summit, 161–162, 205
Nuclear Test Ban Treaty, 199
NZ US Council, 261

O

Obama, Barack
  China's perceptions of, 147, 160
  climate change agreement, 84
  foreign policy priorities, 200–201
  ideals, 31
  influences on, 30–31
  meeting with Shinzō Abe, 83
  meetings, Vietnamese leaders, 224–225, 227–229, 233
  meetings with Xi Jinping, 39, 44, 46–49, 81, 82–85, 202–203, 231, 269, 280, *see also* Sunnylands summit
  Sunnylands summit, 51, 82–83, 86, 215, 216, 222, 232, 269, 280
  views on AIIB, 127
  views on China, 57, 196–197, 200, 287
  views on nonproliferation, 198–199
  visit to China, 52, 82, 84, 200
  visit to Japan, 84
Obama administration
  China policy, 200, 202
  criticism of, 78
  nonproliferation strategy, 196–199, 204–208
  and North Korea, 187–188
  and Pacific, 273–274
  and Vietnam, 227
ocean conservation, 85
Olympics (Beijing), 82
One Belt, One Road, *see also* Maritime Silk Road (China); Silk Road Economic Belt (China)
  and AIIB, 132
  and China–US rivalry, 59, 71, 145, 256
  cooperation opportunities, 75, 102, 148, 272, 278–279
  India endorsement of, 245
  investment in, 93, 97–99
'One Million Strong' initiative, 49, 85
Onodera, Itsunori, 84
opium, 29
ordinary capital resource lending (OCR), 110, 113
Organisation for Economic Cooperation and Development (OECD), *253*
Organski, A.F.K., 61, 65

P

Pacific framework (trade and investment), 260
Pakistan, 98, 241–242, 245
pandemics, 198
Panetta, Leon, 221
Pardesi, Manjeet, 240
Paris Agreement (climate change), 47, 84
Park, Susan, 108
Park Geun-Hye, 176, 180, 188, 203–204
partnerships (benefits of), 66, 68
Patman, Robert, 196
peace treaty (Korean peninsula), 156, 162–165
peacekeeping, 85
People's Bank of China (PBC), 97
perceptions, risks of, 277–278
periphery diplomacy (China), 76–77, 159, 270
Persian Gulf War, 66
Peru, 263
Pham Binh Minh, 226, 227, 230, 233
Pham Quang Nghi, 227
Philippines, 36–37, 69, 148, 157–158, 162, 221, 226, 232, 255–256, 288
Phung Quang Thanh, 221, 225, 226, 227
Poland, 67
polar conservation, 47
policy constraints (US), 62
political differences, 59
political relations, deterioration in, 80
political stability (western China), 77
pollution concerns, 128
Pope Francis (visit to US), 85
population comparisons, 61, 62, 92, 95, 96
Powell, Colin, 261
power (regional vs global), 58
power capabilities (China rise), 102
power preponderance (US in Asia), 273–274
power transition theory, 56, 61, 63, 65
presidential elections (US), 56, 258, 279, 286
productivity, 55, 62, 64–65
protectionism, 264
purchasing power parity (PPP), 61–62
Putin, Vladimir, 218, 285

Q

Qianlong (Emperor), 29
Qiao Guanhua, 53
Qing dynasty, 29, 32, 33
Quadrennia Defense Review (QDR), 161
Quadrilateral Security Dialogue (QSD), 158
Qiyuan Xu, 126

R

rail network development, 78, 91, 92
Reagan, Ronald, 280
rebalancing strategy (US), 48, 146, 150, 156, 158, 187–188, 245, 272
reforms, need for (China), 251–258
refugee fears (of China), 176, 181, 190, 202
Regional Comprehensive Economic Partnership (RCEP), 133, 150, 255–257, 266
regional influence, competition for, 269, 288
regional power grids development, 78
relationship fundamentals, 52–54
restrictiveness (in service sectors), *253*
revenue raising (China), 252
Rhodes, Ben, 203
Rice, Condoleezza, 243
Rice, Susan, 199, 227
rivalry
   China and US, 58–59, 69–71, 189–190
   constraints on, 55, 56, 59–61, 66
   great power (model of), 196–198
   implications of asymmetry, 62–63
   international, 58
   sustainable, 69
   US and Soviet Union, 57
road construction, Afghanistan, 78
Roe Tae-Woo, 176
Roh Moo-Hyun, 164, 176
Romania, 67
Rouhani, Hassan, 205
Rudd, Kevin, 59, 70, 284
Russia, *see also* Soviet Union
   economy, 57
   global role, 63, 285
   and MDBs, 95, 112, 117, 119
   and nuclear nonproliferation, 71, 207
   and One Belt, One Road, 92
   relations with China, 82, 97
   relations with India, 241, 245
   relations with North Korea, 175, 180, 184, 187
   relations with US, 76, 158–159, 199
   relations with Vietnam, 215–216, 218, 222, 232

S

Sardar Sarovar dam project (India), 115
Saudi Arabia, 99
security
   China and Afghanistan, 77–78
   China and Japan, 146–150
   China and Korean peninsula, 164, 179, 183
   China and US, 57, 80, 83, 156
   costs of competition, 60–61
   global, 47, 198–199
   North Korea, 173–174, 176, 188
   regional, 269–270
   sustainable rivalry, 65–67
   US interests, 199, 269–270
Senkaku (Diaoyu) Islands, 80, 81, 83–84, 146–150, 276
service sectors (China), 251–254
Shanghai Cooperation Organisation (SCO), 68, 69, *101*, 245
Shao Yuqun, 75
Silk Road Economic Belt (China), 31, 75–76, 78–79, 91–92, 98, *see also* One Belt, One Road
Silk Road Fund (SRF), 92–94, 96–99, *101*, 102, 132
Singapore, 116, 221, 232, 263
Singh, Jaswant, 243
Sino–Indian War, 241–242
Sino–North Korean Mutual Aid and Cooperation Friendship Treaty, 175
slavery, 32, 35
social safety net needs (China), 252
social stability issues (China), 147, 148
Somalia, 198

South Africa, 63, 95, 119
South China Sea
　artificial island construction, 230–231, 233, 284
　China assertive action in, 146
　China–Japan tension, 150
　China–US tension, 52, 86, 149, 284–285
　China–Vietnam tension, 216–217, 220–222, 227–228
　Code of Conduct, 49, 224, 227
　and New Zealand, 272–273
　US position on, 49, 161, 287–288
　US–India support, 244–245
　US–Vietnam support, 229
South Korea, *see also* Korean peninsula; Korean War
　Chiang Mai Initiative, 133
　Chinese fishing intrusions, 182
　free trade agreements, 147, 150
　and MDBs, 117
　relations with China, *101*, 175–176, 203–204, 255
　relations with New Zealand, 272
　relations with North Korea, 188, 201–202
　relations with US, 69, 156–158, 162–165
　relations with Vietnam, 221, 232
　strategic dilemma, 102, 168, 188
　wealth ranking, 65
Southeast Asia Treat Organisation (SEATO), 157–158
southern oceans, 273
Southgate, Laura, 196
south–south cooperation, 139
South–South Cooperation Fund, *101*, 102
Soviet Union, 57, 67, 76, 156, 175, 197–198, 217, 231, 242
space weaponisation, 66, 67
Spain, 221, 232
Spratly Islands, 217, 276
Stalin, Joseph, 174–175
State Administration of Foreign Exchange, 97
State Development and Reform Commission (China), 78
State Development Bank (North Korea), 181
state-owned companies (China), 99, 251–252
state-*tianchao*, 27–28
Strategic Arms Reduction Treaty (START), 199
strategic competition, 146, 148, 150
strategic interests
　China, 76–77, 99, 154, 159–162, 175, 177–178, 181–182, 184–185, 189
　differences in, 167–168
　global, 65, 158
　India, 241, 244
　United States, 59, 76, 113, 154, 156–159, 161, 245
strategic trust deficit, 75, 83, 202, 227, 232
student exchanges, 49, 54, 70, 86
Sumdorong Chu crisis, 242
Sun Yat-Sen, 33, 35–36, 39
Sunnylands summit, 51, 82–83, 86, 215, 216, 222, 232, 269, 280
sustainable development, 47, 48, 121, 139
sustainable rivalry, 69
Sutton, Jim, 142
Syrian civil war, 207

T

Taean Friendship Glass Factory, 177
Taiping rebellion, 32–33
Taiwan, 81–82, 157, 284
Taiwan military crisis (theoretical consequences of), 60–61
Taiwan Strait, 242, 285
Takahara, Akio, 145
Talbott, Strobe, 243
Taliban, 69
targeted alliances (vs partnerships), 66, 68
tariff elimination, 264
technological diffusion, 62, 64
Terminal High Altitude Area Defence (THAAD) missile defence system, 188
territorial disputes, *see also* Korean peninsula; Senkaku (Diaoyu) Islands
　China–India, 244–245
　China–Japan, 146, 149–150
　China–US, 244–245, 284–285

India, 241–245
India–Pakistan, 245
NZ response to, 272
South China Sea, 49, 146, 149–150, 161
South Korea, 154, 182
Tibet, 241
Vietnam, 216–217, 220–233
terrorism, 66, 69, 158
Thailand, 69, 92, 158, 162, 221, 232
Thayer, Carlyle A., 142, 215
threat perceptions, 161
'Thucydides trap', 44, 52, 61, 86
Tiananmen Square massacre, 242
Tibet, 241, 242, 244
tobacco lobby (US), 265
Tokugawa Shogunate, 34
Tongzhi Restoration, 33
tourism, 49, 70, 85, 225
trade, *see also* free trade agreements; Trans-Pacific Partnership (TPP)
  bilateral, 43, 53
  China, 77, 101, 103, 200–201, 205, 206, 223, 244, 255, 278
  complementarity of, 59–60
  enmeshment, 60
  fragmentation, 132–133, 255
  international, 47, 58, 95, 96, 128–131
  Iran, 205, 206
  North Korea, 182
  NZ business viewpoint, 260, 262
  Pacific framework, 260
  reforms, China, 251–258
  regional, 78, 92, 98, 150, 164, 255–258, 261–266
  restrictiveness, *253*
  tariffs, 264
  US response to China, 254, 257, 266
  Vietnam, 223
Trade in Services Agreement (TISA), 254
trading partners, role in China reforms, 251–253, 255
Tran Dai Quang, 227
transnational highways, 78
Trans-Pacific Partnership (TPP)
  and China, 252, 255–258
  and fragmentation, 133

and Japan, 147, 150–151
and New Zealand, 261–267, 269, 272
and One Belt, One Road, 145
and United States, 158, 159
and Vietnam, 225, 228, 230
transportation, 78
travel, 43, 53
trawler–coastguard incident (2010), 146, 149
Treaty of Amity (ASEAN), 69
Trilateral Strategic Dialogue (TSD), 158
Truong Tan Sang, 222, 224–225, 230–231, 232
Turkmenistan, 97
Twining, Daniel, 159

U

unification (Korea), 162–165
United Kingdom, 71, 158, 221, 232, 245, *see also* Britain
United Nations Climate Conference, *see* Paris Agreement (climate change)
United Nations Command, 162–165
United Nations (UN)
  and China, 53, 288
  Food and Agriculture Organisation, 129
  and MDBs, 111, 113
  and New Zealand, 272
  sanctions, 173–174, 178–179, 182, 183, 186, 188–189, 201, 204–206, 287
  Security Council, 174, 199–201, 203, 205, 218, 269
  and United States, 31, 38, 288
  and Vietnam, 231
United States Forces Korea (USFK), 162–165, 187
urbanisation, 64, 65
US Clean Power Plan, 47
US–China Joint Presidential Statement on Climate Change, 47, 48
US–China Senior Dialogue, 81
US–China Strategic and Economic Dialogue (S&ED), 138, 139, 200
US–India Civil Nuclear Agreement, 243, 245
US–Japan Security Treaty (1952), 83–84,

146, 147, 149, 150
USS Enterprise (ship), 242
USS George Washington (ship), 221

V

Vajpayee, Atal Bihari, 242
values, 59, 155, 159, 165–167
Venezuela, 97
Vietnam, 92, 148, 162
  and ASEAN, 217, 218
  bilateral relations (China), 222–224, 225–227, 229–231, 232
  bilateral relations (US), 218, 224–225, 227–229, 231, 232, 233
  China naval visit, 222
  defence and security cooperation (US), 229
  Defence Policy Dialogue (with US), 220–221
  development assistance to, 217, 218, 225
  diplomatic relations, 216, 217, 229, 231
  espionage allegations, 229–230
  exclusive economic zone (EEZ), 217, 225–227
  goals, 219, 232
  'Goldilocks model,' 215–216, 231–232
  Gulf of Tonkin, 222, 223, 233
  Haiyang Shiyou 981 crisis, 225–227, 232
  human rights issues, 216, 224, 228, 229, 230, 231
  infrastructure development, 223–224
  investment in, 217, 218
  leadership succession, 229–231
  maritime hotline, 222, 225
  military capabilities, 216, 218, 227, 231
  monetary cooperation, 223
  relations with China and US, 215–233
  relations with India, 215–216, 217, 220
  relations with Japan, 215, 217, 220, 222
  relations with Russia, 215, 216, 218
  sanctions against, 225
  security convergence (with US), 220–221, 228, 232, 233
  strategic partnerships, 215–216, 218–222, 224–225, 232
  territorial disputes, 216–217, 220–233
  tourism, 225
  and TPP, 225, 228, 230, 263
  trade, 217, 218, 219–220, 223, 224–225
  and United Nations, 218
  US naval visit, 219, 221
  Vietnam Communist Party (VCP), 217–221, 225–228, 232, 233
  war legacies, 221, 229
Vietnam War, 221, 280
visa statistics (Chinese travellers to US), 49

W

Wang Gungwu, 27, **142**, **250**, **251**, 276
Wang Jiarui, 184
Wang Lutong, 43
Wang Yi, 205–206, 206, 223
Wapenhans Report (World Bank), 115
Warsaw Pact, 58
Washington Consensus, 59
water resource sharing, 78
wealth (global rankings), 64–65
Wen Jiabao, 81–82, 178
western China, 77, 98, 99
western Pacific, 67
wildlife trafficking, 85
Wilson, Woodrow, 35, 36–37, 39
Womack, Brantly, 55, **142**
World Bank
  accountability, 115
  conditionality of loans, 127
  cooperation and co-financing, 120
  country systems approach (CSA), 121
  environmental and social policies, 114–115, 120–121
  funding of, 136
  Global Infrastructure Facility (GIF), 93, 96, 137
  infrastructure funding gap, 116
  and isomorphism, 108
  and new MDBs, 96–99, 103
  role, 128
  statistics, 61–62, 76, 92–93
  structure and governance, 109–111
  Trust Fund, 96
  US influence on, 112–113, 114–115, 117, 122

and Vietnam, 218
World Development Bank, 137
World Development Indicators, 129
world politics, general theory of, 61
World Trade Organisation (WTO), 132–133, 252–255, 257, 258, 263, 265
World War I, 37
World War II, 37, 155, 156, 180, 188, 280
Wu Bangguo, 177
Wu Jianmin, 51, 250, 251, 280
Wu Yi, 177, 181
Wukang Group (China), 181

X

Xi Jinping
  and AIIB, 116
  anti-corruption campaign, 148
  and CCP authority, 286
  climate change agreement, 84
  goals, 31, 39, 56, 159, 160, 245
  influences on, 30–31
  and North Korea, 177–180, 184, 202–203
  One Belt, One Road, 75, 76, 91, 95, 98, 279
  reform intentions, 59
  relations with Japan, 146–147, 151
  relations with South Korea, 203–204
  relations with Vietnam, 222, 226–227, 230, 233
  speeches, 85–86
  Sunnylands summit, 51, 82–83, 86, 215, 216, 222, 232, 269, 280
  US policy, 80–83, 284, 287–288
  views on US, 54
  visits to US, 44, 46–48, 51–52, 69–70, 80–86, 127
Xiao Xian, 205
Xu Caihou, 148

Y

Yamaguchi, Natsuo, 147
Yang Jian, 74
Yang Jiechi, 83, 161, 226, 227
Yongdeung mine (North Korea), 181
Yuan Jingdong, 173
Yugoslavia, 67

Z

zero-sum game, 58, 64, 196, 268, 270–271, 277
Zhou Enlai, 53, 159–160, 176
Zhou Xiaochuan, 97
Zhou Yongkang, 148